Bugaboos, Chimeras, & Achilles' Heels

10,001 Difficult Words and How to Use Them

JOHN L. DUSSEAU

BUGABOOS, CHIMERAS & ACHILLES' HEELS

10,001 Difficult Words & How to Use Them

PRENTICE HALL
Englewood Cliffs, New Jersey 07632

Prentice-Hall International (UK) Limited, *London*
Prentice-Hall of Australia Pty. Limited, *Sydney*
Prentice-Hall Canada, Inc., *Toronto*
Prentice-Hall Hispanoamericana, S.A., *Mexico*
Prentice-Hall of India Private Limited, *New Delhi*
Prentice-Hall of Japan, Inc., *Tokyo*
Simon & Schuster Asia Pte. Ltd., *Singapore*
Editora Prentice-Hall do Brasil, Ltda., *Rio de Janeiro*

© 1993 *by*

PRENTICE-HALL, Inc.

Englewood Cliffs, NJ

10 9 8 7 6 5 4 3 2 1

Library of Congress Cataloging-in-Publication Data

Dusseau, John L.
   Bugaboos, chimeras & achilles' heels: 10,001 difficult words & how to use
them / by John L. Dusseau.
      p.   cm.

Includes bibliographical references.
ISBN 0-13-211350-3
   1. English language—Usage—Dictionaries. 2. English language—Foreign
words and phrases—Dictionaries. 3. English language—Terms and phrases.
I. Title. II. Title: Bugaboos, chimeras, and achilles' heels.
PE1460.D85   1992
423'.1—dc20   92-22959
                                                                                 CIP

ISBN 0-13-211350-3

 PRENTICE HALL
Professional Publishing
Englewood Cliffs, NJ 07632

Simon & Schuster. A Paramount Communications Company

PRINTED IN THE UNITED STATES OF AMERICA

Naturally,
TO SHEILA

Words strain,
Crack and sometimes break under the burden,
Under the tension, slip, slide, perish,
Decay with imprecision, will not stay in place,
Will not stay still.[*]

About the Author

John L. Dusseau received a bachelor's degree from Haverford College and a master's degree from Duke University. He joined W. B. Saunders Company in 1943 and became vice president and editor-in-chief in 1950.

He is also a writer and, with his wife, Sheila Sloane, is the coauthor of *The Business Word Book* and *A Word Book in Pathology and Laboratory Medicine*. Dusseau's many essays have appeared in journals as diverse as *The Sewanee Review* and *Perspectives in Biology and Medicine*.

In another context, Dusseau has said, "We must return to the persuasion of the Renaissance that art and metaphysics stand at the very center of human concerns. We should see that the terrible poverty, strife, and chaos of the modern world cannot be alleviated by still more sophisticated computers or by more astute bombs but only by wisdom in the management of our resources and riches. . . . We need not the guidance of monolithic specialists but of men educated in the humanities, in appreciation of culture, and in understanding of the spirit of wise and compassionate endeavor." In this work, Dusseau has added to that understanding and appreciation.

Preface

It could be said of me that in this book
I have only made up a bunch of other men's
flowers, providing of my own only the string
that ties them together.

Montaigne: *Essays*

The nature of this book is set out in its informal
introduction. Its purpose can be put simply: to suggest proper use
of difficult words by both precept and example. That Thoreau
said "I distrust a man who can spell a word only one way" is a
pleasantry but not a license to misuse words. To write
"compliment" instead of "complement" is to defeat the purpose
of language.

But what is a difficult term and what is good usage?
Is *deus ex machina* a troublesome phrase? Is *solecism* a difficult
word? Even the subject of agreement is subject to disagreement.
Fowler would find "A bunch of boys were sledding on the slope"
a solecism, although Safire would find quotations to allow it,
and Fowler would reply that examples from slipshod writing
do not establish correctness. They prove simply that proper
usage is elusive. In fine, standard English is a myth and the
path to precise use of words a long and tortuous one.

Nonetheless, this is the path we shall hope to pursue. Along its way we shall examine quite a few pairs of similar-seeming words. No doubt even the literate sometimes confuse *principle* and *principal,* but, although several manuals warn against confusion of *extent* and *extant,* it seems improbable that such misuse actually occurs. When it does, it is more likely due to typographical error than to misunderstanding. Nor shall we altogether neglect a new language—the vocabulary of the computer. Its terms are in wide use ("byte" is on every tongue), but we shall confine our attention to common everyday words such as *address* that take on new significance in the language of electronics. Computer terms, like witticisms, should be widely interspersed, and those wary of machine language may wish to note that such terms appear without identifying parts of speech. Throughout the text phonetic pronunciations are given for words whose sound is either difficult or debatable. In a second section of the book we shall include useful and, we believe, interesting foreign words and phrases, for they too are frequently misspelled or misused.

In the use of language no book can pretend to say definitively what is correct or incorrect; and sagacious precepts will not constrain the inadvertent slip. "Graduating with a BFA in painting from Northern Arizona University in 1976, Ernest Wilmeth turned to clay in 1982" (program of the New Mexico Arts and Crafts Fair). Nor is any book ever completed; it simply appears. The appearance of this book means that the midnight light may be dimmed and that the kitchen table, cleared of leftover manuscript and unreadable notes, may be restored to its real use. May use of the book too be real and unencumbered by error or excess in its doing. A fond farewell to it—may its place be secure on the desktop.

J.L.D.

Contents

Appreciation

No book is written alone. All works of reference, especially lexicons, rest to some extent on existing books. Those used in the compilation of this glossary are listed at its end and are cited in abbreviated form in its text. The author has found invaluable help in four of these sources: *The Oxford Dictionary of Quotations, Webster's Dictionary of English Usage,* the second edition of *Fowler's Modern English Usage,* and the *Oxford English Dictionary.* The last is a work of such remarkable scholarship and vivid life that a brief tribute to it appears in the References.

Nor is the author's work solitary. All writers owe debts of gratitude to persons unnamed and named. Among the latter I may put with deep appreciation my friend John Morse, who has read my manuscript with meticulous care and valuable suggestion; my wife, Sheila, who has never faltered in her conviction that a useful book would somehow emerge from my bouts of indecision and despair; my typist Donna Ciccotelli, who has endured indecipherable handwriting and endless changes with smiling fortitude and capable intelligence.

Above all, I wish to acknowledge the patient encouragement and good counsel of my publishing mentor Ellen Schneid Coleman, production editor Eve Mossman, and the staff of the publisher. Together, they keep alive an older tradition of concern for the author and perceptive care of his work. This is not to say that their sage advices have always been followed, for writers have a stubborn preference for their own way of saying things, so that, in the end, the quality of any book rests upon its author whose shortcomings cannot possibly be any more distressing to his critics and readers than they are to him.

J.L.D.

An Informal
Introduction

The first requirement for communication, teaching, and learning is the existence of an agreed-upon vocabulary of terms of established meaning. The first and vital step in understanding any discipline is mastery of its language, but troublesome words (or any words, for that matter) have not descended to us in a state of consistency, uniformity, or perfection. Johnson put this ambivalence bluntly in the preface to his great *Dictionary of the English Language:* "I am not so lost in lexicography as to forget that *words are the daughters of earth and that things are the sons of heaven.* Language is only the instrument of science and words are but the signs of ideas. I wish, however, that the instrument might be less apt to decay and that signs might be permanent, like the things which they denote."

Of course, lexicographers can be unbearable purists. Of "insane asylum" Ambrose Bierce says, "Obviously an asylum cannot be unsound of mind. Say asylum for the insane." Now "insane asylum" is avoided for different reasons. It is too clear and harsh. This writer too knows the hazard of doctrinaire attitudes. After years of trying to persuade reluctant students to say "It is I," he found he had succeeded in teaching them to say "Between you and I."

Even "reminiscence," of which we are all so fond, may have a convenient meaning. "We spent the evening," Tallulah Bankhead said, "reminiscing about the future." Tallulah could use words eccentrically, because she was, in the 1930s,

1

America's only solvent bankhead. At about the same time Leopold Stokowski, approaching the Du Pont Company about sponsoring a series of Sunday afternoon concerts, got to see Pierre Du Pont himself. "Nonsense," said Mr. Du Pont firmly, "at three o'clock on Sunday afternoon, everyone is out playing polo." Clearly to the Du Ponts everyone is not Everyman.

All rules are meant sometime to be broken; otherwise the sun would still be revolving around the earth. So too the canons of rhetoric and good usage may often be wisely disregarded. "Rules and models," said Hazlitt, "destroy genius and art." That gentle iconoclast E. B. White especially distrusted the notion that sentences should not end with prepositions. Hence he liked the story of a father going upstairs to read to his little boy but accidentally bringing along the wrong book. "Why," the boys asks, "did you bring the book that I don't want to be read to out of up for?" Few indeed are sentences that end in five prepositions, but it is said that Don Juan ended almost every sentence with a proposition. The forbidding rule itself forms a curious chapter in the history of grammar. It was devised by Robert Lowth, an eighteenth-century English bishop and gentleman grammarian, whose eccentric but influential *Introduction to English Grammar* urged its complaisant readers never to end sentences with prepositions. Presumably the worthy cleric would have us say, "Up to what are you?" or "I don't know about what you are talking." Even the rules of spelling are sometimes foolish. As Safire has pointed out, the precept "*i* before *e* except after *c*" scarcely makes orthography a sceince.

Language has always been subject not only to growth and decay but to vagaries of taste and to whimsicality. "When I use a word," Humpty Dumpty said in a rather scornful tone, "it means just what I choose it to mean—neither more nor less."

"The question is," said Alice, "whether you can make words mean so many different things."

"The question is," said Humpty Dumpty, "which is to be master—that's all."

Humpty is telling us that the great secret of good speech and good writing is command of language—something not readily taught, for incomprehensible and disorderly writing arises not from the inability to write but from inability to think in appropriate words arranged in a pattern of logical development. Clarity begins at home.

Error, of course, will always be with us, and the wrong word through misprint, misuse, or misunderstanding has a long and curious history. During the Crimean War the British suddenly found themselves allies of France, but in their joint conferences the English admirals—all octogenarian relics of the Napoleonic wars—always called their Russian enemy "the French." Indeed the heroic but witless charge of the light brigade was itself initiated by semantic misapprehension. But the wrong word is not always inadvertent. "Every man," said Churchill to the House of Commons, "should halve his say."

Our language is a capacious carriage whose wayfarers are an ill-sorted lot, Spaniards, Greeks, Muscovites, and streetwalkers nudging the proper English. Even today the tight rules of eighteenth-century pedants, with their absurd grammatical niceties and fanciful etymologies, tend to be preserved. Purists here and in England have long waged a relentless and usually ridiculous battle against infiltration into English English of slang, Americanisms, and vulgarisms. "Britain and the United States are," as Shaw once observed, "two nations divided by a common language." Linguistic puritans cannot admit that a healthy language constantly grows and that additions to it may come from the worlds of television, journalism, cinema, theater, and special callings and even from the subworlds of gypsies, criminals, and prostitutes. Our language is the richer for *bamboozle, flop, dud, sharpshooter, fourflusher, flimflam, tearjerker, scam,* and a thousand others. That many of them are confined to everyday speech does not mean that they should have no place in written English. So fine and elegant a poet as Chaucer did not disdain the speech of street and gutter.

Manuals of style and good usage also recommend plain and discreet prose and will adduce examples to its fine effect, but all will ignore that Shakespeare, Milton, Gibbon, Melville, and Joyce are scarcely fancy-free. Even King James's bishops did not spurn a mellifluent cadence in their unfolding of uncommon phrases for the common ear.

Still, there are few Gibbons and many educators, and the latter often speak and write in impressive polysyllabic jargon. Here is a sample from the department of communications of a presumably functioning university: "Communicologists [absurd word!] have attempted to cull the various perspectives to synthesize salient concepts into an integrated framework. . . . Scholars have established a distinctive field of communication research with a multitheoretical delineation of parameters and orientations" (cited by Gummere). Who among us would care to cull a perspective or synthesize a concept or delineate a parameter multitheoretically?

Despite the example, there is still with us not only a mythic attachment to the word but nothing less than assignment of sublimity to the right word. "A thing said walks in immortality if it has been said well." In the increasingly sophisticated and disillusioned life of Western man, there still persist about the gracefully written and eloquently spoken word the elements of wonder and pleasure. In the finest writing one has the feeling of infusion by a spirit creative and above rules, perceptive and responsive to rules—a spirit pervading the whole domain of culture and intellect.

Could Lord Beaverbrook have had it right? "We have a system, you know, I speak at this end and there is a machine at the other end and it comes out as a leading article." Only a Britannic peer could waive the rules of writing. Whatever the artful ingenuity of Lord Beaverbrook's machine, it cannot capture the primal eloquence that began under a clear firmament on a naked plain. "In Arabia, as well as in Greece, the perfection of language outstripped the refinement of manners; and her speech could diversify the fourscore names of honey, the two hundred of a serpent, the five hundred of a lion at a time when this copious dictionary was entrusted to the memory of an illiterate people."

Gibbon's rolling phrases find their echo in Dr. Johnson's famous *Dictionary*, but neither writer in works of great erudition forwent sly commentary. The dour lexicographer's definition of a fishing line ("A stick and a string with a worm at one end and a fool at the other") was meant not only to amuse but also to bite. And in the pages to follow it is hoped that occasional touches of whimsy will amuse as well as instruct the reader. Of course, not all distinctions are as amusingly drawn as Disraeli's differentiation between misfortune and calamity: "Were Gladstone [his political rival] to fall into the Thames, that would be a misfortune. Were someone to pull him out, that would be a calamity."

In a sense it might be said that language is appearance—the vestment of reasoning, emotion, persuasion; but it is a fabric woven of imprecise and restless words that will not stay neatly in place. As Humpty said of *slithy*, "You see, it's like a portmanteau—there are two meanings packed up into one word."

Difficult Words and Phrases

It is hoped that the quotations here used to illuminate principles of correct usage are apt and in themselves interesting and sometimes amusing. The examples, when not credited, are the inventions of the author. Occasionally, too, quotations have sprung from a memory capacious but not infallible. If these are not always precise, it is believed that they are never unjust.

The reader will notice that English writers of the sixteenth and seventeenth centuries enjoyed a wonderful latitude of orthography, punctuation, and syntax. *Yeoman* is likely to be spelled *yoeman;* sentence subjects of more than two or three words, are invariably followed by commas; and the final *e* in past participles will often be replac'd by an apostrophe. In the original texts s's that look like f's will produce an odd effect. Only the final *s* and capital *S* will be familiar. "I think it fuperfluous to ufe as words of a fubject fo praifed in itfelf as it needs no praifes" (Sidney).

Throughout the text the abbreviations used for parts of speech and the names of foreign languages are familiar and need not be repeated here. However, three acronyms not quite so common are

7

also used: *ODQ, Oxford Dictionary of Quotations; OED, Oxford English Dictionary;* and *WDEU, Webster's Dictionary of English Usage.*

A, An (art's). There is no real problem in use of the indefinite article—*an* before vowels or vowel sounds (*"an* FCC ruling), *a* before consonants or consonant sounds (*a* one-way street)—except for that same "h" that has been troubling the denizens of London's East End for centuries. But even here the rule is simple: Use *a* before an aspirated "h" (*a* house, *a* home) and *an* before words beginning with a silent "h." Of these there are only five: herb, hour, heir, honor, and honest and their derivatives. *"An* honorary doctorate is no longer the nice distinction it once was, for today too many university buildings are being built by degrees" (Comfort). Finally, *h* words with an unstressed first syllable (e.g., *historic, hotel*) may be preceded by either *a* or *an* ("*an historic* occasion" sounding right to most ears).

Abandon (v & n), **Abandonment** (n). The verb *abandon* has two distinct meanings: (1) To forsake completely, to desert, to relinquish, as in Dante's famous inscription over the gates of Hell, *"Abandon* all hope, ye who enter here." (2) To yield to impulses without restraint or moderation, often with the sense of unreasoned or uncontrolled indulgence. "A man might write such stuff forever, if he would *abandon* his mind to it" (Johnson on Ossian). The noun *abandon* means complete surrender to impulse; freedom from inhibition or restraint; exuberance. "The magnificent *abandon* of Harding's brush" (Ruskin).

And the noun *abandonment* shares these meanings. "His manner was frank, even to *abandonment*" (Disraeli). But it also means the act of abandoning. " 'Tis a base *abandonment* of reason to resign our right of thought" (Byron).

Abbreviation (n); Acronym (n); Contraction (n). An *abbreviation* is a shortened word usually followed by a period; but Americans are puzzled by the British practice of omitting the stop in abbreviations such as *Dr, Mr, St,* and other such words but using it after *Prof.* and *Rev.,* for example. Although mysterious even to Englishmen, the practice is governed by a plain principle: when the last letter of the abbreviation is the same as the last letter of the full word no period is required. But this leads to curious-seeming inconsistencies: "*Lat.* for Latin but *Gk* for Greek, sometimes within a single rank or title—the *Rev. Dr* or *Sgt Maj.,* for example" (Bryson). The British might do well to forget this useless distinction or forgo periods altogether. *Contractions* and *acronyms* are also forms of word shortening: the former, words in which some middle letters have been squeezed out, as in *can't* for cannot; the latter, words formed from the initial letters of a group of words, as in *NATO* for North Atlantic Treaty Organization. It may be worth noting that initial letters not forming a pronounceable word (*IBM,* for example) are said by some not be *acronyms* but simply *abbreviations* or "initialisms"—an awkward but established word. However, most dictionaries do not allow this distinction.

Abecedarian (adj). [*Abecedarian* is pronounced variously but most often AB uh suh DARE ee an.] An unusual but handy word meaning either arranged in alphabetical order or elementary. This is an *abecedarian* book. "The earlier chemists who, under the charm of the moment, adopted an *abecedarian* method that led to ambiguity" (Macvicar).

Abhorrence (n), Abhorrent (adj). The noun means hatred, detestation, loathing. Bernstein says it may be followed only by the preposition *of.* "A just and necessary offence does, by giving men acquaintance with war, take off somewhat from the *abhorrence of* it" (*Decay of Piety*). But *to, for,* and *against* may also be used. "Proof of his *abhorrence against* vice" (*Monthly Magazine*). And, of course, *abhorrent* means detestable, hateful as in Dryden's phrase *"abhorrent* to your breeding."

Ability (n); **Capacity** (n). These words should not be used interchangeably. *Ability:* Competence, faculty, skill, dexterity, talent. "To every man according to his *ability"* (St. Matthew). "From each according to his *ability"* (*Communist Manifesto*). *Capacity:* The power to receive, hold, or contain. "A small bucket of slight *capacity."* "He had a certain *capacity* for instruction in violin playing but only slight *ability* to perform."

Abject (adj). Miserable, wretched, despicable, worthless. "I know nothing so *abject* as the behavior of a man canvassing for a seat in parliament" (Smollett). Objection has been raised to *abject poverty* as a cliché, but there can be no real objection to the use of *abject* as an intensifier. "They disguise from themselves the bare and *abject poverty* of the scheme" (Inge).

Abjure (v); **Adjure** (v). The two words are sometimes confused, but their Latin prefixes are a guide to their separate meanings (ab-, away from; ad-, toward). *Abjure:* To renounce, repudiate, avoid, shun. "And other pleasures all *abjure"* (Milton). *Adjure:* To charge or command solemnly—often under oath—to entreat or request. "His friends *adjured* him to take care of a life so valuable to his country" (Macaulay).

Abnegate (v); **Abrogate** (v). To *abnegate* means specifically to deny oneself some privilege, right, convenience, or reward, but it is sometimes used in the broader sense of relinquish or give up. "All honour to those who can *abnegate* for themselves the personal enjoyment of life" (Mill). *Abrogate*, too, has a specific meaning: To repeal or annul by authoritative act. "The negative precepts of man may cease by many instruments; but the negative precepts of God can never cease, except when they are expressly *abrogated* by the same authority" (Taylor's *Rule of Living Holy*).

Abortive (adj). Born prematurely but by extension imperfectly developed or unsuccessful. Safire claims to see in the word an implication of continued failure, so that he objects to calling a failed rescue mission "abortive." But writers from Shakespeare to Toynbee have used the word to describe a single failed event. "Our first design, my friend, has prov'd *abortive*" (Addison).

Abound (v). To exist in great numbers, to be plentiful, to be well supplied—usually followed by *in* or *with*. "Even so, this citie *aboundeth in* wickedness" (Coverdale). "A faithful man shall *abound with* blessings" (Proverbs).

Abscond (v), Abscondence (n). The verb means to hide or flee in order to avoid legal process or consequence. "He did his devilish endeavour, and stayed till he was forced to *abscond* again" (Defoe). The verb carries the preposition *with* when it has an object. "The clerk *absconded with* the petty cash" (Black). The noun means fugitive concealment. "The place of his *abscondence* was a friend's house in Bartholomew Close" (Masson).

Absolute adjectives. Much has been made of the slipshod use of comparative or superlative forms of adjectives that admit no degrees of comparison. There are thousands of them (e.g., absolute, ancillary, complete, correct, eternal, perfect, perpendicular, square, unique, and so on). But writers, however incorrectly, will continue to use the less technical of such words in comparative and superlative forms. One cannot find fault with "a *more perfect* union," for here the word *perfect* is not used in the sense of perfection without limitation but in the sense of having qualities of perfection. The same exception could be made for *correct* but it is difficult to extend the idea to *unique.*

Absolutely (adv). A useful adverb meaning without exception, completely, entirely. But for reasons that are not altogether clear, it has emerged recently as a synonym for *yes.* This is probably a fad that will go away. However, *absolutely* also comes under attack as an overused intensifier. It might well be spared in "I washed my hair and it was *absolutely* glorious" (*Ladies' Home Journal*), but one cannot fault its intensifying force in "What merit they can build upon having joined with a protestant army . . . to defend their own liberties and properties is, to me, *absolutely* inconceivable" (Swift).

Absolve (v), Absolution (n). *Absolve:* To free from guilt or blame, to exempt from the penalties of wrong. It may be followed by either *of* or *from*, but for no good reason *from* has recently increased in incidence of use. "This does not *absolve* him *from* moral blame" (Dale). *Absolution:* The act of freeing from blame or guilt and, in theology, the remission of sin or of the punishment for sin through the sacrament of penance. "Without confession to a Priest there is no *absolution*" (Watson).

Absorb (v), Absorption (n); Adsorb (v), Adsorption (n). *Absorb:* To suck up, to swallow, to engross or engage wholly, to take in without recoil or other reaction. "I have nothing to do today. My practice is never very *absorbing*" (Dr. Watson to Sherlock Holmes). *Adsorb:* An essentially chemical term meaning to condense and hold by *adsorption* as when charcoal *adsorbs* gases. *Adsorption* is the adhesion in thin layers of the molecules of gases or liquids or dissolved substances to the surface of solids with which they are in contact, so that *adsorption* is a technical antonym for *absorption*.

Abstain (v), Abstention (n), Abstinence (n). The verb means to withdraw or hold oneself back from a practice or thing regarded as wrongful or unhealthy. It is usually followed by *from*. "To be perpetually longing and impatiently desirous of any thing, so that a man cannot *abstain from* it, is to lose liberty and to become a servant of meat and drink, or smoke" (Taylor's *Rule of Living Holy*). However, it can also mean to withdraw from a gratification not necessarily unwise or unhealthy. "D'Aubigni was so fond of writing epigrams, that he could not *abstain from* them" (Ferriar). In reference to casting a vote or participating in a poll, no preposition is required. "No less than 213 members *abstained* in the final vote" (cited by *WDEU*). "There were over 7000 *abstentions*" (Clarke). *Abstinence* has the more specific meaning of voluntary withdrawal from the indulgence of appetite and is said to make the heart grow fonder.

Abysm (n), Abysmal (adj); Abyss (n), Abyssal (adj). Both nouns mean the void once believed to exist below the earth and, by extension, any immeasurable space or chasm.

Abyss has somehow come to replace *abysm*, but the latter has had a long life in borrowings from Shakespeare's memorable line "In the dark backward and *abysm* of time." *Abysmal* is used to describe great depth but also, figuratively, to suggest wretchedness or starkly inferior quality. "The *abysmal* living conditions of the people there" (*The New Republic*). *Abyssal*, however, is only used in the technical sense of unfathomable depth. "The coral fauna of the *abyssal* sea" (Lyell).

Accelerate (v); **Exhilarate** (v). This would scarcely seem a necessary distinction—*accelerate* meaning to quicken; *exhilarate* to gladden. Nevertheless, one does hear the *accelerator* of an automobile sometimes called its *exhilarator*. How this must gladden the heart of the car and sadden the heart of the purist.

Accent (v or n); **Accentuate** (v). Both verbs mean to emphasize or give prominence to, but Fowler suggests that the former should be used in a technical or literal sense and the latter figuratively. This is a distinction not always adhered to but borne out in "*accentuate* the positive" and in "For the Preservation of this Rhythm in Music it is necessary that at least one note in every bar be *accented*" (Blair).

Accept (v); **Except** (v & prep). It seems unlikely that these words should ever be confused, but they sometimes are. *Accept* (v): To take or receive, to agree or consent to, to respond affirmatively, or to acknowledge. "'Tis ever thus with simple folk—an *accepted* wit has but to say 'Pass the mustard,' and they roar their ribs out!" (Gill). *Except* (v): To exclude or omit. "You should always *except* the present company" (O'Keefe). *Except* (prep): "All a little daft *except* thee and me and I'm not so sure about thee" (Anon.).

Access (n), **Accessible** (adj). The ability or right to approach, enter, use, or confer with. "When we are wronged, and would unfold our griefs;/We are denied *access* unto his person" (Shakespeare). But in electronics it means the process of obtaining data from a storage device or obtaining instruction from a memory device and following it. *Accessible*: Easy to approach or enter; open to the influence of. "As an island, we are *accessible* on every side, and exposed to perpetual invasions" (Addison).

Accident (n); **Mishap** (n). *Accident:* Any event occurring unexpectedly or without plan or purpose. Hence an *accident* may be either fortunate or unfortunate. "The greatest pleasure I know, is to do a good action by stealth, and to have it found out by *accident*" (Lamb). "For whither is he gone? What *accident*/Hath rapt him from us?" (Milton). *Mishap:* Any unfortunate accident. "Alas for unforeseen *mishaps*" (Cowper).

Accidentally (adv); **Accidently** (adv). *Accidentally:* Unexpectedly, by chance, without conscious purpose. "*Accidentally* is often mispronounced and misspelled. It has five syllables: ac-ci-den-tal-ly" (Shaw). *Accidently:* There is no such word.

Accrue (v), **Accruement** (n). Various style manuals advise that *accrue* is a legal and financial term and should be used only in such contexts. Still, *accrue* has a long history of use in the general meaning of to occur or happen as a natural result of growth or addition. Bernstein says *accrue* takes *to*, but *to* is used to indicate the recipient of *accruing* and *from* or *through* to indicate its source. "*From* innocence a native joy *accrues*" (Anderson).

Achilles' heel. Although the fable of Achilles' vulnerable heel is old, the phrase itself, meaning a defenseless or weak spot, is recent and marked by a small controversy. Should or should it not carry an apostrophe? Usage justifies with or without about equally, but literature favors the possessive form: "A ready wit was his attraction; a sharp temper his *Achilles' heel*" (Thackeray). But medicine will afford the examples of *Achilles* reflex and *Achilles* tendon.

Acid test; Acidulous (adj). Under the headings "Popularized Technicalities" and "Hackneyed Phrases," Fowler gives *acid test* unreserved first place, attributing its faddish use to President Wilson's sentence, "The treatment accorded to Russia by her sister nations in the months to come will be the *acid test* of their good will." No doubt to many every sound sleep is *sleep of the just* and every endeavor put to an *acid test*. Still, Fowler's criticism seems faintly *acidulous* (acerbic, bitter, sharp), for *acid test* as metaphor arises legitimately from the acid testing of gold and has no handy synonym. Sir Leslie Munro was echoing Wilson in both thought and phrase in his "The *acid test* will be whether the members of the United Nations . . . will be able to stop an aggressor." To delete the *acid* would be to deprive the idea of its vigor.

Acknowledgment. The reply given to signals within a computer system where an immediate response is required.

Acoustics (n). As a science it takes a singular verb, as the architectural characteristics that afford distinct hearing a plural verb. "*Acoustics*, or the science of sound, *is* a very considerable branch of physics" (Herschel). "The *acoustics* of the opera house *are* vastly improved" (*The New York Times*).

Acquaintance (n), Acquaintanceship (n). Fowler condemns the word *acquaintanceship* as a needless variant of *acquaintance*, but there still persists a distinction between *acquaintanceship* as the state of being acquainted and *acquaintance* as the person with whom one is acquainted. "His *acquaintanceships* among his fellow students do not appear to have been numerous" (Masson). "An *acquaintance* is a person whom we know well enough to borrow from but not well enough to lend to or a friendship called slight when its object is poor or obscure and intimate when he is rich or famous" (Bierce). *Acquaintance* also persists alone in the sense of knowledge through study. "*Acquaintance* with the works themselves such as only minute and long-continued study could give" (Bryce).

Acquiesce (v), Acquiescence (n). *Acquiesce:* To rest satisfied or apparently satisfied, to concur. Commentators have argued about what preposition the verb should properly carry, all favoring *in* and some disallowing *to* and *with*, but *to* has been in good use since the seventeenth century. "We must *acquiesce to* their sayings, whom we have truly constituted to be Kings over us" (Hobbes). *Acquiescence:* Tacit assent, agreement, compliance. "Neither from the nobility nor the clergy, who were thought most averse from it, there appeared any sign of contradiction, but an entire *acquiescence* in all the bishops thought fit to do" (Clarendon).

Acronym: See **Abbreviation.**

Activate (v); **Actuate** (v). Both words mean to make active or to put in motion, although Fowler disparages the former. Outside their use within technical contexts, the words today are used interchangeably. "This warms and *activates* the spirit in the search of truth" (Walker). "Our passions are the springs which *actuate* the powers of our nature" (Rogers).

Adapt (v); **Adept** (adj); **Adopt** (v). *Adapt:* To make suitable to requirements, to adjust, modify or accommodate: "The reasonable man *adapts* himself to the world; the unreasonable man persists in trying to *adapt* the world to himself. Therefore all progress depends on the unreasonable man" (Shaw). *Adept:* Skilled, proficient. "Whoever is *adept* at the speaking trade will *adapt* himself to inconvenience" (Macaulay). *Adopt:* (1) To choose for oneself, to make one's own by selection, specifically to take as one's own child. (2) To vote upon affirmatively, to accept. (1) "Friends not *adopted* with a schoolboy's haste,/But chosen with a nice discerning taste" (Cowper). (2) "The House *adopted* the resolution because time and truth were running out" (*The New Republic*).

Addendum (n), **Addenda** (n). *Addendum* is a singular noun meaning anything added. "After I had gone over the instructions, I wrote an *addendum*" (Holmes). *Addenda* is its plural, but because of a falling-off in the study of Latin, even literate writers now use *addendums*.

Addicted (pp). The word means habituated obsessively, but it has become so pejorative that its use is now restricted to the harmful. This was not always so: "Ye know the house of Stephanus, that they have *addicted* themselves to the ministry of the saints" (Corinthians).

Address. In computer terminology a letter, number, or symbol designating the location of information stored in a computer memory.

Adduce (v); Deduce (v). *Adduce:* To cite as conclusive or persuasive evidence. "All that I have *adduced* is sufficient to convince any reasonable person" (Holmes). *Deduce:* To reach a conclusion from something known or assumed. "Poirot *deduced* from scanty evidence that the butler did it." (See also *Deduce.*)

Adept: See Adapt.

Adherence (n); Adhesion (n). Both mean a state or act of being attached or devoted to or united with. However, the former is generally used figuratively, the latter literally. "Their firm *adherence* to their religion is no less remarkable than their dispersion" (Addison). "A very slight *adhesion* has taken place between the sigmoid flexure of the colon and the peritoneum" (Abernathy).

Adjacent (adj); Contiguous (adj). The distinction between the words is observed more in law than in common parlance. *Adjacent:* Lying near or close, neighboring. "We furnished ourselves with provisions at the *adjacent* inn" (Tyndall). *Contiguous:* Touching, in contact. When Mrs. Malaprop referred to the contagious countries, she meant *contiguous*—a touching rather than infective example.

Adjure: See Abjure.

Admission (n); Admittance (n). Some argue that *admittance* means merely physical entrance, whereas *admission* signifies formal acceptance with rights and privileges pertaining thereto. But this is a distinction by no means universally observed. "You have to pay *for admission*" is now more common than *for admittance.* The old sense of ceremony is preserved in "This formal *admission* of St. Matthias into the number of the Apostles" (Beveridge), in which *admittance* would not convey the sense intended. *Admission* also has the particular meaning of acknowledgment of error or wrong and of acknowledgment of the truth or validity of something. "The *admission* of supernatural truths is much less an active consent than a cold and passive acquiescence" (Sullivan).

Adopt: See Adapt.

Adopted (pp); **Adoptive** (adj). No question about it: *adopted* children; *adoptive* parents. "Yet I could some *adopted* heir provide" (Dryden). "She is thy mother, *adoptive*, and my natural wife" (Berners).

Adsorb: See Absorb.

Adulation (n), **Adulate** (v). *Adulation* is extravagant praise, but with the overtone of excessive or servile admiration. "*Adulation* ever follows the ambitious, for such alone receive pleasure from flattery" (Goldsmith). It is curious that, although the noun is in common use, the verb *adulate* is but rarely used. "What is there to *adulate* in me? Am I particularly intelligent?" (Gilbert).

Adult (adj). A common and useful word that once meant simply mature or grown up, but it has succumbed to euphemistic use as a synonym for obscene. "What seedy publishers and even seedier filmmakers describe as *adult* is in fact pornographic."

Adumbrate (v). A fancy verb meaning to produce a faint image of or to prefigure. It is not a word of everyday speech but common enough in artistic and political writing. "The duties were very ill defined, or rather not defined at all, but only *adumbrated*" (Mill). Fowler welcomes the circumstance that the word is rarely used, but his suggested substitute ("outline") is not a precise synonym.

Advantage (n), **Advantageous** (adj). The noun means any condition favorable to success or to superiority of position or situation. *Advantage* was formerly followed by *of*. "Lest Satan should get *advantage of* us" (Corinthians), but in modern use *over* has replaced *of*. "Unbelief has no *advantage over* belief" (Martineau).

Adversary (n); **Antagonist** (n); **Opponent** (n). An *opponent* is anyone on the other side of a contest, whether a bridge game, lawsuit, or battle of wits. An *antagonist* is an opponent of determined, hostile opposition, one who seeks with personal antagonism to win the stake at issue. An *adversary* may be either an *opponent* or an *antagonist*, but his opposition is implied to be of long standing. "My desire is that mine *adversary* had written a book" (Job).

Adverse (adj); **Averse** (adj). *Adverse:* Antagonistic, opposing, hostile. "*Adverse* circumstances delayed completion of the Panama Canal." *Averse:* Having distaste or dislike for, reluctant, unwilling. "What female heart can gold despise?/What cat's *averse* to fish?" (Gray). *Adverse* almost always precedes the noun it modifies; *averse* almost always follows. (See also *Averse.*)

Advice (n); **Advise** (v). *Advice* is a noun only, meaning opinion, recommendation, counsel. "*Advice* is seldom welcome; and those who need it the most always like it the least" (Lord Chesterfield). *Advise* is a verb only, meaning to offer suggestion or guidance as worth following. "It's my old girl that *advises*. She has the head. But I never own to it before her" (Dickens). It is a word greatly overused in business correspondence as a genteel substitute for tell or say.

Advisedly (adv). Intentionally, prudently, knowingly. Dogmatic Bierce objected to these meanings, saying the word should mean only "after advice." No one has ascribed to this view. "I am working as a judge at the Los Angeles County Fair, and I use the word 'working' *advisedly*" (cited by *WDEU*). "We speak *advisedly* and from experience when we say that this was the general feeling" (Martineau).

Aegis (n). *Aegis* [EE jis] is a word from classical mythology meaning shield or breastplate but extended to mean protection or support or sponsorship. "He cast over them the *aegis* of his mighty name" (Lecky). "Under the *aegis* of London University colleges have been started in the Sudan and East Africa" (cited by *OED*).

Aerie (n); **Eerie** (adj). Words more often confused in spelling than in usage, *aerie* [AIR ee] meaning a nest, *eerie* weird or inspiring fear. "The buzzard is not very merry,/For he keeps an *eerie aerie*./Clean-picked bones/And somber tones/Make his nest a Stygian ferry."

Affect (v), **Affecting** (adj); **Effect** (n & v). These are words of different meaning and pronunciation. *Affect* (v): To act on, to create a response in. *Effect* (v): To bring about, to cause, to accomplish. *Effect* (n): (1) Result, consequence, influence. (2) A mental impression as produced by poetry or painting. (3) *Effects:* Goods or property. "Hot toddy will not *affect* the course of the common cold, but it will *effect* a pleasant sense of well-being." (1) "I don't know what *effect* these men will have upon the enemy, but, by God, they terrify me" (Duke of Wellington). (2) "That is the bitterness of arts; you see a good *effect*, and some nonsense about sense intervenes" (Stevenson). (3) "He willed his *effects* to charity with his eye not on this world, but the next." The adjective *affecting* has the special meaning of arousing feeling or emotion. "There is something profoundly *affecting* in large masses of men following the lead of those who do not believe in men" (Whitman).

Affective (adj); **Effective** (adj). *Affective:* Caused by or causing emotion, emotional. "He was a judicious preacher, more instructive than *affective*" (Burnet). *Effective:* Adequate to a purpose, producing the intended result. "A more *affective* preacher would no doubt be more *effective*."

Affinity (n). Literally, relationship by marriage or by ties other than blood relationship (distinguished from *consanguinity*). Thus Fowler's contention that *between* and *with* are the only prepositions permitted after it; but the word has also long meant a natural liking for or attraction to a person, thing, or idea—hence *to* and *for* also appropriately follow it. "His *affinity for* controversy got him into further trouble" (*Psychology Today*).

Afflict: See **Inflict.**

Affluent (adj); **Effluent** (adj & n). Words not likely to be confused. The former [pronounced **AF** lo ent] means flowing freely or abounding in riches. "My son was already possessed of an *affluent* fortune" (Goldsmith). The latter as an adjective means flowing forth and as a noun a stream from a lake or reservoir and specifically discharged sewage or waste. "The motion of the *effluent* water will be alike in both cases" (Keill).

"The *effluent* has been drawn off from each tank" (*Pall Mall Gazette*).

Aforementioned (adj); **Aforesaid** (adj). In general they are legal lingo to be avoided, but *aforementioned* does appear in informal writing and in such use is not condemned by Fowler.

Aftermath (n). A result or consequence usually but not necessarily an unpleasant one. "The *aftermath* of the great rebellion" (Coleridge). But also with something of the literal sense of a second crop or mowing: "What tune the enchantress plays/In *aftermath* of soft September" (Housman).

Agenda. A set of computer operations forming a procedure for solving a problem.

Aggravate (v); **Annoy** (v); **Irritate** (v). There is a genuine distinction among these words. *Aggravate/aggravation* (n) is the strongest, meaning to intensify or make worse anything evil, disorderly, or troublesome. "Such threats only serve to *aggravate* hostility" (Thackeray). "I think it's liquid *aggravation* that circulates through his veins, not regular blood" (Dickens). *Annoy/annoyance* (n) is less strong, meaning to pester or disturb. "Speak roughly to your little boy,/And beat him when he sneezes;/He only does it to *annoy*,/Because he knows it teases" (Carroll). "A grain, a dust, a gnat, a wand'ring hair,/Any *annoyance* in that precious sense" (Shakespeare). *Irritate/irritation* (n) has the more specific meaning of arousing impatience or exciting a bodily response or reaction. "Any new taxation may *irritate*" (Ranken). "We come now to those motions which depend on *irritation*" (Darwin).

Aggression (n); **Aggressiveness** (n). The former suggests violence or hostility. "We shall never sheathe the sword until France is secured against the menace of *aggression*" (Lord Asquith). The latter implies merely assertiveness or boldness. "His fearlessness and *aggressiveness* of speech" (Carlyle).

Agreement.
THE INDEFINITE PRONOUNS: *Anybody, anyone, either, everybody, everyone, neither, nobody, somebody,*

and *someone* are in a strict grammatical sense singular but sometimes in a conceptual sense plural. Grammarians from Lowth forward have drummed into our heads that only the singular number is correct. Proper use appears in Mark Twain's definition of a classic: "Something that *everybody wants* to have read and *nobody wants* to read." But before and after Lowth plurality has often seemed appropriate to indefinite pronouns because of their contextually plural meaning. "Nothing was done without clatter, nobody sat still, and *nobody* could command attention when *they* spoke" (Jane Austen). Only a brave Lowth would change "they spoke" to "he spoke" or—worse still—"he or she spoke."

NOUNS JOINED BY *OR*: Everyone agrees that nouns joined by *and* carry a plural verb and all grammarians agree that singular nouns joined by *or* carry a singular verb. But as with indefinite pronouns a plural connotation may justify a plural construction. "Among whose vices ill nature *or* hardness of heart *were* not numbered" (Fielding).

SUBJECT/VERB: Collective nouns are singular in the opinion of many grammarians, but in "*A bunch* of boys *were* sledding on the slope" the fact that the *boys were* sledding, not the bunch, and the mere proximity of *boys* to the verb together suggest propriety of the plural form. In short, the subject of the sentence is really *boys* and *a bunch of* its modifier.

EITHER/OR; NEITHER/NOR: When singular nouns are so joined a singular verb is used and when plural nouns a plural verb. And yet Johnson wrote "*Neither* search *nor* labor *are* necessary" and Ruskin "*Neither* painting *nor* fighting *feed* men." To this Fowler replies, "The right course is not to indulge in bad grammar ourselves and then plead that better men like Johnson and Ruskin have done it before us, but to follow what is now the accepted as well as logical rule." There is also the rule that when nouns of different number or person are so joined, the verb agrees with the nearest noun. Correct or not, there is something awkward about "*Neither* Fowler *nor I am* prepared to admit error." Write instead, "Fowler and I both think we're right."

WHAT CLAUSES: When the pronoun *what* is the subject of its clause, it carries a singular verb. "Our deeds still travel with us from afar/And *what* we have been *makes* us what we are" (Eliot). But when *what* is the object of a clause and when the predicate noun following the verb is plural, this affects the number of the verb, as in "*What* we need in government, in education, in business *are* men who understand issues in all their complexity" (cited by *WDEU*).

COMPOUND SUBJECTS: It is usually agreed that compound subjects require plural verbs. "The bitterness and heartache that *fill* the world" (Sullivan). But in Renaissance England writers seem not to have concerned themselves with whether nouns joined by a conjunction took a singular or plural verb. Shakespeare wrote, "Like to the Pontick sea,/Whose icy current and compulsive course/Ne'er *feels* retiring ebb." Even Lowth grudgingly admits this usage when a singular verb may be said to apply to each rather than all of the preceding nouns, as in "A mutilation, a cruel disappointment, a loss of wealth, a loss of friends, *seems* at the moment untold loss" (Emerson).

Ain't (contraction). Whole forests have been denuded in paper used in condemnation and discussion of *ain't*. Clearly as a contraction for *is not* and *are not*, it is an illiteracy and a blunder. Still, there is the half-wishful notion that at least in conversation it would be nice to have a proper contraction for *am I not*. *I'm not* does well enough for *I am not*, but *am I not* somehow seems too formal for easy talk. Perhaps someday *ain't* for *am I not* will have the standing of *won't I* or *don't I*, for the Scots *amn't I* does not seem likely to take hold elsewhere.

à la (prep). A French importation meaning in the manner of or according to. Spelled *à l'* before a vowel or the letter *h*, it is much used within and without cookery. It has one curious peculiarity: the feminine form *la* is used even when reference is to a masculine noun. "Punning verse *à la* Ogden Nash."

Alas! Poor Yorick! (quotation). Bryson puts the misuse nicely: " '*Alas! poor Yorick, I knew him, Horatio,*' is the correct version of the line from Hamlet which is often wrongly, and a little mysteriously, rendered as '*Alas! poor Yorick, I knew him well.*' "

Albeit (conj). The word *albeit* [awl BEE it], meaning although, or even if, or notwithstanding, has gone in and out of fashion but has never disappeared from use. "Of one whose eyes,/*Albeit* unused to the melting mood,/Drop tears as fast as the Arabian trees/Their medicinal gum" (Shakespeare).

ALGOL (acronym). Originally known as IAL (International Algebraic Language), *ALGOL* is an acronym for ALGOrithmic Language, a computer medium in which information is expressed in Boolean algebraic notation.

Algorithm (n), **Algorithmic** (adj). Originally *algorism*, the word came into use in ninth-century Persia to mean a procedure for solving a mathematical problem. For example, an *algorithm* is employed in dividing 1,347 by 8, a procedure in which the remainders of partial divisions are carried to the next digit or digits—the remainder of 5 in the division of 13 by 8 is placed before 4 and 54 is then divided by 8. In computer technology *algorithm* has a slightly extended meaning in its sense as a set of rules or procedures for solving a problem in a finite number of steps. An *algorithmic* approach may be contrasted with a *heuristic* approach—the methodology of solving a problem by trial and error.

Alibi (n). From its Latin derivation, it means "in or at another place." Hence in law the defense of having been elsewhere at the time of an alleged crime or wrongdoing. "For some of the prisoners an *alibi* was provided" (Macaulay). As an Americanism it has long also meant any kind of excuse, although purists condemn this extended meaning. Ring Lardner made it stick in one of his fine stories *Alibi Ike:* "I've known lots o' guys that had an *alibi* for every mistake they made. . . . But this baby can't even go to bed without apologizin' " (cited by *WDEU*).

Alien (adj & n); **Alienist** (n); **Alienate** (v). *Alien* as an adjective means simply foreign but by extension strange or even hostile. "She stood in tears amid the *alien* corn" (Keats). "A system of confusion remains which is *alien* to all economy" (Burke). *Alien* as a noun means one born in a country other than that in which he resides but of which he has not become a naturalized citizen or subject. "Obsolete statutes prohibiting *aliens* from working in the kingdom" (Macaulay). However, an *alienist* is specifically a psychiatrist who specializes in the legal aspects of sanity and insanity. "Opposing *alienists* confused the jury and the issue." *Alienate* means to turn away, to make apathetic or averse. "No difference of political opinion can *alienate* Cicero" (Macaulay).

Allergic (adj). In its strict medical context it means sensitive to, but it has grown also to mean having a dislike for or aversion to. The word does not appear in the original *OED*, but it does appear in the *Supplement*. Fowler frowns on this use but allows that *I am allergic to* provides an agreeable alternative to the stilted *I have an instinctive antipathy to*. "For some strange reason women continue to be *allergic* to the charms of Mr. Wodehouse's tales" (*Times Literary Supplement*).

Allow (v); **Permit** (v). Although some commentators make a point of distinguishing between *permit* (to give express consent or authorization) and *allow* (to consent where no objection is present), the distinction is rarely observed. One frequently sees *allow* in the sense of *permit*. "This they cannot be *allowed* to do." However, *allow* also has the meaning of acknowledge or admit. "As to what is alleged, that some of the Presbyterians declared openly against the king's murder, I *allow* it to be true" (Swift).

All Ready (phrase); **Already** (adv). *All ready:* Completely ready or prepared. *Already:* Previously or earlier. "He was *all ready* to go, but the train had *already* gone."

All Together (phrase); **Altogether** (adv). Fowler says flatly that *altogether* is used correctly only in the sense of *entirely* or *on the whole*, whereas *all together* alone means *in a group.* "That kept me from being *altogether* wretched" (Trollope). "They came separately but went away *all together*" (cited by *OED*). Indeed, the *all* in *all together* can often be sacrificed without loss of meaning.

Allude (v), **Allusion** (n); **Elude** (v), **Elusive** (adj), **Elusion** (n); **Illusory** (adj), **Illusion** (n). These words are not often confused, but they are sometimes misused. *Allude* means to refer to a person or thing indirectly or by implication, not by name. "Though he never uses your name, the *allusion* to you is obvious" (Fowler). But it is incorrect to say: "When the speaker *alluded* to President Lincoln, his words were received with loud cheers" (*The New York Times*). *Elude* means simply to evade and its adjective *elusive* means evasive. "Is he in heaven?—Is he in hell?/That demmed *elusive* Pimpernel?" (Baroness Orczy). The *illusory* is that which appears to be of greater real or solid value than is so. "The *elusive* mocks its pursuer, the *illusory* its possessor" (Fowler). An *illusion* is a misapprehension, a false mental image. "There wanted not some about him that would have persuaded him that all was but an *illusion*" (Bacon).

Alongside (adv & prep); **Alongside of** (prep). *Alongside* was originally both adverb and preposition meaning side by side with or parallel to something. " 'I thought, Mr. Simple, that you knew by this time how to bring a boat *alongside*' " (Marryat). "She only bowed and kept *alongside* her companion" (MacDonald). But in its prepositional use it has also long been followed by *of*. "A new authority, marching independently, *alongside of* the government" (Jefferson). Many critics have disliked the *of*, believing it unnecessary, and its use does seem to be receding, although it can scarcely be called an impropriety.

Aloof (adj). It means at a distance and, applied to persons, withdrawn or reserved. It usually carries the preposition *from*: "The noise approaches, though our palace stood/*Aloof from* streets, encompass'd with a wood" (Dryden). But *to* and *with* also appear: "He is *aloof to* others" (Rogers). "He is inclined to be *aloof with* strangers" (Thackeray).

Alright; All Right (adj). The question of whether *alright* is or should be a word is a complex one. Few dictionaries give it room, and those that do say it is formed from a false analogy with *already*. Fowler calls it an "inadmissible vulgarism," although there is evidence that it once existed as a proper word but somehow dropped from sight. Why use it when *all right* attracts no puristic scorn and is of established meaning: safe, sound, agreeable, acceptable, and, somewhat informally, as an affirmative meaning very well. " 'Stand firm, Sam,' said Mr. Pickwick, looking down. '*All right*, sir,' replied Mr. Weller" (Dickens).

Alteration. A synonym for *inclusive-or operation*, it is a logical procedure that will produce a result, depending on bit patterns and bit positions of a computer system.

Altercation (n). An *altercation* is a heated exchange of words or a disputatious argument. No one gets physically hurt in an *altercation*. The *Chicago Tribune* misuses the word: "Three youths were injured in the *altercation*" (cited by Bryson).

Alternate (adj, v, & n), **Alternately** (adv); **Alternative** (adj & n), **Alternatively** (adv). *Alternate* (adj): In a state of constant succession. "This battered Caravanserai whose Doorways are *alternate* Night and Day" (Fitzgerald). *Alternate* (v): To change back and forth between conditions and states, to rotate, to occur successively. "We should *alternate* hot compresses with cold" (Beeson-McDermott). *Alternately* (adv): Successively or in rotation. "The laughing hyena may *alternately* laugh and weep." *Alternative* (adj): Affording an option or preference. "The *alternative* courses before us are war or temporary compromise." *Alternative* (n): A choice. "An unhappy *alternative* is before you, Elizabeth. Your mother will never see you again if you do *not* marry Mr. Collins, and I will never see you again if you *do*" (Jane Austen). *Alternatively* (adv): In a way that offers a selection. "The testator doth appoint executors distinctly or *alternatively*, as I make A or B my executor" (cited by *OED*). In general, the distinction between *alternate* and *alternative* is that the former implies one thing *after* the other, the latter one thing *or* the other.

Alumnus, Alumni, Alumna, Alumnae (n's). A male graduate of a specific school or university or (by extension) any institution is an *alumnus*—plural, *alumni*. Such a female graduate is an *alumna*—plural, *alumnae*. When referring to male and female graduates together, the masculine plural *alumni* is used. "The poorer and less steady *alumni* of the school" (Lytton).

Amalgam (n), Amalgamate (v). Technically, the noun means an alloy of mercury with other metals, but by extension it has come to mean any mixture. "They have confounded all sorts of citizens into an homogenous mass, and then they divided this their *amalgam* into republics" (Burke). The verb also has the same technical and extended meanings. "The Romans were ordained by Providence to conquer and *amalgamate* the materials of Christendom" (Burke).

Amanuensis (n). Literally, from its Latin root, a hand servant but specifically a clerk, stenographer, secretary. "Caesar could dictate to three *amanuenses* together" (Tucker).

Amaze (v); **Astonish** (v); **Surprise** (n & v). *Amaze:* To astound, stun, overwhelm with surprise. "Ye gods, it doth *amaze* me" (Shakespeare). *Astonish:* To strike with sudden wonder, to daze or silence, literally to turn to stone. "One of these days I'll loore him on to skittles and *astonish* him" (Byron). *Surprise* (v): To take unawares. Lord Chesterfield caught by his wife in a compromising situation: "Madam, I am *surprised*, you are *astonished.*" *Surprise* (n): An unexpected occurrence or circumstance. "Two lovely black eyes,/Oh! what a *surprise!*" (Coborn).

Ambient (adj), **Ambiance** (n), **Ambience** (var). It is curious that today the adjective is scarcely ever used and the noun both overused and misused. The adjective means surrounding and the noun environment or atmosphere. But for no good reason *ambiance* has come to have the connotation of elegance or pleasantness. Here is the adjective used correctly: "The planets naturally attain these circular revolutions by impulses of *ambient* bodies" (Bentley). Here is use of the noun as a pretentious substitute for *agreeable atmosphere:* "The superlative cooking and the *ambience* of a fine Soho restaurant" (advertisement).

Ambiguous (adj), **Ambiguity** (n); **Ambivalent** (adj), **Ambivalence** (n); **Equivocal** (adj), **Equivocate** (v). *Ambivalent,* a fairly recent word first appearing in translations of Freud, has come into popular use (perhaps overuse) to describe the state of having contradictory feelings or of wavering between polar opposites or of fluctuating between alternatives. "The Soviet attitude toward us is *ambivalent.* They do not wish to miss the opportunity of exploiting the Middle Eastern situation . . . nor do they wish to lose the advantage of peaceful coexistence" (cited by Fowler). *Ambiguous* means susceptible to two or more interpretations and such *ambiguity* may be either intentional or careless. "But what have been thy answers, what but dark,/*Ambiguous*, and with doubtful sense deluding" (Milton). *Equivocal*, on the other hand, also means susceptible to varying interpretations, but it carries with it the connotation of deliberate, even deceptive, intent to obscure. "The greater number of those who held this were misguided by *equivocal* terms" (Swift). The verb *equivocate* means to be ambiguous or to hedge. "I will not *equivocate*—I will not retreat a single inch" (Garrison).

Amenable (adj). Ready or willing to act, open to persuasion, agreeable, tractable—regularly followed by *to*. "The inferior sort were loose and poor, and not *amenable* to law" (Davies).

Amend (v), **Amendment** (n), **Amends** (n); **Emend** (v), **Emendation** (n). *Amend:* To alter, modify, correct. "Patiently adjust, *amend* and heal" (Hardy). *Amendment:* The act of amending or improving but, specifically, alteration in or addition to a legislative act or resolution. "Let us hastily *amend* the amendment." *Amends:* Reparation or compensation for loss or damage. "And doth not a meeting like this make *amends,*/For all the long years I've been wand'ring away?" (Thomas Moore). *Emend:* Although the word was once simply an alternative spelling to *amend*, it has come to mean specifically to edit a manuscript by correcting its flaws and errors, and *emendation* is the act of manuscript editing. "God save me from busybody *emendation.*"

Americanisms. A word in itself objectionable to some, for in use it is confined to words coined in the United States to the exclusion of Canadian or South American coinage, although all agree that USAisms will scarcely do. In the nineteenth century British purists waged a ferocious and often ludicrous battle against the introduction of Americanisms into England's English. In a notably unhumorous passage, *Punch* delivered this ultimatum: "If the pure well of English is to remain undefiled no Yankee should henceforth be allowed to throw mud into it. It is a form of expectoration that is most profane, most detestable" (cited by Thurber). Even the *London*

Medical Times and Gazette joined the fray, seriously alleging that the medical journals of the United States were written in a slang "too outlandish for any decent English physician to understand" (cited by Mencken).

Now that the fury has abated, the attack seems quite senseless. In fact, it is difficult to see how modern communication could manage without these and many other Americanisms: *balance* (in the sense of remainder), *belittle, bookstore, constitutional* (both as adjective and noun), *flop* (in the sense of failure), *governmental, immigrant* (in the sense of incoming migrant), *influential, lengthy, nationality, presidential, reliable, stockholder,* and *systematize.* It is not easy to understand why words so useful as "presidential" and "lengthy" should be stigmatized, but the *British Monthly Anthology* called both barbarisms. The most durable and curious of all American-coined words is *Yankee,* whose disputed etymology has used up whole trainloads of paper. One that keeps cropping up is that the word springs from Persian *Janghe* (a warlike man), although this derivation was actually proposed as a playful hoax by the *Boston Review* in 1910. *Yankee* means a resident of the United States, but it also specifically means a resident of any of the northeastern states that sided with the Union in the American Civil War. "Out of the United States, even the Georgian does not hesitate to call himself a *Yankee*" (Cooper). But in Georgia a northerner is still a *damned Yankee.*

Amiable (adj); **Amicable** (adj). From the same root these words have similar but distinctive meanings. *Amiable* means agreeable, of a kindly disposition; *amicable* means friendly, harmonious. "I cannot help it if I am more delighted with any thing that is *amiable,* than with any thing that is wonderful" (Congreve). "Enter each mild, each *amicable* guest" (Pope).

Among (prep); **Between** (prep). Correct usage presumably requires that *among* be used to indicate a relationship of more than two objects or persons, and *between* a relationship of only two objects or persons. "*Between* the Devil and the deep blue sea." But this is a distinction now as much honored in the breach as in the observance.

Amoral (adj), **Immoral** (adj), **Unmoral** (adj). *Amoral* means without moral quality—neither moral nor immoral. "Birds and animals may justly be considered *amoral*" (Emerson). *Immoral* means wicked, depraved, consciously sinful. "There is no such thing as a moral or *immoral* book. Books are well written, or badly written" (Wilde). *Unmoral* means having no relationship to morality, being unable to distinguish between right and wrong. "The homicidal maniac may be considered *unmoral* and hence not consciously vicious."

Amuck (adv); **Amok** (adv & n). Both adverbs mean in a frenzied manner, but *amok* as a noun means a psychic disturbance characterized by mania and violence. Hence in its adverbial use some commentators prefer the spelling *amuck*, although *amok* is common enough. "He runs *amuck*, stabbing every man he meets" (Marshall).

Analogue (n); **Analog** (var). Something similar to something else. "Humming birds, like the butterflies, whose *analogues* they are, suck the nectar of the flowers" (Kirby). But in computer science an *analog* is the representation and analysis of a system by variable physical entities, such as voltages. Hence an *analog computer* is one designed to perform arithmetical functions upon numbers represented by some physical quality.

Anathema (n); **Anathematize** (v). *Anathema* is a thing or person accursed or a curse itself, especially the solemn ban of excommunication. "To strike with His *anathema* those who made a gain of their virtues" (Morley). *Anathematize* is now rarely used in its particular sense of pronouncing accursed by ecclesiastical authority. "They were therefore to be *anathematized* and, with detestation, branded and banished out of the church" (Taylor).

Anent (prep). A bookish word having its origin in old Scots law and meaning "concerning" or "about." Many critics have called its modern use affected, although it appears often, especially in letters to newspapers: "*Anent* your ill-considered editorial." Fowler gives such use a rough time: "It is a favorite with unpractised writers who, on their holiday excursions into print, like to show that they possess gala attire." One might think he had known the lilting silliness of Spiro Agnew's "The nattering nabobs of negativism will no longer natter negatively *anent* Nixon."

Angry (adj); **Mad** (adj). These words should never be confused. *Angry:* Wrathful, indignant, resentful. "Do no sinful action,/speak no *angry* word" (Alexander). *Mad:* Insane, abnormal, frenzied. "For Allah created the English *mad*—the maddest of all mankind!" (Kipling).

Annoy: See **Aggravate.**

Anoint (v). To sprinkle on or apply an ointment to; to consecrate in a ceremony that includes token application of oil. In either sense *anoint* has only one "n," but the misspelling *annoint* has become so common that it is almost standard. Something of both senses of the word is seen in "*Anointed* let me be with deadly venom" (Shakespeare). Bierce thus defines *anoint:* "To grease a king or other great functionary already slippery enough."

Antagonist: See **Adversary.**

Anticipate (v). Another of those words critics argue about, Bierce saying that it means only to foresee something and take action to prevent, oppose, or fulfill it. In fact, *anticipate* is used often and correctly to mean foresee or predict with no connotation of action to forestall what is expected. "Why should we/*Anticipate* our sorrows? 'Tis like those/That die for fear of death" (Denham).

Antipodes (n). *Antipodes* [an **TIP** uh DEEZ] can mean opposite or contrary things. However, since from its Greek roots the word means "with feet in the opposite direction," it has come particularly to mean places diametrically opposite on the globe or the people who live there. Johnson, in fact, gives only the latter meaning: "Those people who, living on the other side of the globe, have their feet directly opposite to ours." To contemporary Englishmen the term has come to mean Australia and New Zealand and their inhabitants, who with justice contend that it is the British whose feet are in the opposite direction.

Anxious (adj), Anxiety (n). Bryson and others say flatly that *anxious* should carry the connotation of being worried or fearful and not merely eager or expectant. However, if usage is a guide, *anxious* has meant eager for over two hundred years: "The gentle heart, *anxious* to please" (Blair).

Anybody (pron); Anyone (pron). (See also *Agreement.*) All purists agree that these pronouns *should* carry singular verbs but that it is not ungrammatical for them to take plural complementary pronouns. "How fit this retreat is for uninterrupted study. *Anyone* that *sees* it will own that I could not have chosen a more likely place to converse with the dead in" (Pope), but "As *anybody* in *their* senses would have done" (Jane Austen).

Apogee: See Nadir.

Apologize (v), Apology (n); Excuse (n & v); Pardon (n & v). *Apologize* (v): To admit, regretfully, error or wrongdoing. "I never *apologize*" (Shaw). *Apology* (n): Written or spoken regret or remorse for a wrong or insulting act or a malicious deed but also a defense or justification. "An *apology* for the Devil: It must be remembered that we have heard only one side of the case. God has written all the books" (Byron). *Excuse* (n & v): Both noun and verb have the same essential meaning. An *excuse* shifts rather than admits blame; it offers extenuation for a fault. "Let my obedience then *excuse*/My disobedience now" (Cowper). It also asks for forgiveness or indulgence. Like Jonathan Swift, Dorothy Parker wrote her own epitaph: "*Excuse* my dust." *Pardon* (n & v): Both forms signify forgiveness of an offense, wrong, or discourtesy. "Dr. Mudd's heirs and defenders believe that his *pardon* implied guilt and that he should be exonerated" (Dusseau). From the foregoing it is clear that "*Pardon* me" is too strong an expression for use in the instance of a trivial discourtesy. "*Excuse* me" is generally preferable.

Apostrophe (punctuation). The apostrophe is used to indicate omission of a letter (usually a vowel) as in *don't* for *do not.* It also marks the possessive case of nouns and indefinite pronouns, as in *Solomon's* wisdom or *everyone's* privilege. This system still in everyday use was elaborated by Lowth and later

Priestley in the eighteenth century, but Lowth for no clear reason also directed that the possessives *hers, theirs, yours, ours,*
and *its* should be written *her's, their's, your's, our's,* and *it's.*
Even then and without exception now, these pronouns in the
possessive case are written without apostrophes, and this is
helpful in preserving the distinction between elision and possession (*it's* a contraction for *it is* and *its* the possessive; *who's* a
contraction for *who is* and *whose* the possessive). The apostrophe is also used in the plurals of letters (e.g., "Mind your p's
and q's"), numerals (e.g., "She was at 6's and 7's"), and words
(e.g., "Too many nay's and not enough yea's"), but the plurals of
words representing sounds do not carry the apostrophe, as in
"the *oohs* and *aahs* of the crowd" (Bernstein). Perhaps the only
real difference of opinion regarding the apostrophe involves its
use in proper nouns ending with the letter *s*—some preferring
Jones' folly, others *Jones's* folly, the latter having an apparent
recent edge, possibly because *Jones's* sounds roundly possessive.
It may also be worth note that in medicine, there is a curious
new tendency to avoid possessives altogether in the instance of
eponyms, so that what has been known for two centuries as
Addison's disease has suddenly become *Addison disease.* This
folly may arise from a mistaken attempt to distinguish between
Addison's defining the disease and Addison's having the
disease.

Apostrophe (n), **Apostrophize** (v). *Apostrophe:* A
somewhat curious word meaning a digression in speech or writing to address a person or being not present or a personified idea
or thing. In "O Death, where is thy sting?" *O Death* is an *apostrophe.* The verb *apostrophize* means to address through
apostrophe. "There is a peculiarity in Homer's manner of *apos-
trophizing* Eumaeus and speaking of him in the second person; it
is generally applied only to men of account" (Pope).

Apotheosis (n), **Apotheosize** (v). The noun means
the exaltation or elevation of a person to godhood and, by
extension, epitome or quintessence. "Allots the prince of his
celestial line,/An *apotheosis,* and rites divine" (Garth) or "An
Ode to a Nightingale—the *apotheosis* of lyric poetry." The
verb means to deify or glorify. "The rage for accumulation has
apotheosized work" (Spencer).

Appendix (n); **Index** (n). A small controversy may be readily resolved. Both *appendices* and *appendixes*, *indices* and *indexes*, are correct.

Application program. A computer software program written for a specific discipline, such as accounting or astronomy.

Apposite (adj); **Opposite** (adj). *Apposite:* Suitable, well-adapted, relevant. *Opposite:* Opposed, contrary, radically different. "His statement though *opposite* to accepted ideas, was *apposite*."

Appraise (v), **Appraisal** (n); **Apprise** (v), **Apprize** (var). *Appraise* (v): To assess; to estimate the size, quantity, worth, or monetary value of anything. *Appraisal* (n): The act of appraising and, specifically, item-by-item evaluation of property for insurance or tax purposes. *Apprise* (v): To inform or disclose (often followed by *of*). *Apprize* is a seldom-used variant of *apprise*. "When *apprised of* the *appraisal*, he was astonished at the value of his legacy."

Apprehend (v), **Apprehension** (n), **Apprehensive** (adj); **Comprehend** (v), **Comprehension** (n), **Comprehensive** (adj). These words all signify understanding, but they have subtle differences of meaning and of extension as shown in their roots, for *ap-* forms denote *getting* hold or grasping and the *com-* forms *having* hold or possession of. What is beyond one's *apprehension* is beyond perception; what is beyond *comprehension* is not fully understood. *Apprehend* (v): (1) To grasp the meaning of, to perceive. (2) To take into custody, arrest, catch. (3) To be suspicious or fearful of. (1) "He that can *apprehend* and consider vice with all her baits and seeming pleasures" (Milton). (2) "The sheriff *apprehended* the castle thieves in the midst of their dastardly attempt." (3) "From my grandfather's death I had reason to *apprehend* the stone, and, from my father's life, the gout" (Temple). And the noun *apprehension* often has the force of fear. "The sense of death is most in *apprehension*" (Shakespeare). *Comprehend* (v): (1) To understand the nature, meaning, or significance of. (2) To include or comprise. (1) "Our souls, whose faculties can *comprehend*/The wondrous Architecture of the world" (Marlowe). (2) "Such tricks hath strong imagination/That, if it would but *apprehend* some joy,/It *comprehends* some bringer of that joy" (Shakespeare).

Approximate (v & adj), **Approximately** (adv), **Approximation** (n). All take their essential meaning from the verb: Come near to, approach closely to, or, by extension, estimate. It may or may not be followed by *to*. "A narrow valley, almost *approximating to* the character of a ravine" (Stanley). But Follett and others dislike the adverb *approximately* and would replace it with *about* or *nearly* or *almost*, although this disregards substantial and reasonable use: "They will be only *approximately* intelligible to us" (Hawson). *Approximation* is often followed by *to* but sometimes *of*. "Quadrupeds are better placed according to the degrees of their *approximation to* the human figure" (Grew).

Arbitrate (v), **Arbiter** (n), **Arbitrator** (n); **Mediate** (v), **Mediator** (n). The separate meanings of these words are sometimes confused. To *arbitrate* means to hear evidence upon and then make a decision in the matter at hand. "Now who shall *arbitrate*?/Whom shall my soul believe" (Browning). An *arbitrator* decides and is aloof from the parties at dispute. Sometimes too *arbitrator* and *arbiter* are also confused. The former is appointed to reach a judgment; the latter is one whose opinion is valued and sought but in whom there is no vested authority. To *mediate* is to negotiate, and a *mediator* usually shuttles back and forth between the disputing parties to reach not a judgment but a compromise. "Bacon attempted to *mediate* between the Earl of Essex and the Queen" (Macaulay).

Arcane (adj). A useful word but little used, it means secret, abstruse, esoteric and somehow suggests ancient mysteries. "The eximious and *arcane* science of physicke" (Johnson). *Eximious*, by the way, means choice, distinguished, excellent and is characterized by most dictionaries as obsolete, but it still has a pleasant sound and look.

Archaic (adj). Characteristic of an older period, antiquated. *Archaic* words such as *forsooth* are apt to appear in gaudy historical novels, but this is not to say that such words may not have a place in careful writing, although Fowler would not give them much leeway. "*Archaic* words thrust into a commonplace context to redeem its ordinariness are an abomination."

Architecture (n). The art or science of design and construction of buildings, communities, or public areas and, by extension, the style of buildings or the structure of anything. "*Architecture* in general is frozen music" (Von Schelling). For computers, *architecture* is their design and the systems through which hardware and software interact to achieve functional objectives.

Archive (n), **Archivist** (n). In the singular a place for keeping public records and in the plural the records themselves, but the distinction has never been carefully observed. "The Universities, *archives* of all the errors of the age" (Seeley). "He had access to the whole of Lady Astor's *archive*" (cited by *WDEU*). *Archivist*: A keeper of *archives*. "Under the emperors, the *archivist* was an office of great dignity" (Chambers). In computer technology an *archive* is a procedure by which data are transferred from a memory area to a storage medium or a copy of the data so transferred and stored.

Aroma (n), **Aromatic** (adj). An odor or fragrance, especially a pleasant one, arising from spices, flowers, wines, or cookery. "And breathes perfumes no Persian *aromas* can imitate" (cited by *OED*). *Aromatic* has the same meaning; but both words, although they imply an agreeable odor, also imply strong scent. "Now the Jonquille o'ercomes the feeble brain;/We faint beneath the *aromatic* pain" (Anne Finch).

Arrant (adj); **Errant** (adj). Originally both words meant, from their Latin root, wandering or straying. *Errant* has retained this meaning, but *arrant* has come to mean downright or notorious or contemptible. "We are *arrant* knaves all; believe none of us" (Shakespeare). "There are just seven planets, or *errant* stars, in the lower orbs of heaven, but it is now demonstrable unto sense that there are many more" (Brown's *Vulgar Errours*). Notwithstanding the lofty ideals of chivalry, a knight *errant* and an *arrant* knave may still be the same person.

Array (v & n). The verb is used with many prepositions, but in the sense of "dress" or "equip" either *in* or *with*
may be used. "Now . . . the morn *array'd in* gold empyreal"
(Milton). "Deck thyself now with majesty and excellency and
array thyself *with* glory and beauty" (Job). The noun *array*
means arrangement, attire, or dress. "In this remembrance,
Emily ere day/Arose and dressed herself in rich *array*"
(Dryden). But to a computer an *array* is an arrangement of specific items of data identified by a key or subscript in such a way
that a program can extract data relevant to a particular key.

As . . . as (conj). Purists generally insist that *as . . .
as* should be used in positive statements and *so . . . as* negatively. "Sempronius is *as* brave a man *as* Cato" (Addison). "She
is not *so* pretty *as* I expected" (Jane Austen). But if this be rule,
usage often breaks it. "The Church never was *as* rotten *as* the
stock-exchange now is" (cited by *WDEU*).

ASCII. Acronym for American Standard Code of
Information Interchange. A standard computer code used to
facilitate interchange of data between various machines and
systems in teleprocessing. It is curious that Johnson defines the
word ASCII as from the Greek shadow and meaning those
people who, at certain times of the year, cast no shadow at
noon.

As good or better than (phrase). Bernstein and
other purists of course argue that "I am *as good or better than*
you" is slipshod, for it should obviously read, "I am *as good
as* or better *than* you." But the correct version is somehow awkward, and it might be argued that the second *as* is understood.
If hard-pressed, say "I am *as* good *as* you, or better."

Assay (n & v); **Essay** (n & v). *Assay* means, as a
verb, to analyze or to test; as a noun, a test or trial. "The *assay*
disclosed that all that glitters is not gold." *Essay* as verb or
noun means attempt or effort, but the noun has also the specific
meaning of a short literary composition built upon a central
theme. Hence Lord Bacon: "My *essays* come home to men's business and bosoms."

Assembler or **Assembler program.** A program that converts a symbolic language into a machine language.

Assume (v); **Presume** (v); **Presumptuous** (adj), **Presumptive** (adj). The verbs are almost but not quite alike in meaning. To *assume* is to take for granted, to suppose, to accept without proof, whereas *presume*, too, is to suppose but also to undertake something without right or permission or to go too far in acting boldly or taking liberties. "In every hypothesis, something is allowed to be *assumed*" (Boyle). "We *presume* to see what is meet and convenient and good, better than God himself" (Hooker). And, of course, *assume* has the added meaning of taking on duties or responsibilities ("He *assumed* the office of president") and of taking on or being invested with ("The conflict, previously peaceful, now *assumed* a threatening character"). *Presumptuous* and *presumptive* share the meaning of arrogant or confident. "Some will not venture to look beyond received notions of the age, nor have so *presumptuous* a thought, as to be wiser than their neighbours" (Locke). "There being two opinions repugnant to each other, it may not be *presumptive* or skeptical to doubt of both" (Brown), but *presumptive* has the added specific meaning of supposed in relation to titles, as in "the *presumptive* heir," as opposed to heir apparent.

Assure (v); **Ensure** (v); **Insure** (v), **Insurance** (n); **Reassure** (v), **Reassurance** (n). *Assure:* To declare earnestly, to convince, to state confidently, to be certain of. "Drest in a little brief authority,/Most ignorant of what he's most *assur'd*" (Shakespeare). *Ensure:* To make sure or certain. "This letter will *ensure* your admission but hasten your departure." *Insure:* To guarantee or indemnify against loss or harm. "Down went the owners—greedy men whom hope of gain allured;/Oh, dry the starting tear, for they were heavily *insured*" (Gilbert). *Insurance* has the more particular meaning of the act or business of insuring property or person against loss or harm by providing indemnification therefor or the coverage or contract itself. *Reassure:* To assure again or repeatedly but with the connotation of bringing encouragement or comfort or confidence to. "His praise *reassured* me and restored my courage." *Reassurance* is restoration of confidence, removal of doubt, repeated confirmation. "His *reassurances* encouraged my fresh attempt."

Astonish: See **Amaze.**

Asynchronous (adj). Not occurring simultaneously or in correspondence. "When Contractions of the Ventricle become *asynchronous* and inharmonious to those of the Auricle" (Hartley). In computer science *asynchronous* describes the mode of operation of a machine in which the completion of one operation initiates another, contrasted with machine operations synchronized to a schedule by a clocking device.

Attain (v), **Attainment** (n). Generally *attain* has the implication of reaching a desired end or goal, but it can also mean to reach the end (whether desired or not) of a progression or simply to reach: "The heights by great men reached and kept,/Were not *attained* by sudden flight,/But they, while their companions slept/Were toiling upward in the night" (Longfellow). "The heroic marshal, however, *attained* the opposite shore." The noun *attainment* shares these meanings: "We dispute with men who count it a great *attainment* to be able to talk much, and little to the purpose" (Glanville).

Attenuate (v), **Attenuation** (n). To *attenuate* is to make thin, to reduce in force, intensity, or value. "The delightfulness of the one will *attenuate* the tediousness of the other" (Lyly). *Attenuation*, then, means reduction, diminution, or emaciation. "Heat doth rarefy the air by *attenuation*" (Browne). But in electronics *attenuation* means specifically the difference in amplitude between a signal at transmission and at reception.

Attribute (n & v), **Attributive** (adj); **Impute** (v), **Imputative** (adj). The verb *attribute* means to regard as resulting from a specific cause; to consider as a quality of something or someone; to ascribe to a person, time, period, or place. "The sort of mystical character which is apt to be *attributed* to the idea of moral obligation" (Mill). The noun has similar meanings. Something seen as part of the nature of a person or thing; something used as a symbol of a person or office. "But mercy is above this sceptered sway,/It is an *attribute* to God himself" (Shakespeare). "A crown, an *attribute* of sovereign power"

(Wordsworth). *Attribute,* possibly because of association with *tribute,* has come to have a complimentary character, whereas *impute* has come to have the negative connotation of blaming someone or something as a cause. *"Impute* your dangers to your ignorance" (Dryden). The adjective *imputative* (accusatory) is now but rarely used.

Audacity (n), Audacious (adj). The noun means boldness, daring, venturesomeness, but it has also always had the connotation of impudent or improper bravery. "He has had the *audacity* to ask for the hand of my daughter in marriage." And a similar force in the adjective may be seen in Shakespeare's phrase "saucy and *audacious* eloquence."

Audience (n). Early moviegoers in mass were naturally enough called an *audience,* but purists objected that the word derives from the Latin verb "to hear," so that theatergoers are an *audience* but moviegoers are spectators (from "to look"). The battle has long since been lost, just as the poet's *audience* once consisted of listeners whom printing made readers but who are still an *audience.* The word adapts itself to any new technology and becomes a collective noun for all those who see, hear, and read concerts, operas, plays, circuses, books, radio and television performances, and even fashion shows. "Saint Laurent appealed to a more avant-garde *audience"* (cited by *WDEU).*

Auger (n & v); Augur (n & v), Augury (n). Sometimes their spelling is confused but rarely their meanings, for an *auger* is simply a boring tool. "The *Auger* hath a handle and bit. Its office is to make great round holes" (Moxon). "The results of the election do not *auger* well for the President" or for precise use of words in *The New York Times. Augur* derives from the name of ancient Roman officials charged with observing and interpreting omens, and some would argue that as a noun *augur* means only soothsayer or prophet and as a verb to divine or predict from signs or omens, the proper synonym for omen or sign being *augury:* "Whose open, handsome, hardy face *augured* a frank and fearless nature" (Lytton); "From their flight strange *augury* she drew" (Dayton). Still, *augur* is often used to mean sign or portent. Whether overused or not the verb *augur* appears often in the phrase *augur well for*. "It *augurs well for* writing that few writers consult style manuals."

Aural: See Oral.

Authoress (n). A word generally disliked in literary circles because gender is irrelevant to art and the word *author* conveys no distinction of sex. Nonetheless, the word persists, and Jane Austen used it in no chauvinistic sense: "I think I may boast myself to be the most unlearned and uninformed female who dared to be an *authoress*."

Authority (n); **Authoritative** (adj); **Authoritarian** (adj). *Authority* is the power to determine, adjudicate, or control and hence a person or agency in whom or which such power is vested. "Man, proud man;/Drest in a little brief *authority*,/Most ignorant of what he's most assur'd" (Shakespeare). Also then a cited source of validation. "We urge *authorities* in things that need not, and introduce the testimony of ancient writers, to confirm things evidently believed (Brown's *Vulgar Errours*). *Authoritative* describes anyone or anything having *authority* or the air of *authority*. "The two worthies have done much mischief, the mock *authoritative* manner of the one, and the insipid mirth of the other" (Swift). But *authoritarian* describes complete control of or power over the will of others or of another. Hence either a government or a parent may be *authoritarian*. "Men who are *authoritarian* by nature and cannot imagine that a country should be orderly save under a military despotism" (cited by *OED*).

Autochthon (n), **Autochthonous** (adj). *Autochthon* [aw TAHK thun] is a little-used and perhaps somewhat fanciful word for an original inhabitant or an indigenous plant or animal. "There was therefore never any *Autochthon*, or man arising from the earth, but Adam" (Browne). *Autochthonous* too is infrequently used but sometimes misused. In its primal sense it means native or indigenous. "The English have this great predilection for *autochthonous* bread and butter" (Taylor). But in psychology it means pertaining to ideas that arise independently of an individual's usual cast of thought and seem to have some external agency as their source. It is in this extended sense that it is sometimes wrongly used to mean aberrant.

Avenge (v); **Revenge** (v). *Avenge* means to settle a score or redress an injustice. *"Avenge,* O Lord, thy slaughtered saints"* (Milton). *Revenge,* on the other hand, has the connotation of personal animus, of severe retaliation. *"Revenge* his foul and most unnatural murder"* (Shakespeare).

Average: See Median.

Averse (adj), **Aversion** (n). The adjective means having a strong feeling of dislike, antipathy, or repugnance, and, since it has the sense of turning away, Johnson, Lowth, and other puritans of speech say it can be followed only by *from,* but *averse to* has always been common and, if Boswell reported Johnson accurately, even the Great Cham did not disdain its use: "Why, Sir, you cannot call that pleasure *to* which all are *averse."* There is less controversy over the prepositions that may follow *aversion*—*to, from,* and even *for* or *toward* being common. "His *aversion towards* the house of York" (Bacon). And, of course, the noun often stands alone with its object unspecified: " 'Tis safest in matrimony to begin with a little *aversion"* (Sheridan). (See also *Adverse.)*

Avert (v); **Divert** (v); **Evert** (v). The words have the same Latin root (to turn) but different meanings. *Avert:* To turn aside or ward off. "Use any expedient which might *avert* the danger" (Macaulay). *Divert:* To deflect, to distract, or, more broadly, to entertain. "An avocation to *divert* her thoughts, fill her time, and divide her interests" (Brontë). *Evert:* To turn outward or inside out, to overturn. "It is a very simple and easy thing to *evert* the eyelids" (Harlan).

Avid (adj), **Avidity** (n). Barzun tells us that *avid* can mean only hungry, greedy, or moved by physical appetite. In actual use *avid* more commonly means enthusiastic, ardent, or eager without any connotation of physical appetite. "An *avid* reader" is a phrase repeated often—perhaps too often. In "the most *avid* desire for personal power" (Lytton) or in "magazines which I used to read with *avidity* when I was a boy" (Tyndell), psychic, not physical, appetite is meant.

Avuncular (adj). In the manner of or pertaining to an uncle. Although there is no canon for the behavior of uncles, the word has taken on an overtone of mild beneficence. Nevertheless, it is also used (perhaps humorously) to describe a pawnbroker. "If you enter one of these pawnshops . . . you will observe these peculiarities in the internal economy of the *avuncular* life" (cited by *OED*).

Awesome (adj); **Awful** (adj), **Awfully** (adv). Originally *awesome* meant inspiring awe, as in "an *awesome* sight," but the word has been adapted to mean highly impressive. "Finished his season in *awesome* fashion, winning eight of his last nine decisions" (Angell). *Awful* and *awfully* have had a similar decline in intensity. Once meaning only striking with awe or inspiring reverence, *awful* has come to mean dreary or misbegotten, as in "Great God! this is an *awful* place" (Robert Scott), and *awfully* has come, like *terribly*, to mean extremely, as in "It's *awfully* (or *terribly*) hot in Hades and in Haiti." Fowler frowns on both uses.

Backward (adj & adv); Backwards (adv). As an adverb either form may be used. "It is a poor sort of memory that only works *backwards*" (Carroll). But as an adjective, only *backward* may be used. "But I by backward steps would move" (Vaughan).

Bad (adj), Badly (adv). *Bad* is a curious word with its comparative *worse* and superlative *worst* and its wide range of meanings from disagreeable, wicked, and evil, through faulty and rotten, to inadequate, naughty, and ill. "The nature of *bad* news infects the teller" (Shakespeare). Its adverbial form is scorned in its prevalent misuse, "I feel *badly*." If this means anything, it is that one's sense of touch is operating poorly. However, the error is now so common that grammatical distinction between adjective and adverb is breaking down, but resist this temptation and say, instead, "I feel *bad*." Disraeli has one of his characters say, "I rather like *bad* wine; one gets so bored with good wine." Hence it was said of Disraeli that his inverted snobbery was but *badly* disguised.

Bad taste. A phrase that has reasonably clear meaning but no precise definition. Its essence is excess. The Taj Mahal is a work of restrained beauty; its seashore imitation a gargoyle of gaudy finery and overdone ornamentation. Even the sage and witty *Encyclopedia of Bad Taste* must concede that things in *bad taste* have a certain captivating and enduring quality. From the Roman circus to Liberace, unvarnished awfulness often seems funny or alluring. Elvis Presley proved that in the large world of *bad taste* too much is never enough. Hang on to your fin-tailed Cadillac and your elephant's foot umbrella stand. The *bad taste* of excessiveness may appear in language as well as in action. A college president, worried about faculty voting, published a statement, reading in part: "Concern for the need to facilitate a more helpful acceptance oriented vehicle as an antecedent provision to voting" (cited by Gummere). How easily sense becomes nonsense.

Bail out (v); **Bale out** (v). In securing a person's release from custody by guaranteeing his reappearance for trial, the spelling is always *bail out*, and the *OED* stoutly maintains that for emptying a boat of water we should use the same spelling, for the verb derives from the French *baille*, bucket. But the *OED* might as well save its breath, for public usage prefers, indeed insists upon, *bale* both for the boat and for making a parachute descent, and reserves *bail* for prisoners. Perhaps a mania for differentiation has caused this strange distinction.

Baited (pp); **Bated** (pp). To "listen with *baited* breath" is to listen with breath prepared for fishing. The word should be *bated*, a cousin of *abate*—to grow or become less. "*Abate* thy speed, and I will *bate* of mine" (Dryden).

Baleful (adj); **Baneful** (adj). The two words are sometimes used interchangeably, but they do differ in emphasis. *Baleful* means portending or threatening ill or evil, whereas *baneful* means causing ill or evil. " 'Round he throws his *baleful* eyes,/That witnessed huge affliction and dismay" (Milton). "The nightly wolf is *baneful* to the fold,/Storms to the wheat, to buds the bitter cold" (Dryden).

Bamboozle (v). An expressive word of uncertain origin. Although gypsies may have occasionally *bamboozled*, there is no real evidence that the word comes from their world. It means to deceive or cheat and also to confuse or puzzle. "Perhaps if I wanted to be understood or to understand I would *bamboozle* myself into belief" (Greene). Mrs. Gaskell uses it in the sense of puzzle: "He fairly *bamboozles* me. He is two chaps."

Band. In telecommunications a specific range of frequencies, especially a set of radio frequencies. In computer operation one or more tracks or channels on a magnetic drum.

Barbaric (adj); **Barbarous** (adj). The two words are close in meaning, each referring to the customs and ways of barbarians. However, *barbaric* is sometimes used in a favorable sense to mean vigorous, strong, or splendid. "Where the gorgeous east with richest hand/Showers on her kings *barbaric* pearl and gold" (Milton). But *barbarous* always means uncivilized, fierce, cruel, savage. "Twas a *barbarous* deed" (Shelley).

Barbarism (n). A harsh term for misuse of language but one often so employed. There are two kinds of *barbarisms*. The first consists of common errors such as use of *irregardless* for *regardless, presumptious* for *presumptuous, portentious* for *portentous, beneficient* for *beneficent, principal* for *principle*, and so on. The second consists of words coined mostly in America that British purists and pundits universally labeled as "barbarisms." The *Monthly Review* in 1808 denounced "the corruptions and *barbarisms* which are hourly obtaining in the speech of our transatlantic colonies." In British reviews of Bancroft's *Life of George Washington* and of Barlow's *Columbiad*, the coinage of new words was soundly condemned, and in the latter work the *Edinburgh Review* found "a great multitude of words which are radically and entirely new, and as utterly foreign as if they had been adopted from the Hebrew or Chinese" and "the perversion of a still greater number of English words from their proper use or signification" (cited by Mencken). Among the *barbarisms* to which violent objection was taken were *accountability*, to *appreciate* (to rise in value), *backwoodsman*, *balance* (remainder), *bookstore, dutiable, fall* (autumn), to *locate, presidential*, to *progress, squatter, stockholder*, and a thousand others, all of which are in reasonably good taste and common use today. (See also *Americanisms*.)

Bar sinister (n). A somewhat curious phrase. Bierce says there is no such thing in heraldry, and he is right, but it is a phrase in some use with the specific meaning of the condition or stigma of illegitimate birth. "In later years Lawrence treated his bastard status lightly, remarking that *bars sinister* are rather jolly ornaments" (cited by *WDEU*). Once in a great while one sees the expression used as if it meant sinister portent or threat, but there is no justification for this use.

BASIC. An acronym for Beginner's All-purpose Symbolic Instruction Code—a high-level conversational programming language in wide use. It incorporates both common words and commonly used mathematical symbols. The BASIC language consists of two principal parts: the source statements (instructions forming the actual program) and system commands, which allow the user to control the BASIC compiling system.

Bastion (n). The word is sometimes misused to mean a fortress. Actually it is a projecting portion of a rampart or fortification, but in its extended sense it may mean also anything preserving or defending some right, thing, quality, or condition. "The frontier and *Bastion* of the Protestant Religion" (Taylor).

Batch. In computer language a collection of transactions in the form of source documents, punched cards, or records on a magnetic storage device. *Batch processing* is a method for processing data in which transactions (generated data) are prepared for input to the computer for processing as a single unit without provision for user input. An efficient but limited use of computer time and facility, in contrast to *Interactive processing.*

Bathos (n); Pathos (n). *Bathos* (from Greek *bathus,* deep) means the lowest point and by extension triteness or descent from an elevated position to one commonplace or even vulgar. "*Bathos,* the art of sinking in Poetry" (Pope). It is not the opposite of *pathos,* which means the power or faculty of evoking a feeling of pity or compassion. "He descanted on the woes of the land with a *pathos* which drew tears from every eye" (Prescott).

Baud. A unit used to measure the speed of transmission of a telegraph or telephone channel. At one time *baud* was used as a synonym for bits per second, but in multistate signaling, modulation rate and data signaling rate do not have the same value so that *bauds* and bits per second no longer can be used interchangeably.

Bead. In a computer program a small module that performs a specific function.

Bear (v); **Bore, Born, Borne** (pp). *Bear* as a verb has various but distinct meanings. To give birth to, to produce by natural growth, to support, to endure, to take. However, in the use of its past participle curious distinctions are preserved, *borne* being correct in all senses except that of birth. "*Borne,* like thy bubbles, onward" (Byron). But "All men were naturally *born* free" (Milton). However, and unfortunately, *borne* is also used in its active sense to refer to birth, "She has *borne* no children," and in the passive sense when *by* follows, "Several children *borne by* her survive." But in the passive sense without *by, born* is correct: "A *born* fool." This is confusing enough without bringing four-legged carnivora into the picture. "*Bears born* in hibernation are known to have *borne* subzero temperatures nicely."

Beat. A time unit related to the execution of a computer instruction.

Beauteous (adj). A somewhat fancy synonym for beautiful or elegant in form, it has for no apparent reason aroused the scorn of several commentators who call it variously "ugly," "barbaric," "archaic," and "overly poetical." It scarcely seems to deserve these epithets, for it has long been in good use. "I can, Petruchio, help thee to a wife,/With wealth enough, and young, and *beauteous*" (Shakespeare).

Because of, Due to, Owing to, On account of (prep's). *Because of* and *on account of* are clearly adverbial prepositions in good and standard use: "He fell *because of* the slippery ice." But *due to* and *owing to* present a curious problem. *Due* and *owing* are both adjectives and seemingly should hence only modify nouns, so that "His fall was *due to* the slippery ice" is correct, but "He fell *due to* the slippery ice" is incorrect. However, long usage has sanctioned *owing to* in an adverbial character: "He fell from His Grace's grace *owing to* his gracelessness." But this privilege has not yet been accorded *due to*.

"The preposition *due to,* is not more incorrect than the preposition *owing to,* but it is not yet so thoroughly established in the language" (Curme). The only present satisfactory answer to this grammarian's dilemma is to avoid *due to.*

Behalf (n). Some see a genuine distinction between *on behalf of* and *in behalf of.* The first means acting as a representative, agent, or spokesman, whereas the second means acting as a friend or supporter and has a more personal touch. Still, the slight difference is seldom observed although seen here: "Were but my heart as naked to thy view,/Marcus would see it bleed *in his behalf"* (Addison). "An application was made *on behalf of* the prosecutor for a remand" (Mathew).

Behoove (v), **Behove** (v). The former is American spelling, the latter British. Both mean to be necessary or fitting and both are often used in impersonal constructions with *it.* "He did so prudently temper his passions, as that none of them made him wanting in the offices of life, which *it behooved,* or became him, to perform" (Atterbury).

Belie (v). A useful verb meaning to misrepresent, to contradict, to give the lie to. "Their trembling hearts *belie* their boastful tongues" (Dryden). But Follett fears that modern usage has twisted its meaning into the opposite sense of betoken or evince. If so, there is small evidence of such misuse. *Belie* continues on the steady course of its original meaning. "Those who dare *belie* their human nature" (Shelley).

Bellicose, Belligerent, Fractious, Pugnacious, Truculent (adj's). It might conveniently be held that all mean eager and ready to fight, and this is so of *bellicose* and *belligerent,* the former from Latin *bellicosus* (pertaining to war), the latter from Latin *belligerare* (to wage war). But the other adjectives have special meanings of their own. *Fractious:* Unruly, easily angered, peevish. "Men struggling doubtfully with *fractious* cows and frightened sheep" (Wallace). *Pugnacious:* Quarrelsome, contentious. "These *pugnacious* Florentines, whose personal feuds and hatreds were infinitely real" (Oliphant). *Truculent:* Fierce, brutal, harsh, vitriolic. "Pamphlets . . . scarcely less *truculent* or less contemptuous of the Christian virtues" (Marsden).

Bellwether (n). A *bellwether* is literally a male sheep bearing a bell and leading its flock. It has nothing to do with the weather, although it is frequently so misspelled. It means a leader or way-shower, not a harbinger or portent. The *OED* cites it rightly and wryly: "Men are for the most part like sheep, who always follow the *bellwether*." "A *bellwether* of things to come" (cited by Gummere) is nonsense.

Benign (adj), **Benignity** (n); **Condign** (adj), **Condignity** (n). The two adjectives and the noun *benignity* are in steadfast use, but the noun *condignity* has almost disappeared from speech and writing. *Benign:* Specifically, nonmalignant, and, more generally, gracious, kindly, gentle. "Our Creator, bounteous and *benign*" (Milton). *Benignity:* Kindness of heart, goodness of disposition, gentleness. "The king was desirous to establish peace rather by *benignity* than blood" (Haywood). *Condign:* Suitable, deserved, merited. "Consider who is your friend, he that would have brought him down to *condign* punishment, or he that has saved him" (Arbuthnot). *Condignity* may appear occasionally in theological writing in its obsolete sense of merit earned through good works.

Bereft (pp); **Bereaved** (pp). Both are past participles of *bereave*, but each has lately developed a distinctive meaning, *bereaved* generally expressing loss by death of a loved one and *bereft* meaning not to lack something but to be dispossessed of it. In older English literature the words are synonymous. "White as an angel is the English child,/But I am black as if *bereav'd* of light" (Blake). "What would the world be, once *bereft*/Of wet and wildness? Let them be left;/Long live the weeds and the wilderness yet" (Hopkins). But *bereft* is here wrongly used in the sense of lacking: "Many children leave school *bereft* of mathematical skills" (cited by Bryson).

Beside (prep), **Besides** (adv & prep). *Beside* is a preposition only, meaning by the side of, whereas *besides* is an adverb meaning in addition to, but it does have use as a preposition in the sense of except. Hence "I sat *besides* the stream" is incorrect. The old song title has it right: "I Do Like to Be *Beside* the Seaside." "Indeed I too would like to be *beside* the sea, but I have things to do *besides* lolling on the beach."

Betterment (n). Both Fowler and Bernstein speak ill of *betterment,* the latter saying that it is confined to "social welfare work in which it suggests an easing of the lot of unfortunates." They suggest that *improvement* is usually a better choice, and certainly one would not speak of "a *betterment* in the Club's menu." Still, the *OED* ignores the lot of unfortunates and says *betterment* means "the fact of making or becoming better, amendment, improvement, amelioration." It even includes in its definition "improvement of property" (a use Bernstein scorns) and quotes Galt: "He sold off his land and *betterments* in Vermont."

Between: See **Among.**

Biannual (adj); **Biennial** (adj). There is not a great deal to be said for use of either word, and what little there is is complicated by the fact that *bi-* (two or twice) is used ambiguously in these as in other similar hybrids (*biweekly, bimonthly,* and *biquarterly*). Nevertheless, *biannual* means twice a year, whereas *biennial* means once every two years. Even the *Bulletin of the International Association of Professors of English* fails to keep the distinction in mind: "An annual bulletin is our aim, but *biennial* issues may become necessary if the Association enlarges." Since *semi-* means half, we might gain by replacing *biannual* with "semiannual" or even "twice a year." And for all we know, the professors of English do hope to publish once every two years instead of annually.

Bias. In electronics the application of a steady voltage to any active device. In computer operation an error range having a value of more than zero.

Billi-. A prefix denoting one thousand million or 10^9, synonymous with *giga-.*

Billion (n); **Bullion** (n); **Bouillon** (n); **Million** (n). It should be kept in mind that *billion* for many nations (e.g., United States and France) means a *thousand million* (1,000,000,000), whereas for the British it means a *million million* (1,000,000,000,000). The English stubbornly persist in calling our *billion* a *milliard.* "Billions for defense" must have meant to the British an overwhelming commitment. *Bullion* simply means gold or silver in mass and has no connotation of value. Hence there is no such thing as a bullionaire. For those who can't spell, the word is sometimes confused with *bouillon* [**BOOL** yahn], a clear broth.

Binary, Binary code, Binary notation. *Binary* is an adjective that means consisting of or involving two or a pair. Hence the *binary code* is the most fundamental of codes using only 0 and 1 to represent data. *Binary notation* is a system for representing numbers in which the positional representation for each digit is 2. In the decimal system displacement of one digit to the left means multiplication by 10, so in the *binary* system displacement means multiplication by 2 so that the *binary* number 10 represents 2 and 100 represents 4.

Biodegradable (adj). Capable of being broken down by natural decomposition and hence not causing pollution. A word no doubt necessary to ecologists and environmentalists but now taken up as a vogue and vague word by politicians and other childlike people.

BIOS. An acronym for Basic Input/Output System— that part of a computer's operating system that communicates with input/output devices such as printers or keyboards.

Bit. An acronym for *binary digit*, one of the two digits used in *binary notation* (see *Binary*). The term is extended to representation of a *binary digit* in different forms, for example, a pulse or an electronic circuit.

Blast. To release external or internal memory areas so that they become available to other computer programs.

Blatant (adj); **Flagrant** (adj). *Blatant* means obtrusive, brazenly obvious, offensively noisy, clamorous, whereas *flagrant* means glaringly evident or notorious. "Maledictions, *blatant* tongues, and viperous hisses" (Southey). But, "Many individuals were cut off on account of their *flagrant* wickedness" (Fletcher).

Blazon (v). A verb sometimes misused. It means literally to blow or sound a trumpet, hence to set forth conspicuously, to proclaim, to make known far and wide. "What's this but libelling against the senate,/And *blazoning* our injustice everywhere" (Shakespeare). The word has nothing to do with *blaze* and is here misused: "She *blazoned* a trail in the fashion world which others were quick to follow" (cited by Bryson).

Bleed. The printing of computer characters for optical recognition.

Bloc (n); **Block** (n & v). *Bloc* (n): A French word meaning specifically a coalition or political group, that is, the farm *bloc*. *Block* (n): A word of numerous meanings—a mass of wood, metal, or stone, a cube-shaped toy; a hollow masonry building unit (i.e., a concrete *block*), a pattern used in the making of woodcuts, and a part of a city or town enclosed by four adjoining streets. In its basic meaning, "Awaiting the sensation of a short, sharp shock/From a cheap and chippy chopper on a big black *block*" (Gilbert). *Block* (v): Also a word of many meanings, but its most common is to hinder or obstruct. "No visible political force can *block* the power of the labor *bloc*."

Bludgeon (n & v). The noun means a short club heavier at one end than the other and the verb to strike or bully or threaten. "Democracy means simply the *bludgeoning* of the people, by the people, for the people" (Wilde).

Blunderbuss (n). Originally a short musket of large bore and short, inexact range. By extension, perhaps from large bore, now a stupid person, a blunderhead, a noisy talker. "He must be a numbskull, not to say a beetle, nor yet a *blunderbuss*" (Tucker).

Boat (n); **Ship** (n). The difference is simply put. A *boat* is a small vessel, a *ship* a large vessel. The height of misuse would be calling the *Queen Elizabeth II* a *boat*, and yet "slow *boat* to China" does not suggest a small craft.

Bodacious (adj). A word unrecognized in all style manuals and most dictionaries. Apparently a combination of *bold* and *audacious* and in use especially in the southern United States, it means blatant (a *bodacious* liar), remarkable (a *bodacious* tale), brazen or impudent (a *bodacious* gossip).

Boggle (v). Barzun and others have said that *boggle* is an intransitive verb and that therefore nothing can grammatically *boggle* the mind. In the sense of overwhelm or bewilder, things have been *boggling* minds and spirits for a long time ("Our budget deficit *boggles* the imagination") and will no doubt continue to do so.

Boolean algebra. An algebraic system named after the mathematician George Boole that uses algebraic notation to express logical relationships in the same way as conventional algebra expresses mathematical relationships. In *Boolean algebra* variables do not stand for numbers but for words that demonstrate the relationship of statements, such as *and, but, or, not, nor,* and so on.

Boondoggle (n & v). There is an unlikely story that the noun was coined by a scoutmaster, Robert H. Link, out of "Boone" and "joggle" to describe the useless plaited leather cord worn by Boy Scouts. Whether so or not, the word came into wide use in the 1930s to describe futile tasks performed in government make-work projects. It continues in this use, but as a verb it has taken on the meaning of to deceive, in the sense of *hornswoggle:* "A scheme to *boondoggle* unwary investors."

Bootstrap (n). A *bootstrap* is a device to help pull on boots and, metaphorically, a means for accomplishment or advancement. "To pull oneself up by one's own *bootstraps*" is to use one's own resources, to advance without the aid of others. Even electronic wizards use the *bootstrap*—the technique of loading a program into a computer by means of preliminary instructions that in turn motivate instructions to read programs and data.

Born and Borne: See Bear.

Borrow. The carry signal in subtraction when the difference between digits is less than zero.

Both . . . and. *Both* and *and* in this construction are correlative conjunctions so that they should link elements grammatically identical. Hence the sentence cited by Fowler, "He was *both* deaf to argument *and* entreaty," is incorrect. It should be recast thus: "He was deaf to *both* argument *and* entreaty."

Bottleneck (n). A word that came into wide use in World War II to mean anything that impedes progress or defies resolution. However, the word thus used is a metaphor, and its inherent meaning should not be disregarded. Phrases like "a worldwide *bottleneck*" or "a *bottleneck* that needs to be ironed out" are absurd. But still a useful word when employed discreetly. Harry Truman had it right in his message to Congress: "To increase supplies of scarce materials, break *bottlenecks*, and channel production to meet essential needs."

Bottom line (n). The phrase is business jargon for profit or profitability. It is now a much overworked fad word for almost any kind of result. It is to be hoped that it will soon drop from favor and languish in the unread reports of accountants. "A small cloud appeared over publishing, once the pursuit of right words but becoming the pursuit of right numbers—a goal marked by a tasteless but revealing term, 'the *bottom line*'" (Dusseau).

Bourgeoisie (n), **Bourgeois** (adj). The *bourgeoisie* [boor zhwah ZEE] is simply the middle class and *bourgeois* [boor ZHWAH] describes people, things, and ideas of middle-class taste and value. But in the heyday of Marxist double talk, *bourgeois* came to mean crass and crawling and the *bourgeoisie* a class of people brutish, witless, and nasty. Suddenly the Hungarian (no longer People's) Republic, borne aloft on new-found wings of freedom, announces in its new constitution the enduring "value of *bourgeois* democracy." Imagine the Left having veered so far to the Right. But beware, Hungary, for the "booboisie," as Mencken called us, is also subject to word manipulation: The price of *fish* doubles as *seafood*, triples as *poisson*, and quadruples as *truite fumée aux fines herbes*.

Brake (n); **Break** (n & v). The words signifying bracken, thicket, harrowing implement, or decelerating device are all spelled *brake*. "The heath, with withering *brake* grown o'er" (Crabbe). *Break* as a verb has innumerable meanings, but they all involve the idea of splitting, smashing, penetrating, and, fleeing from. *Break* as a noun has similar meanings but a few not inherent in the verb (i.e., a lucky stroke of fortune or a blank line between paragraphs). In its usual meaning, "Thou wast up by *break* of day" (Herbert).

Bravado (n). Ostentatious display of courage (often fake)—a Spanish word in use in English since the early seventeenth century. "Spain, to make good the *bravado,*/Names it the invincible armado" (Anon.).

Breach (n); **Breech** (n). *Breach:* A break, rupture, or gap. An infraction or violation of law, trust, or promise. A severance in relationships, as of friendship. "Once more unto the *breach,* dear friends; once more;/Or close up the wall with our English dead!" (Shakespeare). *Breech:* The rear or lower part of anything. Hence *breeches* become trousers. "Sir, it is no matter what leg you shall put into your *breeches* first" (Johnson).

Breakdown (n). Everyone will allow us *breakdown* in the sense of collapse or loss of ability to function, but some, notably Bernstein, will fault use of the word in the meaning of itemization or division into categories. The objection to this use of the word seems to rest on its overuse, and no doubt this was once so. However, its faddishness has passed and there can be no objection to a "breakdown of the data" in the sense of division into classes.

Breath (n); **Breadth** (n); **Breathe** (v). *Breath:* Air inhaled and exhaled in respiration. Hence, figuratively, life or vitality: "Poetry is the *breath* and finer spirit of all knowledge" (Wordsworth). *Breadth:* Width but, more specifically, the second largest dimension of a plane or solid figure. Hence, figuratively, freedom from restraint or from narrowness of view. "Simplicity, harmony and *breadth* combine in these pictures with a restfulness which is truly admirable" (Ruskin). *Breathe:* To inhale and exhale in respiration. Hence, figuratively, to inject as if by breathing, to infuse. "She can *breathe* life into any dull party." These words are seldom confused in meaning but occasionally in spelling.

Bridging. The conversion of systems written for one kind of computer for use in another kind.

Broach (v); **Brooch** (n). *Broach:* To mention or suggest for the first time. *"Broach* me no broaches, and I'll but you no buts" (Anon.). *Brooch:* A jewel or clasp having a pin at the back for securing the ornament to cloth. "I will make you *brooches* for your delight" (Stevenson).

Brobdignagian (adj). From the inhabitants of the land of Brobdignag, which Lemuel Gulliver visits, it means tremendous, huge, gigantic, for the *Brobdignagians* were as tall as steeples and, unlike the petty Lilliputians, of a stately turn of mind. When told by Gulliver of European customs and institutions, the king of Brobdignag observes, "I cannot but consider the bulk of your natives to be the most pernicious race of little vermin that nature ever suffered to crawl upon the face of the earth." (See also *Swiftian.*)

Buffalo (n & v). The *buffalo* is a formidable but not a notably deceptive beast. "He thought he saw a *Buffalo/*Upon the chimney-piece;/He looked again and found it was/His sister's husband's niece" (Carroll). But the verb *buffalo* in American slang has somehow come to mean to confuse another purposely, to take advantage of, to cheat, to intimidate as in "She's got him *buffaloed.*"

Buffer. Also called *buffer store,* it is a means of temporarily storing computer data when information is being transmitted from one unit to another.

Bugaboo (n); **Bugbear** (n). Both words may spring from the Welch *bug,* a frightful object, and in folklore a *bugbear* is a goblin that eats up naughty children. Hence a *bugbear* is the source, real or imagined, of anything that terrifies or annoys. "To the world, no *bugbear* is so great,/As want of figure, and a small estate" (Pope). *Bugaboo* shares this meaning with the added sense of a fancied or actual obstacle, a nemesis, something that causes failure or bad luck. "Fear is the major *bugaboo* of novice skiers."

Bull (n). *Bull,* neither as male animal, stock-market optimist, nor shortened derisory expletive, needs explanation. But perhaps it does in its legal sense of a seal (deriving from the Latin *bulla*) attached to an official document. Within the Roman Catholic Church, it refers specifically to a formal proclamation by a pope, that is, a papal *bull*. "A *bull* is letters apostolick, strengthened with a leaden seal, and containing within them the decrees or commandments of the pope or bishop of Rome" (Ayliffe).

Bur (n); **Burr** (n). The words are often used interchangeably, but they do have distinct meanings. *Bur:* (1) The spiky rough outer case around seeds. (2) Anything that adheres like a *bur*. "Whither betake her/From the chill dew, amongst rude *burs* and thistles" (Milton). (3) A rotary cutting tool used in dentistry and surgery. *Burr:* (1) A guttural pronunciation of the "R" sound. (2) A rough or irregular protuberance as on a tree or on a ragged metal edge after punching or cutting. Nevertheless, no one really faults two r's when one is meant: "I am a kind of *burr;* I shall stick" (Shakespeare).

Burgeon (v). To *burgeon* is literally to bud or to sprout, not to mushroom or expand, and it also means to thrive or flourish. One should not speak of a *"burgeoning* population" in the sense of one expanding greatly, for this ignores the sense of budding or thriving. "Beneath whose fragrant dews all tender thoughts might bud and *burgeon*" (Kingsley).

Burlesque (n); **Parody** (n). A *burlesque* is a vulgarization of lofty material or the treatment of ordinary material with mock or exaggerated dignity. Hence any grotesque caricature or a bawdy, slapstick, provocative stage show is a *burlesque*. A *parody* is a more subtle, often literary, device designed to criticize or ridicule by slightly askew imitation. "We may find that they were Satirique Poems full of *Parodies,* turn'd into another Sence than the Author intended them" (Dryden).

Bust (v); **Burst** (v). *Burst* is a verb in good repute. "Let me not *burst* in ignorance" (Shakespeare). But *bust* (as verb only, not as noun) is in ill repute, is in fact an illiteracy, but who will gainsay "spring is *busting* out all over" or even "blockbuster"? However, slang usage does condone *bust* (to fail an examination or to demote a military person in rank) and *bust up* (to disagree or break up) and to *go bust* (to become bankrupt).

Byte. A basic unit of information in a computer. A *byte* usually represents one character and is normally eight bits in length. It carries enough information to represent useful instruction to a central processing unit.

Cache (n & v); Hide (n & v); Stash (v); Cache buffer. *Cache* [KASH] as a noun means hiding place; as a verb to conceal: "He accordingly *cached* enough provisions to last them back" (Kane). *Hide* as a verb also means to conceal, but as a noun it has the unrelated meanings of the skin of larger animals or trace of something: "The police were unable to find *hide* nor hair of the murder weapon." *Stash* is a word of unknown origin—perhaps a corruption of *cache*—for it shares its meanings: "The squirrel *stashes* away nuts for winter." But a *cache buffer* is a portion of the memory of a computer network into which disk files are read, thus allowing each terminal quick access to the files.

Cacophony (n), Cacophonous (adj); Euphony (n), Euphonious (adj). *Cacophony* [kah KAHF uh nee] is a harsh or discordant sound and hence also dissonance. *Euphony* [YOOH fuh nee] is a pleasing or melodious sound or series of sounds. "The continual holding down of the loud pedal produces unutterable *cacophony*" (Goddard). *Euphony* is often ascribed to mellifluous prose, poetry, or speech. "The majestic *euphony* of Milton's verse." The adjectives correspond to the meaning of the nouns: *cacophonous* (discordant, strident, raucous) and *euphonious* (of agreeable or pleasant sound). "Thus divesting itself of its harsh *cacophonous* effects" (Black) and "Those *euphonious* hexameters" (Taylor).

Caid: See **Qaid.**

Calamity: See **Misfortune.**

Calculate (v), **Calculated** (pp). To *calculate* is to compute or to determine by mathematical means, to estimate. "A cunning man did *calculate* my birth,/And told me that by water I should die" (Shakespeare). Its meaning of adapt, adjust, or make fit for a purpose is most often seen in the past participle *calculated*. "The reasonableness of religion clearly appears, as it tends so directly to the happiness of men, and is *calculated* for our benefit" (Tillotson). However, in its meaning of suppose, think, or even intend *calculate* has attracted censure from many commentators. Still, the verb is often so used and the use recognized in the original *OED*. "Mr. Crane requested those who *calculated* to join the singing school to come forward" (*Knickerbocker Magazine*).

Calligraphy (n). From its Greek roots, says Bernstein, the word means not handwriting but beautiful handwriting so that tasteless *calligraphy* is an impossibility and handsome *calligraphy* a redundancy. But almost all dictionaries recognize use of the word to mean penmanship in general and the *OED* cites *Household Words:* "His *calligraphy* suggests the skating of an intoxicated sweep over a sheet of ice." Surely there is no sense of inborn beauty here, but Greek roots do not always make English meanings.

Callow (adj). Johnson defines *callow* as naked, without feathers, and he cites Dryden: "Then as an eagle, who, with pious care/To her now silent airy does repair/And finds her *callow* infants forc'd away." But by extension the word has come to mean green, untried, inexperienced: "Teaching young and *callow* orators to soar" (Walpole).

Callus (n); **Callous** (adj). A *callus* is simply a hard thickened part of the skin or a new growth of bone at a fracture site (also called a *callosity*), and the adjective *callous* describes such a hard skin area and so comes to mean thick-skinned, unsympathetic, unfeeling. For no discernible reason Dr. Scholl persists in calling his product a *"callous* remover." If this means anything, it suggests a cold-hearted van line or an unfeeling wallpaper scraper.

Calvary (n); **Cavalry** (n). These are words more apt to be confused in spelling than in meaning. Everyone knows that *cavalry* is an army unit traditionally mounted on horseback. "Their *cavalry*, in the battle of Blenheim, could not sustain the shock of the British horse" (Addison). But *Calvary* is a more complex word. Capitalized, it is the hill near Jerusalem where Jesus was crucified, but in lowercase it means either a series of representations in a church or chapel of the Passion of Christ or a life-size depiction of the Crucifixion in open air. "By the side of the high-road is one of those *cavalries* so associated with the landscape of Catholic countries" (*Harper's Magazine*). However, in lowercase *calvary* also means the experience of extreme mental grief or anguish. "They suffer the *calvary* of a foretold doom" (Masserman).

Can (v); **May** (v); **Might** (v or n); **Must** (v). Critics have for centuries dunned into our not-so-receptive heads that *can* connotes power or ability to do something and *may* permission or opportunity to be or do something. "Malt does more than Milton *can*/To justify God's ways to man" (Housman). "It is not what a lawyer tells me I *may* do; but what humanity, reason and justice tell me I ought to do" (Burke). *May* also expresses contingency and possibility. "There *may* be heaven; there must be hell:/Meantime there is our earth here—well!" (Browning). *Might* is a form of *may* in its sense of possibility. "If it was so, it *might* be; and if it were so, it would be; but as it isn't, it ain't" (Carroll). *Might* as a noun has no sense of the contingent; it is a word meaning absolute strength. "Ev'n that same Lord, that great in *might* and strong in battle is" (Scottish Metrical Psalm). *Must* means to be obliged or required to do or be something by force of duty, law, custom, conscience, or circumstance. "Genius does what it *must* and talent does what it *can*" (Lytton).

Cannot but, Cannot help, Cannot help but, Cannot choose but (phrases). A fair amount of nonsense has been written about these phrases, but in fact they all mean the same thing (to be unable to do otherwise) and are all in common and reasonable use. *Cannot choose but* is probably the least common of the four, but the *OED* attests its ancient use and quotes Wordsworth in modern times: "The eye—it *cannot choose but* see;/We cannot bid the ear be still"; nor the tongue for that matter. For some reason Bernstein characterizes *cannot but* as pompous, though it seems quite natural in Jane Austen's "I *cannot but* think of Dear Sir Thomas's delight."

Canon (n); Canonical (adj); Canonicals (n). *Canon* is a word of various but related meanings, many of which have a religious significance; in general, however, any law, decree, principle, or criterion that is accepted as fundamental and universal: "They are the rules and *canons* of that law, which is written in all men's hearts" (Hooker). But, more specifically, a *canon* is an ecclesiastical decree or code and in the Roman Catholic Church a rule of doctrine enacted by an official council and approved by the pope. "They were looked upon as lapsed persons, and great severities of penance were prescribed them . . . by the *canons* of Ancyra and many others" (Stillingfleet). A *canon* is also a clergyman on the staff of a cathedral. "Swift much admires the place and air,/And longs to be a *canon* there" (cited by *OED*). *Canon*, too, denotes any of "those books of the scripture, which are received as inspired and *canonical,* to distinguish them from either profane, apocryphal or disputed books. Thus we say that Genesis is part of the sacred *canon* of the Scripture" (Johnson). *Canonical* means pertaining to or conforming to a *canon,* especially one of ecclesiastical force. "York anciently had a metropolitan jurisdiction over all the bishops of Scotland, from whom they had their consecration and to whom they swore *canonical* obedience" (Ayliffe). And, finally but not completely, *canonicals* are the garments prescribed by *canon* law for clergymen when performing their office. "The chaplain in full *canonicals* led the toast: 'On this the great anniversary of the sacred coronation of their majesties, may God help us to serve with them our beloved Russia' " (Dusseau). (See also *Catholic* and *Ecclesiastical.*)

Canvas (n); Canvass (v & n). *Canvas* is a rough cloth, often used in the making of sails and hence the sails themselves. "Thou comest, much wept for: such a breeze/Compell'd thy *canvas*" (Tennyson). *Canvass* (v): To solicit funds, votes, opinions, or the like. *Canvass* (n): A solicitation for funds or orders; a campaign for election to office. "In short, their success in the *canvass* quite astonished them" (Lord Sheffield).

Capacity: See Ability.

Capital (n & adj); **Capitol** (n). The first of these words has a wide variety of meanings, the latter only two. *Capital:* A city or town that is an official seat of government. An uppercase letter as in capital "C." An accumulation of stock or other wealth. Wealth employed in productive facility or in the earning of more wealth. As an adjective, *capital* also has various meanings: Pertaining or relating to investments or assets; principal or important; excellent or first rate; and, from its Latin root, fatal or serious or punishable by death as in *capital* error or a *capital* crime. *Capitol,* on the other hand, has only the meaning of a specific building. Capitalized it means either the meeting place of the United States Congress or the Temple of Jupiter in Rome. In lowercase it means specifically a building used for the meetings of state legislatures or the statehouse. "The state *capital* boasted a neo-Grecian facade of marble columns."

Carat (n); **Caret** (n); **Carrot** (n); **Karat** (n); **Karate** (n). A *carat* is a unit of weight used in the appraisal and evaluation of jewelry, as in a diamond solitaire of three *carats*. A *caret* is a printer's or proofreader's mark used to indicate an omission. It arises from the Latin *carere*—to be without or lacking. *Carrot* is a vegetable considered edible by all rabbits and some people. *Karat* is simply a variation of *carat*, but for obscure reasons it is preferred as the unit for measuring the fineness of gold. *Karate* is a system of defense developed in Japan in which an opponent is rendered powerless without use of weapons but by striking sensitive areas of an attacker's body.

Careen (v); **Career** (v). To *careen* is to tilt or sway dangerously or to cause a ship to roll or keel over. "Wildly *careening* boxcars were once a fixed feature of Saturday-afternoon movies" (Dusseau). "The heavy blows of the sea upon the sides of the vessel *careened* and shook her" (Marryat). To *career* is to run rapidly or in uncontrolled motion. "The little

Julian was *careering* about the room for the amusement of his infant friends" (Scott).

Carton (n); Cartoon (n). A *carton* is a box or other container made of corrugated kraft paper. It is also the small white disk within the bull's-eye of a target. *Cartoon* has two somewhat different meanings. The first is of a drawing usually in caricature and meant to be humorous or satirical. The second is of a drawing on heavy paper meant to be reproduced and completed in same size as a tapestry or fresco. "How fine the *cartoons* of the tapestries for the Sistine Chapel" (Jameson).

Casual (adj); Causal (adj). Words often confused, mispronounced, and misused. *Casual:* Accidental, occurring by chance, indifferent, occasional, not serious, informal, relaxed. "And we, light half-believers in our *casual* creeds" (Arnold). *Causal:* Implying or constituting a sufficient cause. "A *casual* approach to duty can be the *causal* force in downright dereliction."

Category. A group of computer disks containing a given set of information.

Catholic (n & adj); Ecumenical (adj), Oecumenical (var); Orthodox (adj), Orthodoxy (n). The lowercased adjective *catholic* and *ecumenical* have virtually the same meaning: universal or general, affecting mankind as a whole, comprehensive in understanding, or pertaining to the whole body of Christian doctrine or to the ancient undivided Christian church. "Doubtless the success of those your great and *catholic* endeavours will promote the empire of man over nature" (Glanville). "No other literature exhibits so expansive and *oecumenical* a genius as the French" (Mallock). Capitalized, *Catholic* means any member of the Roman Catholic Church or the Church itself. After the Great Schism of 1472, the Western Church formally assumed the designation *Catholic* and the Eastern Church the title *Orthodox.* Like *catholic*, lowercase *orthodox* also means conforming to universal beliefs, attitudes, or modes of conduct or correct in doctrine, especially theological doctrine. The noun *orthodoxy* shares the meaning of universally accepted or religiously correct code of behavior or doctrine. "I do not attempt explaining the mysteries of the christian religion; since Providence intended there should be mysteries, it cannot be agreeable to piety, *orthodoxy*, or good sense, to go about it" (Swift).

Cavort (v).   The word means simply to prance about, but it has always had a faintly disreputable tilt as if a satyr were doing the prancing. It has been justly said of champagne that "two pints make one *cavort*" (*Philadelphia Inquirer*). In its pure sense, " 'Every man for himself,' said the elephant, as he *cavorted* among the chickens." It is noteworthy that the elephant's phrase is almost always spoken by someone not at risk in the presenting situation.

Celebrant (n); **Celebrator** or **Celebrater** (n).   A *celebrant* is a person participating in public religious rites or other ceremonies and, specifically, the officiating priest in celebration of the Eucharist. "There cannot be more than one *celebrant* or one chief consecrator" (*The [London] Times*). One who celebrates festive occasions by merrymaking or one who praises effusively and widely is a *celebrator*. "I am really more a well-wisher to your felicity than a *celebrator* of your beauty" (Pope).

Celibate (adj), **Celibacy** (n); **Chaste** (adj), **Chastity** (n).   *Celibate* does not mean, as is generally supposed, abstaining from sexual relations. It means, rather, unmarried or bound by vow not to marry. "Marriage has many pains, but *celibacy* has no pleasures" (Johnson). But *chaste* does mean not engaging in sexual intercourse or free from indecency or offensiveness. "Man is the chaser, and woman is *chaste*" (Beaumont).

Cellar.   Computer storage that works on the principle of a push-down list, so that when new items of data are added, previous items move back.

Censer (n); **Censor** (n), **Censorship** (n); **Censure** (n & v).   *Censer:* An incense burner. *Censor:* A person, usually but not necessarily official, who examines plays, books, motion pictures, television programs, to suppress parts objectionable on moral, military, or legal grounds. Hence any supervisor of public customs and morals and, in Freudian analysis, the force that represses ideas or impulses in their undisguised forms. "Assassination is the extreme form of *censorship*" (Shaw). *Cen-*

sure as a noun or verb means blame, reproach, rebuke. "Those who durst not *censure* scarce could praise" (Johnson).

Ceremonial (n & adj); **Ceremonious** (adj). Both words as adjectives mean characterized by formal ceremony or ritual, but *ceremonial* is applied to events, whereas *ceremonious* describes people or human character and means carefully observant of ceremony and also elaborately courteous. "Entered the room with a most *ceremonious* bow" (Cowper).

Chafe (v); **Chaff** (v & n). As Bryson says, "the one may lead to the other, but their meanings are distinct." To *chafe* means to make worn or sore by rubbing or to warm or heat and, by extension, to irritate or annoy. "To vex and *chafe* me is part of her nature" (Dickens). But *chaff* means to tease in a good-natured way, to banter. "The Regent treated the affair as a sort of joke . . . and *chaffed* the supposed author of the satire" (Dicey). The noun *chaff* means the husk or grains that are separated by threshing and winnowing and hence anything worthless or useless. "Pleasure with instruction should be joined;/so take the corn and leave the *chaff* behind" (Dryden).

Chapter. A self-contained section of a computer program.

Character (n). *Character* is usually the distinctive nature, quality, or attribute of a person or thing and any conventional mark, sign, or symbol used in writing. But in electronics *character* has a more specific significance. It is one of a set of symbols in a data-processing system used, for example, to denote the numerals 0 to 9, letters of the alphabet, or punctuation marks. Such *characters* are represented by unique bytes or holes in punched tapes. A *character set* is composed of the *characters* available to any computer or peripheral device, some devices having only a limited set. For example, a 64-*character* machine code might consist of ten numerals (0–9), 26 letters (A–Z), and 28 *special characters*, probably including a blank.

Chaste: See Celibate.

Check digits. In most data-processing procedures numbers are ascribed to persons or objects, but such numbers are meaningless to those who use them in processing so that the possibility of transcription error is substantial. A *check digit* is one or more digits added to a number as a checking device. Thus if the number 7 is used to generate *check digits*, 127 is written 1271, 1 being the remainder when 127 is divided by 7. Thereafter each time the number is processed, a machine check of the remainder ensures accuracy.

Childish (adj); **Childlike** (adj). These words illustrate the difference in connotation between the suffixes -ish and -like, the former unfavorable or disparaging and the latter favorable or neutral. "The wife was pretty, trifling, *childish*, weak;/She could not think but would not cease to speak" (Crabbe). "Newton, *childlike*, sage! sagacious reader of the works of God" (Cowper).

Chimera (n), **Chimeric** (adj). The *Chimera* [kye MIR uh] was a female monster spewing forth flames and usually represented with lion's head, goat's body, and serpent's tail. Hence a *chimera* is a fantastic creature or frightful fancy arising from the imagination. "In short, the force of dreams is of a piece,/*Chimeras* all; and more absurd, or less" (Dryden). *Chimeric* hence means fanciful, fantastic, imaginary. "Notwithstanding the fineness of the allegory, I cannot think that persons of such a *chimeric* existence are proper actors in an epic poem" (Dryden).

Chopper. In electronics a device interrupting a beam of light to produce a pulsating signal.

Chord (n); **Cord** (n). Perhaps only inadvertent misspelling confuses these words. A *chord* is various things: (1) In music a combination of two or more notes struck simultaneously. (2) In geometry the line between two points on a curve. (3) In life an emotion or feeling. "His story struck a *chord* of pity in his listeners." (4) In aeronautics the straight line between the edges of an airfoil section. *Cord* too has various meanings: (1) In practice a string or thin rope made of several strands. (2) In anatomy a cordlike structure as in spinal *cord* or umbilical *cord*. (3) In life a restraining influence. "The very sight of the island had relaxed the *cords* of discipline" (Stevenson). (4) A unit of measurement of firewood.

Circumlocution: See Locution.

Cite (v); **Site** (n). The words sound alike and should not be confused but sometimes are. To *cite* is to quote from, refer to as support or authority, to use as an example—"To *cite* those instances only which have come within my own knowledge" (Abernethey)—whereas *site* means the position or location of anything, especially with reference to its environment: "How shines your tower, the only one/Of that especial *site* and stone" (Blake).

Claque (n); **Clique** (n); **Coterie** (n). *Claque* derives from the French verb to applaud and means specifically a group of persons hired to applaud a public performance, as in a theater, nightclub, or symphony hall. "He organized in 1820 the first Parisian *claque*" (Brewer). *Clique* is a small group of self-selected people, and so is a *coterie*. But *clique* has a derisive connotation of persons self-appointed as authorities or banded together for selfish purposes: "Choose well your set; our feeble nature seeks/The aid of Clubs, the countenance of *Cliques*" (Holmes). *Coterie* is not so contemptuous a term and usually applies to small groups interested in specific aspects of art or literature. "Fame is but a lottery/Drawn by the blue-coat misses of a *coterie*" (Byron).

Classic (n & adj); **Classical** (adj). *Classical* means pertaining to or typical of the art, literature, and culture of the ancient Greeks and Romans. "*Classical* quotation is the parole of literary men all over the world" (Johnson). *Classic* means of the highest or preeminent excellence. "Homer's *Iliad* is a *classic*, but World Series homers should not be called such." In short, *classic* is a word to be used somewhat sparingly.

Clear. To replace data in a storage device with a standard character, often a zero or blank.

Clench (v); **Clinch** (v). These words are sometimes confused, because they both refer to holding or securing. But *clench* means to close tightly or grind together, as in *clenching* one's hands or teeth. *Clinch* means to secure or fasten down as in *clinching* an argument, contest, or contract or in *clinching* nails. "He drove in the nails and *clinched* them flat." *Clinch* also has the meaning in boxing of body entwinement and its extended slangy meaning of passionate embrace.

Climacteric (n), **Climactic** (adj); **Climatic** (adj). *Climacteric* and *climactic* refer to climax, whereas *climatic* refers to climate. *Climacteric:* Any critical period, hence the time of decrease in reproductive capacity of men and women and the specific year in which such change is likely to occur—usually called the grand *climacteric*. *Climactic:* Pertaining to or forming a climax in an ascending series. "Give the history of development a *climactic* form" (Whitney). *Climatic:* Of or pertaining to weather. "No *climatic* action has significantly changed the hues of the lava" (Reid). *Climatic* arises from the Greek *klima* (zone), whereas *climactic* has its root in the Greek *klimax* (a ladder) and, hence, implies gradual ascent to a peak or culmination.

Clock. An easy-enough word, though an uneasy making gadget. It also is an electronic device that provides pulses at fixed intervals to monitor or synchronize other circuits or units operating within the same system.

COBOL. An acronym for COmmon Business-Oriented Language—a symbolic, international programming language developed for general commercial use under the sponsorship of the U.S. Department of Defense.

Code. Representation of data or instructions in symbolic language.

Cohort (n). Bernstein says correctly enough that *cohort* derives from the Latin word for enclosure and was originally applied to a division of the Roman army and so has come to mean a group or company. "The Assyrian came down like a wolf on the fold,/And his *cohorts* were gleaming in purple and gold" (Byron). Hence Bernstein argues that *cohort* cannot be used to mean an individual, but almost all dictionaries allow the meaning of a companion or associate, an accomplice or abettor. "His *cohort* in the crime was never apprehended"

(*Philadelphia Inquirer*). Latin roots do not always determine the singularity of their flower.

Collaborate (v), **Collaborator** (n); **Corroborate** (v), **Corroborative** (adj). *Collaborate* is a useful word meaning to assist in the doing of something, to cooperate; but the subtle sense of words does change with time, and history has given *collaborate* and especially *collaborator* a bad name. However, just as time wounds all heels, it also heals all wounds, and perhaps *collaborate* will soon be restored to innocent use. "Composers who *collaborated* with Metastasio in the opera of the eighteenth century" (Lee). *Corroborate* means to verify, to confirm, and *corroborative* means validating, authenticating. "Merely *corroborative* detail, intended to give artistic verisimilitude to an otherwise bald and unconvincing narrative" (Gilbert).

Collide (v), **Collision** (n). A score of style manuals and commentators like Bernstein and Bryson tell us that a *collision* can occur only when two or more *moving* objects *collide*. Hence if a motorcar runs into a wall, this is not a *collision*. They all might just as well have spared us their advices, for the requirement of *two* or more *moving* bodies has never been met in literature. This is particularly true in those common instances where privileges, ideas, theories, searing glances, and the like *collide*, for in such figurative use motion cannot be a consideration. "Our interests would be about as likely to *collide* as those of a shark and a tiger" (Duff).

Collusion (n), **Collusive** (adj); **Connivance** (n). *Collusion* means furtive agreement for the carrying out of some deceitful or fraudulent act. "The *collusion* of the false Templars with the infidels" (Fuller). Both noun and adjective have a pejorative connotation, and one would not speak of scientists working in *collusion*. "He would not have lent himself to any *collusive* trickery" (Horn). *Connivance*, from its Latin root, means winking at—hence intentionally averting one's eyes from wrongdoing and so assisting it. "What was this but his *connivance* at wicked and licentious acts?" (Sandys).

Comment. Written notes that can be included in coding of computer operations.

Compare (v), Comparable (adj); Contrast (v). The two verbs are sometimes confused, although they have quite different meanings. To *compare* things or ideas or people is to examine them for similarities. "I have been studying how I may *compare* this prison where I live unto the world" (Shakespeare). *Comparable* means having features or characteristics in common with something or someone else. "There is no blessing in life *comparable* to the enjoyment of a discreet and virtuous friend" (Addison). *Contrast* means to compare in order to note unlikenesses or differences or opposing characteristics. "Perpetually *contrasting* it with systems with which it has nothing in common but the name" (Whately). Commentators have been at some pains to differentiate between *compare to* and *compare with* and between *contrast to* and *contrast with*. The distinction in each instance is simple but often disregarded. *Compare to* means to liken. "Shall I *compare* thee *to* a summer's day?" (Shakespeare); whereas *compare with* means to search for similarities or differences. Bernstein and Safire contend that *contrast to* has a stronger implication than *contrast with;* but *with* is in more common use and often has the force of strong, even opposing, difference. "To *contrast* the optimism of Teilhard de Chardin *with* the pessimism of Pascal" (cited by *WDEU*).

Compend (n), Compendium (n), Compendious (adj). *Compend* is simply a variation of *compendium* and is usually used correctly, but *compendium* and *compendious* are not, perhaps because the latter sounds like commodious. A *compendium* is an abridgement or a concise treatment of a subject, but it is not necessarily brief—rather, comprehensive and succinct. It can, for example, be an inventory or a list. George Eliot used the phrase "A *compendium* of extravagances and incongruities." Its plural is *compendia*, but *compendiums* is in good use, although purists wince at the "ums." Noah Webster called the first edition of his *Dictionary of the English Language* "*Compendious*"—not small but concise. Latin *compendium* is a shortcut, and so one of Johnson's definitions of *compendious* is "by which time is saved and circuition cut off," and he quotes Woodward: "They had learned more *compendious* and expeditious ways, whereby they shortened their labours and so gained time." *Circuition* is scarcely these days in common use, but it is the kind of

Latinized word Johnson loved, and it simply means the act of doing anything in a circuitous way. Perhaps it is a word to which the deliberations of our legislators may give new life.

Compiler. A *compiler* is one who puts together documents or selections from which to create a book or anthology or one who puts together data with which to make a graph or tabulation. In electronics a *compiler* is a program that translates a high-level language into a machine-readable language, thus enabling a computer to execute a program more rapidly.

Complacent (adj); **Complaisant** (adj). The latter adjective is no longer in great use, but when it is used it is often confused with the former. *Complacent:* Pleased with oneself or circumstances or surroundings; contented, self-satisfied. "Whenever Gibbon was going to say a good thing, he announced it by a *complacent* tap on his snuff-box" (Hunt). *Complaisant:* Obliging, eager to please. "The most affable, *complaisant,* and cheerful creature in the world" (Charleton).

Complement (n & v); **Compliment** (n & v). *Complement* (n): Anything that completes or improves as an addition to. " 'The grand tour' was considered the *complement* of English education" (Smilee). *Complement* (v): To complete or supplement. "Information from other documents will *complement* these" (Stubbs). *Compliment* (n): An expression of praise, admiration, or approbation. "You're exceedingly polite,/And I think it only right/To return the *compliment*" (Gilbert). *Compliment* (v): To felicitate or praise. "Monarchs should their inward souls disguise,/By ignominious arts, for servile ends,/Should *compliment* their foes, and shun their friends" (Prior).

Complex (n & adj). Time was when the adjective *complex* meant complicated or intricate and the noun a whole made up of interrelated parts, but modern psychiatry has made *complex* a fad word for repressed ideas or emotions leading to abnormal mental states or aberrant behavior. The *OED* quotes from the *Athenaeum:* "A *complex* is now a polite euphemism for a bee in one's bonnet." But faddish or not, the word is often misunderstood in a particular sense. Many seem to believe that the mark of an *inferiority complex* is diffidence; actually it is aggressiveness.

Compose, Comprehend, Comprise or **Comprize, Constitute** (v's). Each of the words involves the concept of containment, but each has a distinctive meaning. *Compose:* To make, form, or create by combining things or elements. Hence to create a literary or musical work. Also to induce calmness or quiet and, specifically, to set type (i.e., to create something by combining discrete elements). "Were it a Caske *compos'd* by Vulcan's skill,/My Sword should bite it" (Shakespeare). *Comprehend:* To understand the nature of something but also to include. "Such tricks hath strong imagination,/That, if it would but apprehend some joy,/It *comprehends* some bringer of that joy" (Shakespeare). *Comprise:* To comprehend in its sense of containing. "The People's Republic of China *comprises* several separate republics." The whole *comprises* its parts and not the other way around, so that the phrase *comprised of* meaning consisting of is always incorrect. *Constitute:* To compose in the sense of creating, to form, to establish: "Ordained and *constituted* the Services of Angels and men in wonderful order" (*Book of Common Prayer*). But *constitute* also means to form a constituent element, as "Vivacity *constitutes* her greatest charm."

Comprehend: See also **Apprehend.**

Comprehensible or **Comprehendible** (adj); **Comprehensive** (adj). *Comprehensible* means simply capable of being comprehended or understood. "For reasons not easily *comprehensible*" (Wilson). But *comprehensive* means of large scope, inclusive. "He was the man who of all modern and perhaps ancient poets had the largest and most *comprehensive* soul" (Dryden).

Compulsive (adj); **Compulsory** (adj). At one time the two words were synonymous, but psychopathology has made *compulsive* refer to an inward irresistible impulse toward some behavior or action usually irrational, whereas *compulsory* continues in its sense of obligatory or enforced. "Kindly it would be taken to comply with his request, although not *compulsory*" (Swift).

Concave (adj); Convex (adj). Words sometimes confused, although they have opposite meanings. *Concave:* Curved inward. "For his verity in love, I do think of him as *concave* as a covered goblet, or a worm-eaten nut" (Shakespeare). *Convex:* Curved outward. "A *convex* mirrour represents its images smaller than the objects" (Chambers).

Concept (n), Conceptual (adj). These have become fad words in great demand by advertisers, politicians, sociologists, and popularizers. Originally *concept* belonged to philosophers and meant an idea or theory derived from analysis of specific instances. "*Concepts* are merely the results, rendered permanent by language, of a previous process of comparison" (Hamilton). And *conceptual* describes what is conceived by the mind. "The *conceptual* incongruities of Paradise Lost" (Pattison). But philosophy has lost its hold on *concept*, and the word is now put to menial tasks. "A new *concept* in makeup, blessing your skin with its incredible beauty benefits" (cited by Fowler).

Condemn (v); Contemn (v). The former means to disapprove of, to censure, to pronounce a legal verdict of guilt, to sentence to punishment, "*Condemn* the fault and not the actor of it?" (Shakespeare), whereas *contemn* means to view or treat with scorn or contempt, "One who *contemn'd* divine and human laws" (Dryden).

Condign: See Benign.

Condone (v). To *condone* is to pardon or overlook but not to approve or endorse. "That fact alone would *condone* many shortcomings" (*Daily News*).

Confidant (n); Confident (adj); Confidential (adj). Sources of mild confusion. *Confidant* [KAHN fuh dant]: A person with whom secrets or intimate thoughts are shared. The word *confidant* is, however, not much used, for its female form is *confidante*. *Confident:* Assured, certain, bold. "She was unwisely *confident* that her *confidante* was trustworthy and discreet." *Confident* also means sure of oneself or assured of some thing or idea. "There is not so impudent a thing in Nature, as the saucy look of an assured man, *confident* of success"

(Congreve). *Confidential* means spoken or written in secret or entrusted with hidden or private matters, as in a *confidential* secretary. "I am desirous of beginning a *confidential* correspondence with you" (Lord Chesterfield).

Congenial (adj); **Congenital** (adj); **Genial** (adj). *Congenial:* Of similar nature, compatible, suited in character or temperament, agreeable, "Poetry and music are *congenial* companions" (Wharton). *Congenital:* Existing from birth or hereditary as in *congenital* defect. *Genial:* Cheerful, cordial. "No lily-handed Baronet he,/A great broad-shoulder'd *genial* Englishman" (Tennyson).

Connote (v), **Connotation** (n); **Denote** (v). *Connote:* To suggest meanings or implications beyond a primary meaning. "The word 'fireplace' *connotes* hospitality and good fellowship." A *connotation* is an implication or an inference, hence a secondary or associated meaning of a word or phrase. "A proper definition is an extension of the *connotation* of a term" (Fowler). *Denote:* To indicate, to be a sign or mark of something. "This line shall be the Equinoctial line and serve to *denote* the hour distances" (Maxon).

Consensus (n).   Avoid phrases like *general consensus* or *consensus of opinion,* for the idea of accepted opinion is contained in the word itself. It derives from consent, not census, and means general agreement or unanimity. A *consensus,* said Abba Eban, signifies that "everyone agrees to say collectively what no one believes individually."

Consequent: See Subsequent.

Construct.   A statement in a source program that will produce a predetermined effect.

Contemptible (adj); **Contemptuous** (adj).   It is curious that these words are sometimes confused, for *contemptible* means deserving of contempt or despicable. "A little group of wilful men have rendered the great Government of the United States helpless and *contemptible*" (Wilson). But *contemptuous* means having or showing contempt, scornful, disdainful.

"Sometimes she was hard and cold and *contemptuous*" (Garrett).

Contention. The condition that arises in time sharing among computer users when more than one unit attempts to transmit simultaneously.

Contiguous: See Adjacent.

Continue: See Resume.

Contraction: See Abbreviation.

Contumacy (n); **Contumely** (n). *Contumacy* [KAHN too muh see] is perversity or rebelliousness, obstinate disrespect for authority. *Contumely* [KAHN too muh lee] is contemptuous display of dislike or disdain, humiliating or condescending behavior. "Such acts/Of *contumacy* will provoke the Highest" (Milton). "The oppressor's wrong, the proud man's *contumely*" (Shakespeare).

CORAL. A high-level computer language in which the processing of data obtains a result virtually simultaneous with the event generating the data.

Core (n); **Corps** (n). They sound alike, but their distinctive meanings arise from their Latin roots—*cor* (heart) and *corpus* (body). *Core:* The central or essential part of anything, especially that of a fleshy fruit containing its seeds or of a magnet or induction coil. "Sweet as the rind was, the *core* is" (Swinburne). *Corps:* A military unit or a group of any persons associated together in a common cause, as in signal *corps* or diplomatic *corps.*

Corroborate: See Collaborate.

Corruption. Mutilation of computer data caused by failure of hardware or software.

Coterie: See Claque.

Council (n), **Councilor** (n); **Counsel** (n or v), **Counselor** (n); **Consul** (n). A *council* is a group of persons formed or convened for consultation or deliberation in some issue of common concern and a *councilor* is a member of such a body. "The *Council* of Trent convoked to meet the crisis of the Protestant Reformation" (*Columbia Encyclopedia*). *Counsel* is advice or opinion and to *counsel* is to offer advice, opinion, or recommendation. "Take my *counsel*, happy man;/Act upon it, if you can" (Gilbert). A *counselor* is any advisor but the word also has the specific meaning of attorney, as in the phrase "*counselor*-at-law." *Consul* is an official appointed by a government to look after commercial affairs of its citizens in a foreign country, as in the phrase "*consul* general."

Covert (adj); **Overt** (adj). Although these words are sometimes confused, they have opposite meanings. *Covert* means secret, hidden, disguised, whereas *overt* means open to view or inspection, acknowledged. "The beaver has *covert* ways beneath the ice" (Steele). "Whereas human laws can reach no further than to restrain *overt* action, religion extends to the secret motions of the soul" (Rogers).

Crazy (adj). A somewhat elastic word meaning anything from befuddled through impractical and enthusiastic to psychotic. In *Annie Hall* Woody Allen gives it a double-edged meaning. "Doctor, Doctor, I have a terrible problem. My brother thinks he is a chicken." The doctor says, "That's *crazy*. Your brother's not a chicken. Just tell him that." "I can't. I need the eggs."

Credible (adj); **Creditable** (adj); **Credulous** (adj). *Credible:* Worthy of confidence, believable. "He had the fate to be disbelieved in every *credible* assertion" (Sterne). But *creditable* means deserving credit or esteem or praise, although the word sometimes has the connotation of just barely deserving honor. The phrase "*creditable* performance" does not suggest the highest excellence. *Incredible* is the opposite of *credible*, and *discreditable* that of *creditable*. But *credulous* means too ready to believe. "The most positive men are the most *credulous*" (Swift).

Criterion (n), **Criteria** (n). The latter is simply the plural of the former. *Criterion* means a standard of judgment or a measure by which anything is rated. "The only infallible *cri-*

terion of wisdom to vulgar judgments—success" (Burke). "We have here sure, infallible *criteria*, by which every man may discover the gracious or ungracious disposition of his own heart" (South).

Cue (n & v); **Queue** (n & v). The words are sometimes used interchangeably, but they shouldn't be. A *cue* is anything said or done in the theater that is to be followed by a specific passage or action and hence a hint, intimation, or suggestion. " '*Cue* for the soldier's entrance,' shouted the prompter" (Edwards). *Cue* is also the playing rod used in billiards and pool. "On a cloth untrue/With a twisted *cue*/And elliptical billiard balls" (Gilbert). A *queue* is a line or a file of people awaiting their turn for anything from tickets to thingamajigs. It is also a braid of hair. "The Chinaman's *queue* was once the *cue* to his station in life, you see./But gone is the *queue* and so is the clue to what he might or mightn't be" (Tang).

Cylinder. An area of storage that permits rapid access to specified records. Also called a *seek area.*

Cynosure (n). Cynosura was one of Zeus's handmaidens. Upon her death he transformed her into the constellation *Cynosura* that contains the North Star—beacon guide to mariners and travelers. Hence a *cynosure* [CY nuh shoor] is a focus of attention or a center of attraction. "Where perhaps some beauty lies,/The *cynosure* of neighboring eyes" (Milton).

Dais, Lectern, Podium, Rostrum (n's). A *dais* is a platform for several people. A *podium* is a platform for only one person. A *rostrum* is a platform of any size—for one person or more. A *lectern* is not a platform but a stand holding written material (lecture notes, musical scores, etc.) for a performance.

Dance (n & v). Scarcely a difficult word but nonetheless a fascinating one, for in its connotations it has meant different things to different people at different times. "To move the body in rhythm, accompanied or unaccompanied by music or drumbeat" is a common definition of the verb, but it does not convey the shadings of its overtones. The *dance* among primitive people tells a story, performs the rites of magic, marks momentous occasions, invokes the help of the gods, or asks for success in love or war. It is only in recent times that the *dance* has become a social pastime or a healthful exercise. It is curious too that in Victorian England, where the revealed ankle was considered indecent exposure, staid burgers watched undismayed the French and Russian ballerinas in their skimpy tutus. Perhaps they felt all foreigners were wicked and beyond redemption in any event. There has always been about the *dance* a feeling of carnal pleasure and expression—a feeling that lingers in the modern definition: "A navel engagement without loss of semen."

Dangling participle. The participial phrase is a common construction in English and is here used correctly. "A sexton now appeared and, leaving the clergyman at his devotions on the porch, made his way along a muddy track" (Palliser). This is a proper construction, for it is the sexton who is leaving the clergyman. But if the subject of the phrase is omitted when it is different from that of the main clause, the participial phrase is then called a *dangling participle,* and it has aroused the censure of many critics who have more often invented than found examples of its absurdity, as in Barzun's "Quickly summoning an ambulance, the corpse was carried to the mortuary" or Bryant's "Walking over the hill on the left, the clubhouse can be clearly seen." Nonetheless, *dangling participles* and other dangling modifiers appear often in literature and are unnoticed except by grammarians. One does not stumble over Jane Austen's ". . . wanting to be alone with his family, the presence of a stranger must have been irksome." The trick is not necessarily to avoid the dangling modifier but to avoid the howler so evident in this newspaper account: "Jerry Remy then hit an RBI single off Haas' leg, which rolled into right field" (cited by *WDEU*).

Dastard (n), Dastardly (adj). *Dastard* is a rare word. It first meant dullard and then coward: "A laggard in love and a *dastard* in war" (Scott). "A coward; a man infamous for fear" is the definition Johnson gave in the eighteenth century, and Fowler insists that both noun and adjective should retain the idea of cowardice. However, the coward has somehow slipped into the past and *dastard* has come to mean a villain, and *dastardly* describes underhanded or treacherous villainy. "A girl who took the wrong turning when some *dastard* . . . had worked his own sweet will on her" (Joyce). "Since the unprovoked and *dastardly* attack by Japan on Sunday, December 7th, a state of war has existed" (F. Roosevelt).

Data (n); Datum (n). *Data* is a peculiar word. Actually an English word formed from a Latin plural, it has come to lead a life of its own. Long before it was adapted by computer specialists to be synonymous with information (as in *data* processing), *data* had taken on the quality of an aggregate of facts and figures, so that increasingly it carried a singular construction, however frowned upon by Fowler and others. For this reason it is never used with cardinal numbers. One may speak of five *criteria* but not five *data*. Perhaps we shall all soon be saying, "*Data* from the new census *is* not yet available," just as we now say, "The news *is* not good," although nineteenth-century purists regarded *news* as a plural noun. And then too perhaps *datum* will become a synonym for fact. The latter is often said to be little used, but it occurs frequently in the literature of mathematics, philosophy, engineering, and the social sciences to mean a specific finding or observation. "The omission of a material *datum* in the calculation . . . namely, the weight of the charge of powder" (Hutton).

Database. A file of computer data so structured that appropriate applications can be drawn from it but do not themselves constrain the file design or its content. In general, any collection of related data organized for convenient access.

Deadly (adj); **Deathly** (adj & adv). *Deadly* means causing or tending to cause death, as in a *deadly* poison. It also means implacable—a *deadly* enemy—extremely accurate—*deadly* aim—and excruciatingly boring as well—*deadly* conversation. Here Mark Twain in one use manages both its first and second meanings: "Soap and education are not as sudden as a massacre, but they are more *deadly* in the long run." *Deathly* (adj) means resembling death as in *deathly* pallor. "Let no night seal thy sense in *deathly* slumber" (de la Mare). As an adverb it means extremely, as in *deathly* afraid.

Deadly embrace. Only within the world of electronics is this a condition in which processes simultaneously active within a computer become suspended.

Debar (v); **Disbar** (v). *Debar* means to exclude or prohibit. "The love which Fate so enviously *debars*" (Marvell). *Disbar* has the specific significance of excluding from the practice of law or from the bar of a particular court. "*Disbarring* a barrister from the bar, a power vested in the benches of the four inns of the court" (Wharton).

Debauchee (n). "One who has so earnestly pursued pleasure that he has had the misfortune to overtake it" (Bierce).

Debut (n & v). *Debut* is a French noun meaning specifically the formal introduction of a young woman into society and, more generally, a first public appearance, as on stage or television, or the beginning of a career or campaign. "I saw at once that my *debut* into the House of Commons was a failure" (Disraeli). But the word is in acceptable use in both French and English as a verb. "He *debuted* at Naples and has since performed in the principal theatres of Italy" (*Fraser's Magazine*). Nevertheless, critics have called such use jargon, and *debut* rarely appears in literature as a verb.

Decimate (v). The word literally means to reduce by a tenth from the Roman practice of punishing the mutinous or cowardly by killing one of every ten men, and purists continue to hold that it should still mean to "destroy every tenth man." But in fact the verb *decimate* has rarely been used in English with such mathematical exactitude. It has long been used to denote either great loss of life or drastic reduction in numbers. "Cholera was then *decimating* the country" (Oliphant). "Though the buffalo herds have been *decimated*, this is still the frontier" (Updike).

Declaration. A computer instruction written as part of a source program.

Decrement. In electronics a quantity used to decrease the magnitude of a variable.

Deduce (v), Deduction (n); Deduct (v), Deduction (n); Induce (v), Induction (n). *Deduce* is to reason from the general to the particular but, more loosely, also to arrive at a conclusion from known facts. Hence *deduce* and *deduction* are favorite words in detective fiction. "When a fact appears opposed to a long train of *deductions*, it invariably proves to be capable of some other interpretation" (Conan Doyle). *Deduct* means simply to subtract. "His Master might buy him bow and arrows and *deduct* the price out of his wages" (Gouge). In logic a *deduction* is a conclusion following inevitably from its premises so that the conclusion cannot be false if its premise is true. If we know that all red fruits are edible, then the *deduction* may be made that the tomato is edible, but we cannot *deduce* that the orange is inedible. This we could *deduce* only from the premise that all edible fruits are red. *Induction*, on the contrary, is reasoning from the particular to the general and hence secures conclusions not absolutely certain but of highly probable certainty. If seen planets are observed to revolve around suns, then the *induction* may be made that all planets revolve around suns whether visible or not. "*Induction* from experience may provide us convenience, not science" (Locke). To *induce* also is to persuade, but *induction* into the armed services has been on occasion something more than persuasive. In general, *induction* starts from observed instances and derives generalizations therefrom or exercises the principle of applying to new or unseen instances what has been confirmed in old, seen instances, whereas *deduction* starts from a general principle, whether established or assumed, and arrives at some less general principle or some individual fact that inherently follows from the broader principle. (See also *Adduce.*)

Default. A legal term transferred to electronics. It means a value or option assumed by a computer system when no other value is specified.

Defect (n), **Defective** (adj); **Deficit** (n), **Deficient** (adj). A *defect* is a fault or flaw. Bernstein tells us categorically that *defect* is followed by *in* for a thing and *of* for a person. But use does not bear out this distinction: "Language is alive only by a metaphor drawn from the life of its users. Hence every *defect in* language is a *defect in* somebody" (Barzun). "A permanent aristocracy, possessing the merits and *defects of* the Spartans" (Russell). A *deficit* is, in general, a lack or shortage, especially the amount by which liabilities or expenditures exceed income or assets. "*Deficits* have been repeatedly recurring, and debt has been steadily and surely accumulated" (Fawcett). To distinguish between the two adjectives, one need only think of their noun forms—*defect* and *deficit*. When something is faulty in operation, it is *defective,* as in *defective* wiring; when something is missing a necessary part or an essential quality, it is *deficient.* "Every man of any education would rather be called a rascal than accused of being *deficient* in the graces" (Johnson).

Defenestration (n). It is simply the act of throwing a thing or person out a window. The *Defenestration* of Prague is a famous incident in which Bohemian rebels threw commissioners out windows of an imperial castle in Prague, thus initiating the Thirty Years' War. Some say that there should then be an accompanying verb *defenestrate,* and indeed there is, but it appears in no lexicons and its use is rare indeed: "Perhaps the chief distinction of the picture is the number of things being *defenestrated* in it" (cited by *WDEU*).

Deference (n), Deferential (adj); Differential (n & adj). To *defer* is to yield to, and *deference* and *deferential* carry the connotations of respectfulness and courtesy. "Though trunkless, yet/It couldn't forget/The *deference* due to me" (Gilbert). *Differential* arises from *difference* and means diverse, distinctive, constituting a difference, as in *differential* diagnosis. Hence a *differential* is also a set of gears designed to allow two or more shafts to revolve at differing speeds, and in mathematics an infinitesimal difference between two consecutive values of a variable quantity.

Defile (n & v). A curious word in that noun and verb have no relationship in meaning. A *defile* (from Latin *filum,* a thread) is a narrow passage, especially one through mountainous terrain. "Constantine had taken post in a *defile* between a steep hill and a morass" (Gibbon). But the verb *defile* (perhaps from the archaic *defoul*) means to pollute, debase, or tarnish. "He that toucheth pitch shall be *defiled* therewith" (Ecclesiastes), and specifically it means to violate sexually: "The Son of Hamor took her and lay with her and *defiled* her" (Genesis).

Define. A common-enough word of everyday use and one of the functions of this book. But in electronics it means to specify in user/human language a problem and how to solve it through a computer.

Definite (adj); Definitive (adj). *Definite:* Clearly defined or determined, precise, exact. "Even the serfs had now acquired *definite* rights" (Tyndall). *Definitive:* Exhaustive, reliable, complete, as in a *definitive* biography. "Other authors write often dubiously, even in matters wherein is expected a strict and *definitive* truth" (Brown's *Vulgar Errours*).

Degradation. A lowered level of service in a computer system due to equipment failure.

Delectable (adj). *Delectable* has been called a "club woman gush word" (*WDEU*), and Fowler says that it is only used ironically. Still, it appears often without irony to mean enjoyable or delightful. "Of which original journey, a most *delectable* narrative will be given in the course of this work" (Sterne).

Delimit: See Limit.

Delusion (n); **Illusion** (n). *Delusion* once meant simply a false belief or opinion as in *delusions* of grandeur, but psychiatry has made it a stronger word denoting an intractable, even dangerous, belief contrary to both fact and reason. "Nihilistic *delusion:* A depressive *delusion* in which the victim imagines that the world and all that relates to it have ceased to exist" (Stedman). *Illusion* is a milder word meaning a false or misleading impression without connotation of mania. Indeed *illusion* can even be thought of as beneficent, only its shattering causing distress. "Youths green and happy in first love,/So thankful for *illusion*" (Clough). (See also *Allusion.*)

Demean (v). *Demean* is two verbs. The earlier, deriving from *demeanor,* is to conduct oneself in a specific or appropriate manner. "It shall be my earnest endeavour to *demean* myself with grateful respect towards her Ladyship" (Jane Austen). "Stephen had long perplex'd his brains/How with so high a nymph he might/*Demean* himself the wedding night" (Swift). The later significance, deriving from the adjective *mean,* is to debase, to lower in honor or dignity. Some critics hold that only the first meaning is correct, but the second has been in wide and continuing use since the eighteenth century: "A woman is looked upon as *demeaning* herself if she gains a maintenance by her needle" (Fielding).

Denote: See **Connote.**

Deny: See **Refute.**

Deprecate (v); **Depreciate** (v); **Deprecatory** (adj). *Deprecate* means literally to pray against and hence to urge reasons against or to protest, but it also commonly means to express strong disapproval of. Something of both meanings is apparent in "To persist in such a *deprecated* and odious innovation" (Shaw). *Depreciate* means to belittle, to represent as of small value or merit. "Our architectural reputation, never high, is still more *depreciated* by the building at South Kensington" (*Fraser's Magazine*). And, of course, *depreciate* also means to claim depreciation (lessening of value) on a property for tax purposes. *Deprecatory* once shared the meaning of *deprecate* and was related to prayer, but Swift took it into the secular world and gave it the modern meaning of apologetic or belittling: "I performed the due discourses, expostulatory, supplicatory, or *deprecatory*, with my good lords the criticks."

Derisive (adj); **Derisory** (adj). Bryson draws a distinction between the two adjectives: "Something that is *derisive* conveys ridicule or contempt. Something that is *derisory* invites it." Originally, though, both words meant mocking or scoffing. "*Derisive* taunts were spread from guest to guest" (Pope). The garrulous grasshopper sits, pouring out her *derisory* song" (Chapman). But modern use does justify *derisive* as expressing contempt, *derisory* as deserving contempt. "Even our President permitted himself some *derisive* remarks about intellectuals" (Stevenson). "They prefer decorous security to *derisory* notoriety" (*The [London] Times*).

Desert (n & v); **Deserts** (n); **Dessert** (n). *Desert* (n): An arid region supporting sparse or no vegetation. "Wherein of antres vast and *deserts* idle/It was my hint to speak" (Shakespeare). *Desert* (v): To leave, abandon, forsake. "*Deserted* at his utmost need/By those his former bounty fed" (Dryden). *Dessert* (n): Any sweet as the final course of a meal. "The pastry cook is very useful. He supplies such *dessert* as an ordinary cook could not be expected to make" (*Scribner's Magazine*). But *deserts* has nothing to do with confections or defections. It arises from the same root as *deserves* and means either rewards or punishments, as in just *deserts*. It is also, in the sense of deserving, used in singular form. "Use every man after his *desert*, and who should 'scape whipping?" (Shakespeare).

Desideratum (n). From its Latin root it clearly means what is desired or needed. "The fitness of the animal for food is a great *desideratum*" (Jowett). Just as clearly its plural is *desiderata*, or, permissibly *desideratums*, but the latter rarely appears in literature. Here is one example cited by *OED:* "One of the great modern *desideratums* in oriental literature . . ." (Southey).

Designation. Coded information forming part of a computer record, or special punching in a card column.

Detract (v); **Distract** (v). *Detract* is commonly used to mean to take away from, but it is also used to mean to deflect or divert. "These exaggerated reports tend to *detract* attention from the real issues" (Scott). *Distract* is a stronger word meaning to divert the mind or attention from some object or pursuit, to trouble greatly, or even to drive mad, and, oddly, to provide a pleasant diversion as in "I have few interests in life, but bridge and golf *distract* me." Its stronger meanings are seen in "He possesses a quiet and cheerful mind, not afflicted with violent passions or *distracted* with immoderate cares" (Johnson) and "You shall find a *distracted* man fancy himself a king" (Locke).

Deus ex machina (n). A literary device explained by Fowler: "The 'machine' is the platform on which, in the ancient theatre, the gods were shown suitably aloft and from which they might descend to take a hand in settling the affairs of mortals." Hence the phrase means intervention— providential, human, or material—that appears suddenly to solve an otherwise insoluble difficulty of plot in a play or novel. In a typical Dickens novel the compression of the final pages often does not permit an altogether satisfactory explanation of exactly how every complexity is resolved and happiness is established. A *deus ex machina* came often opportunely to the beleaguered novelist, but the reader was no less captivated by the felicity so achieved.

Device (n); Devise (v). Any confusion between the words is probably more an error of orthography than of understanding. *Device* is a noun meaning primarily an invention, contrivance, gadget. But it still retains its older meanings of word configuration used to evoke desired responses, as in "rhetorical *devices*," or of an emblem or a heraldic symbol, as in Dryden's "Then change we shields, and their *devices* bear." It still also means a scheme or stratagem. "This is our *device*,/That Falstaff at that oak shall meet with us" (Shakespeare). *Devise* is a verb meaning to invent or contrive. "More ingenious than his father in *devising* warlike engines" (Knolles), and also in law to give or bequeath property by will. "The Testator gave, *devised* and bequeathed all his furniture, goods, chattels and effects, whatsoever they might be and wheresoever situate" (Black).

Dialect, Jargon, Lingua franca, Patois (n's). *Dialect* is a form of language spoken by any group of people but differing in some way from the standard form of language. Almost everyone uses *dialectical* words, sometimes for comical effect, in informal conversation. *Jargon* is a special form of language, appropriate to and often devised by a particular group of people—physicians, lawyers, musicians, mechanics, and the like. *Lingua franca* is any language widely used as a means of communication among speakers of differing languages. Capitalized, the phrase means specifically the Italian-Provençal speech once used widely in Eastern Mediterranean ports. *Patois* [PAT wah] does not differ greatly in meaning from *dialect*, but it does have the connotation of a rural or provincial form of speech, especially in France. " 'He spoke the *patois* of Yorkshire' is at best jocular" (Bryson).

Dichotomy (n), Dichotomous (adj). There has been a good deal of fussing about use and overuse of these faddish words. *Dichotomy* means division into two parts and hence a separation or cleavage. "The French Revolution deepened the *dichotomy* between radical and conservative" (cited by Fowler), and *dichotomous* shares this meaning. "The division may be not only *dichotomous* but polytomous, as, for example—angles are right, or acute, or obtuse" (Hamilton). But *dichotomy* can also mean division into opposing or mutually exclusive parts, as in "the *dichotomy* between mind and body" (*Psychology Today*), and so has come to be loosely used as a synonym for paradox or contradiction, but this is an extension of meaning difficult to support, although *WDEU* does cite Davis in this sense: "The *dichotomy* or contradiction within the American mind." Let us return to the eighteenth century and use *dichotomies*, trichotomies, and polytomies, if we must, strictly as divisions of things.

   Dickensian (adj). At the age of twelve Charles Dickens was put to work in a shoe-blacking sweatshop in the slums of London while his father was imprisoned for debt. The overwork, loneliness, and near starvation Dickens endured forged forever in his heart a sense of abandonment and desolation and an implacable hatred of oppression that gave his life and his work a tone of heightened emotion and sadness. "That I suffered in secret," he wrote, "and that I suffered exquisitely no one ever knew." In his very first work, Pickwick begins as a buffoon but emerges in his struggle against injustice as a man steadfast and heroic in principle, compassionate, and fine in feeling. The scenes of Pickwick in Fleet Prison redeem excess, and the picture Dickens draws of the poor wretches confined forever for paltry debts is all the more agonizing for its truth. Nor is Mr. Micawber (Dickens's portrait of his improvident father) an entirely comic figure. Despite his engaging sprightliness, there is in his bewildered hopefulness a feeling of despair and loss. And so in *Dickensian* there is not only the sense of the wonderfully comic but also the sense of the grotesquely and bitterly ironic. "In all the great galaxy of Shakespeare's creations, Falstaff is the only *Dickensian* character—the rascally clown become despairing and forsaken" (Reitzel).

   Dictionary (n). A book containing the words of any language or subject in alphabetical order, with explanations of their meaning, a lexicon, a word book. "A *dictionary* is not merely a home for living words; it is a hospital for the sick; it is a cemetery for the dead" (Dale). "The *dictionary* is the only place where success comes before work" (Brisbane).

Die (n). "The singular of 'dice.' We seldom hear the word, because there is a prohibitory proverb, 'Never say die' " (Bierce).

Different from, Different than, Different to (phrases). *Different than* is not the illiteracy it is commonly supposed to be and is defended by the *OED*, but *different from* has somehow become accepted usage. "Miss Buss and Miss Beale/Cupid's darts do not feel./How *different from* us,/Miss Beale and Miss Buss" (Anon., describing the headmistress of the North London Collegiate School and the principal of the Cheltenham Ladies College). *Different to* is in more common use in Great Britain than elsewhere: "It is quite a *different* thing within *to* what is without" (Fielding).

Digit (n), **Digital** (adj). A *digit* is a toe or finger but in mathematics a character used to designate a quantity numerically—in the decimal system 0 to 9, in the binary system 0 and 1. "Not only the numbers 7 and 9, from considerations abstruse, have been extolled by most, but most or all other *digits* have been mystically applauded" (Brown's *Vulgar Errours*). In electronics a *digit* is a component of an item of data or a character that may assume one of several values. For example, the number 991 comprises three digits but is composed of two characters. *Digital* describes the use of discrete signals to represent data in the form of numbers or characters. Most forms of *digital* representation in data processing are based on use of the binary system, and a *digital* computer is a machine capable of performing operations on data represented in *digital* or number form.

Dilapidated (pp). A word sometimes misspelled but rarely misused, although Bierce tells us that *dilapidated* can refer only to a stone structure since it derives from the Latin *lapis*, stone. Before, during, and after Bierce's time *dilapidated* has described structures of every conceivable kind that are in disrepair, falling down, or decayed. "A *dilapidated* old country villa" (Dickens).

Diligence (n). *Diligence* in its ordinary meaning of industriousness, assiduity, or perseverance scarcely needs definition. "*Diligence* is the mother of good luck" (Franklin).

But it does have an older meaning evident only in past literature: a public stagecoach. "I shall make my lord very merry with our adventures in the *diligence*" (Smollett).

Diminution (n), Diminutive (adj). This common-enough word is often mispronounced and misspelled as "dimunition." Correctly spelled, it means a lessening or decrease. "The gravitating power of the sun is transmitted through the vast bodies of the planets without any *diminution*" (Newton). Its adjective *diminutive* (small, little, contracted, tiny) has somehow attracted the wrath of Fowler, who calls it a "favourite of the polysyllabic humourist" and says "a faint aura of facetiousness hangs about it." Not so with Shakespeare's "The poor wren,/The most *diminutive* of birds, will fight,/Her young ones in the nest, against the owl."

Directly (adv). The meaning of the word is plain enough: in a direct way, manner, or method. "There is no other place assigned to this matter, than that whereinto its own gravity bore it, which was only *directly* downwards" (Newton). But some commentators have objected to the extended use of *directly* to mean immediately, although it has been so used for centuries. Jane Austen offers a typical example: "With undoubting decision she *directly* began her adieus."

Directory. A device in standard file-processing programs used to specify the size and structure of the file to be processed.

Disability: See Inability.

Disassemble (v); Dissemble (v). To *disassemble* is to take apart, but it may also mean by extension to separate or disburse. Its antonym is *assemble*. "He who *disassembles* a motor may well so scatter its parts that he cannot *assemble* it again." To *dissemble* is to conceal, hide, or feign. "Perhaps it was right to *dissemble* your love,/But—why did you kick me downstairs?" (Bickerstaff).

Disassociate (v); Dissociate (v). Both verbs mean to sever an association, to separate, and both have been in long use with the preposition *from*. "I can never *disassociate* the opinion *from* the person" (Cook). "Our very wants and desires, which first bring us together, have likewise a tendency to *dissociate* us" (Tucker).

Disburse (v); **Disperse** (v). It seems unlikely that so different-meaning verbs could be confused, but they sometimes are. To *disburse* is to pay out, to distribute, to expend. "As Alexander received great sums, he was no less generous and liberal in *disbursing* them" (Arbuthnot). *Disperse* means to scatter, to send or take off in various directions. "And I scattered them among the heathen, and they were *dispersed* through the countries" (Ecclesiastes). But *Biological Abstracts* has it wrong: "Cottontail management study indicates that marked rabbits *disburse* widely." There must be Alexanders among them.

Disclose (v); **Divulge** (v). These verbs have essentially the same meaning: to make known or reveal, although often *divulge* has the connotation of private revelation, *disclose* that of public revelation. "No farther seek his merits to *disclose;*/Or draw his frailties from their dread abode" (Gray). However, several commentators have objected to use of *divulge* as a synonym for say or tell. In fact it is scarcely ever so used and almost always means to reveal a secret or something unknown. "The cabinets of the sick, and the closets of the dead, have been ransacked to publish our private letters, and *divulge* to all mankind the most secret sentiments" (Pope).

Discomfit (v), **Discomfiture** (n); **Discomfort** (n & v); **Discompose** (v), **Discomposure** (n); **Disconcert** (v), **Disconcertion** (n). *Discomfit* is commonly misused. To purists it means to defeat completely, to rout, or to thwart. "Kings with their armies did flee, and were *discomfited*" (*Book of Common Prayer*). But there is recent evidence that *discomfit* has come to mean *disconcert,* and perhaps a valuable distinction has been lost, but T. S. Eliot's use of the word seems right enough: "His habit of *discomfiting* an opponent with a sudden profession of ignorance." *Discomfiture* means not the act but the result of *discomfiting*—defeat, rout, frustration. "Sad tidings bring I to you out of France,/Of loss, of slaughter, and *discomfiture*"

(Shakespeare). *Discomfort* means anything that disturbs comfort—uneasiness or mild pain—and the verb shares this meaning. "Does the want of the cushion *discomfort* you?" (Couch). *Discompose* means to disarrange, unsettle, disturb, agitate. "It was better that Passion never *discomposed* the mind" (Walpole). *Discomposure*, like *discomfiture*, means not the act but the state of being *discomposed*, that is, agitation or perturbation. *Disconcert* means to disturb self-possession, to ruffle. " 'Tis part of the Devil's business to *disconcert* our minds" (Collier). *Disconcertion* may mean either the act of *disconcerting* or the state of being *disconcerted*. "To his still greater *disconcertion*, he was asked to make a speech" (Thompson).

Discreet (adj), Discretion (n); Discrete (adj). The sound-alike adjectives have completely different meanings. *Discreet:* Prudent, cautious, circumspect. "It is the *discreet* man, not the witty, nor the learned, nor the brave, who guides the conversation and gives measures to society" (Addison). *Discretion:* The power to act according to one's own judgment, also the quality of being *discreet*, prudent, or sensible. "The better part of valor is *discretion*" (Shakespeare). *Discrete:* Separate, distinct, particulate. "To hold together, and keep *discrete*, simultaneous phenomena" (Barratt).

Disinterested (adj); Uninterested (adj). *Disinterested* means impartial, not influenced by selfish or partisan motives: "A nation of shopkeepers are very seldom so *disinterested*" (Adams). But *uninterested* simply means having no interest in and *uninteresting* creating no interest. "A Republic is a government in which attention is divided among the *uninterested* many, who are all doing *uninteresting* things" (Bagehot). Unfortunately in modern times *disinterested* has come to mean *uninterested*. "Doctors seem curiously *disinterested* in what happens to the patient afterwards" (cited by Fowler). A genuinely useful distinction is thereby lost.

Disk (n); Disc (var). A storage device consisting of a number of flat circular plates coated on both surfaces with some magnetizing material. A *disk* may be either floppy or hard as determined by performance requirements. A *disk drive* is an electromechanical device designed to read and write data onto a *disk*. A *disk emulator* is either a hardware or software device designed to read or write data for a particular range of computers but also used with computers of another range in, for example, bridging from one generation of computers to another.

Disorganized: See Unorganized.

Disparity (n); **Disparate** (n & adj). *Disparity* means lack of similarity or a difference in degree, but it also means inequality. The first meaning is seen in "Between Elihu and the rest of Job's familiars, the greatest *disparity* was but in years" (Hooker). The second in "Some members must preside and direct, and others serve and obey; and a *disparity* between these is necessary to keep the several orders in mutual dependence on each other" (Rogers). The adjective *disparate* is then almost always defined as essentially different or dissimilar in character, and Johnson's definition of the now rarely used noun *disparate* supports this meaning: "*Disparates:* Things so unlike that they cannot be compared with each other." But Safire contends that the adjective *disparate* means unequal rather than unlike, and there is some justification for this view, for its use often conveys a sense of both the dissimilar and the unequal. "Paul proceeds to the acknowledgment that his authority was in no sense *disparate* with theirs" (Lamb).

Disposal (n); **Disposition** (n). The two nouns overlap in meaning, but each has its special uses. *Disposal* means the getting rid of or destruction of something. "The *disposal* of 300 tons of solid waste" (cited by *WDEU*). But it also means the power or right to control or dispose. "Are not the blessings both of this world and the next in his *disposal?*" (Atterbury). *Disposition* means the arrangement or administration or ordering of things. "Under the head of invention is placed the *disposition* of the work, to put all things in beautiful harmony and order" (Dryden). *Disposition* too has its own special meaning of temperament or state of mind. "A reader seldom peruses a book with pleasure until he knows whether the writer of it be a black man or a fair man, of a mild or choleric *disposition,* married or a bachelor" (Addison).

Disqualified: See Unqualified.

Dissatisfied: See Unsatisfied.

Dissemble: See Disassemble.

Dissimilate (v), **Dissimilar** (adj), **Dissimilarity** (n); **Dissimulate** (v), **Dissimulation** (n); **Simulate** (v), **Simulation** (n). *Dissimilate* is not a frequently used word. It means to make unalike or to become unalike. Its meaning is clearly conveyed in the more frequently used words *dissimilar* and *dissimilarity.* "It is far easier for distinct languages grouped and used together to assimilate than to *dissimilate*" (Catlin). *Dissimulate* means to disguise under a false appearance, to dissemble. It too is more frequently used in its noun form, *dissimulation.* "Let love be without *dissimulation*" (St. Paul's Epistles to the Romans). *Simulate* means to make a pretense of or to assume the character or appearance of. "He *simulated* the manners and mannerisms of the aristocracy." *Simulation* is imitation or pretense or deception. "A deceiving by word is commonly called a lie; and deceiving by actions, gestures, or behaviour, is called *simulation*" (South).

Distaff (n & adj). The *distaff,* a stick with a cleft end, is used for holding yarn when spinning flax or wool—once strictly the work of women. "Weave thou to end this web which I begin;/I will the *distaff* hold, come thou and spin" (Dryden). Hence the adjective came to mean female, as in the *distaff* side of a family as opposed to the now rarely used *spear* or male side. "In my civil government some say the *distaff* side was too busy" (Howel). However, in recent times, *distaff,* like *authoress* (q.v.), has been disparaged as pretentious, quaint, or offensive to women. Nevertheless, it continues in use, as in this 1940 example: "The first *distaff* jockey to win a race in Mexico" (cited by *WDEU*).

Distinct (adj), **Distinctive** (adj); **Distinguished** (adj). These words similar in root and connotation do have separate meanings. *Distinct:* Clear, separate, unmistakable in identity.

"Not more *distinct* from harmony divine,/The constant creaking of a country sign" (Cowper). *Distinctive:* Characteristic, individual. "Progress, man's *distinctive* mark alone" (Browning). *Distinguished:* Preeminent by reason of excellence or renown, as in *distinguished* guests or *distinguished* scholar.

Distrait (adj); **Distraught** (adj). The first means inattentive, absent-minded, abstracted in thought. "One of those Sort of Men who are very often absent in conversation and *distrait*" (Budgell). The second means deeply agitated. "With present fear and future grief *distraught*" (Fletcher).

Diversity. A logical computer operation intended to produce a result dependent on its bit patterns.

Divert: See **Avert.**

Divulge: See **Disclose.**

Documentation (n). *Documentation* is the provision of evidence or references or citations to validate a position or statement. "The author is very painstaking in his *documentation*" (Fawcett). But in electronics *documentation* is instruction regarding the effective operation of a computer program. Such a program may be capable of fulfilling the tasks for which it is designed, but only if its operator understands its necessary input, the types of processing it performs, and the output it produces. The *documentation* that accompanies a program ensures this usefulness. It is interesting that almost all computer *documentation* or instruction is by written word.

Dominate (v), **Domination** (n); **Domineer** (v). *Dominate:* To rule or govern, to tower over, to prevail. "I thus conclude my theme,/The *dominating* humour makes the dream" (Dryden). *Domination:* Rule, sway, control, often with the connotation of arbitrary domination. "Until the military *domination* of Prussia is wholly destroyed" (Lord Asquith). *Domineer:* To rule arbitrarily or despotically. "With a certain conscious despotism he rules, nay *domineers*, over us" (Oliphant).

DOS. An acronym for Disk Operating System—any of several operating systems, especially for microcomputers, contained only in disk storage.

Dot matrix. A method of using an array of dots to create characters. A small array will suffice for alphanumeric characters, and a larger array may provide upper- and lowercase letters, underscoring, punctuation, or other symbolic devices of communication.

Double negative. Lowth in his early and pedantic grammar outlawed the *double negative:* "Two negatives destroy one another, or are equivalent to an affirmative." "No one isn't here" can logically mean only that someone is here. But it should not be forgotten that in other languages (Greek, for example) the *double negative* is deliberately used as an intensifier and so may explain its frequent appearance in past literature. "I cannot by no means allow him this argument" (cited by Lowth). "She cannot love,/Nor take no shape nor project of affection" (Shakespeare). Examples too may be found in Jane Austen, but whether deliberate or not is difficult to say, for this most subtle of writers was neither a very good speller nor grammarian. Of course, there is the intentional *double negative* used affirmatively, but often with coy intent. "My not-inconsiderable resources" suggests the speaker's abundant resources—and is meant to.

Draft (n & v); Draught (v); Drought (n). *Draft* (n): (1) A drawing or sketch. (2) A preliminary piece of writing subject to revision. (3) A current of air. (4) A device to regulate the flow of air. (5) The force required to pull a load or the team of animals to pull it. (6) A levy or conscription. (7) A selection of persons for military or other purpose. (8) An order directing the payment of money. The verb *draft* shares these meanings, but it also means specifically to write legislation. "It is not *drafting* a bill, but passing it that is the difficulty" (Seeley). *Draught* is an older spelling of *draft* and is now regarded as archaic except in Great Britain, where one often feels a cold *draught*. *Drought* is an extended, often injurious, period of dry weather or any extensive shortage, as in a *drought* of good writing.

Dryad, Hamadryad, Nereid, Oread (n's). In classical mythology these are the names of various nymphs, lovely semideities who populated the meadows, seas, and woodlands of the ancient world. The *dryads* inhabited the forests; the *hamadryad* was the spirit of a particular tree; the *nereids*, daughters of the sea god Nereus, occupied the seas, and the *oreads*, attendants on Artemis, charmed the mountains. "That thou, light-winged *Dryad* of the trees,/In some melodious plot/Of beechen green, and shadows numberless,/ Singest of summer in full-throated ease" (Keats).

Dubiety (n); **Dubious** (adj); **Doubtful** (adj). Many commentators have argued that an action or a statement or an idea may be *dubious* but only the person who harbors or alleges the *dubiety* [dooh BYE uh tee] is *doubtful*. This distinction may be logical enough but is supported neither by dictionary definition nor by usage. Both *dubious* and *doubtful* are frequently used to refer to the object of doubt. *Doubtful* means full of doubt about some object of scrutiny, but may imply a lack of conviction or certainty, and *dubious* means lacking in quality or value but may imply hesitation, uncertainty, or even mistrust. In fine, the two adjectives are used interchangeably despite the objection of purists. "No quick reply to *dubious* questions make" (Denham). "Almanackmakers are wise to wander in general and *dubious* talk and leave to the reader the business of interpreting" (Swift). "Methinks I should know you, and know this man;/Yet I am *doubtful*" (Shakespeare). "Our manner is always to cast a *doubtful* and a suspicious eye towards that, over which we know we have least power" (Hooker).

Due to: See **Because of.**

Dummy. A feature of a computer routine to satisfy a specific logical or structural requirement but that, in a particular circumstance, may not be used.

Duplex. A *duplex* is not only a twin house or an apartment on two levels, it is also an interface that allows simultaneous two-way communication between a computer and an auxiliary or peripheral device.

Each (adj & pron). *Each* as an adjective (specifying one of two or more) presents no real problem, for there is general agreement that it should be followed by a singular noun, verb, and possessive. "*Each* house shall keep a journal of *its* proceedings" (U.S. Constitution). Although *each* as a pronoun generally takes a singular verb and singular possessive: "Let *each/His* adamantine coat gird well, and *each/*Fit well *his* helm" (Milton), it is also clear that *each,* like other indefinite pronouns, has often a plural sense. Fowler allows "We *each have our* own nostrums," and one cannot object to "*Each* of Mr. Fugard's plays . . . *are themselves* acts of contrition" (cited by Simon).

Easy (adj & adv); Easily (adv). *Easy* and *easily* scarcely require definition, but some have raised objection to *easy* as an adverb, although it has been in good and reputable use in this capacity for centuries. "Vacant heart and hand and eye,/*Easy* live and quiet die" (Scott), and in some instances it has a force quite different from that of *easily:* "She bid me take love *easy,* as the leaves grow on the tree" (Yeats).

Ecclesiastical (adj); Evangelical (adj). *Ecclesiastical* means pertaining or relating to a church, its organization, or its clergy. "Is discipline an *ecclesiastical* matter or civil? If *ecclesiastical,* it must of necessity belong to the duty of the minister" (Hooker). But *evangelical* has much more specific

102

significance, primarily meaning contained in the Gospels, or first four books of the New Testament, and, secondarily, descriptive of those Protestant churches that emphasize salvation by faith in the atonement of Christ and reject the efficacy of the sacraments and good works alone. *Evangelical* has also taken on the meaning of marked by zealous or even fanatical enthusiasm. "*Evangelical* zeal in the cause of liberty may lead to license" (Dunbar). (See also *Canonical*.)

Echelon (n). Originally a French word meaning the rung of a ladder, *echelon* [ESH uh lahn] was early adapted into English to mean a formation of troops, ships, or artillery or a level in the chain of military command. However, it soon came into civilian use to mean a level in any chain of command or authority. Fowler objects to this use as "slipshod," but it is not far off its original French meaning and is in constant, steadfast use. "The twelve men who formed the party's top *echelon*" (*Newsweek*).

Economic (adj), Economical (adj). The first means having to do with the study or theory of economics. "Our country has deliberately undertaken a great social and *economic* experiment" (Borah). The second means simply inexpensive or thrifty. "The most *economical* application of the public revenue" (Thirlwall).

Ecstasy (n), Ecstacy (var). *Ecstasy:* Ebullient joy or rapture; "Any passion by which the thoughts are absorbed, and in which the mind is for a time lost" (Johnson). "O, love be moderate! Allay thy *ecstasy*" (Shakespeare). *Ecstacy:* Actually a misspelling but now so common that it has become an acceptable variant, arising no doubt from parallel noun endings in such words as celibacy, delicacy, fallacy, and others. "I get carried away in an *ecstacy* of mendacity" (Shaw).

Edifice (n). *Edifice* has been called a pompous synonym for building, but in past literature it is usually used to mean a structure vast and intricate. "He must be an idiot that cannot discern more strokes of workmanship in the structure of an animal than in the most elegant *edifice*" (Bentley).

Eerie: See Aerie.

Effect: See **Affect.**

Effective: See **Affective.**

Effete (adj). From its Latin root it should mean no longer fruitful and was once so used. "All spent and exhausted, the animal becomes *effete*" (Raymond). In modern usage *effete* has come to mean decadent, weak of character, effeminate, ineffective. "She cannot manage masculine men. Her males are overtly *effete*" (Sackville-West).

Effluent: See **Affluent.**

Egoism (n); **Egotism** (n). Both words have similar meanings, for they derive from Latin *ego* (the "I" or "self"). But there is preserved a distinction between *egoism* and *egotism*, the former meaning the practice of valuing things only in reference to one's personal interest (as opposed to *altruism*), the latter meaning preoccupation with oneself, hence self-conceit, boastfulness, excessive reference to one's status and accomplishment. "The mature man, hardened into skeptical *egoism*, knows no monition but that of his own frigid caution and interest" (Carlyle). But "His absorbing *egotism* was deadly to all other men" (Emerson on Napoleon). "*Egotism* is the anesthetic nature gives us to deaden the pain of being a fool" (Shofield).

Egregious (adj). *Egregious* once meant eminent, remarkable, extraordinary. "*Egregious* prince! Whose manly childhood portended joy unspeakable" (Phillips). However, the word at the end of the eighteenth century became pejorative and began to mean conspicuously bad or flagrant or even vicious. "We may be bold to conclude that these times, for insolence, pride and *egregious* contempt of all good order, are the worst" (Hooker). Alas, too, it has become a faddish word so that every folly is now an *egregious* folly and it should not likely be added to such ordinary follies as excessive devotion to television, "*Egregious* habit—the chewing gum of the eyes" (Wright).

Either (adj, pron, conj). As an adjective *either* means one or the other of two or each of two, as in "You may dine at *either* end of the room" or "There are paths on *either* side of the courtyard." As a pronoun it means one or the other, as in "There are two trains to London and you may take *either*." Disagreement arises only in its use as a coordinating conjunction. Bryson and others contend that *either* expresses duality and that "*Either* Chicago, New York, or Philadelphia will be the site of the convention" is incorrect. It is true that the meaning of the sentence is clear if *either* is deleted, but in actual usage the rule of duality is rarely observed. "Scanty attention from *either* biographers, scholars, or critics" (Wilson). There is also some disagreement about the number of the verb governed by *either* as a conjunction, but a simple rule applies to most situations: When *either* and *or* join singular subjects, the accompanying verb is singular, as in "*Either* soup *or* salad *precedes* the entrée." When a singular and a plural subject are so joined, the plural should be the second in order and the verb plural, as in "*Either* the principal *or* the *teachers determine* when instruction shall begin."

Elapse (v); **Lapse** (n). *Elapse* was once used as a noun to mean the duration or termination of a period of time, but it is now commonly used only as a verb meaning to slip or glide away, to pass, as in the passage of time: "Twenty-seven years had *elapsed* since the Restoration" (Macaulay). But *lapse* has a broader meaning than the obsolete noun *elapse*. It not only signifies an interval of time, it also has a great variety of extended meanings: (1) An accidental or temporary decline from an expected standard. (2) A fall from rectitude. (3) A decline into a lower grade or condition. (4) A falling into disuse. (5) In law, the termination of a right through failure to exercise it. (6) In insurance, the discontinuance of coverage of a policy either through its termination or failure to pay premium thereon. Perhaps the most common example of these extended meanings is in "*lapse* of memory." A more severe connotation is apparent in "Evil is represented to have been brought upon the human race by the *lapse* of Adam" (Tucker).

Elder, Eldest, Older, Oldest (adj's). These words have obvious-enough meanings, but correct use is not always observed, because *elder* and *eldest* apply only to persons, whereas *older* and *oldest* apply to both persons and things. A brother may be either *older* or *elder* but his house may only become *older*.

Elegy (n); **Elegiac** (adj); **Eulogy** (n). From their Greek roots, *elegy* means a song of mourning and *eulogy* a funeral oration in praise of the deceased. "When death is nigh,/The mournful swan sings her own *elegy*" (Dryden). "Fontenelle pronounced his *eulogy* more than fifty years afterwards" (Lyell). *Elegiac* means not only resembling or suitable to an *elegy* but also expressing sorrow or lamentation in any manner. "Hast thou no *elegiac* verse/For Brunswick's venerable hearse?" (Scott).

Elemental (adj); **Elementary** (adj). Although the words share a common root, they have different meanings. *Elemental:* Pertaining to ultimate constituents; simple; uncompounded; basic or primitive. "For the *elemental* creatures go/About my table to and fro" (Yeats). *Elementary:* Simple, easy, introductory, plain. " 'Excellent,' I cried. '*Elementary*,' said Holmes" (Conan Doyle).

Elicit: See Illicit.

Eloquence (n); **Grandiloquence** (n). These words are rarely confused, but it is not always realized that *grandiloquence* has a pejorative connotation. *Eloquence* is the art of using language, especially verbally, with fluency and power. "The beauty of the mind is *eloquence*" (Cicero). But *grandiloquence* is speech so lofty in tone as to become bombastic or foolish. "One cannot help smiling sometimes at his affected *grandiloquence*" (Boswell).

Else (adj & adv). *Else* as an adjective means other than or in addition to the person or thing at hand or implied. "Sweating with desire to see him; thinking of nothing *else*, putting all affairs *else* in oblivion, as if there were nothing *else* to be done but to see him" (Shakespeare). As an adverb it means in some other way or at some other place or time. "What do they do *else*, but scrape and scramble?" (Barrow). The only real problem with *else* is in use of the possessive in compound pronouns such as *someone else, nobody else, anybody else*. Grammarians and usage once steadfastly made the pronoun possessive, and *somebody's else* book and *everybody's else* business were standard English, but this has come to seem awkward and *somebody else's* book is now allowed even by fastidious purists.

Elude: See Allude.

Emanate (v); Emerge (v); Emerse (v); Immerge (v); Immerse (v). *Emanate:* To flow forth, to issue from a source, to emit. *Emanate* is usually used in reference to immaterial things or intangible forces. "The feudal idea views all rights as *emanating* from a head landlord" (Mill). *Emerge:* To rise or come forth (as from water or other liquid); to come into view from obscurity; to arise or appear as a problem or difficulty. "Strong against tide, th' enormous whale *emerges*" (Smart). *Emerse:* The verb is no longer used except in its past participle *emersed:* Standing out from a medium into which something has been plunged or from which it naturally *emerges.* A water lily standing out of surrounding water is *emersed. Immerge:* To plunge into, as in water or other fluid, to disappear by entering into a different medium. "They pour not water upon the heads of infants, but *immerge* them in the Font" (Fuller). *Immerse:* To plunge into a liquid; to become deeply absorbed. "A youth *immersed* in Mathematics" (Cowper).

Embargo (n). Not a difficult word but an interesting one. Spanish in derivation, it means generally restraint and specifically the act of a government prohibiting movement of merchant ships into and out of its ports. "After an *embargo* of our trading ships in the river of Bordeaux, and other points of sovereign affront, there did succeed the action of Rheez" (Wotton). *Embargo* is also a palindrome for "O Grab Me"—a phrase much used in debate on the United States *Embargo* Act of 1807, which attempted to deal with impressment of American seamen on the high seas and other violations of the rights of neutrals by both the British and French during the Napoleonic wars.

Embellish (v). To *embellish* is to adorn, to beautify, to grace with ornaments. "That which was once the most beautiful spot of Italy, covered with palaces, *embellished* by emperors, and celebrated by poets, has now nothing to show but ruins" (Addison). But, like many words that carry a connotation of elegance, *embellish* can be misused. One does not *embellish* a Christmas tree; *decorate* will do.

Emend: See Amend.

Emigrate (v), Emigrant (n); Immigrate (v), Immigrant (n). To *emigrate* is simply to leave one's country or region for another, and whoever does so is an *emigrant*. "The mountaineers *emigrate* during the summer to the Tuscan coast" (Spalding). To *immigrate* is to enter a new country or region as residence or temporary abode. "The *immigrants* to Australia *emigrated* mostly from the British Isles."

Eminent (adj); Imminent (adj); Immanent (adj), Immanence (n). Spelling similarity often confuses these words of entirely different meanings. *Eminent* means distinguished, famous, outstanding, of high rank or repute: "He above the rest/In shape and gesture proudly *eminent*/Stood like a tower" (Milton). *Imminent*, however, means impending, likely to occur soon, or overhanging, often in a threatening sense: "Oppose, first of all, the nearest and most *imminent* danger" (Robertson). And *immanent* means being or acting within the subject considered—inherent, indwelling, innate. It is a word often used in theology in the sense of indwelling: "It remains then that we conceive of God as at once transcending and *immanent* in nature" (Illingworth), and in the sense of innate: "Judging the infinite essence by our narrow selves, we ascribe intellections, volitions, and other such *immanent* actions, to that nature which hath nothing in common with us" (Southey). The noun *immanence* shares these meanings. "Bruno anticipated Spinoza in his conception of the *immanence* of the Deity" (Lewis).

Emotional (adj); Emotive (adj). Both words have long had the same meaning: pertaining to, affected by, or revealing feelings or emotions. "The playwright makes conscious use of *emotional* language" (Sheridan), and Fowler went so far as to say that hence *emotive* was a superfluous word. However, in recent years *emotive* has taken on the particular meaning of appealing to or evoking emotion. "The *emotive* passionate quality of epic diction" (cited by *OED*), and some commentators now object to the use of *emotional* in this sense. But such distinction is essentially artificial, and *emotional* is still widely used to mean appealing to the emotions. "Every musical mode had its own peculiar *emotional* influences" (Grote).

Empathy (n); **Sympathy** (n). *Empathy* is a relatively new word meaning primarily intellectual or emotional identification with or vicarious experience of the feelings, thoughts, or moods of another or, in an extended sense, the ascription to natural objects or works of art of the feelings or attitudes of the beholder. In its primary sense, "The psychiatrist must bring to his analysis a profound *empathy* with the anxieties and emotional disturbances of his patient" (Hebb). *Sympathy* is not only the perception but the harmonious sharing of the feelings and emotions of another, especially those of grief and sorrow. "Pleased, it returned as soon, with answering looks/Of love and *sympathy*" (Milton).

Emulation (n). In everyday speech the effort or desire to imitate, compete with, or excel others. "Aristotle allows that some *emulation* may be good, and may be found in good men; yet envy he utterly condemns" (Spratt). But in electronics, *emulation* is the process of using a computer to operate on data produced for a computer of different type. Special hardware and software are required to effect such transition.

Enclose (v); **Endorse** (v). The two words have nothing to do with each other except that both are ill used in business jargon. "Enclosed, please find" is an essentially silly expression; say, instead, "I am enclosing." Equally absurd is "Endorse on the back," for *dorse* means back. Say, instead, "Endorse the check."

Encode. To represent data in digital form as impulses denoting characters or symbols.

Endemic (n & adj); **Epidemic** (n & adj); **Pandemic** (n & adj). *Endemic:* Peculiar to a region or people, indigenous. Often used to describe disease but by no means confined to such use. "An unreflecting habit of routine that seems *endemic* among official men in our country" (Blackie). *Epidemic:* Affecting simultaneously a large number of people in a given locality by spreading from person to person. Usually said of disease, but one may speak of an *epidemic* of fads or even of riots. "The *epi-*

demic and *endemic* diseases in Scotland fall chiefly, as is usual, on the poor" (Malthus). *Pandemic:* Prevalent throughout an entire country, continent, or the world. Used principally in medicine but appearing also in its general sense of universal as in "the *pandemic* fear of nuclear war" (*The New York Times*).

Endogenous (adj); **Exogenous** (adj). *Endogenous* means arising from within and *exogenous* arising from without an organism or system. "No chemist has prospered in the attempt to crystallize a religion. It is *endogenous*, like the skin" (Emerson). "The doctor made no examination to ascertain whether her disorder was *exogenous* but merely gave that as his impression" (Block).

End result. A common-enough phrase, especially in journalism, meaning simply result and, hence, as Bryson says, "inescapably redundant." But the *end* can be justified as an intensifier suggesting finality of the *result*. "Only the *end results* of changes over many thousands of years can be seen" (cited by *WDEU*).

Enervate (v); **Innervate** (v). To *enervate* is to weaken or enfeeble. "Great empires while they stand, do *enervate* and destroy the forces of the natives which they have subdued" (Bacon). *Innervate* means literally to furnish with nerves or nervous force and, by extension, to communicate nervous energy, to stimulate. "The spiritual essence fair/Which doth *innervate* the outward show of things" (Morris).

Ensure: See Assure.

Enthuse (v). *Enthuse* means simply to be or become enthusiastic, but it is a word that has never quite obtained respectability. It has been called "ridiculous" and to be "studiously shunned by those careful in the selection of their language." It does somehow have a coy ring, and the original *OED* gives it but a grudging entry: "An ignorant back formation from *enthusiasm*. To go into ecstasies." Still, it does cite five examples, including a somewhat convincing one from Kimball in the *Pall Mall Gazette*: "I don't get *enthused* at all, sir, about all this Greek business." And now *WDEU* finds *enthuse* in common use and provides eighteen citations to suggest its acceptability.

Entropy (n). A technical word from thermodynamics that has wandered into cosmology and electronics and thence into fashionable use. In its technical sense it is a measure of unavailable energy in a thermodynamic system. In electronics it is a measure of the loss of information in a transmitting signal or message. In cosmology it is a hypothetical tendency for the universe to attain a state of homogeneity in which all matter is at a uniform temperature (thermal death). Hence *entropy* in faddish use has come to mean increasing loss and complexity, inevitable decline, and degeneration. "*Entropy* is also a hot topic among information theorists, who point out that if increased complexity leads to varied richness of thought, more power to it. Besides, according to the concept of *entropy*, the world should be falling apart by now, and apparently it isn't" (Edwards).

Enviable (adj); Envious (adj); Invidious (adj). *Enviable* is a quality in the thing beheld, meaning highly desirable or to be envied. "Unlike the *enviable* ostrich, I cannot shut my eyes to danger when it is near" (Tyndall). *Envious* is a quality in the beholder, meaning full of envy often of a spiteful or malicious kind. "*Envious* Displeasure against an Harmless, Suffering People" (William Penn). *Invidious* means causing resentment or animosity, but it often has the connotation of arousing *envious* dislike. "I must speak what wisdom would conceal/And truths, *invidious* to the great, reveal" (Pope).

Envisage (v); Envision (v). Both words suggest the calling up of a mental image, but *envision* is the loftier of the two. One may *envision* a better life for humankind and *envisage* the effect of new wallpaper in the dining room. Neither word should be followed by "that," for this usage implies foreseeing rather than *envisioning*. It is incorrect to say "He *envisaged* that there would be no access to the school from the main road" (cited by Gowers). Also the sense of both verbs (to have a picture of) is so strong that their direct objects should be things rather than ideas.

Epitaph, Epigraph, Epithet, Epigram (n's). Both *epitaph* and *epigraph* mean an inscription on a tomb or elsewhere memorializing the dead. However, *epigraph* has the additional meaning of a quotation introducing any piece of writing, for example, a book or chapter in a book. "I must say, I don't care for any of the *epigraphs* you have suggested in your essay" (Core). However, *epithet* means a word or phrase describing succinctly any person or thing, but it often has a censorious or vindictive connotation. "The frog is justly sensitive/To *epithets* like these" (Belloc). An *epigram* is a pointed, witty saying, often antithetical as in "Weeping is the refuge of plain women but the ruin of pretty ones." "What is an *Epigram*? a dwarfish whole,/Its body brevity, and wit its soul" (Coleridge).

EPROM. An acronym for Erasable, Programmable, Read-Only Memory—a clumsy phrase for a long-term computer memory that can, under special conditions, be erased and rewritten.

Equable (adj); Equitable (adj). *Equable:* free from variation, uniform, calm, undisturbed. "Thus the *equable* climates of Western Europe are accounted for" (Maury). *Equitable:* Just, right, fair, reasonable. In law, pertaining to or valid in equity as distinguished from validity in common law. "Their punishment, if tyrannical in form, was *equitable* in substance" (Froude).

Equivocate: See Unequivocal.

Equinox (n), Equinoctial (adj); Solstice (n), Solstitial (adj). *Equinox* is the point of equal duration of night and day, an event that transpires twice a year when the sun is directly overhead at the Equator. The *equinox*, occurring on or about March 21, is called vernal in the northern hemisphere and autumnal in the southern. "And since the vernal *equinox*, the sun/In Aries twelve degrees or more had run" (Dryden). *Equinoctial:* Pertaining to the *equinox* or to equal duration of day and night, but in poetic use sometimes meaning vernal or springlike, as in Pope's "gentle *equinoctial* wind." The *solstice* also occurs twice a year when the sun is directly above the Tropic of Cancer (about December 22) or the Tropic of Capricorn (about June 21). "The point at which the day is longest in Summer or shortest in Winter" (Johnson). *Solstice,* by extension, can also mean a turning point: "This being the *Solstice* of his Fortunes" (Heath). *Solstitial* means pertaining to or happening at the *solstice.* "From the North to call/Decrepit Winter; from the South to bring/*Solstitial* Summer's heat" (Milton).

Eristic (adj). Argumentative, disputatious. "The Great Cham, *eristic* arbiter of eighteenth-century letters" (Dusseau on Johnson).

Erotic (adj); **Esoteric** (adj); **Exoteric** (adj); **Exotic** (adj). *Erotic:* Pertaining to or arousing sexual desire or activity, the word deriving from the god Eros. "The *Erotic* passion is allowed by all learned men to be a species of Melancholy" (Charleton). *Esoteric:* Recondite; understood by or meant for a select few or elite; secret, confidential. "Walls covered with mythological representations and *esoteric* texts, explanatory of the old religion" (Birch). *Exoteric:* Suitable to the general public, not confined to a select group. "His *exoteric* teaching admitted fable and falsehood; the *esoteric* only what he believed to be true" (Warburton). *Exotic:* Of foreign origin, strange, unusual, glamorous; of remarkable appearance or effect. "The Italian opera, an *exotic* and irrational entertainment" (Johnson).

Errant: See Arrant.

Erstwhile: See Quondam.

Eruption (n); **Irruption** (n). An *eruption* is a forceful breaking *out,* an *irruption* a forceful breaking *in.* "This bodes some strange *eruption* in our state" (Shakespeare); but "The Goths made *irruptions* into Gaul" (Humphrey).

Escalate (v). This is a modern word—a back formation from *escalator*—that has attracted stringent criticism, both here and abroad. Nevertheless, it has settled comfortably into good usage with the meaning of to increase in size or magnitude, sometimes with the implication of undesirable and successive increase, and it was so used to describe the growing American involvement in the Vietnam war: "The possibility of local wars *escalating* into atomic wars" (cited by *OED Supplement*).

Especial: See **Special.**

Essay: See **Assay.**

Eulogy: See **Elegy.**

      Euphemism (n), **Euphemistic** (adj); **Euphuism** (n). *Euphemism* is a figure of speech meaning the substitution of a word or phrase of favorable or indefinite implication for a harsher, more demeaning or disagreeable one that more precisely designates what is intended. "The American seldom believes that the trade he follows is worthy of his virtues and talents. Since it is often impossible for him to escape, he invents a sonorous name for his trade to set himself off from the common herd" (Mencken). Hence a thousand American *euphemisms*. The foot doctor has progressed through chiropodist to podiatrist; the dog catcher has become a humane officer, the undertaker a mortician, the garbage man a sanitation engineer, the janitor a service superintendent, and the gardener a landscape architect. These are, although pretentious, harmless, but the *euphemism*, especially in advertising and statecraft, can be used to deceive. An announcement from a local shop reads, "For your greater convenience this store will hereafter be closed on Wednesday afternoons." Honesty would have knocked the "y" off *your*. In the vocabulary of diplomacy and warfare, wholesale carnage has become liquidation, and the accidental or witless killing of one's own forces is by "friendly fire." How nice it is to be the secretary of defense rather than the secretary of war. The adjective *euphemistic* shares the meaning of the noun. "He is entitled to claim, or to negotiate, or to arrange—or whatever *euphemistic* phrase may be more suitable—for a retiring competency" (*Saturday Review*). *Euphuism* [YOOH fuh iz um] is sometimes mistakenly used as a synonym for *euphemism*, with which it has no connection except a vague look of similarity. It means affected artificiality of language, preciousness, overuse of similes and conceits. "As soon as men begin to write on nature, they fall into *euphuism*" (Emerson).

      Euphony: See **Cacophony.**

Evanesce (v), Evanescent (adj). *Evanesce:* To disappear gradually, to fade away, as in Steele's "the night's bold plans that *evanesce* with day." *Evanescent:* Becoming imperceptible, vanishing, and hence fleeting, transitory, ephemeral. "The Duke of Rothsay, whose virtuous feelings were as easily excited as they were *evanescent*" (Scott).

Evangelical: See **Ecclesiastical.**

Event (n). An ordinary word of ordinary meaning: occurrence, happening, outcome. "Or sign that they were bent/By paths coincident/On being twin halves of one august *event*" (Hardy). But in the physics of relativity an occurrence sharply localized at a single point in time or space, and in sports any of the contests in a series or program, and in computer operation any circumstance that affects an item on a file of data.

Evert: See **Avert.**

Everybody (pron); Everyone (pron). Grammarians from Lowth to Simon say that indefinite pronouns should carry singular verbs and possessives, but the problem is that *everybody* and *everyone* are sometimes plural in implication. There is really nothing wrong with "Give *everyone* credit for having the courage of *their* convictions," but Bernstein will not sanction the plural possessive although common sense does. Jacques Barzun joins the sensible: "It seems clear to me that good sense requires us to say, '*Everybody* took *their* hats and filed out.' "

Exceedingly (adv); Excessively (adv). Similarity of sound obscures the altogether different meanings of these words. The former means extremely or very much; the latter, too much or unduly. One can be *exceedingly* or even *excessively* generous, and one can be *exceedingly* talented but scarcely *excessively* so. "I like *exceedingly* your Parthian dame" (Hood), but "The scenery seemed *excessively* rudimentary" (Lady Brassey). However, it may be worth note that this distinction, however sound and useful, is new, *excessively* having once had both meanings. "I am *excessively* obliged to you" is not now good usage, but was a popular phrase of the eighteenth century.

Except: See **Accept.**

Exceptionable (adj); **Exceptional** (adj). *Exceptionable* describes something to which exception or objection may be taken. "The only piece of pleasantry is where the evil spirits rally the angels upon the success of their artillery. This Passage I look upon as the most *exceptionable* in the whole Poem" (Addison on "Paradise Lost"). *Exceptional* describes something forming an exception, hence unusual, extraordinary, superior, or excellent. "The founders of the thirteen colleges were almost all of them *exceptional* men" (Pattison).

Excite (v), **Excitement** (n); **Incite** (v), **Incitation** or **Incitement** (n). To *excite* is to rouse or stir up emotions or feelings, to stimulate. "I'll come no more behind your scenes, David, for the silk stockings and white bosoms of your actresses *excite* my amorous propensities" (Johnson to Garrick). *Incite* is to urge on or to exhort to action. "The Pope *incited* the King of Spain to make war upon the Republick" (Bramhill). *Incitation* or *incitement* means the act of *inciting* or motive or incentive. "The mind gives not only license/but *incitation* to the other passions to act with the utmost impetuosity" (*Decay of Piety*).

Excuse: See **Apologize.**

Execution time. Unrelated to capital punishment, it is in electronics the time required to complete the cycle of events necessary to perform an instruction.

Exemplify (v); **Exemplar** (n), **Exemplary** (adj). The verb *exemplify* means to show or illustrate by example. "The author has *exemplified* his precepts in the very precepts themselves" (Addison). An *exemplar* is a person or thing worthy of imitation, a model or pattern, as in Jowett on Plato, "The *Republic* is the pattern of all other states and the *exemplar* of human life." *Exemplary* means serving as a model or pattern, laudable, meritorious, worthy. "If all these were *exemplary* in the conduct of their lives, religion would receive a mighty encouragement" (Swift on clerics).

Exercise (v); **Exorcise** (v). The words are rarely confused, and, when they are, the confusion is probably due to misspelling rather than misunderstanding. Nevertheless, to *exercise* is to train or condition faculties either mental or physical. "Whenever I have the impulse to *exercise,* I find if I lie down for a while it will pass over" (Shaw). It is also to make use of privileges or powers, and to discharge duties or functions. "Their consciences oblige them to submit to that dominion which their governours had a right to *exercise* over them" (Locke). *Exorcise* is to expel evil spirits or demons by prescribed ceremony and, by extension, to drive out any malign person, thing, or influence. "The spirit which devised it, is not *exorcised* either from the priesthood or the population" (Gladstone).

Exhausting (adj); **Exhaustive** (adj). These look-alikes are misused with some frequency. Whatever is *exhausting* drains off energy, wears out, uses up, or fatigues. "The misfortune of coming after this *exhausting* generalizer" (Emerson). Whatever is *exhaustive* is complete, comprehensive, thorough, detailed, and if it be an *exhaustive* twenty-volume treatise may well also be *exhausting.*

Exhilarate: See Accelerate.

Exit (n & v). A simple-enough word, although some have objected to its use as a verb, but its Latin form seems appropriate in Elizabethan and later stage directions (e.g., "*exit* Falstaff"). In electronics it is the last instruction in a routine or program, usually a branch from the routine into another part of the program.

Exogenous: See Endogenous.

Expatiate (v); **Expostulate** (v). The first means to enlarge on in discussion or in writing or to be copious in detail and is often followed by *on* or *upon.* "Those who *expatiate* with delight *on* the wonders of creation" (Chalmers). The second means to argue earnestly or vehemently with someone about something he intends to do or has done. "Stay not to *expostulate,* make speed" (Shakespeare).

Expatriate (n & v). The verb means to banish from or to withdraw from one's country. "This minister, after having been *expatriated,* outlived his enemy" (Disraeli). The noun signifies anyone banished from his country or anyone who has withdrawn allegiance from his native land. *"Expatriates* are the children of circumstance" (*Quarterly Review*). But the noun *expatriate* is curious in often being misspelled *expatriot,* possibly from analogy with *compatriot.*

Explicit (adj); Implicit (adj). *Explicit:* Clearly expressed, leaving nothing implied, hidden, or obscured. "How impossible it is to have a clear and *explicit* notion of that which is infinite" (South). *Implicit:* Implied rather than specifically stated; also absolute, unreserved, as in *implicit* trust. As opposed to *explicit:* "Yet, because it is but *implicit,* I send again to know more clearly" (Harington).

Expression (n). A word of manifold meanings, but they all relate to the representation (by word, act, symbol, gesture, or art) of ideas, thoughts, and feelings. "There is nothing comparable to the variety of instructive *expressions* by speech, wherewith man alone is endowed, as with an instrument suitable to the excellency of his soul, for the communication of his thoughts" (Holder). *Expression* in the sense of squeezing out is no longer in much use except in medical writing, as in "the *expression* of pus." In electronics an *expression* is specifically the symbolic representation of a mathematical or logical statement.

Extant (adj); Extent (n). *Extant* means still in existence, not destroyed. "The story is *extant,* and writ in very choice Italian" (Shakespeare). *Extent* means the space anything occupies or the degree which anything achieves, hence, scope, volume, range, length, area. "The English Bible, if everything else in our language should perish, would alone suffice to show the whole *extent* of its beauty and power" (*Edinburgh Review*).

Extemporize: See **Temporize.**

Extern (n); Intern or Interne (n); Intern (v), Internment (n). *Extern:* Anyone associated with an institution (usually of learning) but not residing in it. "The matter affecting the congregation alone, he puts to the good sense of *externs*" (cited by

OED). *Intern:* A resident member of the staff of a medical school or hospital and, more broadly, any resident trainee or student. "How can the *intern* cope with the bewildering complexities of clinical medicine?" (Beeson). To *intern* is to confine or detain within a limited area. "Overly zealous nations often *intern* aliens in time of war." And *internment* is such detention. "It may be hoped that *internment* in their own capital is all the confinement the army of Paris will have to submit to" (cited by *OED*).

External memory. Also called *external store,* it is a backing store of larger capacity but slower access time than the main memory or immediate access store of a computer. It is under the control of but not permanently connected to a central processor and holds data or programs acceptable to the processor.

Extract (v); Extract instruction; Extricate (v). To *extract* is to pull or draw out with force or with skill or to make excerpts from written matter. "Out of the ashes of all plants they *extract* a salt which they use in medicines" (Bacon). "To see how this case is represented, I have *extracted* out of that pamphlet a few notorious falsehoods" (Swift). *Extract instruction* is, in computer operation, an instruction that will place selected parts of information in a specified location. To *extricate* is to free or release from entanglement or danger. "Every Sunday Hairbreadth Harry *extricated* Belinda Blinks from the wiles and guiles of Rudolf Rassendale."

Extraneous (adj); Intrinsic (adj). These are antonyms, *extraneous* meaning irrelevant, not pertinent, coming from without, and *intrinsic* meaning innate, indigenous, proper to the very nature of something. "Hastings attributed the weakness of his government to *extraneous* interferences" (Burke). But "Then came out the *intrinsic* rottenness of the whole system" (Kingsley).

Fabulous (adj). From its root *fable*, the adjective clearly means mythical, legendary, imaginary, fictitious. "A person terrified with the imagination of spectres, is more reasonable than one who thinks the appearance of spirits *fabulous* and groundless" (Addison). However, *fabulous* has become a popular word, especially in advertising and journalism, as a synonym for extraordinary, marvelous, or superb. "I stood with an array of Cunard executives to greet Mr. Hicks and Lady Pamela after their *fabulous* wedding" (cited by Fowler). But Fowler holds out hope that *fabulous* may someday be restored to its pristine meaning, for, he says, in advertising "the vogue of *fabulous* is passing. *Fantastic* and *sensational* and *stupendous* are beginning to contest its leadership."

Facility (n); Faculty (n). These words are near synonyms in the sense of ability, but there is also a difference between their separate connotations. *Facility* has the extended meanings of anything designed to serve a specific function, as in "educational *facilities*," or anything that permits readier performance of an act, as in "providing every *facility* for accomplishing our purpose," or ability due to skill and practice, as in "writing with great *facility*." But *faculty* is more restricted in its basic meaning of ability. "Though old, he is in full possession of his *faculties*." It also has the extended meaning of the teaching staff of any educational institution. "The *faculty* of the Sorbonne was acknowledged to be the first in Europe" (Simmonds).

Factitious (adj); **Fictitious** (adj). *Factitious:* Artificial or contrived. "The acquisition was invested with a *factitious* value" (Mill). *Fictitious:* False, not genuine, pertaining to fiction. "It has come, I know now how, to be taken for granted that Christianity is *fictitious*" (Butler).

Faker (n); **Fakir** (n). A *faker* is anyone who fakes anything, hence a fraud or swindler. "We never call them thieves here, but prigs and *fakers*" (Borrow). A *fakir*, however, is a Muslim or Hindu religious devotee, often one who dedicates his life to contemplation and self-denial. "A *fakir* would hardly be an estimable figure in our society" (Morley).

Fallacy (n), **Fallacious** (adj); **Fallible** (adj). Many commentators contend that *fallacy* applies only to a fault in logic, but all dictionaries allow that it may also mean any error or a false notion or belief. "All men, who can see an inch before them, may easily detect gross *fallacies*" (Dryden). The adjective *fallacious* not only means erroneous but has also the connotation of consciously deceptive. "They believed and assented to things neither evident nor certain, nor yet so much as probable, but actually false and *fallacious*" (South). But *fallible* means liable or open to error, exposed to the chance or danger of deception. "Our intellectual or rational powers need some assistance, because they are so frail and *fallible*" (South).

Fallow (adj). *Fallow* describes land left unseeded. "Her predecessors did but sometimes cast up the ground; and so, leaving it *fallow*, it soon became overgrown with weeds" (Howel). Hence too it means neglected or inactive. "Shall saints in civil bloodshed wallow and let the cause lie *fallow*?" (Butler). *Fallow* has also an older meaning in which it is rarely used today: pale yellow or light brown. "The king, who was excessively devoted to hunting, had a desire to make a great park for red as well as *fallow* deer" (Clarendon).

Familiar (adj & n). *Familiar*—meaning generally known or commonly seen or well acquainted with—when used as a predicate adjective carries either the preposition *with* or *to*. Someone is *familiar with* something, something is *familiar to* someone. "The senses at first let in particular ideas; and the mind growing *familiar with* them, they are lodged in the memory" (Locke). "That war, or peace, or both at once, may be/As things acquainted and *familiar to* us" (Shakespeare). *Familiar* may also mean affable, informal, friendly. "Be thou *familiar* but by no means vulgar" (Shakespeare). And it may also mean overly friendly. "A poor man found a lord *familiar* with his wife, and because he spake it abroad and could not prove it, the lord sued him for defamation" (Camden). But *familiar* as a noun meaning a friend or intimate is no longer in current use. "The king is a noble gentleman and my *familiar*" (Shakespeare).

Fancy (n); **Fantasy** (n). *Fancy* is the product of imagination and implies also an artistic ability to create whimsical ideas or decoration. It is also a capricious image, preference, or inclination. "The soldier of today is not a romantic animal, dashing at forlorn hopes, full of *fancies* as to a love-lady or a sovereign" (Bagehot). Whereas *fantasy* is the product of unrestrained, unreal, or extravagant imagination. "Yea, faileth now even dream;/Even the linked *fantasies*, in whose blossomy twist/I swung the earth a trinket at my wrist" (Thompson).

Farther (adj & adv); **Further** (adj & adv). Although the distinction between the two words is gradually breaking down, the purist will still insist that *farther* refers only to a measurable space or distance, "O my brave soul!/O *farther, farther* sail!" (Whitman), but that *further* means only greater in degree or additional: "Without *further* Preface, I am going to look into some of our most applauded Plays" (Addison).

Fatal (adj); **Fateful** (adj). The two words both deriving from "fate" have, nevertheless, distinct meanings. *Fatal:* causing death, destruction, or misfortune, "It was that *fatal* and perfidious bark/That sunk so low that sacred head of thine" (Milton), whereas *fateful* primarily means momentous or decisively significant; "That *fateful* inability to review their position" (*Pall Mall Gazette*).

Fatuous (adj), **Fatuity** (n); **Foolish** (adj), **Foolishness** (n). Both adjectives mean lacking in judgment or common sense, stupid, asinine, silly, but *fatuous* [FACH you us] implies also a sense of complacency about one's *foolishness.* "The moment the very name of Ireland is mentioned, the English bid adieu to common feeling, common prudence, and common sense and act with the *fatuity* of idiots" (Smith). "The veteran courtier, *fatuous* as he was, was not duped by professions of regard" (Morley).

Faze (v); **Phase** (n & v). These sound-alikes are rarely confused, because they have completely different meanings. *Faze:* To disconcert or to disturb. "This blow, altho' a fearful one, did not *faze* me" (*Columbia Dispatch*). *Phase:* Any of the various major aspects in which a thing of varying appearances manifests itself or a stage in the process of growth or development. "He saw her in the most attractive *phase* of her character" (Lytton). However, the verb *phase* has meanings somewhat unrelated to the noun: (1) To schedule so that a product will be available when needed. (2) To synchronize. (3) *Phase in:* To incorporate or put in use gradually. (4) *Phase out:* To withdraw slowly out of use or service. "*Phase out*" has become something of a fad phrase. Nothing is any longer gradually reduced—it is *phased out.*

Feasible (adj); **Possible** (adj); **Probable** (adj). *Feasible* means capable of being done or suitable to being done. "To an infinite power all things are equally *feasible*" (Ward). But *possible* means capable of happening, and *probable* means likely to happen. "The Prohibition amendment can be revoked only by the same methods as secured its adoption. I met no one in America who deemed this *probable,* few who thought it even *possible*" (Fowler). *Possible* is often misused, as in "Our thanks go to the committee for making this affair *possible.*" Nonsense—the affair was always *possible;* the committee transformed possibility into reality.

Feature (n & v). There is no real problem with the noun *feature* in its various meanings as a prominent or characteristic part, the main motion picture in a movie presentation, a column or cartoon appearing regularly in print, or in plural form the face or countenance. "Though various *features* did the sisters grace/A sister's likeness was in every face" (Addison). It is only as a verb meaning to give prominence to that it has attracted criticism, Fowler finding it a "repulsive Americanism." However, the verb has fought its way into respectability both here and in Britain and no one would now fault Erica Jong's "The exhibition will *feature* first editions and related manuscripts."

Fecund (adj); **Fecundity** (n). *Fecund:* Fruitful, prolific. "The more sickly they are, the less *fecund* or fruitful of children they also be" (Graunt). *Fecundity:* Fruitfulness, the power of producing or bringing forth. "Some of the ancients mention some seeds that retain their *fecundity* forty years; and I have found that melon seeds, after thirty years, are best for raising of melons" (Ray).

Feign (v); **Fain** (adj & adv); **Feint** (n & v); **Faint** (v & adj). *Feign:* To put on the appearance of, to imitate deceptively, to pretend. "*Feigned* necessities, imaginary necessities, are the greatest cozenage that men can put upon the Providence of God" (Cromwell). *Fain* as an adjective: Willing, eager, content, also obliged to do or be something. "I was *fain* to forswear it; they would have else married me to the rotten medlar" (Shakespeare). As an adverb, gladly, willingly, rather. "The wills above be done! but I would *fain* die a dry death" (Shakespeare). *Feint:* Any movement made to deceive or disconcert an adversary. As a verb, to simulate, to distract. "*Feint* him—use your legs" (Hughes). *Faint:* As a verb, to grow weak or lose consciousness. "Oh lift me from the grass!/I die! I *faint*. I fail!" (Shelley). As an adjective, lacking strength or brightness, feeling weak, or lacking courage. "*Faint* heart never won fair lady!/Nothing venture, nothing win—/Blood is thick but water's thin—/In for a penny, in for a pound—/It's love that makes the world go round!" (Gilbert).

Felicitous (adj); **Fortuitous** (adj); **Fortunate** (adj). The words have somewhat similar but nevertheless distinctive meanings. *Felicitous:* Apt, appropriate, well suited to the occasion or circumstance. "This striking essay abounds in *felicitous* comparisons" (Felton). *Fortuitous:* Happening by chance.

"Accidental and *fortuitous* concurrence of atoms" (Viscount Palmerston). *Fortunate:* Resulting favorably, receiving a good or benefaction from an unexpected source, lucky, auspicious. "Of all axioms this shall win the prize/'Tis better to be *fortunate* than wise" (Webster).

Femto-. A prefix used especially in mathematics and electronics to denote units of measurement that are 10^{-15}—one quadrillionth smaller than the base unit.

Ferment (v); **Foment** (v). These two verbs in extended meaning may both signify to cause trouble, but *ferment* literally means to cause or undergo fermentation, whereas *foment* means to instigate or encourage anything, especially discord or rebellion. "All love at first, like generous wine,/*Ferments* and frets until 'tis fine" (Butler). But "These evil commotions were constantly *fomented* by the monarchs of Blefescu" (Swift).

Fictitious: See **Factitious.**

Field. In electronics a subdivision of a record containing a unit of information.

Filter. In computer operation a pattern of characters designed to alter or isolate specific bit patterns in another bit pattern.

Flag. A piece of information added to a computer data item—or an error *flag* indicating that the data item has given rise to error.

Flagrant: See **Blatant.**

Flair (n); **Flare** (n & v). *Flair:* The word originally meant keen scent, the capacity to get on the scent of something desired, and has so come to mean also a sense of discernment or a natural inclination, talent, or ability. "I see you have the true *flair*" (Braddon). *Flare* means to burn with an unsteady flame or to blaze forth with a sudden flash. "Forth John's soul *flared* into the dark" (Browning). As a noun, it means the flame or flash itself. "*Flares* of dazzling crimson and purple shot up from the mouth of the crater" (cited by *OED*).

Flammable (adj); **Inflammable** (adj); **Inflammatory** (adj). *Inflammable*, from *inflame*, is a sensible and useful word meaning capable of being set on fire, combustible, or capable of being aroused or excited. "This is the gas which was formerly known as *inflammable* air, and is now called hydrogen" (Huxley). Some presumed ambiguity in *inflammable* must have led to the coining of *flammable*—a word that has no philologic justification and is little used except for the signs on gasoline tank trucks. However, if people believe *inflammable* to mean incapable of being set afire, then *flammable* becomes a live-saving, if senseless, alternative. *Inflammatory* is somehow more fortunate in its meaning of tending to arouse hostility, anger, or passion, and no one seems to feel the need for *flammatory* as its replacement. "People read poisonous and *inflammatory* libels" (Junius).

Flaunt (v); **Flout** (v). Words often confused but of distinctly different meanings. *Flaunt:* To show off, to display ostentatiously. "Here's to the maiden of bashful fifteen;/ Here's to the widow of fifty;/ Here's to the *flaunting*, extravagant queen;/And here's to the housewife that's thrifty" (Sheridan). *Flout:* To scorn, scoff at, disregard, show disrespect to. "*Flout* 'em and scout 'em; and scout 'em and *flout* 'em;/ Thought is free" (Shakespeare).

Float. To add origins to data in a computer program, thus determining its area of memory.

Floating point representation. A method of electronic number representation in which a number is expressed by two sets of digits known as the fixed point part and the exponent.

Floppy disk. A flexible storage device consisting of a cylinder coated with magnetic material and storing data that can be read by a computer.

Flotsam (n); **Jetsam** (n). Although the words have become almost inseparable, they do have different meanings. *Flotsam* (from Old English float) is that part of a wreck or wreckage floating on the water surface, whereas *jetsam* (same root as jettison—from Latin throw) means cargo or gear thrown overboard to lighten a ship and then found on shore. Under the old laws of salvage *flotsam* belonged to the king of subjects who reclaimed it and *jetsam* to the lord of the manor on whose land it was found. In modern times the words used together have taken on the meaning of useless trifles or junk and, figuratively, of human down-and-outs.

Flounder (v); Founder (v). *Flounder*, thought to be a curious amalgam of founder and blunder, means to flail about helplessly, either literally as of a man in quicksand or figuratively as might be said of a nervous blundering performer. "He dashed off to a ball in time enough to *flounder* through a Cotillion" (Irving). *Founder* means simply to sink or fall and, like *flounder*, can be used literally as with a ship or figuratively as of a plan or an ambitious project. "The seamen every now and then cried out she would *founder*" (Defoe). "In this point/All his tricks *founder*; and he brings physic/After his patient's death" (Shakespeare).

Flout: See Flaunt.

Fluctuate (v); Vacillate (v). Each of these verbs means to change back and forth, to be irregular or unstable, but *fluctuate* can be applied to actions, persons, and objects, whereas *vacillate* usually applies only to persons. "Mr. Nickleby's income *fluctuated* between sixty and eighty pound per annum" (Dickens). "He may pause and tremble—but he must not *vacillate*" (Ruskin).

Foment: See Ferment.

Foolish: See Fatuous.

Forbear (v); Forebear (n). *Forbear:* To abstain or desist from, to refrain, to be patient with. "A fair region round the traveller lies,/Which he *forbears* to look upon" (Wordsworth). *Forebear* (but usually *forebears*): Ancestors, forefathers. "A yeoman whose *forebears* had once owned the land" (Murray).

Force. To intervene in the operation of a computer program by executing a branch instruction.

Forcible (adj); **Forceful** (adj). *Forcible* describes that which is achieved by force or violence. "Compel, by *forcible* means, submission to authority" (Wilson). But *forceful* means powerful, vigorous, effective: "Melodious and *forceful* verse" (Ruskin).

Forego (v); **Forgo** (v). The first means to go before or precede; the second to do without. "The *foregoing* distinction is a simple one, and it should be readily possible to *forgo* the questionable privilege of confusing the two look- and sound-alikes."

Foreword (n); **Forward** (adj); **Forwards** (adv). There is no possible reason except phonetic untidiness for these words to be misused, but they are still often confused. A *foreword* is a word that goes before—hence a preface or introduction. "The translator has felt no hesitation in placing his *Foreword* at the end of the volume" (Dasent). But *forward* means onward, in front, ahead. "They carried them out of the world with their feet *forward*" (Browning). *Forwards* is an adverb and should only be used as such. "Swings backwards and *forwards*,/ And tilts up his chair" (Holmes).

Former (adj); **Latter** (adj). The *former* is the first of two, the *latter* the second of two. The *former* should never be used as the first of three or more or the *latter* as the last of three or more.

Forthcoming (adj). A curious word whose two essential meanings are unrelated. Its primary meaning is likely to happen, about to occur, approaching. "He had forgotten all about the *forthcoming* execution" (Lang). But it also means frank or candid and outgoing or agreeable. "The publisher, a pale languid man of thirty, was even more *forthcoming*. 'I'm in it for the money,' he said" (cited by *WDEU*). "Viennese girls are attractive, amusing, *forthcoming*" (Fleming).

FORTRAN. An acronym for FORmula TRANslation—a high-level programming language, oriented to mathematics and other hard sciences, in which a source program is written in algebraic formulas and standard English.

Fortuitous and **Fortunate:** See **Felicitous.**

Founder: See Flounder.

Fractious: See Bellicose.

Frame.   Any transverse section of magnetic tape.

Frequent: See Recur.

Fulsome (adj).   *Fulsome* is a word that once had a clear and distinctive meaning. Johnson defines it as "1. Nauseous; offensive. 2. Of a rank odious smell. 3. Tending to obscenity." But it has also long meant gross or excessive as in *"fulsome* flattery" or *"fulsome* praise." Perhaps its frequent joining with "praise" has somehow given rise to the mistaken notion that *fulsome* itself means praiseworthy or full of praise. To be sure, it is not often so misused, but the error seems to be catching on. Here is an example from a *New Yorker* column filler: "Nick Schenk is at work now drafting the letter of L. B. Mayer's resignation—to make it so *fulsome* that even Mr. Mayer will like it (Leonard Lyons in the *Post*)." The *New Yorker* adds, "You mean so coarse, gross, foul, nauseating, sickening? Or do you mean so repulsive, disgusting and offensive to moral sensibility?"

Funeral (n & adj); Funereal (adj).   *Funeral* means the ceremonies attending burial of the dead and, as an adjective, pertaining to such services, as in *funeral* director, but *funereal* means mournful, gloomy, dismal, doleful. "Man in portions can foresee/His own *funereal* destiny" (Byron).

Funny (adj); Peculiar (adj); Strange (adj).   *Funny* is often used incorrectly to mean odd or strange. It should be used only to mean witty, droll, humorous. "He became very social and *funny*" (De Quincey). But, of course, there are defenders of *funny* as a synonym for strange, peculiar, odd, and one must admit that "A *funny* thing happened on the way to the Forum" has a certain aptness about it. *Peculiar* means uncommon, odd, eccentric. "Mr. Weller's knowledge of London was extensive and *peculiar*" (Dickens). But it also means (followed by *to*) characteristic of, as in "an expression *peculiar* to Canadians." *Strange* means abnormal, bizarre, foreign, extraordinary, unfamiliar. "But Lord! to see the absurd nature of Englishmen, that cannot

forbear laughing and jeering at everything that looks *strange"*
(Pepys).

Further: See **Farther.**

Fustian (n & adj). Originally the noun *fustian*
meant a stout fabric, but it has come to mean pompous, bombastic, or inflated language. "*Fustian* can't disguise the author's
meager talent." The adjective too means turgid, blustering,
extravagant. "Virgil would have thought Statius mad in his
fustian description of the statue on the bronze horse" (Dryden).

Gage (n); **Gauge** (n). In the sense of measurement these words are interchangeable, as in a narrow-*gauge* railway, but *gage* can also mean a greengage plum or a pledge or challenge. "A gauntlet flung down is a *gage* of knightly battle" (Scott).

Gain (n). Profit or advantage. "Shakespeare/For *gain*, not glory, wing'd his roving flight,/And grew immortal in his own despite" (Pope), but in electronics *gain* is the ratio of the output signal from a circuit to the original input signal.

Gambit (n). A *gambit* is historically an opening move in chess by which a player hopes to gain an advantage by sacrificing a pawn or other minor piece. Hence Follett, Bryson, and others believe that a *gambit* must involve a sacrifice or concession. In actual use the word almost always means any device, ploy, or stratagem intended to secure an advantage. "The Emperor's genius in the art of war had devised a brilliant military *gambit*" (Lennox). *Gambit* also means a telling remark or one made to open a conversation, often with the implication of seeking to direct its subsequent course. "He uses a foxier *gambit* to achieve his ends. He employs the infantile, or blubbermouth approach" (Perelman).

Gantlet (n); **Gauntlet** (n); **Gamut** (n). A *gantlet* is an old and cruel form of military punishment in which an offender was made to run between two rows of men who struck at him with swords. *Gamut* is the entire musical scale—hence any range, as in the *gamut* of emotion from gaiety to grief. Thus one may run either a *gantlet* or a *gamut* but not a *gauntlet*, for the last is a medieval metal glove and, by extension, a challenge. "Civic independence flings/The *gauntlet* down to senates, courts and kings" (Campbell).

Garnish (v); **Garnishment** (n), **Garniture** (n). To *garnish* is to decorate or supply something ornamental. But it is also to summon to litigation or to attach property that belongs to a debtor but is in the hands of a third party. "It will be a miracle if no one finds out who the trustee is; and as soon as his name is known, he will be *garnished* to a certainty" (*Pall Mall Gazette*). It is curious that the noun *garnishment* carries both meanings of the verb, whereas *garniture* means only a decoration or adornment. "Stomachers, Caps, Facings of my Waistcoat Sleeves and other *Garnitures* suitable to my Age and Quality" (Addison).

Gender (n). In grammar *gender* means a distinction (partly based on sex) that determines agreement with other words. It represents a problem in the study of languages, especially French, because *jeune fille* (girl) is obviously feminine and takes the article *la* and the feminine *jeune*, but it is not so obvious why *plume* (pen) should be feminine and *crayon* (pencil) masculine. The French, who at heart believe there is no other language, are entirely satisfied with "*la* plume de ma tante" and "*le* crayon de mon oncle." In English the problem is less severe, but that a table should be *it* and a ship *she* is a distinction closed to logic. Purists have contended that *gender* should be used only in a grammatical context and never used to mean either feminine or masculine sex. Fowler is particularly severe on such misuse: "To talk of *persons* or *creatures of the masculine* or *feminine gender*, meaning of the *male* or *female sex*, is either a jocularity or a blunder." Nevertheless, knowledgeable writers have long used *gender* to mean sex. Here is Lady Mary Wortley Montagu writing, with customary asperity, to a friend: "Of the fair sex . . . my only consolation for being of that *gender* has been the assurance of never being married to any one among them."

Generous to a fault (phrase). An overworked cliché sometimes construed to mean giving freely to the San Andreas Society.

Genial: See **Congenial.**

Genitive (adj). The word *genitive* (describing a case of nouns and pronouns that expresses the idea of possession) is no longer in great use because Lowth in the seventeenth century replaced *genitive* with *possessive.* However experts have continued to study and write about the *genitive* case, though some of their findings are more elaborate than useful. In general the *genitive* case is marked in nouns by an apostrophe and an *s* or simply by an apostrophe after an *s* ending. There is little to choose from between *James's* house and *James'* house. The preposition *of* may also be used to denote the *genitive* case of nouns— either the *president's* house or the house *of* the president. Personal pronouns have their own possessive forms (*my, our, your, his, her, their*) and the impersonal pronouns (*its, their*) that are the equivalent of *genitive* noun forms. Subtleties that go beyond these simple prescriptions are in the province of the grammarian, but it should be added that *whose* and *its* are possessives, *who's* and *it's* contractions. Perhaps an unnecessary advice but one that might have been heeded by the *Mayflower Quarterly* in its instruction to benefactors, "Be sure to include all of the deceased members full names for *whom's* memory the Memorial or Gift is given."

Germane (adj); **Material** (adj); **Relevant** (adj). *Germane* and *relevant* both mean pertinent to a matter under discussion or to a hope or plan, "The advantage most *relevant* to the present purpose" (Gladstone). "The phrase would be more *germane* to the matter if we could carry cannon by our sides" (Shakespeare). But *material* has a further implication of necessity or essentiality. "A slight contrast of character is very *material* to happiness in marriage" (Coleridge).

Gibe: See **Jibe.**

Giga-. A prefix denoting one billion (10^9), as in *gigabyte*, a measure of storage capacity equal to one billion bytes.

Gild (v); Gilt or Gilded (pp); Guild (n). To *gild* something is to overlay it with gold or gold leaf, and its past participle means covered with gold or golden-hued, as in Pope's "Where the *gilt* chariot never mark'd its way" or "*Gilded* wood may many worms infold" (Shakespeare). But "the bonds of matrimony are often *guilt*-edged" (Anon.). A *guild* is a union of workers or a trade, professional, or business association. "There were at least as early as the twelfth century *guilds* of weavers in London" (Prescott).

Glitch.   An unwanted electronic pulse that causes errors.

Glutton (n), Gluttony (n), Gluttonous (adj); Gourmand (n), Gormandize (v); Gourmet (n). A *glutton* is anyone who eats excessively or who has an excessive capacity or desire for something. "Of praise a mere *glutton*, he swallow'd what came" (Shakespeare). *Gluttony* is excessive eating or drinking. "The inhabitants of cold moist countries are generally more fat than those of warm and dry; but the common cause is too great a quantity of food, and too small a quantity of motion; in plain English *gluttony* and laziness" (Arbuthnot). A *gourmand* is a person overly fond of good eating, whereas a *gourmet* is a connoisseur of fine and delicate foods, an epicure. "Greedy *gourmands* that cannot eat moderately" (Prescott). But "the most finished *gourmet* of my acquaintance" (Thackeray). To *gormandize* is to eat greedily or ravenously. "Moderate Fare and Abstinence I prize in publick, yet in private *Gormandize*" (Congreve).

Gobbledygook (n). Although *gobbledygook* is a word of recent origin, it describes a venerable disorder—the use of turgid, grandiose, and generally incomprehensible prose. Perhaps because educators seem often to be educated in education and little else, they are often guilty of an obscurantism that can only be called *gobbledygook*. A high-school principal recently said in public: "I am apologizing to the faculty via my own volition and by no method of prompting. I adhere to the dictum that professionalism must be maintained at all costs, and by no means would I thrust any aspect of our profession which may be construed as negative" (cited by Gummere). If this be English, make the most of it, for it is difficult to envision what prompting would induce anyone to thrust an aspect, even via his own volition.

Gomorrean: See Sodomite.

Graceful degradation. Not the onset of genteel senility but a computer breakdown that is not complete and allows continued limited operation.

Graduate (v); Matriculate (v). The verb *graduate* has three distinct meanings: (1) To change gradually. (2) To arrange in gradations according to a scale. (3) To receive a degree, diploma, or certificate marking completion of a course of study. It is only in the third sense that *graduate* is now prevalent. "I married her a month after I *graduated* from college into underpaid teaching" (O'Hara). To *matriculate* is to enroll in or be admitted to a college or university as a candidate for a degree. "He, after some trial of his manners and learning, was thought fit to *matriculate* at the university" (Walton).

Grandiloquence: See Eloquence.

Grandiose (adj), Grandiosity (n). *Grandiose* originally meant producing an effect of grandeur, characterized by greatness of plan or largeness of vision. "This *grandiose* character pervades his wit and his imagination" (Emerson on Carlyle), but it has also come to mean pompous, overblown, pretentious. "He carried into the bookselling craft something of the *grandiose* manner of the stage" (Irving on Goldsmith). The noun *grandiosity* tends usually to be used in the pejorative sense of *grandiose.* "Mr. Balme's book is disfigured in regard to style by a pervading *grandiosity* of manner" (cited by *OED*).

Graphics. The science or art of drawing and also the ability of a computer to construct line drawings, graphs, charts, or diagrams on a cathode ray tube or a printer.

Grateful (adj); Gratify (v); Gratuitous (adj). These words are sometimes misused. *Grateful* means appreciative or thankful, but we are *grateful to* other persons and *grateful for* benefits. "I came to be *grateful* at last *for* a little thing" (Tennyson). To *gratify* is to give pleasure, to indulge one's self, or to humor the whims of someone else. Hence its past participle, *gratified*, does not mean thankful but rather pleased or indulged. "The lineaments of *gratified* desire" (Blake). *Gratuitous* has nothing to do with gratitude. It means either given or bestowed without charge or occurring without sufficient reason, as in *gratuitous* insult. "Prophecy is the most *gratuitous* form of error" (Eliot).

Grisly (adj); Grizzly (adj). The adjective *grisly* means inspiring fear, terror, or horror. "My *grisly* countenance made others fly;/None durst come near, for fear of sudden death" (Shakespeare). The adjective *grizzly*, from French *gris*, means gray. "Old squirrels that turn *grizzly*" (Bacon). The *grizzly* bear is so named because of his grayish color, but many think his name arises from his fierce and *grisly* character.

Grubstreet (n & adj). "Originally the name of a street in Moorfields in London, much inhabited by writers of small histories, dictionaries, and temporary poems, whence any mean production is called *grubstreet*" (Johnson).

Guild: See Gild.

Gulp. A mouthful, as in "We take large *gulps* of air to cool our hearts, overcharged with love and sorrow" (More), but also a group of binary digits consisting of several bytes.

Habitat (n); Habitant (n); Habitan (n). The *habitat* is the natural environment for anything from man to mango. "All things are good for nothing out of their natural *habitat*" (Lowell). A *habitant* is anyone who inhabits any place. "The little city of which he was now an *habitant*" (Disraeli). But the word also has the curiously specific meaning of a French settler in Canada or Louisiana or the descendant of such a settler, although in this sense usually spelled *habitan*. "A hamlet of cottages, occupied by Acadians, or what the planters call *habitans*, French Creoles" (Olmsted).

Hail (n & v); Hale (v & adj). There is some confusion in the use of these words. *Hail* as a noun means precipitation in the form of icy pellets. "I wield the flail of the lashing *hail*,/And whiten the green plants under" (Shelley). It is also an interjection, now not often used, meaning health to or greetings. "*Hail* to the sun, from whose returning light/The cheerful soldier's arms new lustre take" (Dryden). The verb means to salute or call out to. "A galley well appointed with a long boat was *hailed* by a Turk, accompanied with a troop of horsemen" (Knolles). From the sense of the noun the verb also means to fall in profusion, to rain down. "He set thee in a shower of Gold, and *hailed* Rich Pearles upon thee" (cited by *OED*). The confusion arises with *hale*, which is the established spelling for the verb meaning compel to appear. "Give diligence that thou may

137

be delivered from him, lest he *hale* thee to the judge" (Luke). *Hale* as an adjective means healthy, robust, vigorous. "His stomach too began to fail;/Last year we thought him strong and *hale*" (Swift). But *WDEU* does cite instances in which *hail* is used in these contexts. It should also be added that in the alliterative cliché "*hale* and hearty," hearty is often misspelled *hardy*.

Halcyon (adj & n). The adjective *halcyon* [HAL see un] means peaceful, serene, tranquil. "When great Augustus made war's tempests cease/His *halcyon* days brought forth the arts of peace" (Denham). The noun *halcyon* means a mythical bird supposed to breed during the winter solstice in a nest floating on the sea and to have the power to calm stormy winds and waves. "Amidst our arms as quiet you shall be/As *halcyons* brooding on a winter sea" (Dryden).

Half duplex. In computer operation an interface that allows either reception or transmission of data but does not allow both to occur simultaneously.

Hang (v), **Hanged** (pp), **Hung** (pp). The meaning of *hang* is clear enough, but there is an odd distinction preserved in use of its past participle. *Hung* applies to everything except a victim of the gallows. Pictures are *hung*, but felons are *hanged*. "Men are not *hanged* for stealing horses, but that horses may not be stolen" (Lord Halifax).

Happenstance (n). A relatively recent word formed from *happen* and circum*stance*, it means a chance happening or event, a fortuitous occurrence. Some critics dislike the word, but its colloquial use continues. "By circumstance and *happenstance*, I chanced upon a great romance" (Nash).

Harangue (n & v); **Tirade** (n). A *harangue* may not be vituperative, merely prolonged and tedious, but it does require more than one listener. A purist would not allow one person to *harangue* another. "I heard Sir Samuel Tuke *harangue* to the House of Lords" (Evelyn). A *tirade* may be abusive and be directed to one person or several. "She listened with a melancholy smile to the guide's *tirade* against oppression" (Scott).

Harbinger (n); **Herald** (n & v). A *harbinger* is literally a person who precedes another and makes known his approach—hence anything that foreshadows the future, a sign or omen. "Make all our trumpets speak, give them all breath,/ Those clam'rous *harbingers* of death" (Shakespeare). A *herald* is also a person or act that announces the approach of someone or something, hence anything that proclaims or foretells. "It was the lark, the *herald* of the morn" (Shakespeare). The verb *herald* means to signal a coming event, to announce, to usher in. "And *heralding* his way,/Proclaims the presence of the Power divine" (Southey).

Harbor: See **Port.**

Hardware. The physical units making up a computer system—the apparatus as opposed to the program—in contrast to *software*. It has this meaning in the phrase *hardware availability ratio*—a measure of the availability of a computer system to provide productive work, usually expressed as the ratio of difference between accountable time and downtime.

Hare-brained (adj). Not hair-brained. The allusion, alas, is to the furry fecund rabbit whose wits are often sharp enough. Who outfoxed the fox?

Hash. Meaningless information put into computer storage to satisfy length requirements.

Healthful (adj); **Healthy** (adj). *Healthful* means conducive to health or wholesome; *healthy* means possessing or enjoying good health. "No warmth, no cheerfulness, no *healthful* ease" (Hood). But "Everybody saw with joy/The plump and hearty, *healthy* boy" (Hoffman).

Heathen (n & adj), **Heathenish** (adj); **Pagan** (n & adj). The *heathen* and the *pagan* are persons of neither the Judaic, Christian, nor Muslim faith. "In vain with lavish kindness/The gifts of God are strown;/The *heathen* in his blindness/Bows down to wood and stone" (Bishop Heber). But the adjective *heathen*, especially in its form *heathenish*, has the pejorative connotation of uncivilized, fierce, savage. "The

Moors did tread under their *heathenish* feet whatever little they found yet there standing" (Spenser). *Pagan* as noun and adjective somehow escapes contempt, perhaps because *pagan* is often used to refer to the polytheistic religions of ancient Greece and Rome and is hence also associated with hedonism. "The Christian missionaries go out to convert the *heathens*, all loincloths and pulsating jungle rhythms, while the *pagans* hold orgies, debate the relative merits of wines, and explore the connection between pain and pleasure" (Wilson).

Helpmate (n); **Helpmeet** (n). King James's bishops in their precise sonorous way, referring to Adam's need for a wife-companion, have the Lord say, "I will make him an *help meet* for him." A perfectly good sentence in which *help* means someone who provides assistance or comfort and *meet* means suitable or appropriate. Somehow lexicographers did not perceive the meaning of the two words and made them one, *helpmeet*. Still later lexicographers deciding that *helpmeet* doesn't make much sense—which it doesn't—changed it to *helpmate*, which doesn't make a great deal of sense either in respect to the original *help meet*. Of the two corrupted words *helpmate* is more common and sounds as if it meant something. "A waiting woman was generally considered the most suitable *helpmate* for a parson" (Macaulay).

Hertz. In the International System of Units a unit of frequency equal to one cycle per second. Named after the German physicist Gustav Hertz.

Heterodox (adj), **Heterodoxy** (n); **Orthodox** (adj), **Orthodoxy** (n). *Heterodox* means differing from or not in accord with established doctrine or currently held ideas. *Orthodox* means conforming to established theological doctrine or other widely held beliefs. "Admissions which recommended him to neither the *orthodox* nor the *heterodox* classes" (Stubbs). *Heterodoxy* is deviation from established beliefs or doctrines. *Orthodoxy* is the practice of or belief in accepted dogma or ideas. "The establishment of Christianity as the State Religion turned the attention of rulers to minute questions of *heterodoxy* and *orthodoxy*" (Rawlinson). See also *Catholic*.

Heuristic (adj); **Heuristic program** (n). *Heuristic* [hew RIS tik] means encouraging or stimulating investigation or solving problems by a trial and error method. "The ideas of reason are *heuristic:* they enable us to ask a question, not to give the answer" (cited by *OED*). A *heuristic program* in electronics is an approach to solving problems by trial and error in which each attempt at solution is assessed until one acceptable within defined limits is reached—in contrast to *algorithmic program.*

Hexadecimal system. A notation of numbers to the base of 16. The ten decimal digits 0 to 9 are used, and the letters a, b, c, d, e, and f represent 10, 11, 12, 13, 14, and 15 as single characters.

Hide: See **Cache.**

High-level language. A computer language with characteristics of English words, decimal system arithmetic, and common mathematical symbols. *High-level languages* allow users to write in a notation with which they are familiar (e.g., FORTRAN in mathematics, COBOL in English).

Hindrance (n), **Hinderance** (var). *Hindrance* (an impediment, obstruction, obstacle) is a word in good and steadfast use. "The legal subordination of one sex to another is wrong in itself and now one of the chief *hindrances* to human improvement" (Mill). Many writers in language scorn *hinderance* as an ignorant misspelling, but it is an acceptable variant and was the approved spelling in the eighteenth century. "He must conquer all these difficulties, and remove all these *hinderances* out of the way that leads to justice" (Atterbury).

Historic (adj), **Historical** (adj); **Histrionic** (adj). The first words overlap in meaning but not in connotation, for *historic* means broadly known, important, or significant in history, as in the *historic* meeting between Livingstone and Stanley, whereas *historical* means simply pertaining to or characteristic of history. "In such tales as *Kenilworth,* Scott created the *historical* novel" (Brooks). *Histrionic* means pertaining to actors or acting and hence unreal or artificial. "He loved the theatre and everything which savoured of the *histrionic*" (Ward on Dickens).

Hither, Thither, Whither (adv's). These similar-sounding adverbs mean *to here, to there,* and *to where.* "Who brought me *hither*/Will bring me hence, no other guide I seek" (Milton). "There Phoenix and Ulysses watch the prey;/And *thither* all the wealth of Troy convey" (Dryden). "I strayed I knew not *whither*" (Milton). *Whither* is often used interrogatively, meaning *to what place.* "And *whither* fly the gnats, but to the sun?" (Shakespeare).

Hoard (n); **Horde** (n). A *hoard* is a supply or a store of materials for future use carefully guarded and usually hidden. "Our *hoard* is little, but our hearts are great" (Tennyson). A *horde* is any large multitude but especially a tribe or troop of nomads. "Can history offer a more terrifying prospect than that of a *horde* of ruffians led by a fanatic? Yes, that of a band of Presbyterians rising from their knees to do the Will of God" (Gregg).

Hobson's choice (phrase). *Hobson's choice* is sometimes taken to mean a difficult choice or alternative. Actually it means no choice at all, for it is an eponym from Thomas Hobson, a seventeenth-century English stable-keeper whose customers were allowed to take the horse nearest the stable door or none at all.

Homeostasis. In biology the tendency or capacity of the physiologic system of higher animals to maintain internal stability. In electronics the state of a system in which input and output are exactly balanced.

Homesickness: See Nostalgia.

Homogeneous (adj); **Homogenous** (adj). *Homogeneous* [HOH muh JEE nee us] describes things that are consistent and uniform or essentially alike. "Between the world and mind there is no comparison; the things are not *homogeneous*" (Bain). *Homogenous* [HOH **MOJ** en us] is employed in a scientific, usually biological, context in which it describes common ancestry or similarity of structure due to common descent. "Thus the forelimbs of Mammals and Fishes may be called *homogenous*" (Darwin).

Homograph, Homophone, Homonym, Synonym, Antonym (n's). A *homograph* is a word of which there is one spelling but diverse meanings, like the noun *quail* and the verb *quail*. A *homophone* is a word that sounds like another but of different spelling and meaning (*to, too, two; complement, compliment*). A *homonym* is either a *homograph* or a *homophone*. A *synonym* is a word equivalent in meaning and use to another (e.g., *loathe* and *hate*). An *antonym* is a word opposite in meaning to another (e.g., *cowardly* and *courageous*), but it is curious that there are a few *antonyms* sometimes used as *synonyms* (e.g., *flammable* and *inflammable, valuable* and *invaluable*).

Hooligan (n). *Hooligan* (a ruffian, hoodlum, or bully) derives from the perhaps-apocryphal Patrick Hooligan, notorious roughneck scion of a prolific Irish family of London. For some reason the eponymic "H" is now reduced to "h." "In the 1978 border warfare between the Cambodians and the Vietnamese, the Cambodian government always indignantly referred to the other side as *hooligans*" (Espy).

Hopefully (adv). *Hopefully* is a useful word meaning with hope, in a hopeful manner. "To travel *hopefully* is a better thing than to arrive" (Stevenson). But in modern times *hopefully* has somehow taken on the unlikely meaning of *it is to be hoped*. Used in this loose way, *hopefully* then fails to modify the word or phrase it should. "Consider this sentence: '*Hopefully* the sun will come out soon.' Taken literally, it is telling us that the sun, its manner hopeful, will soon emerge. Even if we accept the meaning '*It is to be hoped that* the sun will come out soon,' it is still grammatically amiss. Would you say, 'Hopelessly, the sun will come out soon,' if you hoped it wouldn't?" (Bryson).

Human (adj); Humane (adj). *Human* means characteristic of man or consisting of men and women, as in the *human* race. "All *human* things are subject to decay./And, when fate summons, monarchs must obey" (Dryden). *Humane* means characterized by tenderness, compassion, or sympathy. "The *humane* spirit of the law which supposes every man innocent till proved guilty" (Edgeworth).

Humbleness (n); **Humility** (n). *Humbleness* suggests a state of feeling or being inferior or insignificant. "Shall I bend low, and in a bondsman's key,/With bated breath, and whispering *humbleness*,/Say this:—/'I'll lend you thus much moneys'?" (Shakespeare), whereas *humility* suggests not only a modest sense of one's place and importance but also an acceptance of low station or rank: "And the Devil did grin, for his darling sin/Is pride that apes *humility*" (Coleridge).

Hunting. In computer operation an unstable condition that results from the attempt by an automatically controlled loop to find equilibrium.

Hurdle (v); **Hurtle** (v). *Hurdle:* To leap over, to overcome. "To *hurdle* this obstacle, we must exert our utmost force" (Gladstone). *Hurtle:* To move speedily or rush violently. "An avalanche *hurtled* down the mountainside" (*The New York Times*).

Hyperbole (n), **Hyperbolic** (adj). *Hyperbole* is a figure of speech consisting of exaggerated or extravagant statement, often not intended to be taken literally. "An Arabic interpreter expatiated in florid *hyperbole* on the magnanimity and princely qualities of the king" (cited by *OED*). *Hyperbolic:* Exaggerated, overstated, unduly rhetorical. "Eternal gratitude is his word, among others still more *hyperbolic*" (Richardson).

Hypnosis: See Somnolence.

Hypothesis (n); **Hypothesize** (v); **Hypothecate** (v); **Hypothetical** (adj). An *hypothesis* is an explanation of phenomena or a theoretical proposition offered as conjectural rather than proved. "It is the nature of an *hypothesis*, when once a man has conceived it, that it assimilates every thing to itself, as proper nourishment" (Sterne). The verb *hypothesize* shares the meaning of the noun: to assume, to offer a theory of. "They *hypothesize* a vacuum through which the emanative particles pass" (Thompson). The adjective *hypothetical* means arrived at by *hypothesis*, presumed, imagined. "He that can set *hypothetical* possibilities against acknowledged certainty, is not to be admitted among reasonable beings" (Johnson). The verb *hypothecate* has no relationship to *hypothesis* and means to mortgage or to pledge as security. "The assembly adopted a system of paper money secured and *hypothecated* upon the public lands" (Scott). That *WDEU* can dredge up a couple of examples in which *hypothecate* is used as a synonym for *hypothesize* means only that able writers sometimes stray into error.

Iconoclast (n), Iconoclastic (adj). An *iconoclast* is a breaker of images or icons, hence any disturber of accepted doctrine, and *iconoclastic* is disruptive or destructive to established dogma, especially religious belief. "Respectable vices, which take shelter under the eaves of the Church, need nothing so much as the stern *iconoclast*" (Reynolds). And "In their *iconoclastic* rage they hewed and broke the images of the cathedrals" (cited by *OED*).

Idiosyncrasy (n). Listed here only because its *idiosyncratic* spelling is almost universal. Even *The New York Times* and the London *Economist* consistently misspell one of their favorite words. "The international fashion world has accepted the *idiosyncracies* of the British." That second *c* should be an *s*.

If (conj); Whether (conj). *If* introduces a single condition; *whether* introduces alternate conditions and is often followed by *or not*, either implied or expressed. "*If* you can keep your head when all about you/Are losing theirs and blaming it on you" (Kipling). But "*Whether* 'tis nobler in the mind to suffer/The slings and arrows of outrageous fortune/Or to take arms against a sea of troubles" (Shakespeare). There is also an old rule of obscure origin that *if* may not introduce a noun clause, whereas *whether* may. If indeed it is a rule, it is disdained by most grammarians and violated by the ablest writers: "He sent forth a dove from him, to see *if* the waters were abated from off the face of the ground" (Genesis).

Ignoramus (n). "A person unacquainted with certain kinds of knowledge familiar to yourself, and having certain other kinds that you know nothing about" (Bierce). A small controversy swirls about *ignoramus*. Should its plural be *ignoramuses* or *ignorami*? The vote here is for *ignoramuses*, for the word is a Latin verb, not a noun. In its legal sense *ignoramus* means literally "We do not know" and is written on a bill by a grand jury when there is insufficient evidence to authorize finding a true bill.

Illicit (adj); Licit (adj); Elicit (v). *Illicit:* Unauthorized, unlawful, unlicensed. "A more profitable but *illicit* trade was carried on with the Spanish settlements" (Yeats). *Licit:* A word meaning the opposite of *illicit* but little used—lawful, permitted, proper. "To obtain the recognition of Christianity as a *licit* religion of the empire" (Baring-Gould). But the verb *elicit* means to draw out or bring forth, to evoke. "A corrupt heart *elicits* in an hour all that is bad in us" (Robertson).

Illusory: See Allude.

Imaginary (adj); Imaginative (adj). A score of writers have been at pains to differentiate between *imaginary* (existing only in the imagination, fancied, not real) and *imaginative* (produced by the imagination, fanciful, artfully inventive), and this is a just distinction. "Don't let us make *imaginary* evils, when you know we have so many real ones to encounter" (Goldsmith). "Poetry included then the whole exertion of its *imaginative* faculties" (Blair). But there are instances in which the words approach each other in meaning. "His canvases, chiefly *imaginary*, somber landscapes" (cited by *WDEU*). "His righteousness is not an *imaginative* but a true righteousness" (Cartwright).

Imbue: See Infuse.

Immanent (adj); Imminent (adj). *Immanent:* Indwelling, inherent. A word not often used and usually within the context of theology or philosophy. "What of the *Immanent* Will and its designs?—/It works unconsciously" (Hardy). *Imminent:* Likely to occur soon, impending. "Presaging their intended and *imminent* destruction" (Fuller). (See also *Eminent.*)

Immerge, Immerse: See Emanate.

Immigrate: See Emigrate.

Immoral: See Amoral.

Immune (adj), **Immunity** (n), **Immunize** (v); **Impugn** (v), **Impunity** (n), **Impunitive** (adj). The meanings of the first three words all derive from *immune:* protected from disease, especially by inoculation, or exempt from. "We are never altogether *immune* from contagion" (Cobbs). However, the last three words are not related in meaning. *Impugn:* To assail the truth of, to challenge veracity of, to call into question. "The *impugned* department will send down a cohort of witnesses" (*The Saturday Review*). *Impunity:* Exemption from punishment or freedom from legal restraint and, by extension, from unpleasant consequences. "Any nose/May ravage with *impunity* a rose" (Browning). *Impunitive* has a meaning, special to psychology, of not condemning oneself or others and of justifying actions as the reflection of inner feelings.

Immured (pp); **Inured** (pp). *Immured* from its basic root "wall" means confined, imprisoned, enclosed, "Love . . . lives not alone *immured* in the brain, but . . . courses as swift as thought in every power" (Shakespeare). Whereas *inured* means accustomed to or habituated to by exercise or convention. "Why should not the habit of youth be that of middle age, and the wont of middle age be the *inured* custom of advanced age?" (Pusey).

Impact (n & v). Although *impact* as a noun (forceful contact, collision) and as a verb (to strike forcefully, to collide with) has always been in good favor, use of the noun as a synonym for influence or effect has attracted severe criticism, both Follett and Bernstein calling it "faddish abasement." Still, such use is by no means new or faddish. When historian Stubbs speaks of "the *impact* of the barbarian conquest," *impact* has the sense of both force and influence. It is in reality the verb that is now figuratively and sometimes foolishly overused. *The Wall Street Journal* quotes Ruckelshaus as talking of ways in which "to advantageously *impact* the auto pollution problem." This is journalese become bureaucratese.

Imperial (adj); **Imperious** (adj). *Imperial:* Of or pertaining to an empire or emperor, hence also grand, magnificent, domineering. "There is nothing so bad or so good that you will not find Englishmen doing it. They do everything on principle. They fight you on patriotic principles; they rob you on business principles; they enslave you on *imperial* principles" (Shelley). But *imperious,* from the same root and once meaning befitting an emperor, has in modern times come to mean imperative or urgent. "The laws of honour make it an *imperious* duty to succour the weak" (Bentham). From its earlier sense it also means domineering, haughty, dictatorial. "This *imperious* man will work us all/From princes into pages" (Shakespeare).

Implicit: See Explicit.

Impractical (adj); **Impracticable** (adj). What is *impractical* is neither practical nor useful. What is *impracticable* is unsuitable to practical purposes or incapable of being put into effect. "Many cargoes are of such a nature as to make air transportation *impractical*" (cited by *WDEU*). "To preach up the necessity of that which our experience tells us is utterly *impracticable,* were to affright mankind with the terrible prospect of universal damnation" (Rogers).

Impresario (n). *Impresario* derives from the Italian word *impresa* (an undertaking or event) and means anyone who directs or manages public entertainments. But many, especially journalists, must believe that the word has something to do with *impressive,* for it is frequently so misspelled: "*Impressario* Ricardo Muti has left for Milan" (*Philadelphia Daily News*).

Impudent (adj); **Impertinent** (adj). *Impudent:* Bold, rude, arrogant, shameless. "There is not so *impudent* a thing in Nature, as the saucy look of an assured man, confident of success" (Congreve). But *impertinent* has the connotation of rudeness inappropriate, uncalled for, intrusive, or presumptuous. "I'm privileged to be very *impertinent*, being an Oxonian" (Farquhar).

Inability (n); **Disability** (n). *Inability* means lack of ability or of power or means. "My distressing *inability* to sleep at night" (Dickens). Whereas *disability* means incapacity due to physical weakness, flaw, or handicap. "The author labours under many *disabilities* for making a good book" (*Westminster Review*).

Inaudible (adj). Incapable of being heard, muffled, soundless. "Why is *o* the loudest vowel?" "Because all the others are *in audible*."

Inchoate (adj). *Inchoate* [in **KOH** ayt] means not yet fully developed, rudimentary, immature. "All was as yet in an *inchoate* state" (Burgon). Not unnaturally it has taken on the extended meaning of disorganized or incoherent. "They had to seek the help of their conquered subjects, or of more vigorous foreigners, to administer their ill-knit and *inchoate* empires" (Lawrence).

Incidentally (adv); **Incidently** (adv). *Incidentally:* Happening by chance in connection with something else or in addition to the main point or circumstance. "The supreme object of learning should be truth, and *incidentally* self-improvement" (Douglas). *Incidently* no longer exists as a word and is now considered an illiteracy although it was once in good use.

Incite: See **Excite**.

Incredible (adj); **Incredulous** (adj). *Incredible:* Unbelievable, seemingly impossible, not credible. "The *incredible* sums paid in one year by the great booksellers for puffing" (Emerson). *Incredulous:* Not believing, skeptical, disposed to doubt. "Thou hast, in truth, a most *incredulous* mind" (Cowper).

Incriminate (v); **Recriminate** (v). *Incriminate:* To charge with a crime or fault, to implicate. "Evidence which *incriminates* others while it clears themselves" (*Manchester*

Examiner). *Recriminate:* To bring a countercharge, to accuse an accuser, to reply to an accusation with a counteraccusation. "How shall such hypocrites reform the state,/On whom the brothels can *recriminate*?" (Dryden).

Inculcate (v). To *inculcate* is to impress upon the mind by repetition of statement or admonition and is followed by the preposition *in* or *into* when the direct object is what is *inculcated.* "The blatant irrationalism and blind violence *inculcated into* the dupes of totalitarian despots" (cited by *WDEU*).

Indict (v), **Indictment** (n); **Indite** (v). *Indict* means to charge with an offense or crime and *indictment* an accusation or formal charge. "I do not know the method of drawing up an *indictment* against an whole people" (Burke). *Indite* means simply to write or compose. "Men far too well acquainted with their subject to *indite* such tales of the Philistines as these" (Disraeli).

Indubitably (adv). *Indubitably* is a stuffy synonym for undoubtedly and is used in everyday speech only with jocular intent, but in literature *indubitably* is sometimes used for emphatic effect. "*Indubitably*, execution deters its victim from repeating his crime" (Stevens).

Induce: See Deduce.

Ineluctable (adj). Irresistible, inescapable, inevitable. "She and he were alike helpless, both struggling in the grip of some force outside themselves—inexorable, *ineluctable*" (Ward).

Infidel (n). "In Rome one who does not believe in the Christian religion; in Constantinople, one who does" (Bierce).

Inflammable, Inflammatory: See Flammable.

Inflict (v); **Afflict** (v). *Inflict* means to lay on or impose and has the connotation of imposing something burdensome, unwelcome, or grievous. "It is almost a definition of a gentleman to say that he is one who never *inflicts* pain" (Newman). *Afflict* means to trouble or to distress. "The mind is free, whate'er *afflict* the man,/A king's a King do Fortune what she can" (Drayton).

Informer (n); **Informant** (n). The distinction between these words is gradually disappearing. An *informer* is anyone who provides information but is also a person who informs against another for money or other reward, as in the great cinema classic *The Informer*. An *informant* is also one who informs but in law is a person who provides information to civil authorities in order to lead to successful prosecution of those guilty of wrongdoing or criminal acts. "The matter of such information shall be substantiated by the oath or affirmation of the *informant*" (Blackstone). *Informant* is also loosely used to mean a tipster.

Infrastructure (n). Originally *infrastructure* meant the permanent installations that support a military force, but it has come to mean, somewhat vaguely, the underpinning of any enterprise or the organized structure of society. The bombing of Iraq during "Desert Storm" was almost always referred to as destruction of its *infrastructure,* not with the meaning of military installations but of the whole organized fabric of the nation.

Infuse (v), **Infusion** (n); **Imbue** (v). To *infuse* is literally to penetrate, to instill, and is usually followed by *into*. One can *infuse* courage *into* a person or *imbue* him *with* courage but should not *infuse* him *with* courage. "*Infuse into* their young breasts such a noble ardour as will make them renowned" (Milton). *Infusion* is the act of pouring into, instillation. "Our language has received innumerable elegances and improvements from the *infusion* of Hebraisms out of the poetical passages of holy writ" (Addison). To *imbue* is to moisten or tinge and by extension to impregnate, pervade, or inspire, as with opinions, feelings, or ideas. "Thy words with Grace Divine *imbued*" (Milton).

Ingenious (adj); **Ingenuous** (adj). *Ingenious:* Cleverly inventive, resourceful, original in creation. "I like you and your book, *ingenious* Hone!" (Lamb to the editor of the *Every-Day Book*). *Ingenuous:* Artless, innocent, free from ordinary reserve or dissimulation. "These were fine notions to have got into the head of an *ingenuous* country maiden" (Black).

Inhibit (v), Inhibition (n). To *inhibit* is to hold back, restrain, hinder, impede, or repress. "Criticism is never *inhibited* by ignorance" (Harold Macmillan). *Inhibition* is constraint, guardedness, impediment, restriction, prohibition. "Those extreme measures which he had hitherto been restrained from taking by the Pope's *inhibition*" (Carte). But modern psychology has given *inhibition* a turn for the worse, for it now means inappropriate conscious or unconscious restraint of behavior, especially sexual response, due to guilt, fear, or rigidly puritanical background. Kinsey describes *inhibition* as "depending to a great extent upon longstanding and sometimes ancient social codes regarding various types of sexual activity." "So then Dr. Froyd said that all I needed was to cultivate a few *inhibitions* and get some sleep" (Anita Loos).

Innervate: See Enervate.

Inscribe (v). To *inscribe* is to write, print, mark, or engrave and also to dedicate informally by personal note or to enroll formally on a list. "This writer knows as much about computers as could be *inscribed* on the head of a pin by a clumsy engraver." In computer operation, to *inscribe* is to rewrite data that can then be read by a character-recognition device.

Insidious (adj); Invidious (adj). *Insidious* describes the stealthy spread of something undesirable. "Some deep *insidious* design against the states" (Watson). *Invidious* describes animosity, resentment, or envious dislike. "He had ever an *invidious* eye upon the Clergy and Men Eminent for Virtue" (Puckle).

Insure: See Assure.

Intelligent (adj); Intellectual (adj & n). *Intelligent:* Having strong mental capacity and quickness of comprehension. "Politics we bar,/They are not our bent;/On the whole we are/ Not *intelligent*" (Gilbert). *Intellectual:* Pertaining to the intellect and hence characterizing any highly rational pursuit or a person who studies the more complex and rigorous fields of knowledge, especially on an abstract or philosophical level. "Oxford! Beautiful city! So venerable, so lovely, so unravaged by the fierce *intellectual* life of our century" (Arnold). "The silent person who astonished Coleridge at a dinner of *intellectuals*" (Watts).

Intense (adj), **Intensive** (adj). *Intense:* Existing in an extreme degree, acute, strong, vehement. "Love thy country, wish it well,/Not with too *intense* a care" (Baron Melcombe). *Intensive* has much the same meaning as *intense* except that it adds the element of great concentration or compression. "*Intensive* thinking is tedious and tiresome" (Woodhead).

Intensifier. An *intensifier* is not a part of speech but simply a word or phrase that strengthens or enlarges the meaning of an accompanying word or statement. Adverbs, indispensable to the art of graphic writing, are the largest class of *intensifiers*. "Recorded data" means one thing, but "*meticulously* recorded data" something else. "A knit blouse" means something, but "a built girl" means nothing; it is only when the adverb *well* or *superbly* or *gloriously* is added that an image arises in the mind. Adjectives too can be *intensifiers*, as in *dramatic* increase or *bloody* fool or *complete* jackass, and participles also may play this role, as in *raving* maniac or *overweening* confidence. Even prepositional phrases can be *intensifiers:* "What *in the world* is the point of talking about *intensifiers?*" Simply this: they can be overdone. Not every cherished hope is *egregiously* optimistic. "A stunning hairdo" suffices. "An *absolutely* stunning hairdo" is the beautician's ploy.

Interactive (adj). *Interactive* means acting one with or upon another, interacting, performing mutually reciprocal tasks. "The *interactive* stimulus that always goes on between writer and reader" (Barzun). In electronics it means maintaining communication between a computer in operation and its human user, generally by speech.

Interface (n). An *interface* is literally a surface regarded as the common boundary between two objects or spaces, but in recent times it has become a faddish synonym for interplay, interaction, or communication between disciplines, theories, institutions, and even human beings. "In this technological century, we need an *interface* between science and the public" (Sagan). In such use the word has been viewed with considerable alarm, but it does have a more specific significance in electronics: the connection between a central processor and its peripheral units.

Intern: See Extern.

Internecine (adj). However controversial its pronunciation [usually IN turn NEE sin], *internecine* has the clear meaning of murderous, sanguinary, slaughterous, often with the implication of mutually destructive. "The Egyptians worship'd dogs, and for/Their faith made *internecine* war" (Butler). Fowler contends that the word is sometimes mistakenly used to mean intense rather than bloody. Such misuse seems rare but is perhaps evident here: "For all their *internecine* squabbling, trade unionists always call one another 'brother' " (Grundy).

Interpret. To read the patterns of holes in a punched computer card and printing the *interpreted* data on the same card.

Intractable (adj). *Intractable* has various meanings that are essentially related: not easily managed or directed, undisciplined, ungovernable, willful, obstinate, or difficult to cure or relieve, as in *intractable* pain. "To love them who love us is so natural a passion that even the most *intractable* tempers obey its force" (Rogers).

Intrinsic: See Extraneous.

Inured: See Immured.

Invidious: See Enviable, Insidious.

Irrefutable: See Refute.

Irregardless (adj). There is no such word. Use *regardless* instead, followed by *of*. "In gallant trim the gilded vessel goes,/*Regardless of* the sweeping whirlwind's sway" (Gray).

Irritate: See **Aggravate.**

Irruption: See **Eruption.**

Its (poss pron); **It's** (cont).   Perhaps an unnecessary entry, for *its* is the possessive of it and *it's* a contraction for it is. But even the *Washington Post* more than occasionally confuses the two: "*Its* the worst *its* been in the last five years." To neglect the necessary apostrophe twice in the same sentence is no mean feat of ill usage.

Jabberwocky (n). Here are the final lines of Lewis Carroll's *Jabberwocky:*

Twas brillig, and the slithy toves
Did gyre and gimble in the wabe;
All mimsy were the borogoves,
And the mome raths outgrabe.

"It seems very pretty," Alice said, "but it's *rather* hard to understand. . . . Somehow it seems to fill my head with ideas— only I don't exactly know what they are!" Hence *Jabberwocky:* Playfully inventive words that imitate real words; gibberish, nonsense.

Jackanapes (n). From its obsolete meaning of ape, it takes on a sense of an impudent, impetuous, frisky young person; a whippersnapper, an upstart. "A whiskered *Jackanapes* like that officer set to command grey-headed men before he can command his own temper" (Kingsley).

Jargon: See **Dialect.**

Jealous (adj), **Jealousy** (n); **Zealous** (adj), **Zeal** (n), **Zealot** (n). The two adjectives are in fact rarely confused, but "rarely" is enough to merit their distinction. *Jealous:* Characterized by resentment of a rival or animosity at another's success. "Who wit with *jealous* eyes surveys,/ And sickens at

157

another's praise" (Churchill). *Zeal:* Fervor for a cause, institution, or person. "Above all, gentlemen, not the slightest *zeal*" (advice of Talleyrand on the conduct of politics). *Zealous:* Ardently active, devoted or diligent, full of zeal. "One always *zealous* for his country's good" (Gray). However, the noun *zealot* has the distinct connotation of excessive zeal, of fanaticism. "I do not aspire to the glory of being a *zealot* for any particular national Church" (Burke).

Jejune (adj). *Jejune* [ji JOOHN], one of many words of curiously different meanings, derives from Latin *jejunus* (hungry or empty) and so means devoid of nutriment or substance and hence also trite, uninteresting, or inadequate. "He gives what seems a very *jejune* and unsatisfactory reason" (Blackstone). But perhaps because of confusion with French *jeune* (young), it has also come to mean immature, juvenile, naive. "We pass in the world for sects and schools, for erudition and piety, and we are all the time *jejune* babes" (Emerson).

Jetsam: See Flotsam.

Jibe (n & v); **Gibe** (n & v). Many commentators draw a strict distinction between the two words, giving the verb *jibe* the meaning of to agree or be in accord or harmony with. "The piece you happened to be playing didn't seem to *jibe* with the picture that was passing" (Mark Twain). Only *gibe*, they insist, can be used as a noun to mean a sarcastic or scornful remark and as a verb to mean taunt or deride. "But the dean, if the secret should come to his ears,/Will never be done with his *gibes* and his jeers" (Swift). In fact *jibe* as both noun and verb has long been interchangeable with *gibe*. "Alas, poore Yorick, . . . Where be your *Jibes* now?" (Shakespeare). "A blasphemous boy *jibes* at them" (Craft).

Jocose, Jocular, Jocund, Jovial (adj's). These adjectives have similar but slightly different meanings. *Jocose:* Jesting, playful, humorous. "If the subject be sacred, all ludicrous turns, and *jocose* or comical airs, should be excluded" (Watts). *Jocular:* Full of quips, waggish, facetious. "These *jocular* slanders are often as mischievous as those of deepest design" (cited by Johnson). *Jocund:* Cheerful, merry, blithe. "A poet could not but be gay/In such a *jocund* company" (Wordsworth). *Jovial:*

Convivial, characterized by hearty humor or good fellowship. "Men of the present age are merry or *jovial*, rather than joyous" (Taylor).

Judge (n); **Jurist** (n). These words are not synonyms. A *jurist* is anyone learned in the law. "The doctrines of the Mohammedan *jurists* are somewhat at variance in this matter" (Wilson). Whereas a *judge* is a public officer authorized to hear causes and actions in a court of law. He may well be a lawyer but may not be a *jurist*. " 'I'll be judge, I'll be jury,' said cunning old Fury,/ 'I'll try the whole cause and condemn you to death' " (Carroll).

Judicial (adj); **Judicious** (adj), **Judiciously** (adv). The words have a common base but distinctive meanings. *Judicial* characterizes only judges or courts of law and the judgments of either. "A *judicial* rent was a rent fixed by a *judicial* body, a dispassionate and impartial body" (Gladstone). Whereas *judicious* means characterized by good judgment, prudence, or wise understanding. "The art of reading is to skip *judiciously*" (Hamerton).

Juggernaut (n). In twelfth-century India the god Vishnu's idol *Juggernaut* was taken in a vast car from one temple to another. On the last day of festival pilgrims are said to have cast themselves under the wheels of the car to be crushed to death. Hence a *juggernaut* is anything monstrously powerful or any object of worship demanding blind devotion or cruel sacrifice. "Practical politics, that revolutionary *Juggernaut* that grinds us all under its car" (cited by *OED*).

Junction (n); **Juncture** (n). *Junction:* The act of joining or the place or point at which two or more things converge. "Upon the *junction* of the two corps, our spies discovered a great cloud of dust" (Addison). *Juncture:* A point of time, especially one made critical by concurrent circumstance. "At this critical *juncture* in history only the fullest resources . . . can do the job" (cited by *WDEU*). Because of this critical sense, to use "at this *juncture* in time" as a synonym for now seems unduly pompous.

Just (adj & adv). The adjective *just* has a primary meaning of lawful, rightful, equitable, impartial, and a host of derivative secondary meanings: appropriate, accurate, precise, correct, merited, well founded. In its primary sense, *"Just* are the ways of God" (Milton), and in the sense of appropriate or merited, it is often used with punishment: "Whose damnation was *just"* (Romans). As an adverb it means exactly, precisely, no more than, barely, really, a short time ago, and merely. "Give me, ye gods, the product of one field,/That so I neither may be rich nor poor;/And having *just* enough, not covet more" (Dryden). *Just deserts* is a cliché favored by many but spelled correctly by few. The phrase has nothing to do with pie à la mode. Hence it is not *just desserts.* Its root is the French word "deserté"—past participle of "deservir"—to deserve. A reader who gets as far as the references that close this book may note an essay called *"Just* Words" and wonder whether *just* here means precise or merely.

K or **Kilo-**. The symbol or prefix for 1,000. In computer language 1K actually means 2 to the tenth power, or 1,024.

Karat and **Karate:** See **Carat.**

Kernel. A set of procedures controlling the resources of a computer system.

Kind of, Sort of (phrases). The two phrases are interchangeable, and, if not whole volumes, at least lengthy disquisitions have been written about their proper use. In vernacular employment both phrases may be used quite loosely, but by any standards "He is *kind of* stupid" is an illiteracy. In writing, use should be restricted to the literal sense of the words. "Amber is a *kind of* fossil resin" (Strunk). In general *kind of a* should be avoided, and we should think of *kind* or *sort* as meaning a species or category or division of a category. "All the world is divided into two *kinds of* people. Those who divide the world into two *kinds of* people and those who don't" (James). "Stockbrokers, sugar bakers—that *sort of* people" (Thackeray).

Kinesis (n), **Kinesics** (n); **Kinetic** (adj), **Kinetics** (n). *Kinesis:* The movement of an organism in response to a stimulus. "We shall find *kinesis* (especially in response to light) in many

161

forms of life" (Gray). *Kinesics* is the study of body movements in general and, specifically, as means of communication. *Kinetic:* Pertaining to, caused by, or characterized by motion. "I still remember that the spinning of a top is a case of *kinetic* stability" (Stevenson). *Kinetics* is the study of the relationship between the motions of bodies and their activating forces.

Kith (n); **Kin** (n). "Your *kin* are your relatives. Your *kith* are your relatives and your acquaintances. Individually the words are antiquated. Together they are redundant and hackneyed" (Bryson). "For every trite balloon a pin,/None quite so bad as *kith and kin*"—unless it be *kith and tell*.

Knot (n). *Knot* in nautical use, unlike mile, is not a measure of distance but a unit of speed: one nautical mile an hour. "The carrier *Wasp* is limping home at eight *knots* an hour" is incorrect. The words *an hour* or *per hour* should never follow knot. "A torpedo-boat destroyer has made a record speed of 35 *knots,* almost exactly equal to 41 miles an hour" (*Daily News*).

Know: See Realize.

Knowledge (n). *Knowledge* means simply knowing, but it is a word of subtle variations in meaning. The phrase "carnal *knowledge*" implies something beyond mere knowing. Here are some of the principal senses of the word: (1) Perceptivity, acumen. "*Knowledge* consists in the perception of the truth of negative or affirmative propositions" (Locke). (2) Learning or illumination of the mind. "Ignorance is the curse of God,/*Knowledge* is the wing wherewith we fly to heav'n" (Shakespeare). (3) Acquaintanceship with things, persons, or facts. "To my *knowledge,*/I never in my life did look on him" (Shakespeare). (4) Awareness, cognizance. "A state's anger should not take *knowledge* of either fools or women" (Jonson). (5) Information, lore. "If a little *knowledge* is dangerous, where is the man who has so much as to be out of danger?" (T. Huxley). (6) The sum of what is known or a body of truth. "Our soul whose faculties can comprehend/The wondrous Architecture of the world,/And measure every wand'ring planet's course,/Still climbing after *knowledge* infinite" (Marlowe). But particulate *knowledge* can be more stultifying than illuminating. "Where is the wisdom we have lost in *knowledge;/*Where is the *knowledge* we have lost in information?" (T. S. Eliot).

Kudos (n). *Kudos* is a Greek word meaning praise or renown and is singular, so that "the *kudos* that were his due" is ungrammatical. But there is a word *kudo* (accolade)—an illiterate back formation from *kudos* in the mistaken belief that the latter is plural. "There is no such thing as one *kudo*" (Bryson). Still, "the *kudos* that *was* his due" is sufficiently awkward to suggest that we forego the word altogether.

Lapse: See Elapse.

Lascivious, Lecherous, Lewd, Libidinous, Licentious, Lubricious or Lubricous (adj's). *Lascivious:* Lustful, wanton. "He on Eve/Began to cast *lascivious* eyes, she him/As wantonly repaid" (Milton). *Lecherous:* Inciting to lust. "The sapphire should grow foul, and lose its beauty, when worn by one that is *lecherous*" (Derham). *Lewd:* Morally loose, coarsely vulgar, unchaste, salacious. "He is not lolling on a *lewd* love bed,/But on his knees at meditation" (Shakespeare). *Libidinous:* Characteristic of the libido, carnal, sensual. "A *Lewd* youth advances by Degrees into a *Libidinous* old man" (Steele). *Licentious:* Sexually unrestrained, dissolute. "How would it touch thee to the quick,/Shouldst thou but hear I was *licentious*?/ And that this body consecrate to thee,/With ruffian lust should be contaminate" (Shakespeare). *Lubricious* [LUE brish us]: Oily, slick but also ruttish, bawdy, erotic. "The *lubricious* fantasies of a half-demented daydreamer" (*Quarterly Review*).

Laudable (adj); Laudatory (adj), Laudative (adj). *Laudable:* Worthy of praise, commendable. "In the sight of Reason nothing is *laudable* but what is guided by Reason" (Steele). *Laudatory* and *laudative* mean the same thing: Full of praise or expressing praise. "An artist is not apt to speak in a very *laudatory* style of a brother artist" (Hawthorne).

Lead (v), **Led** (pt). Confusion here arises almost entirely from a problem of pronunciation, for the verb *lead* is pronounced "leed," but its past tense *led* is sounded like the metal *lead*. "Education makes a people easy to *lead,* but difficult to drive; easy to govern, but impossible to enslave" (Baron Brougham). "The original mistake was inventing the Calendar; this *led* to Mondays" (Wade).

Learn (v); **Teach** (v). It should scarcely be necessary to distinguish between the two. However, to *learn* is to acquire knowledge or skill by study or practice, whereas to *teach* is to impart knowledge or skill. "*Learn* to write well or not to write at all" (Dryden). "Sir, it is no matter what you *teach* children first, any more than what leg you shall put into your breeches first" (Johnson). In colloquial speech, *learn* is sometimes used to mean *teach.* "That'll *learn* him!"

Least (adj); **Less** (adj); **Lest** (conj). *Least* is the superlative degree of *little,* and *less* its comparative degree, whereas *lest* is a conjunction meaning for fear that. "For I am the *least* of the apostles" (Paul to the Corinthians). "There is now *less* flogging in our great schools than formerly, but then *less* is learned there; so that what the boys get at one end they lose at the other" (Johnson). "There are five reasons we should drink;/Good wine—a friend—or being dry—/Or *lest* we should be by and by—/Or any other reason why" (Aldrich). We shall not confuse the basic issue by introducing the circumstance that, of course, *littler* and *littlest* can also be the comparative and superlative degrees of *little* and that *less* and *least* can also be adverbs. Perhaps one example of the last-named use is justified by its truth. "Whatever we anticipate seldom occurs; what we *least* expect generally happens" (Dryden).

Leave (v & n); **Let** (v & n). *Leave* (v): To depart from; to quit a person, place, or thing. "This very night I am going to *leave* off tobacco!" (Lamb). *Let* (v): To allow or permit. "Rob me, but bind me not and *let* me go" (Donne). Confusion between the verbs may arise from the fact that the noun *leave* means permission to do something, as in "by your *leave*," while *let* as a noun means an obstruction or impediment, although this use is becoming rare. "At last all *let* and hindrance ceased for the merry lady upon the sudden death of her husband" (Lover).

Lectern: See **Dais.**

Legible: See **Readable.**

Lesbian: See **Sapphic.**

Lexicographer (n). "A writer of dictionaries; a harmless drudge that busies himself in tracing the original, and detailing the signification of words" (Johnson).

Liable (adj); **Libel** (n & v). *Liable:* Likely or subject or exposed to something—especially something unpleasant. In law, under legal responsibility or obligation. "Difficulties, I am sensible, may be *liable* to occur" (Ruskin). And "Every one of the partners is *liable* to the full extent of his fortune for all debts incurred by the partnership" (Pearson). *Libel* as a noun and verb means technically defamation by or to defame by written or printed words or pictures, but not by spoken words or gestures. Loosely, however, it means any damaging misrepresentation. "Convey a *libel* in a frown,/And wink a reputation down" (Swift).

Liaison (n). *Liaison* [LEE uh zahn *or* lee **AY** zahn] is a French word meaning communication, connecting link, or coordination; it has also come to mean an intimate, usually illicit, relationship between a man and a woman. "You ask me what it is I do. Well, actually you know,/I'm partly a *liaison* man and partly P.R.O." (Betjeman). " 'If it were but a temporary *liaison*,' the excellent man said, 'one could bear it. But a virtuous attachment is the deuce' " (Thackeray). The word is in both senses usually used correctly but often misspelled. The second *i* has a tendency to disappear.

Licit: See **Illicit.**

Lie (v), **Lay** (pt), **Lain** (pp); **Lie** (v), **Lied** (pt); **Lay** (v), **Laid** (pt & pp); **Lay** (adj), **Lay** (n). Confusions surround the proper use of these words, most of them arising from the fact that *lay* and *lain* are the past tense and the past participle of the intransitive verb *lie*, while *laid* is both past tense and past participle of the transitive verb *lay*. *Lie* means (1) to be in a recumbent position and (2) to make a false statement. Its past tense is illustrated in "And his lifeless body *lay*/A worn-out fetter" (Longfellow); its past participle in the fine verses from the Book of Kings: "For now should I have *lain* still and been quiet, I should have slept; then had I been at rest,/With kings and counsellors of the earth, which built desolate places for themselves." A small confusion at once arises in the circumstance that the past tense of *lie*—to utter falsehood—is *lied*. "I said to Heart, 'How goes it?' Heart replied:/'Right as Ribstone Pippin!' But it *lied*" (Belloc). *Lay* means to put in place, usually in a horizontal position or a position of rest, as in *lay* the book on the table. Its past tense and past participle is *laid*. Hence "The best *laid* schemes o' mice and men/Gang oft a-gley" (Burns). *Lay* in its adjectival and noun forms is alone in not going readily a-gley. As an adjective: of or belonging to the laity as opposed to the clergy, as in a *lay* sermon. As a noun: a short narrative poem, especially one that is sung—"He touch'd the tender stops of various quills,/With eager thought warbling his Doric *lay*" (Milton). We shall not mention the colloquial *lay*.

Lifelong (adj); **Livelong** (adj). *Lifelong* means continuing through life, but *livelong* means whole or entire, especially when tediously slow. "Plato . . . in his *lifelong* effort to work out the great intellectual puzzle of his age" (Jowett). And "For though it seems so little a time . . . it hath been a whole *livelong* night" (Marvell).

Lightening (pres p); **Lightning** (n). *Lightening* is the present participle of *lighten:* To brighten or become less dark or to make lighter in weight. "*Lightening* the steamer *Amaryllis* ashore at Savannah will enable her to get off" (*Daily News*), but *lightning* (a noun) is a luminous electrical discharge in the sky. "When I'm playful . . . I scratch my head with the *lightning* and purr myself to sleep with the thunder" (Mark Twain).

Light-year (n).   In astronomy, the distance traveled by light in space during one solar year, about 5,878,000,000 miles. Perhaps because of the word "year" the unit is sometimes used incorrectly as a measure of time: "They are two minutes and yet light-years away from the crowded village" (cited by *WDEU*).

Like. As an adjective, adverb, verb, noun, and preposition, *like* is open to no objection, but as a conjunction it is intensely disliked. Some time ago when cigarette smokers weren't being burned at the stake in Salem, an advertising line, "Winston tastes good *like* a cigarette should," stirred up a furor of popular puristic disapprobation—probably what the agency intended in the first place. The furor died down, and the Surgeon General took up other cudgels, but commentators still lambasted *like* as a conjunction. "*Like* has long been widely misused by the illiterate; lately it has been taken up by the knowing and well-informed, who find it catchy and liberating, and who use it as though they were slumming" (Strunk and White). That puts it strongly and doesn't give much recognition to the circumstance that *like* has been used as a conjunction for centuries by writers from Shakespeare to Winston Churchill. Harry Truman's "It looks *like* we were a pretty good combination" does not suggest a slumming expedition. Still, be on the safe side and don't write *like* Shakespeare did but *as* Strunk and White do. *Like* used as conjunction is still slovenly. The fact that Darwin wrote "Unfortunately few have observed *like* you have done" does not really excuse misuse. *Like* as a preposition is unobjectionable. " 'There's nothing *like* eating hay when you're faint.' . . . 'I didn't say there was nothing better,' the King replied, 'I said there was nothing *like* it' " (Carroll).

Limit (n & v); **Delimit** (v). To *limit* is to restrict or constrain, and the noun *limit* is the farthest point of extent, amount, procedure, and the like. "There is, however, a *limit* at which forbearance ceases to be a virtue" (Burke). To *delimit* is to set boundaries or to mark the *limits* of. "The question of *delimiting* the Russo-Afghan frontier" [*The (London) Times*].

Linage (n); **Lineage** (n). *Linage* is simply the number of printed lines contained in a newspaper or magazine article or advertisement. "One of the terms of the reporter's engagement was that he should have half the *linage*" (*Mercury*). *Lineage* means line of ancestry or descent. "We Poets of the proud old *lineage*/Who sing to find your hearts, we know not why" (Flecker).

Lingua franca: See **Dialect.**

Link. A branch instruction used to return to some desired point in a computer program.

Liquor (n); **Liqueur** (n). *Liquor* is any liquid but especially a distilled or spirituous beverage as opposed to a fermented drink like beer. "Candy's dandy, but *liquor's* quicker" (Parker). *Liqueur* designates a special class of alcoholic liquors, usually sweet, highly flavored and aromatic, and often served after dinner. "At dinner we had different sorts of wine and a *liqueur*" (Boswell). You bet they did.

Litany (n); **Liturgy** (n). A *litany* is a ceremonial form of prayer consisting of invocations or supplications with responses that are repeated, and hence any continuous repetition resembling a *litany*. "The *Litany* of the Saints is chanted on the feast of St. Mark and on the three Rogation days" (*Catholic Dictionary*). "She had to listen to a *litany* of the unrecoverable debts he was owed" (cited by *WDEU*). *Liturgy* is a form of public worship or ritual and hence also a compendium of formularies for worship. "We have a Calvinistic creed, a Popish *liturgy*, and an Arminian clergy" (William Pitt).

Little (adj, adv). *Little* as an adjective scarcely needs the definition of tiny, small, not large. "There isn't much to be seen in a *little* town, but what you hear makes up for it" (Hubbard). However, the adverb *little* is the subject of some confusion. It is in good and constant use to mean slightly, somewhat, or quite, although the *Dictionary of American Slang* wrongly calls such use colloquial. "The tongue of the just is as choice silver; the heart of the wicked is *little* worth" (Proverbs). What is not always realized is that the comparative and superlative forms of *little* are usually *less* (or *lesser*) and *least*. "His *less*-known novels today attract *little* attention" (Elwyn on Charles Reade).

Livid (adj); **Vivid** (adj). The words are scarcely ever confused, but *livid* is sometimes misused. It means having the discolored bluish appearance of a congestion of blood vessels or it means deathly pale. Although it does not mean suffused with red, it is often so used. *Livid* with rage and *livid* with fear demonstrate its true meanings—"His trembling lips are *livid* blue" (Scott)—whereas *vivid* means strikingly bright or intense—"Trusty, dusky, *vivid,* true,/With eyes of gold and bramble-dew" (Stevenson).

Loath (adj); **Loathe** (v). *Loath* means reluctant, disinclined, unwilling. "His relations being *loath* to part with the estate they had gotten by his supposed death" (Bargrave). *Loathe* means to abhor, detest. "We fix our eyes upon his graces and turn them from his deformities, and endure in him what we should in another *loathe* or despise" (Johnson on Shakespeare).

Lobotomy (n). A *lobotomy* is an incision into any lobe. Severe depression or anxiety can be effectively reduced by a deep cut in each frontal lobe of the brain—a *frontal lobotomy.* But this procedure is not without hazard, and there are other means of alleviating such mental states. An Irish wit, given to spirituous relief of his depression/anxiety, is said to have said, "I'd rather have a bottle in front of me than a *frontal lobotomy.*"

Lock. A method by which a process is given exclusive use of a resource within an operating computer system.

Locution (n); **Circumlocution** (n). *Locution* is a style of speech or phraseology or a particular form of phrase or expression. "A permanent Philological Board to watch over the introduction of new words or *locutions*" (*Illustrated London News*). *Circumlocution* could be described simply as roundabout *locution* or use of excessive words. "After much *circumlocution* and many efforts to give an air of importance to what he had to communicate" (Scott).

Longshoreman (n); **Stevedore** (n). These words are often used interchangeably, but "to waterfront people a *longshoreman* is a laborer and a *stevedore* is an employer of *longshoremen*" (Bernstein). However, almost all dictionaries define *stevedore* as a person engaged in the loading and unloading of vessels.

Loop. A series of computer instructions performed repeatedly until some specified condition is satisfied.

Loquacity (n), Loquacious (adj). The noun *loquacity* [loh **KWAS** uh tee] means talkativeness and the adjective *loquacious* [loh **KWAY** shus] means garrulous. "When a preacher was once in the pulpit, the only limit to his *loquacity* was his strength" (Buckle). "In council she gives licence to her tongue,/*Loquacious*, brawling, ever in the wrong" (Dryden). But the question might be asked whether the noun and adjective (from the Latin *loquor*, to speak) may be applied to writers as well as speakers. They may be in the extended sense of wordy: "They that glut the Press with their canting *loquacities*" (Power).

Loss. In electronics the difference in amplitude between the transmission and reception of a signal.

Lustful (adj); Lusty (adj). *Lustful* means greedy or lecherous, whereas *lusty* means vigorous, robust, hearty. "There are also *lustful* and chaste fishes, of which I shall give you examples" (Walton). But "Though I look old, I am strong and *lusty*" (Shakespeare).

Luxuriant (adj); Luxurious (adj). *Luxuriant:* Abundant, exuberant in growth, flourishing vigorously. "Wit's like a *luxuriant* vine" (Cowley). *Luxurious:* Characterized by, conducive to, or having intense liking for luxury. "Men are conservatives when they are least vigorous, or when they are most *luxurious*. They are conservative after dinner" (Emerson).

MAC. An acronym for MultiAccessing Computing. A *MAC* mode is a method of using an operating system in which units of work are submitted from remote terminals with immediate response to input.

Machiavellian (adj). More than 450 years ago, banished from his precious city of Florence, Niccolo Machiavelli died. Author of *The Prince* and the riotous comedy *The Mandrake*, he was then, as now, an enigmatic figure. For almost half a millennium he has been known as astute political philosopher and as subtle defender of political guile. The Elizabethans naturally admired his masterful prose and his level-headed realism. "We are," said Francis Bacon, "much beholden to Machiavel and others, that write what men do, and not what they ought to do." The Victorians were made of sterner moral stuff and had an eyes-averted disinclination to look at the actual, so to them the sardonic humanist became a cognomen for wily double-dealing. Lord Macauley, from his lofty perch, summed up the prevailing character of Machiavelli: "Out of his surname they have coined an epithet for a knave, and out of his Christian name a synonym for the Devil." Justly or not, *Machiavellian* means expedient, crafty, duplicitous, or cunning, especially in relation to statecraft. "Where men follow their natural impulses, they would not bear the odious maxims of a *Machiavellian* policy" (Burke).

172

Machine language. A language that a computer can respond to directly without translation, usually a series of binary or hexadecimal numbers or, more generally, any symbolic instruction written for a computer.

Mad: See **Angry.**

Magazine. A computer input hopper that holds punched cards.

Magdalene: See **Maudlin.**

Magic (n & adj), **Magical** (adj). The noun *magic* has three distinctive meanings: (1) The art of producing illusions, conjuring. (2) The art or method of producing desired effects through incantation or other recourse to supernatural beings. (3) Enchantment, charm, or power. (1) "Oh! My name is John Wellington Wells,/I'm a dealer in *magic* and spells" (Gilbert). (2) "If this be *magic,* let it be an art/Lawful as eating" (Shakespeare). (3) "The moon gilds the brow of night/With the *magic* of reflected light" (Rogers). However, commentators have written extensively about *magic* and *magical* as adjectives, most saying that *magic* is an attributive adjective, as in *magic* carpet, spell, or ring, and should not be used predicatively. The effect was *magical,* not *magic.* In actual use this nicety is not carefully observed, but *magical* does seem to have an extended, even figurative, meaning beyond that of *magic.* "All its hues/Their *magical* variety diffuse" (Byron). "Looked more and more *magical* and silvery as it danced away" (Chesterton).

Majority (n). *Majority* (the greater part or number) is clearly a singular noun, but it sometimes carries a plural verb when it is followed by *of* and a plural noun. "The *majority of* its members *were* girls" (Gogarty). *Majority* can also mean the status of being of legal age. "A Cuban of twenty-two years of age, who by the law of his own country would not attain *majority* until twenty-five" (Gillespie).

Malapropism (n); **Spoonerism** (n); **Irish bull** (phrase). The word *malapropism,* the ridiculous misuse of words, is coined from Mrs. Malaprop of Sheridan's *The Rivals* and came into wide use in the nineteenth century, though the phenomenon is as old as language itself. Of course, examples abound. "I hope inexperience will not *mitigate* against my chances" and "His capacity for continuous work is *incredulous*" (cited by Fowler). Even writers on language may drop into hazy, lazy use of words. "Safire is neither an *entomologist* nor an expert on usage" (*The Saturday Review*). Like Mrs. Malaprop's famous *contagious* countries, Safire the *entomologist* needs to be debugged. The *spoonerism* (transposition of initial letters or sounds) is named after a real person, the Reverend W. A. Spooner, who stumbled into transposal frequently. Perhaps the best-known instance of his indulgence, "Permit me, madam, to sew you to another street," was more contrived than accidental as was his reference to Victoria as "our queer old dean." *Irish bull*, a phrase of no clear derivation, means any statement ludicrously self-contradictory. "May you never live to see your wife a widow" (cited by Urdang) and "Rich or poor, it's nice to have money." Freud was fond of the nimble octogenarian who said to his equally aged wife, "When one of us dies, I'm going to Paris to live."

Manifold (adj); **Multiform** (adj); **Multiple** (adj & n). *Manifold:* Of many kinds; numerous, varied; suggesting also complexity. "*Manifold* stories, I know, are told not to thy credit" (Byron). *Multiform:* Having many forms. "The variations so common and *multiform* in organic beings under domestication" (Darwin). *Multiple:* Consisting of or having many parts or elements or individual components. "Why should not solvent thieves and cheats be rather punished with *multiple* restitutions than death, pillory and whipping?" (Petty). *Multiple* as a noun has a purely mathematical significance: any number divisible by another number without remainder. Twelve is a *multiple* of 2, 3, 4, and 6.

Manner born (usually preceded by *to the*) (phrase). The phrase means accustomed by birth to high position or having a lifelong acquaintance with certain customs and conditions. It is frequently misspelled as *manor born* under the mistaken notion that the meaning is born to feudal aristocracy, whereas the idea intended is that of habituation or practice. Indeed in its broadest meaning the phrase signifies destined by birth to be subject to a specific custom. "But to my mind, though I am native here/And to the *manner born*, it is a custom/More honor'd in the breach than the observance" (Shakespeare).

Marginal (adj); **Minimal** (adj). Fowler would have us use these words quite literally. He calls them favorites "with writers who find *small* too drab for their taste." *Marginal* literally describes what is situated on a border or edge or what is so close to the division between opposing states that it is difficult to say on which side it will or should go, and *minimal* describes the least or smallest possible form of something. But both words have taken on similar extended meanings that are in fact quite sensible: barely acceptable, just about adequate, a shade more than sufficient. "*Marginal* banks engage in frenzied borrowing and lending" (*Fortune*). "The *minimal* virtues of good poetry are those of good prose" (Krutch). "The nursing homes afford but *minimal* care of chronic disease" (Beeson).

Marital (adj); **Martial** (adj). With good reason the words are sometimes confused. *Marital* means pertaining to marriage, "What a deal of *marital* discomfort might have been avoided" (Thackeray), whereas *martial* means pertaining to war or warfare. "All the delusive seduction of *martial* music" (Burney).

Martyr (n); **Victim** (n). A martyr is anyone who willingly suffers torture or death because of his faith or beliefs or one who endures hardship in defense of a principle, cause, ideal, or conviction. "And the bitter groan of the *martyr's* woe/ Is an arrow from the Almighty's bow" (Blake). A *victim* is the unwilling or unknowing sufferer of wrong or injury or one cheated or deceived by others. "The *wictim* o' connubiality, as Blue Beard's domestic chaplain said ven he buried him" (Sam Weller in *Pickwick Papers*).

Mask. In computer operation a pattern of characters devised to alter or isolate specific bit positions.

Masochist: See Sadist.

Mass storage. A storage medium (e.g., a large magnetic disk file) of great capacity directly on line to a central processor.

Masterful (adj); **Masterly** (adj). Fowler and others have contended that the words have distinctive meanings. *Masterful:* Having the qualities of a master, hence authoritative, arbitrary, imperious, forceful. "Some children are very *masterful* and disobedient" (Whateley). *Masterly:* This word also derives from master but in the restricted sense of mastery of a skill or art. "The Commons, faithful to their system, remained in a wise and *masterly* inactivity" (Mackintosh). In fact, though, the distinction has never been observed in literature, and *masterful* is frequently used in the sense of *masterly.* "The same *masterful* hand which carved the anguish of the dawn" (Oliphant). "Ross has done a *masterful* job of making his people act like humans" (*The Saturday Review*).

Material: See **Germane.**

Matriculate: See **Graduate.**

Maudlin (adj); **Magdalene** (n). *Maudlin* (effusively sentimental, tearfully emotional, mawkish) is a corruption of *Magdalene,* pronounced *maudlin* by the British, as in Magdalene College. In medieval iconography Mary Magdalene is always depicted with eyes swollen and features distorted from weeping for the lost Jesus. "Is this a time for *maudlin* tenderness?" (Sheridan). But *maudlin* has also always had the connotation of befuddled with liquor. "Another ill-looking fellow, *maudlin* drunk" (Mulock). It is difficult to explain how this implication of intoxicated silliness arises—perhaps from the *maudlin* peach sometimes used in the distillation of spirits. And uncertainty is confounded by confusion of Mary Magdalene (a faithful follower of Christ) with the unnamed harlot who anointed the feet of Jesus. From this confusion arises the meaning of *magdalene* as a reformed prostitute. "A poor abused creature . . . with very little of the *magdalene* about her" (Trollope). Although now rarely seen in print a *magdalene* is also a home for prostitutes.

May: See **Can.**

Mean (adj, v, & n); **Meant** (pt & pp); **Mien** (n). *Mean* as an adjective signifies inferior, unimposing, ignoble, vicious, malevolent. As a verb *mean* denotes intention or signification. The noun *mien* [MEEN] signifies countenance, aspect, or bearing. "He *meant* to be *mean;* but his kindly *mien* belied the intent." The noun *mean* is, in its technical sense, an average. (See also *Median.*) "The *mean* of Buenaventura's elevated temperature is *mean* indeed." But in plural form it has the specific meaning of an agency or method to attain an end or of available resources, especially monetary. "Increased *means* and increased leisure are the two civilizers of man" (Disraeli).

Media (n). Purists will continue to growl that *media* is the plural of *medium* and should carry a plural verb. However true that may be, *media* has become a collective singular noun originally applying to the press but now applicable to all means of mass communication and advertising. "I understand the *media* and *it* understands me" (Reggie Jackson in *Sports Illustrated*).

Median (adj); **Average** (adj & n); **Medium** (n). *Median* as adjective means being in the middle, hence pertaining to a plane dividing something (especially the animal or human body) into two equal parts. "His physician does still let blood in the *median* vein of the heart" (Hall). Hence also in statistics describing a point in a series at which half the individuals in the series are on one side of it and half on the other, as distinguished from *average.* To illustrate, if five persons have respective hourly wages of $3, $4, $5, $7, and $11, the *average* hourly wage is $6, and the *median* wage is $5. *Medium,* whose plural may be either *mediums* or *media,* has a wide variety of meanings: (1) A middle state or condition. (2) An intervening substance through which a force acts. (3) An element that is the natural habitat of an organism. (4) Surrounding objects, conditions, or influences. (5) A means, agency, or instrument. (6) In biology the substance in which specimens survive or are preserved. (7) A person serving as an agent through whom a deceased person or supernatural force manifests itself. (8) In photography, the middle distance. Of these varied significations, one of the most common is that of an agency or instrument, well exemplified in Wilde's famous critical dictum: "Meredith is a prose Browning, and so is Browning. He used poetry as a *medium* for writing in prose."

Mediate: See **Arbitrate.**

Meet (adj & v); **Met** (pt); **Meet with; Mete** (v). *Meet* as an adjective (see also *Helpmate*) is now somewhat sparingly used but is still a useful word meaning suitable or appropriate. "The Eye is very proper and *meet* for seeing" (Bentley). The verb *meet* has various meanings that are essentially related. (1) To encounter. (2) To notice in passing. (3) To become acquainted with. (4) To join at an expected place of arrival or at an appointed time. (5) To come into the company of a person or group of persons. (6) To confront directly. (7) To come into physical contact with. (8) To encounter in opposition or conflict; to oppose. (9) To form a junction, as with lines, planes, or areas. (10) To cope with effectively. (11) To come together face to face. (12) To assemble for conference or action. Of these varied meanings the most common is seen in the phrase from the *Book of Common Prayer:* "When we assemble and *meet* together." *Meet with,* however, has the more restricted meanings of encounter, join the company of, and undergo. "Continually we *met with* many things worthy of Observation and Relation" (Bacon). *Mete* is a verb no longer much in use. It means to distribute, to measure out, to allot. "I *mete* and dole unequal laws unto a savage race" (Tennyson).

Mega-; Megalo-. As a prefix *mega-* is a variant of *megalo-,* but it also has the specific meaning of one million, as in "10 *mega*cycles per second," meaning 10 million cycles per second. *Megalo-* is a combining form meaning huge, vast, as in *megalo*mania—delusions of grandeur, of great wealth or power or obsessive extravagance or profligacy.

Meiosis (n). In biology *meiosis* is part of the process of gamete formation by chromosome conjugation and cell division. But in rhetoric *meiosis* is the use of understatement not to mislead but to enhance an impression as in such phrases as "not unlikely event" or "not inconsiderable influence." It is also seen in the odd British expression. "He wasn't rich, *by half.*" "Some condemne Rhetorick as the mother of lies, speaking more than the truth in Hyperboles, lesse in her *Meiosis*" (cited by *OED*).

Melancholia (n); **Melancholy** (n & adj). *Melancholia,* from Greek "black bile," is "A mental disorder marked by apathy, indifference to one's surroundings, mental sluggishness and depression" (Stedman). Although the noun *melancholy* is a synonym for *melancholia,* it is generally conceived to be less a disorder than a cast of mind—gloomy, pensive, dismayed, dejected. "This *melancholy* flatters, but unmans you;/What is it else but penury of soul,/A lazy frost, a numbness of the mind?" (Dryden). For Robert Burton in his famous "Anatomy of *Melancholy,*" it was a state of mind embracing everything from raving lunacy to philosophical indifference and fleeting pessimism. "*Melancholy,*" he said, "is the character of mortality" and even a kind of forbidden pleasure. "All my joys to this are folly,/Naught so sweet as *Melancholy.*" Here is the adjective *melancholy:* "What do you get if you cross a honeydew with Lassie?" "A *melancholy* baby."

Memorandum (n). A *memorandum* is a short note, a record, an informal message, a reminder to aid the memory, and in diplomacy a summary of the state of a foreign affairs issue. "Nature's fair table-book, our tender souls,/We scrawl all o'er with old and empty rules,/Stale *memorandums* of the schools" (Swift). As a Latin noun its plural is *memoranda,* but *memorandums* has long been in good use even by so capable a Latinist as Jonathan Swift. But there can be no such word as *memorandas.*

Memory (n). The high-speed electronic components in a computer that store information. It is also the thing we forget with. "Everyone complains of his *memory,* but no one of his judgment" (Anon.).

Mendacity (n), **Mendacious** (adj); **Mendicity** (n); **Mendicant** (n & adj). *Mendacity* is the conduct of a liar; *mendicity* that of a beggar. "Notwithstanding his *mendacity* (and it must be owned he is the most brilliant liar under heaven)" (cited by *OED*). "During the reign of Louis XIV, *mendicity* had existed to a frightful extent" (Ainsworth). "There is a certain class of clergyman whose *mendicity* is only equalled by their *mendacity*" (Archbishop Frederick Temple). *Mendacious* means habitually lying, untruthful. "The pagan ages were not *mendacious* and distracted, but in their own poor way true and sane"

(Carlyle). There is no word *mendicious*, only the adjective *mendicant* that serves also as a noun meaning beggar and, specifically, a member of orders of friars forbidden to own property and subsisting on alms. *"Mendicant* prophets go to rich men's doors" (Jowett).

Menu. A term used in computer programs to indicate a list of choices. *Menu* selection is a method of using a terminal to display a list of optional facilities that can be selected to carry out different functions in a system.

Mercury (n), **Mercurial** (adj); **Mercer** (n). *Mercury,* messenger of the gods, conductor of souls to Hades, patron of commerce and travel, protector of vagabonds, thieves, and rogues, was kept constantly on the go. Hence quicksilver, a highly volatile metal, is called *mercury,* and *mercurial* means mobile, capricious, ingenious, fluctuating, erratic, restless, sprightly. "The gay, gallant, *mercurial* Frenchman" (Disraeli). From *Mercury* too, comes *mercer:* a merchant, especially a dealer in fabrics. "The draper and *mercer* may measure religion as they please, and the weaver may craft her upon what loom he please" (Howel).

Meretricious (adj). *Meretricious* has to a considerable extent lost its original meaning of alluring, flashy, vulgar, or whorish (from the Latin *meretrix,* harlot) and has come to mean insincere, deceptive, false, sham. "The *meretricious* ornaments with which the minstrelsy of the East is usually attended" (Prescott).

Metal (n); **Mettle** (n). Although both spring from the Greek word *metallon* (a mine), the words have come to have distinctive meanings—the first meaning any of the basic elements such as iron, gold, or copper; the second meaning courage or spirit. "Why now I see there's *mettle* in thee" (Shakespeare).

Metamorphose (v), **Metamorphosis** (n). *Metamorphose:* To change the nature or form of something, to transform. But *metamorphosis* has the connotation of complete or profound change and, in biology, the meaning of the alteration in development of an organism from one stage to another. "From such rude principles our form began;/And earth was *metamorphos'd* into man" (Dryden). "By a singular *metamorphosis* the secular principle was now represented by the Catholics, and the theological principle by the Protestants" (Buckle).

Metaphor: See **Simile.**

Meticulous (adj); **Scrupulous** (adj), **Scrupulosity** (n). Fowler devotes a column to excoriation of *meticulous:* "In the nineteenth century it was given a new sense for which it was not in the least needed, and freely used as a synonym for careful, exact, scrupulous, precise, etc." Well, it has indeed come to have those meanings for which it is "an unneeded" synonym: painstaking, careful, or exact. "The *meticulous* care with which the operation in Sicily was planned has paid dividends" (Franklin Roosevelt). *Meticulous* may also mean fussy, finicky, or overelaborate. "The decadence of Italian prose composition into laboured mannerisms and *meticulous* propriety" (Symonds). *Scrupulous* means having scruples or showing a strict regard for the principles of right and honesty. However, *scrupulous* may also mean minutely careful, and *scrupulosity* carries the implication of excessive zeal. "He washed himself with oriental *scrupulosity*" (Johnson).

Micro instruction. A computer instruction at machine-code level that directly controls the functioning of hardware independently of the operative system.

Microwave. An electromagnetic wave of extremely high frequency and hence also describing an electronic communications system using ultrahigh-frequency wave forms to transmit messages.

Mien: See **Mean.**

Might: See **Can.**

Mighty (adj & adv). As an adjective *mighty* means strong, powerful, huge, exceptional. "Who is the King of Glory: it is the Lord strong and *mighty*, even the Lord *mighty* in battle" (*Prayer Book*, 1662). As an adverbial intensifier, *mighty* has come under criticism and been called incorrect, but it has long been so used, although this is Johnson's definition in his *Dictionary of the English Language:* "*MIGHTY.* adv. In a great degree. Not to be used but in very low language." This is surprising because he too, like everyone else, used *mighty* as a synonym for very or extremely: "An ancient estate should always go to the males. It is *mighty* foolish to let a stranger have it because he marries your daughter" (Boswell). So scrupulous a writer as Oliver Wendell Holmes did not disdain such use in *The Autocrat at the Breakfast Table.* "But he said a *mighty* good thing about mathematics." Certainly *mighty* as an intensifier will go on its sturdy colloquial way, perhaps because "*mightily* fine" or *mightily* like a rose" seems improbable.

Militate (v); **Mitigate** (v). These words are needlessly confused. *Militate* means to exert effect on or to influence; to act either against or in favor of, but more often in the negative sense of in opposition to. "To incur the displeasure of his father and Sir David by disobeying the one and *militating* against the peace of the other was what he could not bear" (DuBois). *Mitigate* means to make less severe, to lessen the force or intensity of. "The envoys interposed to *mitigate* the king's anger" (Prescott).

Million: See Billion.

Mimetic (adj). Characterized by mimicry or make-believe; imitative. "A false and merely *mimetic* poverty" (Stevenson).

Minimal: See Marginal.

Minuscule (adj); **Miniscule** (var). *Minuscule* (very small, tiny) derives from Latin *minusculus* (little), and so the first *u* is correct. Perhaps due to confusion with the Latin prefix *mini-*, the word is now often spelled *miniscule*—a variant so popular that the misspelling has become almost standard. "The *miniscule* profits of ill-founded ventures in bioengineering" (*The Wall Street Journal*).

Misfortune (n); **Calamity** (n). *Misfortune* has the connotation of mischance, whereas *calamity* that of grievous affliction or very serious misfortune. Asked to distinguish between the two, Disraeli replied: "Were Gladstone to fall into the Thames, that would be a *misfortune*. Were someone to pull him out, that would be a *calamity*."

Mishap: See **Accident.**

Missal, Missile, Missive (n's). A *missal* is a book of prayers or devotions: "By the rubrick of the *missal*, in every solemn mass, the priest is to go up to the middle of the altar" (Stillingfleet). A *missile* is any object thrown, hurled, or propelled, usually as a weapon. "The *missiles* which the engines of war threw consisted of leaden balls" (Tyler). A *missive* is any written message, usually a letter. "The marquis had dispatched *missives* requesting the support of the principal lords" (Prescott).

Mnemonic (adj). *Mnemonic* [nee **MAHN** ik] means assisting or intended to assist memory. "Many of the North American tribes had invented a set of *mnemonic* signs, by which the words of songs, once learned, could be recalled to memory" (cited by *OED*). "Spring forth—fall back" is a *mnemonic* device to keep people from being an hour late in April. In computer operation *mnemonic* describes a symbolic code easier for the programmer to remember than the numeric code forming the basic machine code. The operation *multiplication*, for example, might be represented as MULT.

Modem. An acronym for MOdulator/DEModulator, a device that enables computer data to be transmitted over long distances (usually by telephone).

Monitor. A component, such as a cathode ray tube, for use with a screen for viewing data at a computer terminal.

Moral (adj & n); **Morale** (n). *Moral* as adjective means pertaining to right conduct or to the distinction between right and wrong. Hence also conforming to the rules of good conduct, virtuous. "An Englishman thinks he is *moral* when he is only uncomfortable" (Shaw). As a noun *moral* means the ethical teaching or practical lesson contained in a fable, maxim, or experience. "He left the name, at which the world grew pale,/To point a *moral*, or adorn a tale" (Johnson). *Morale* refers to the state of mind or spirit of a person or group of persons, usually with the connotation of cheerfulness or zeal or high intention. "The *morale* of the troops is excellent" (*The [London] Times*).

Moslem (n); **Muslim** (n). Both words mean a believer in Islam, a religious faith founded by the prophet Mohammed and taught through the Koran. For obscure reasons, *Moslem* is the common spelling in newspaper and magazine publication. However, students of religion and adherents to the faith prefer the spelling *Muslim*. "The mosque of the Sultan Hassan, perhaps the most beautiful in the *Moslem* world" (Edwards). But "All the *Muslim* wants is a courtyard with a tank for ablution" (Forrest).

Motion: See Resolution.

Motive (n); **Motif** (n). The words are not often confused. A *motive* is anything that prompts a person to act in a certain way; an incentive or, by extension, a goal. "Our country has undertaken a great social and economic experiment, noble in *motive* and far-reaching in purpose" (Hoover on the Prohibition Amendment). *Motif* is a recurrent feature, theme, or idea or a recurring form or figure in a design or the basic theme of a musical composition. "I feel original. I have got hold of a *motif*! Oh, if we had a sheet of scored paper!" (Mrs. A. Edwardes).

Mountebank (n). In its Italian derivation a *mountebank* is one who climbs on a bench—hence a quack or charlatan. "There was an impudent *mountebank* who sold pills which (as he told the country people) were very good against an earthquake" (Addison). The word, though, is sometimes misused to mean a clown or buffoon. "The crafty *mountebank* is ever in demand as jester to crown, court or corporation" (Downey).

Mugwump (n). A *mugwump* is an indecisive person, one who cannot make up his mind especially on a political issue, a shilly-shallier. "A bird who sits on a fence with his mug on one side and his wump on the other" (Anon.).

Multiform and Multiple: See Manifold.

Musical (adj); **Musicale** (n). *Musical:* Of or pertaining to music; hence also harmonious, melodious; fond of or skilled in music. "We were none of us *musical*" (Gaskell). A *musicale* is a program of music forming part of a social occasion. The word has something of an emphasis on the sociability of such occasions. "The ladies' receptions are of a different character. Some are *musicales*" (*Cosmopolitan*).

Must: See Can.

Mutual (adj). Some purists maintain that *mutual* in the sense of shared in common or jointly shared is incorrect because *mutual* implies the idea of reciprocity. But when Dickens published *Our Mutual Friend,* the adjective *mutual* was already well established without the sense of reciprocal. "*Mutual* cowardice keeps us in peace. Were all mankind brave, all would be continually fighting; but being all cowards we go on very well" (Johnson).

Nadir (n); Zenith (n); Apogee (n). The three words come from astronomy, the first meaning a point on the celestial sphere directly below a position or observer and the second a point directly above. In their extended meanings *nadir* is the lowest point of adversity, failure, or despair and *zenith* the highest point of accomplishment or achievement. "The seventh century is the *nadir* of the human mind in Europe" (Walpole). "In St. Augustine's time, Christian affairs seem to have been in their *Zenith* of Prosperity" (Morgan). *Apogee* is the point at which an astral body in orbit is farthest from the earth, hence also a highest point, climax, apex, pinnacle. "The trade of the Netherlands had, however, by no means reached its *apogee*" (Motley). Curiously, one sometimes sees *apogee* used as if it meant lowest point, but this is in the figurative sense of extreme point, as in "the *apogee* of doubt, sorrow and despair" (Eachard). (See also *Zenith*.)

Nano-; Nanno- (var). A prefix denoting one billionth or 10^{-9}, but it is also a combining form meaning very small or minute, as in *nannofossil*, a fossil of size at or below the limit of resolution of a light microscope.

Narcissism (n), Narcissistic (adj). In Greek mythology, Nemesis punished Narcissus by making him fall in love with his own reflection in the water of a fountain. He died in vain desire for himself and was turned into a cluster of trumpet-shaped flowers—the narcissus. *Narcissism* is hence fascination with the self, morbid self-admiration, erotic gratification through contemplation of one's own physical or intellectual attributes. "Dominance of the individual's *Narcissism* tends always to regressive behavior" (Jones). *Narcissistic:* Characterized by excessive love of self. "Character reactions which bridge the gulf between the two sets of *Narcissistic* and sublimating desires" (Low).

Narrative (n). A pleasant word meaning an account, whether true or fictitious, of experiences, events, happenings. It is also in electronics a statement included in the coding of a program that serves as explanation of the coded procedures.

Nauseate (v), **Nauseated** (pp), **Nauseous** (adj). To *nauseate* is to affect with nausea, to make queasy or sick, to disgust. "Castor oil is very repulsive to the palate, so much so as to *nauseate* some susceptible individuals" (Wood). Hence the past participle *nauseated* means sickened, queasy, disgusted and is not to be confused with *nauseous* (causing nausea or queasiness). People may feel *nauseated* but not *nauseous* unless they regarding themselves as sickening. The distinction is not always observed even in medical works: "She was able to fly in the helicopter without getting *nauseous*" (Kabat-Zim).

Naval (adj); **Navel** (n). Another easy distinction. *Naval* means pertaining to warships or to affairs of a navy. " 'It was a maxim of Captain Swosser's,' said Mrs. Badger, 'speaking in his figurative *naval* manner, that when you make pitch hot, you cannot make it too hot' " (Dickens). But the *navel* is the depression in the middle of the abdomen marking the point of attachment of the umbilicus and thus, by extension, meaning also the middle of anything. "Thy *navel* is like a round goblet" (Song of Solomon). And "Within the *navel* of this hideous wood,/Immur'd in cypress shades, a sorcerer dwells" (Milton).

Necromancy (n), **Necromancer** (n). *Necromancy* [NEK ruh MAN see] is the art or act of revealing future events by communication with the dead and, by extension, any kind of sorcery, witchcraft, black magic. A *necromancer* is a sorcerer, conjurer, or medium. "The resurrection of Samuel is nothing but delusion in the practice of *necromancy* and popular conceptions of ghosts" (Brown's *Vulgar Errours*). "I am employed like the general who was forced to kill his enemies twice over, whom a *necromancer* had raised to life" (Swift).

Neither (pron). Neither serves as the negative of *either* and like *none* (q.v.) requires in theory a singular verb but in practice is often followed by a plural. "Our adversaries boast of Conquests in this Island, yet *neither* of them *was* just or total" (Parker). But "*Neither* of your letters *mention* these disagreeable circumstances" (cited by *OED*), or "*Neither* of us *are* proper judges" (Wakefield). In general, the singular number of *neither* is likely to be ignored when it is followed by *of* and a plural noun. "*Neither* of these indicators *are* particularly accurate" (cited by *WDEU*). (See also *Agreement*.)

Nemesis (n). In Greek mythology *Nemesis* is the goddess of divine retribution, hence in English an agent or act of retribution and also a thing, person, or obstacle that cannot be overcome. "Guilt naturally produces a fear of divine *Nemesis*" (Crawford). "The drunk-driving test proved to be his *nemesis*" (*Daily News*).

Network (n). Johnson's famous definition, "Any thing reticulated or decussated, at equal distances, with interstices between the intersections," might just as well have been written in Latin but is not far off the mark for *network* as it is used in telecommunications and electronics: Any system that represents reticulated points and the interconnections between their interstices. Still, *decussated* (intersected at right angles) is a word not much seen today.

Neurosis (n); **Psychosis** (n). A *neurosis* is a "psychological or behavioral disorder in which anxiety is the primary characteristic. Defense mechanisms or any of the phobias are the adjustive techniques that an individual learns in order to cope with this underlying anxiety" (Stedman). A *psychosis* is a "mental disorder causing gross disorientation or disorganization of a person's mental capacity, affective response, and ability to recognize reality" (Stedman). "As it is very necessary to keep a clear distinction between these processes, let the one be called *neurosis* and the other *psychosis*" (Huxley).

Nexus. The point in a communications or information system at which interconnections occur.

Nidor (n). A word more likely to turn up in puzzles than in prose although an accepted synonym for odor or aroma, especially the rank smell of cooked or cooking food. Johnson is even more specific, defining it as the smell of roasted meat or fat, but perhaps this is more a matter of gustatory-olfactory preference than of precise definition. "Evil Demons or Devils were delighted at the Blood and *Nidors* of Sacrifices" (Cudworth).

Nocturnal (adj); Diurnal (adj). *Nocturnal* means pertaining to or occurring or active at night and *diurnal* pertaining to or occurring or active by day. "The *nocturnal* owl but rarely sees the *diurnal* bear."

Node. The location within a computer system of information about an object.

Noisome (adj); Noxious (adj); Obnoxious (adj). *Noisome* has nothing to do with noise. It means offensive, disgusting, or sickening and is often applied to odors. "For he shall deliver thee from the snare of the hunter, and from the *noisome* pestilence" (*Book of Common Prayer*). *Noxious* means harmful, injurious, or pernicious. "It blows over the whole island steadily—a cold, *noxious* wind" (Haughton). *Obnoxious* means objectionable, giving offense or annoyance. "I know of no method to secure the repeal of bad or *obnoxious* laws so effective as their stringent execution" (Grant).

None (pron); Nobody (pron). *None* is one of many words whose use defies its rules. Assuming its literal sense of "not one," almost all usage experts agree that it should carry a singular verb and a singular predicate or possessive pronoun. Here it is in classical construction: "*None* of the least advantages of hope *is* its great efficacy in preserving us from setting too high a value on present enjoyments" (Addison) and, more recently, "*None* of the inhabitants *expects* to become a millionaire" (De Voto). But usage has long recognized that *none* often is plural in implication, "But *none* of these things *move* me" (Acts), and, later, "*None* of these *are* love letters in the conventional sense" (Auden), and with a plural pronoun, "*None go* to *their* homes till the waning of the moon" (Sitwell). Even Strunk and White in their revised edition grudgingly agree that *none* may carry a plural verb when more than one thing or person is suggested, and they wryly add this example: "*None are* as fallible as those who are sure they're right." The same ambiguity applies to *nobody*, which usually carries a singular verb but may be referred to by either a singular or plural pronoun. Only purists will fault Jane Austen's "*Nobody* was in *their* right place."

Nostalgia (n), **Nostalgic** (adj); **Homesickness** (n), **Homesick** (adj). From its Greek root *nostalgia* originally meant a desire to return home, but it has come to mean the desire to return to a former period of one's life or to some other past circumstance or time. "The terror, the agony, the *nostalgia* for the heathen past were a constant torture to her mind" (Lawrence). The adjective *nostalgic* shares the broadened sense of longing for familiar circumstances. "The desire to hear it once more became *nostalgic*—almost an ache!" (du Maurier). *Homesickness* is specifically a longing for home so intense as to become an illness, and the adjective *homesick* describes such feeling. "I am *homesick*. I am not accustomed to be away from mamma for so long" (Trollope).

Notable (adj); **Noted** (adj). *Notable* means worthy of note or attention, especially on account of excellence or distinction, "David obtained *notable* victories" (Golding), whereas *noted* means celebrated, eminent, famous, renowned. "That evening Clarendon and several other *noted* Jacobites were lodged in the Tower" (Macaulay). Usually, if not necessarily, *notable* is applied to objects or things and *noted* to persons: "Dr. Tompkins is a *noted* scientist whose practical inventions have had *notable* success."

Not only . . . but also (conj). The principal care in good use of these correlative conjunctions concerns their proper placement, and this is purely a matter of parallelism, for the part of speech or grammatical construction following *not only* must be paralleled by the part of speech or construction following *but*. To illustrate, "They hope to discover *not only* how the antibiotic attacks pathogenic microorganisms *but also* to learn how it produces its other remarkable effects." This is incorrect; it should be recast thus: "They hope to discover *not only* how the antibiotic attacks pathogenic microorganisms *but also* how it produces its other remarkable effects."

Notorious (adj), **Notoriety** (n). *Notorious* once meant simply well known, not secret, but beginning in the eighteenth century, the word took on the pejorative sense of unfavorably known, infamous. "His subjects, many of whom were *notorious* robbers, . . . " (Wilson), and this sense of the word continues: "A biography of someone as *notorious* as Adolf Hitler" (Galbraith). But in the phrase *it is notorious that* the adjective retains its neutral character of meaning well known. "The bishops have procured some small advancement of rents, although *it be notorious that* they do not receive the third penny of the real value" (Swift). The noun *notoriety* has followed a similar course. Once meaning the state or quality of being well known, it has come to mean disrepute or ill repute. "In *A Tale of Two Cities* Dickens gave the idea of violent revolt a *notoriety* that impeded the progress of reform" (Forster).

Noxious: See **Noisome.**

Nuance (n). A *nuance* (a French word meaning color or hue) is a very slight difference or distinction in color, tone, style, or character and, by extension, a subtlety or nicety. Some critics find it an overused word, but it is still a useful one without a precise synonym. "Much of the obscurity arises from our having lost the finer *nuances* of Athenian feeling respecting the persons satirized in the old Comedy" (Symonds). "A *nuance* of doubt is worth a pound of certainty."

Nubile (adj). *Nubile* originally meant of marriageable age or status and was applied either to men or women, but it came also to have the extended meaning of sexually mature or attractive and now describes only women or girls. "The cowslip smiles, in brighter yellow drest,/Than that which drapes the *nubile* virgin's breast" (Prior).

Nuncupative (adj). A fancy word for oral and a favorite of crossword puzzlers. "Testaments *nuncupative* that are afterwards reduced to writing" (Ayliffe). A *nuncupative* will is one spoken but unwritten by a testator ad may be held to be valid. The word is from the Latin verb *nuncupare* (to call or name) but is quite often misspelled as *noncupative*, apparently under the impression that *cupative* means written.

Nymphomania: See **Satyr.**

Objective (adj & n); **Subjective** (adj). *Objective* as an adjective means pertaining to reality, not influenced by personal feeling or bias, concerning the object of thought or perception rather than the perceiver, as in *objective* truth. *Subjective* means belonging to the perceiving subject, existing in the mind, personal. "In the philosophy of mind, *subjective* denotes what is referred to the thinking subject, the Ego; *objective* what belongs to the object of thought, the Non-Ego" (Hamilton). In rhetoric *objective* appears as an adjective in *objective case:* denoting the object of a verb or preposition. "You may my *glories* and my *state* depose,/But not my *griefs;* still am I king of *those*" (Shakespeare). Similarly, *subjective case* denotes the subject of a sentence or clause. As a noun meaning aim, goal, or purpose, *objective* has been objected to by several commentators, Fowler saying that "love of the long word has led to the popular use of *objective* for *object*," but it is so defined in all current lexicons and is seen here in its customary sense: "The Atomic Energy Commission laid down six *objectives* for the development of nuclear research" (cited by *WDEU*).

Oblivious (adj). The word derives from the Latin verb *oblivisci* (to forget) so that some language experts insist that the correct meaning of *oblivious* is forgetful and that it should not be used to mean "unaware of." This may be true, but the objectors must be *oblivious* to the circumstance that in cur-

193

rent use *oblivious* does mean "not conscious of." "Father was *oblivious* to the man's speculative notice of his wife" (Doctorow).

Obnoxious: See Noisome.

Observance (n); **Observation** (n). *Observance* is the act of following or conforming to customs, laws, creeds. More specifically, it also means the celebration of ceremonies or rites. "Dublin-born Maureen O'Hara joins Andy Williams in *observance* of St. Patrick's Day Thursday night on Channel 4" (*The New York Times*). *Observation* is the act of noticing or perceiving and also whatever is learned in such perception. "To *observations* which ourselves we make,/We grow more partial for th' observer's sake" (Pope).

Obsolete (v & adj), **Obsolescent** (adj). *Obsolete* is today primarily an adjective meaning out of use or fallen into disuse. "Of things *obsolete*, the names become *obsolete* also" (Harris). *Obsolete* as a verb (to discard or render useless) was once in wide use but now appears generally in a technical context: "A reimaging process that would *obsolete* the ones we work with now" (Tobias). *Obsolescent* means becoming *obsolete* or falling into disuse. "This stronghold of *obsolescent* opinions and decaying sects" (Kirk). In biology *obsolescent* means not only gradually disappearing but also imperfectly developed. "The Law of Parsimony, whereby all unnecessary organs become *obsolescent*" (cited by *OED*). "In another generation the *obsolescent* will have become the *obsolete*" (Wright).

Obtain (v). A commonly used verb meaning to get, acquire, or procure. "Whatever once is denied them, they are certain not to *obtain* by crying" (Locke on children). However, *obtain* as an intransitive verb (to be prevalent, customary, or established) is viewed with caution by some critics who think it too literary, but the usual synonym "to prevail" is no less literary and in many instances *obtain* seems precisely right as in Bishop Berkeley's "A practice which *obtains* only among the idle part of the nation."

Obtund (v); **Obtend** (v). To *obtund* is to blunt, dull, deaden, weaken. "No man at his pleasure can *obtund* or invigorate his senses" (Johnson). But *obtund* does not mean to deter or repel, although it is occasionally used in this mistaken sense, perhaps through confusion with the archaic verb *obtend* (to oppose). *Obtend*, though no longer in much use, is a curious word, for it has the secondary meaning of to implicate falsely or ascribe to, seen in Dryden's "Thou dost with lies the throne invade,/*Obtending* Heav'n for whate'er ills befall."

Obtuse (adj). A good useful adjective meaning dull or dull-witted. "Thy senses then/*Obtuse*, all taste of pleasures must forego" (Milton). Through some unimaginable confusion with *obscure* or *abstruse* or both, the word has suddenly stopped meaning unable to comprehend and begun to mean difficult to comprehend, murky, unclear. "His answer, often phrased in *obtuse* language, was in brief that a child learns by discrete stages" (cited by *WDEU*). Let us hope that this vapid misapprehension may soon fade away lest tons of piously recycled paper be wasted in its vain correction.

Obviate (v). To *obviate* is to foresee and prevent difficulties, hindrances, or obstruction. "To lay down every thing in its full light, so as to *obviate* all exceptions, would carry me out too far" (Woodward). "Robs a dealer of gems to *obviate* his being slaughtered by yeggs" (Perelman). Although Follett and Bernstein think *obviate* does not carry the implication of anticipating and preventing but only the meaning of removing an obstacle, neither dictionaries nor usage supports this view. The *OED* gives the definition "to prevent by anticipatory measures, to forestall."

Occident (n). "That part of the world lying west (or east) of the Orient. It is largely inhabited by Christians, a powerful subtribe of the Hypocrites, whose principal industries are murder and cheating, which they are pleased to call 'war' or 'commerce.' These, also, are the principal industries of the Orient" (Bierce).

Octal. Describing a numerical system using 8 as a base or radix. In digital computer operation, the *octal* system employs the numbers 0 to 7, and each digit position represents a power of 8.

Official (n & adj); **Officious** (adj). An *official* is anyone elected or appointed to a position charged with certain duties and responsibilities, and the adjective *official* describes an office or position of trust and authority, "The heavy footfall of the *official* watcher of the night" (Dickens), whereas *officious* means objectionably forward in offering services or advice, meddlesome, overeager to oblige: "One of those *officious*, noisy, little men who are always anxious to give you unasked information" (Disraeli).

Older, Oldest: See **Elder, Eldest.**

On account of: See **Because of.**

Only (adv). All purists spend paper and time discussing and complaining about misplacement of the adverb *only*. *Only*, it is all wasted because inadvertence, not misunderstanding, is the culprit. Even in the moving and eloquent preface to his *Dictionary of the English Language,* Dr. Johnson stumbled: "Every other author may aspire to praise; the lexicographer can *only* hope to escape reproach." Every schoolboy knows that the *only* should follow *hope.*

Onomatopoeia (n). A figure of speech signifying the formation of words whose sound resembles that of an object or action. *Quack, croak, sizzle, buzz, caw,* and *cluck* are reasonable examples. The figure is also applied to a phrase or sentence whose sound suggests what is described. "The moan of doves in immemorial elms,/And murmur of innumerable bees" (Tennyson).

Opaque (adj); **Transparent** (adj); **Translucent** (adj). These words are of different meanings that are not always carefully distinguished in use. *Opaque* means impenetrable to light, not transparent, and, by extension, hard to understand, obscure. "The lions . . . having the advantage of thick and *opaque* jungle" (Baker). *Transparent:* Admitting the passage of light; easily seen through; hence also obvious and open. *Translucent:* Permitting the passage of light but diffusing it so that objects cannot be seen readily through it. The *OED* quotes this passage from *The (London) Times:* "The windows of this classroom were once *transparent;* they are now *translucent,* and if not cleaned very soon will be *opaque."*

Ophthalmologist, Oculist, Optometrist, Optician (n's). *Ophthalmologist* is frequently misspelled as *opthalmologist* and mispronounced to coincide with the incorrect spelling. The *ophthalmologist* and *oculist* are doctors specializing in diseases of the eye. An *optometrist* is not a doctor of medicine but is trained to test or refract eyes. An *optician* makes corrective lenses.

Opponent: See **Adversary.**

Opposite: See **Apposite.**

Optimism (n), **Optimist** (n), **Optimistic** (adj); **Pessimism** (n), **Pessimist** (n); **Sanguine** (adj), **Sanguinary** (adj). *Optimism:* "The doctrine, or belief, that everything is beautiful, including what is ugly; everything good, especially the bad; and everything right that is wrong" (Bierce). An *optimistic* person (or *optimist*) is one who takes a favorable view of life in general and expects things to turn out favorably. "The *optimist* proclaims that we live in the best of all possible worlds and the *pessimist* fears this is true" (Cabell). "*Pessimism* is only the name that men of weak nerves give to wisdom" (Mark Twain). A *sanguine* person is cheerful and hopeful, but he may or may not be *optimistic. Sanguine* from its Latin root means bloody, and in ancient physiology, blood as a predominating humor was the cause of both ruddy countenance and cheerful disposition. "These faults differ in their complexions, as *sanguine* from melancholy" (Addison). However, *sanguinary* retains its basic meaning of bloody, even of eagerness to shed blood, and is often applied to warfare, as in a *sanguinary* conflict.

Optimization (n). Design or modification of a computer system or program to achieve maximum efficiency. The efficiency sought for in *optimization* may involve any of the basic factors of time, cost, speed, or storage capacity. In everyday speech *optimization* has essentially the same meaning: making some device or action as effective or useful as possible and is here used ironically. "We have the *optimization* of two faults in this blundering and witless act" (*Kansas City Gazette*).

Optimum (adj); **Optimal** (adj). *Optimum* is the neuter form of Latin *optimus* (best) and has become in English an adjective meaning not only the best but also most favorable, most opportune, most desirable. "The *optimum* time for learning a particular thing is when the child begins to wonder about it" (Rush). No serious fault can be found with this use, but, since *optimum* is also a noun, a certain nicety would prevail if *optimal* were to replace *optimum* as an adjective. "There is probably an *optimal* temperature at which the process proceeds most rapidly or most favourably" (Sibley).

OR. In electronics an acronym for Operational Research—the applied science of electronics that uses statistical and mathematical methods to solve operational problems.

Oral (adj); **Verbal** (adj); **Verbosity** (n); **Aural** (adj). *Oral* means of or pertaining to the mouth and hence spoken rather than written. "Temptations to petulance . . . which occur in *oral* conferences" (Johnson). Whereas *verbal* means of or pertaining to words and so can refer either to what is written or to what is spoken and hence is the root of *verbosity:* excessive wordiness. "A sophistical rhetorician, inebriated with the exuberance of his own *verbosity*" (Disraeli on Gladstone). *Aural,* on the other hand, means primarily of or pertaining to the ear and is used mostly in medicine, but *aural* can also be the adjectival form of *aura* and so means characterized by a distinctive or pervasive quality. "Magnetic power of personality depends upon an *aural* impression" (Hook).

Orchestrate (v). To *orchestrate* is to arrange music for performance by an orchestra, but it has taken on the extended meaning of to arrange for maximum effect or even to arrange or manipulate through clever planning, as in "to *orchestrate* a profitable exchange of currencies." It is this latter figurative meaning to which some critics object, but no objection can be taken to the extended sense of to arrange for better effect. "Lacquers in which the lovely detail of fairy-land was *orchestrated*" (Hilton).

Ordinance (n); **Ordnance** (n).   An *ordinance* is a law or regulation or a public decree. "Wilt thou have this woman to be thy wedded wife, to live together after God's *ordinance* in the holy estate of matrimony?" (*Book of Common Prayer*). But *ordnance* means artillery or military weapons of any kind and, specifically, the branch of an army that procures and distributes military supplies, including munitions. "Armor, weapons, and all other *ordnance* expedient for war" (Hall).

Origin (n).   A source, beginning, fountainhead. "Man with all his noble qualities . . . still bears in his bodily frame the indelible stamp of his lowly *origin*" (Darwin). In electronics, the location of specific items in computer storage.

Ornate (adj); **Ornamental** (adj).   *Ornate:* Elaborately or excessively adorned. "But who is this, what thing of sea or land?/Female of sex it seems,/That so bedeck'd, *ornate* and gay,/Comes this way sailing" (Milton). *Ornamental* has no implication of excess and means simply of or pertaining to ornament, decorative. "The male dress of the time is more or less *ornamental*" (Saunders).

Orthodox: See Catholic and Heterodox.

Oscar (n).   The gold statuette awarded each year for outstanding achievement by the Academy of Motion Picture Arts and Sciences. Why *Oscar?* Mencken's account seems faintly far-fetched, but it's the only one. Here it is, pared down a little: "Donald Gledhill, Secretary of the Academy, and his wife were in his office discussing the impending arrival of a relative, Uncle Oscar. A newspaper man was meanwhile waiting in the outer office. Just then a jeweler arrived with a sample statue. At first glance Gledhill mistook him for the missing relative and said to Mrs. Gledhill, 'Here's Oscar now.' The newspaper man, thinking he referred to the statue, wrote in his column the next day: 'The gold awards are referred to as *Oscars* by Academy officials.' "

Oscillate (v); **Osculate** (v).   *Oscillate:* To swing back and forth as a pendulum does or to fluctuate between differing views or opinions. "The language *oscillates* between bombast and bathos" (Hazlitt). *Osculate:* To come into contact and, in archaic use, to kiss. "Professedly prudish . . . they mutter, nod, *osculate*" (*St. Paul's Magazine*).

Overlay.   A technique by which the same area of computer storage is used to contain successively different parts of a program.

Overlook (v); **Oversee** (v).   *Overlook:* (1) To fail to notice. (2) To disregard. (3) To look over from a higher position. (4) To rise above. (5) To excuse or pardon. (6) To inspect or peruse. These varied meanings all derive from the basic idea of looking over. But *oversee* has a more restricted meaning: to observe unintentionally or to supervise. "He *oversees* all and *overlooks* none" (Spurgeon).

Overly (adv).   *Overly* is a reasonably sensible adverb meaning excessively or inordinately. Nevertheless, critics have attacked it with what seems unnecessary asperity, Follett calling it "useless, superfluous, and unharmonious." To most writers this would seem *overly* critical, for in many instances, *overly* provides precisely the meaning intended. "To my eye it seems not to be *overly* peopled" (Cooper). "*Overly* indulgent" somehow has a ring of excessiveness that "overindulgent" does not quite manage.

Oversight (n).   A strange word, for its two meanings are essentially opposed: (1) supervision, watchful care; (2) omission, error. "They gave the money . . . that had the *oversight* of the house" (Kings). "What one hath gotten more honor than the book in which he carefully owns his *over-sights* and fiercely condemneth them" (Hooker on St. Augustine).

Overt: See Covert.

Overwrite.   Who isn't guilty of *overwriting*? But in computer operations, to *overwrite* is to erase data by recording new data over a storage area.

Owing to: See Because of.

Owner.   In computer operation a user or process that has overriding control of resources or data.

Oxymoron (n). A figure of speech signifying a combination of contradictory or incongruous words, as in "make haste slowly" or "his cheerful pessimism." The word has suddenly become faddish, especially in correspondence columns. "How's this for the newest *oxymoron:* respected journalist" (*Time* magazine, "Letters"). So far "honest lawyer" hasn't appeared. "Holy War: The grandfather of all *oxymorons*" (*Philadelphia Inquirer*).

Pachyderm (n), **Pachydermatous** (adj). *Pachyderm* is a nice and proper synonym for elephant. "A mighty creature is the germ,/Though smaller than the *pachyderm*" (Nash). But some critics have objected to the adjective *pachydermatous* (elephantine, thick-skinned) as ponderous and a favorite of "polysyllabic humourists" (Fowler). The critics overlook that *pachydermatous* arouses an image of cumbersome hugeness that elephantine does not quite achieve—an image that Wodehouse happily lights on in "one of his saber-toothed, *pachydermatous* aunts."

Pagan: See **Heathen.**

Paid (v); **Payed** (v). *Paid* is the past tense and past participle of *pay* in all its usual and various meanings. "Till Noah said: 'There's wan av us that hasn't *paid* his fare!' " (Kipling). But *payed* is the past tense and past participle of *pay* only in the sense of releasing slowly, or uncoiling. "We *payed* out the hawser by which we were riding" (Smeaton).

Palimpsest (n). In the Middle Ages parchment and vellum were scarce and expensive so that the words of Latin classics were quite frequently removed from manuscripts and the parchment reused for scriptural text or pious homilies. Later, it was discovered that the faint images of the original could be restored, and thus were recovered important texts of Cicero, Livy, Gaius, Plautus, and many others. The term *palimpsest* [PAL imp sest] was given to any parchment or like material from which original writing had been erased and replaced by newer writing. *Palimpsest* has taken on metaphoric meanings such as faint or layered images. But the essential meaning remains: material written on, erased, and overwritten, with the underlying writing still discernible. Here De Quincey uses the word in both literal and figurative sense: "What else than a natural and mighty *palimpsest* is the human brain?"

Palindrome (n). A sentence, phrase, or even word that reads the same forward or backward, as in Napoleon's apocryphal phrase, "Able was I ere I saw Elba." Some purists insist that the sentence *palindrome* must be a word-for-word reversal, as in the veterinarian's sign, STEP ON NO PETS. By this rigid standard, "Madam, I'm Adam" would not qualify as a pure *palindrome*.

Palpable (adj). The primary meaning of *palpable* is capable of being touched or felt, but it has taken on the figurative meaning of perceptible by the other senses and by the mind as well, as in *palpable* error or *palpable* nonsense. Many commentators have objected to the extended meaning, especially that of perceptible to the intelligence. Though it may be a metaphor overextended, there is something vivid and just in such a phrase as *palpable* lie. It suggests a grossness of deceit almost touchable. We find many writers use the word figuratively. "They grant we err not in *palpable* manner, we are not openly and notoriously impious" (Hooker). Hardy uses it in a figurative, almost-literal sense. "To persons standing alone on a hill during a clear midnight such as this, the roll of the world eastward is almost a *palpable* movement."

Panacea (n). A *panacea* is literally a medicine that heals all ills, a cure-all, and hence also a solution that magically solves any problem. It is in this sense that the word is sometimes used in a depreciatory way to suggest a nonsensical belief in the magical properties of the cure proposed. "The official *panacea* for managing social conflict at home was economic growth" (Barnet).

Pandemic: See Endemic.

Pandemonium (n). Milton called the site of Satan's palace *Pandoemonium*, from the Greek word for demon. However, *pandemonium* has come to mean chaos, tumult, wild disorder, a center of lawless violence. "Ribald songs, quarreling, and blasphemy made a veritable *pandemonium* of the place" (Bullen).

Paradigm (n). The original meaning of *paradigm* [PAR uh dim *or* PAR uh dyme] was example or pattern, but it has become a popular jargon word meaning anything from model, through theory, to paragon. Johnson gives *paradigm* a one-word definition, "Example," and clarity would be served in return to the older, simpler meaning. "Louis XIV, the *paradigm* of absolute monarchs" (cited by *WDEU*).

Parallel communication. A technique for the input/output of computer operation that allows bytes to be transmitted simultaneously.

Parameter (n); **Perimeter** (n). A *parameter* is a mathematical term originally deriving from crystallography and meaning a quantity to which an arbitrary value may be assigned, as opposed to variable. The word has become a darling of faddists and has suddenly come into mistaken use as a synonym for radiating points of influence or for far-reaching extensions. It is a word that should be left to mathematicians, and it should not be confused with *perimeter*—the circumference, boundary, or outer limit of a two-dimensional figure but, by extension, any outer limit. Gummere quotes an educator who speaks of "a distinctive field of communications research with a multi-theoretical delineation of *parameters* and general orientations." Nothing makes gibberish understandable, but perhaps here we see *parameters* mistakenly used for *perimeters* (boundaries). It may not be too far off the mark to use *parameter* as a synonym for an arbitrary but not necessarily fixed value. Certainly it is nonsense to speak of the *parameters* of a problem when all that is meant is its distinguishing features or outlines. Even scientists use the term loosely: "There has been a good deal of monitoring of circulatory and respiratory *parameters* of native highlanders" (quoted from *Nature* by *WDEU*).

Paramount (adj). A word deriving from Old English meaning above and hence supreme, preeminent, it is used today widely and indiscriminately. Every consideration is now *paramount* and every issue of *paramount* importance. It was inevitable that Paramount Pictures would build in its image the gaudy Paramount Building in the city of *paramount* affluence and influence. At its opening ceremonies, Harry K. Thaw was overhead to say, "I shot the wrong architect."

Paramour (n). From Old French *par amour* (by or through love), *paramour* once meant simply a lover, but it has also long carried the sense of an illicit lover, especially of a married person, and that sense of the illicit is meant in Shakespeare's strange metaphor "Shall I believe/That unsubstantial death is amorous/And that the lean abhorred monster keeps/Thee here in dark to be his *paramour*."

Paraphernalia (n). *Paraphernalia,* meaning equipment or apparatus or furnishings, is a plural Latin noun for which there is no singular in English. It should, therefore, carry a plural verb, but, as with many nouns that are collective in sense, it is often used with a singular verb: "Transistorized *paraphernalia gleams*" (Croce).

Pardon: See Apologize.

Pariah, Pharisee, Philistine (n's). The three words have in common that capitalized each has a specific eponymic meaning and in lowercase a derivative more general meaning. A *Pariah* [puh RYE uh] is a member of a low caste in India and Burma; a *pariah* is an outcast, one despised or avoided by society: "The sparrow, a very *pariah* amongst the feathered tribes" (*Expositor*). A *Pharisee* is a member of a strict Jewish sect of the first century A.D. differing from the Sadducees in rigorous observance of religious rites and Talmudic law; a *pharisee* is a sanctimonious, self-righteous person, a religious zealot: "The true spirit of a *pharisee* betrays itself" (Trench). A *Philistine* is a native of Philistia, a region of ancient Palestine comprising fertile lowlands along the Mediterranean coast; a *philistine* is a person indifferent to cultural, intellectual, and artistic values: "Though the *philistines* may jostle, you will rank as an apostle in the high aesthetic band,/If you walk down Piccadilly with a poppy or a lily in your medieval hand" (Gilbert). (See also *Puritan.*)

Parity bit. A bit added to a group of bits to make their sum (including the *parity bit*) always even or always odd. With a set of six bits (010110), a *parity bit* of 1 or 0 is needed to give the set even or odd parity.

Parody: See **Burlesque.**

Partial (adj), **Partially** (adv), **Partiality** (n), **Partly** (adv). *Partial* is an adjective of two quite different meanings. (1) Of or pertaining to or affecting a part only; incomplete, as in a *partial* eclipse. (2) Inclined to favor one party or thing or faction more than another; biased; foolishly fond. "I do hope I shall enjoy myself with you. . . . I am *partial* to ladies if they are nice" (Ashford). The noun *partiality* has no sense of incompleteness but only of preference for, undue or special fondness of, favorable bias toward. "His *partiality* for St. John's Chapel had prevented it from being desecrated by the Vicar-General" (Ainsworth). *Partly* as an adverb is near synonymous with *partially* in the meaning of incompletely and is preferred to *partially* in this sense by purists, but it should not be overlooked that *partially* alone has the meaning of to a limited degree, as in his *partially* restored health.

PASCAL. A relatively new high-level computer language named after the seventeenth-century French philosopher and mathematician Blaise Pascal, who invented one of the first mechanical calculators. The language is an offshoot from ALGOL and is designed to facilitate structural programming.

Pass. Passage of magnetic tape across read heads, or a single execution of a loop.

Path. The logical sequence of instruction in a computer program, or an instruction added to a program to correct errors.

Pathos: See **Bathos.**

Patois: See **Dialect.**

Peaceable (adj); **Peaceful** (adj). *Peaceable* should literally mean disposed toward peace and *peaceful* characterized by peace. "These men are *peaceable,* therefore let them dwell in the land and trade" (Genesis). "The *peaceful* power that governs love repairs,/To feast upon soft vows and silent pray'rs" (Dryden). In actual practice the two adjectives are used interchangeably with no real loss to understanding. Here *peaceful* is used where *peaceable* would be more precise: "Congo natives are *peaceful,* and the drums often mean an invitation to a dance" (cited by *WDEU*).

Peculiar: See **Funny.**

Pedagogue (n); **Pedant** (n). In its older sense *pedagogue* meant simply a teacher—never an advantageous calling. "Few *pedagogues* but curse the barren chair,/Like him who hang'd himself for mere despair/And poverty" (Dryden). It has not lost this meaning but also has come to be a synonym for *pedant*—anyone who makes ostentatious show of his learning or is fussy about the rules of grammar or about any other rules for that matter. "A Man who has been brought up among Books and is able to talk of nothing else is what we call a *Pedant*" (Addison).

Pejoration (n), **Pejorative** (adj). In linguistics a change in the meaning of a word to one of less established or less agreeable sense. In general, a lessening in worth or value, depreciation. "What ameliorations and what *pejorations* are to be taken into account?" (cited by *OED*). *Pejorative:* Tending to make or become worse, depreciatory. "Poetaster is a word *pejorative*—a petty, temporary poet of slight merit" (Hotson). *Pejoration* is occasionally misspelled *perjoration,* but this may be simply a typographical error rather than confusion with *perjuration* (the act of perjury).

Pendant (n); **Pendent** (adj); **Pennant** (n). A *pendant* is any hanging ornament: "Stoles and maniples all with *pendants* of gold and gems" (Chalmers). *Pendent* is an adjective describing something hanging or suspended: "The *Pendent* Barometer is a machine rather pretty, and curious, than useful" (Chambers). A *pennant* is any tapering flag, especially those used aboard naval or other vessels for signaling and those used to designate college football teams: "A squire's mark was a long *pennant* similar to the coach-whip *pennant* of modern ships of war" (Preble).

Penultimate (adj). A simple-enough word meaning next to last. "One more revise—positively the last—at any rate, the *penultimate*" (Byron). Possibly because *penultimate* sounds even more final than ultimate, it is quite often used incorrectly to mean final, last, concluding, as in "the *penultimate* days of the event" (Taylor), where the plural *days* suggests not next to last but final or concluding.

Percept (n), **Perceptive** (adj); **Precept** (n), **Preceptive** (adj). *Percept:* The mental result or effect of perceiving. "Word-images as integral components of *percepts* and concepts" (*System of Medicine*). *Precept:* A commandment or direction for action or conduct; hence also a maxim or guide. "Example is always more efficacious than *precept*" (Johnson). Hence *perceptive* means having the faculty of perception, or the character of intuitive understanding. "Our active and *perceptive* powers are improved and perfected by use and exercise" (Reid). And *preceptive* means instructive, mandatory, or didactic. "The whole treatise is *preceptive* and hortatory" (Friend).

Peripatetic (adj). In its primary meaning: Itinerant or walking about. "*Peripatetic* mountebanks used to include a goat among their stage properties" (cited by *OED*). But also, and now rarely, *peripatetic* means of or belonging to the Aristotelian school of philosophy, for Aristotle taught his pupils while walking in the Lyceum at Athens. "The old *peripatetic* principle that Nature abhors a vacuum" (Johnson).

Peripheral unit. Any machine that can be operated under computer control, for example, input, output, and storage devices. A *peripheral control unit* is a device that acts as a medium of communication between a *peripheral unit* and a central processor and interprets and acts on instructions from the processor.

Periphrasis (n), **Periphrastic** (adj). *Periphrasis:* Roundabout speech or writing, circumlocution. "The *periphrases* and circumlocutions, by which Homer expresses the single act of dying, have supplied succeeding poets with all their manners of phrasing it" (Pope). *Periphrastic:* Prolix, wordy, verbose. "A way of putting it—not very satisfactory:/A *periphrastic* study in a worn-out poetical fashion" (T. S. Eliot).

Perpetrate (v), **Perpetration** (n); **Perpetuate** (v), **Perpetuity** (n), **Perpetuation** (n). *Perpetrate:* To perform or do; to commit (often as an offense). "The auspicious hour to *perpetrate* the deed" (Smollett). *Perpetration:* The act of doing or performing. "A man whose passions might impel him to the *perpetration* of almost any crime" (Radcliffe). *Perpetuate:* To make long-lasting or to preserve from extinction. "Medals, that are at present only mere curiosities, may be of use in the ordinary commerce of life, and at the same time *perpetuate* the glories of her majesty's reign" (Addison). *Perpetuity* (often preceded by *in*) is the state of indefinitely long duration. "But the iniquity of oblivion blindly scattereth her poppy, and deals with the memory of men without distinction to merit of *perpetuity*" (Browne). *Perpetuation* is the act of securing long or indefinite life. "This invention [printing] contained within itself a self-preserving power which assured it *perpetuation*" (Smilee).

Perquisite (n); **Prerequisite** (n & adj). *Perquisite is* a noun only, meaning some inducement beyond salary, an incidental privilege or benefit. "The *perquisites* of his position—a chauffeured limousine, a chef" (cited by *WDEU*). *Prerequisite* is both noun and adjective, as a noun meaning precondition or requirement and as an adjective necessary to or required beforehand. "The essential *prerequisites* for striking a balance" (Westcott). "There must be a pre-existence of active principles, necessarily *prerequisite* to mixing these particles of bodies" (Hale). The two words are sometimes confused, but such misuse is rare.

Persecute (v); **Prosecute** (v). Although writers may fail to distinguish between the two verbs, each has a distinctive meaning. To *persecute* is to harass persistently or to oppress with punishment, especially for belief in unpopular creeds or principles, "Princes have *persecuted* me without a cause" (*Book of Common Prayer*), whereas *prosecute* means either to take legal action against or to carry forward (usually to its completion) anything begun. "If you lodge this charge, you will be bound over to *prosecute* this gang" (Scott). "The Dutch war commenced without necessity and *prosecuted* with ill-judged parsimony" (Coleridge).

Personal (adj); **Personnel** (n). *Personal:* Pertaining to or coming from a particular person; hence also individual or private. "No *personal* considerations should stand in the way of performing a public duty" (Grant). *Personal* is one of the considerably overused words of our language and is unnecessary in such phrases as "*personal* friend." How many of us have impersonal friends? The adverb *personally* is also overused in such phrases as "*Personally*, I believe." How else can one believe except *personally*? *Personnel:* The body of persons jointly engaged in any work or undertaking. "He knew the *personnel* of the University" (Thackeray).

Perspective (n); **Prospective** (adj). *Perspective* is the technique of depicting spatial relationships on a flat surface so they appear three dimensional; hence also a picture or a scene having this quality. *Perspective* is also the faculty for seeing all the data of a specific problem or situation in their relationship to the whole; hence also insight. "We need a new *perspective* in the matter of unilateral disarmament" (*The New York Times*). But *prospective* means likely, potential, expected. "Not only a large *prospective* but even a large immediate profit would be returned" (Fawcett).

Perspicacity (n), **Perspicacious** (adj); **Perspicuity** (n), **Perspicuous** (adj). These words are often confused but shouldn't be, for the first two concern the ability to see through, the second two the capacity to be seen through. *Perspicacity:* Keenness of mental perception; acute intelligence or discernment. "She showed the same *perspicacity* in the selection of her agents" (Prescott). *Perspicacious:* Keen-witted, discerning, perceptive. "He was far too *perspicacious* to be imposed upon by any such false analogy" (Rogers). *Perspicuity:* Clearness, lucidity, intelligibility. "There is nothing more desirable in composition than *perspicuity*; and in *perspicuity* precision is included" (Southey); "His *perspicuous* philosophy" (Johnson), that is, philosophy penetrable or understandable.

Pertinacity (n), **Pertinacious** (adj); **Audacity** (n), **Audacious** (adj). *Pertinacity* is stubbornness, persistence; *pertinacious* is obdurate or disagreeably tenacious. "In this reply was included a very gross mistake, and if with *pertinacity* maintained, a capital errour" (Brown). "He had never met with a man of more *pertinacious* confidence and less ability" (Walton). *Audacity* means bold disregard of convention, safety, or other restraints. Like *pertinacity*, it has the connotation of willfulness or arrogance. "Where the populace rises at once against the *audacity* of elected persons" (Whitman). *Audacious* carries this same sense of boldly confident, assured, and daring. "Young students, by a constant habit of disputing, grow impudent and *audacious*, proud and disdainful" (Watts).

Pessimism: See Optimism.

Phase: See Faze.

Phenomenon (n). A *phenomenon* is any observable or extraordinary fact, circumstance, or event, and its plural may be either *phenomenons* or *phenomena*. Here the plural is used in the sense of observed or observable reality: "Short-sighted minds are unfit to make philosophers, whose business is to describe in comprehensive theories, the *phenomena* of the world and their courses" (Burnet); and the singular in the sense of the extraordinary: "Language was not powerful enough to describe the infant *phenomenon*" (Dickens). Regrettably, in recent times *phenomena* is being used as a singular noun, as in "a fine analysis of this *phenomena*" (*Publisher's Weekly*). However, the case can be made that the singular *phenomena* is no more singular than the singular *agenda, stamina, data*, and a dozen others. Perhaps purists should more often recognize the rightness of wrongness when wrongness is so prevalent.

Pico-. A prefix denoting one trillionth or 10^{-12}.

Pilot. A high-level computer language used especially for classroom instruction.

Pitiable (adj); **Piteous** (adj); **Pitiful** (adj). *Pitiable* means deserving of pity or compassion. "The champion of injured and *pitiable* women" (Milman). *Piteous* means evoking pity by reason of suffering or misery: "Behold, a silly tender Babe/In freezing winter night./Alas, a *piteous* sight!" (Southwell). *Pitiful* means such as to excite pity but also such as to evoke contempt by its mean or inferior quality: "It is no more than a *pitiful* village" (Lovell). But *pitiful* also means characterized by pity, compassion, tenderness: "For the Lord is full of compassion and mercy, long-suffering and very *pitiful,* and forgiveth sins, and saveth in time of affliction" (Ecclesiastes).

Plagiarism (n). To steal from one source is *plagiarism;* from many, research. Accused of *plagiarism,* Molière is said to have replied, "I do not steal things from others, I improve them."

Plant. To place the result of an operation where it will be used later in a computer program.

Platitude (n), **Platitudinous** (adj). *Platitude:* "The fundamental element and special glory of popular literature. A thought that snores in words that smoke. The wisdom of a million fools in the diction of a dullard. A fossil sentiment in artificial rock. All that is mortal of a departed truth. A jellyfish withering on the shore of the sea of thought. The cackle surviving the egg. A desiccated epigram" (Bierce). *Platitudinous:* Commonplace, trite, stale, insipid. Here is Peter Traill on Laurence Sterne's *Sermons:* "They are of the most commonplace character, *platitudinous* with the *platitudes* of a thousand pulpits."

Plenitude (n); **Plentitude** (var). *Plenitude,* from Latin *plenus,* means fullness or abundance. "Relaxation from *plenitude* is cured by spare diet" (Arbuthnot). The point can be made that *plentitude* is scarcely a real word, for it arose from confusion of *plenitude* with plenty. Still, it is in fairly frequent use and is not likely to go away. "Like undertakers, they have a *plentitude* of gravity, a deficiency of true seriousness" (cited by *WDEU*).

Pleonasm: See Redundancy.

Podium: See Dais.

Poignancy (n), **Poignant** (adj). *Poignancy:* Sharpness of pain, regret, sorrow, or other deeply felt emotion. "The tiding were received with a peculiar *poignancy* of grief" (Barlow). *Poignant* [**POYN** yunt]: Keenly distressing to or affecting the emotions. "There are few sorrows, however *poignant*, in which a good income is of no avail" (Logan Pearsall Smith).

Policy (n); **Polity** (n). A *policy* is a formulated course of action calculated to assure some end or to conform to principles of prudence or practical wisdom. "Honesty is the best *policy;* but he who is governed by that maxim is not an honest man" (Whately). A *policy* is also a contract of insurance, whose originators must have adopted the word because of its connotation of prudence, just as they thought of the unlikely euphemism of calling a bill a premium. *Polity* is a broader term signifying either a particular form of government, as in ecclesiastical *polity,* or governmental or administrative regulation. "The original constitution of the American Colonies possessing their assemblies with the sole right of directing their internal *polity*" (Jefferson).

Politician (n), **Politics** (n). A professional in party politics, a political careerist, an officeholder or officeseeker, and (rarely these days) a statesman. "A *politician* will do anything to keep his job—even become a patriot" (Hearst). He will also become immersed in *politics:* "A strife of interests masquerading as a contest of principles. The conduct of public affairs for private advantage" (Bierce).

Poll. A technique of data transmission through which several terminals share communication channels.

Popular (adj); **Vulgar** (adj). These words once meant the same thing, but *popular* has come to have a favorable connotation: regarded with approval or affection by people in general. "He had but one eye and the *popular* prejudice runs in favour of two" (Dickens). *Vulgar* has taken on the implication of poor taste, low breeding, or coarse ignorance. " 'Father' is rather *vulgar*, my dear. The word Papa besides, gives a pretty form to the lips. Papa, potatoes, poultry, prunes and prism are

all very good words for the lips; especially prunes and prism"
(Mrs. General in *Little Dorrit,* Dickens).

Population (n); **Populace** (n); **Populous** (adj). *Population:* The total number of persons within a specific area; also the number or body of inhabitants belonging to a particular class, race, or creed, as in working-class *population.* "*Population,* when unchecked, increases in a geometrical ratio. Subsistence only increases in an arithmetical ratio" (Malthus). *Populace:* The common people of a nation or community, as distinguished from the more elevated classes. "Now swarms the *populace,* a countless throng,/Youth and hoar age tumultuous pour along" (Pope). *Populous:* Full of residents or inhabitants. "As one who long in *populous* city pent,/Where houses thick and sewers annoy the air" (Milton).

Port (n); **Harbor** (n). A *port* is a place where ships load or unload. "In every *port* he finds a wife" (Bickerstaff). But a *harbor* is a safe body of water deep enough for the passage and anchorage of ships and usually providing access to a *port.* "A ship is floating in the *harbour* now,/A wind is hovering o'er the mountain's brow;/There is a path on the sea's azure floor,/No keel has ever ploughed that path before" (Shelley).

Portability. A characteristic of code or data that can be used in more than one computer system.

Portentous (adj), **Portentious** (adj). Of the nature of a portent, ominously significant, and hence also marvelous, amazing. Perhaps something of both meanings is seen in Shakespeare's "This *portentous* figure/Comes armed through our watch so like the king/That was." There is no such word as *portentious,* which somehow arises through analogy with *pretentious,* but it does occur in speech, very rarely in writing.

Positive (adj). A word of various technical meanings but of a clearly understood popular sense: "Mistaken at the top of one's voice" (Bierce).

Possible: See **Feasible.**

Practical (adj), **Practically** (adv); **Practicable** (adj). The two adjectives are not identical in meaning. *Practical* means adapted to actual use or engaged or experienced in actual practice of a trade, profession, or calling; hence also both efficient and sensible. "Out of the range of *practical* politics" (Gladstone). The adverb *practically* has the natural meaning of in a *practical* manner, but it also means virtually or in effect. "The application was supported by *practically* all the creditors" (*Law Times*). *Practicable* means capable of being done or used or put into effect: "The only *practicable* pass through these mountains to the upper settlements on Connecticut River" (Belknap).

Precede (v); **Proceed** (v). *Precede* means to go before in order, rank, place, or time. "All the sons of viscounts and barons are allowed to *precede* baronets" (Rees). *Proceed* means to go forward or onward, especially after an interruption, or to carry on any course of action or intention. "We will *proceed* no further in this business" (Shakespeare).

Precedence or **Precedency** (n); **Precedent** (n). *Precedence* or *precedency* is the act or fact of going before; priority in rank or importance. "Sir, there is no settling the point of *precedency* between a louse and a flea" (Johnson). *Precedent:* A preceding instance or case that serves as an example or, in law, acts as an authoritative rule. "Every public action which is not customary, either is wrong or, if it is right, is a dangerous *precedent*. It follows that nothing should ever be done for the first time" (Cornford).

Precept: See **Percept.**

Precious (adj); **Preciosity** (n). *Precious* deserves a detailed entry because it is a word of varied meanings, is apt to be overused, and is sometimes misused. It has the primary meaning of highly valuable and describes jewels or other costly ornament. "This *precious* stone set in the silver sea" (Shakespeare). By extension it takes on the natural meanings of highly esteemed or deeply cherished. "All that's *precious* in our joys, or costly in our sorrows" (Sterne). And "I often wonder what the Vintners buy/One half so *precious* as the Goods they sell" (Fitzgerald). But then things begin to go downhill, *pre-*

cious meaning, half sardonically, wonderful or exquisite: "Her little house is just *precious.*" Also it takes on the meaning of flagrant or gross, as in a *precious* fool. Finally, it becomes excessively delicate or refined: "An apparent desire of Admiration, . . . a *precious* Behaviour in their general Conduct are almost inseparable Accidents in Beauties" (Steele). It is difficult to explain its meaning of very or extremely, as in *precious* few. In any event it does not here mean the few that are deeply cherished, simply the exceedingly few. And, ultimately, it takes on the ironic meaning of worthless. " 'Well, Sir Peter, I have seen both my nephews. A *precious* couple they are!' " (Sheridan). It is curious that the noun *preciosity* has almost the sole meaning of affected refinement in language or taste. " 'Circle' he pronounced 'circul' with a certain affected *preciosity* which was noticeable in the other parts of his behaviour" (Carlyle).

Precipitate (v, adj, & n); **Precipitous** (adj). *Precipitate* as a verb means to hasten the occurrence of. "Men will not bide their time, but will insist on *precipitating* the march of affairs" (Buckle). It also means to plunge headlong. Hence the adjective *precipitate* means either rushing headlong and without deliberation or proceeding with great haste. "She set my heart into a palpitation, like a *precipitate* pendulum in a clock case" (Richardson). The noun *precipitate* has entirely the technical meanings of a substance *precipitated* from a solution or the fall of rain, snow, or hail on the earth's surface. But *precipitous* means extremely steep. "Down the *precipitous* rocks they sprung" (Moore). In general, *precipitous* is usually reserved for physical characteristics, as in a *precipitous* cliff, and *precipitate* for actions, as in his *precipitate* departure.

Predator (n); **Prey** (n & v). A *predator* is any animal or organism that lives by *preying* on others. "Species that behave in this manner are not true parasites but extremely economical *predators*" (Wheeler). A *prey* is the object of the hunt, especially by carnivores; a victim. "You think you are Anne's suitor; that you are the pursuer and she the pursued. . . . Fool: it is you who are the pursued, the marked down quarry, the destined *prey*" (Shaw). To *prey* is to stalk or hunt an animal or other organism for food, to attack for plunder, to victimize. "A cowardly non-Sabbath-observing dragon who only *preyed* on weak knights" (Omni).

Predicate (v); **Predict** (v), **Prediction** (n). *Predicate* means to proclaim or affirm or to assert as an attribute or quality of something or to imply, as in snow *predicates* whiteness. "Your mentality, too, is bully, as we all *predicate*" (Beerbohm). To *predict* is simply to foretell or prophesy. "Mr. Turnbull had *predicted* evil consequences . . . and was now doing the best in his power to bring about the verification of his own prophecies" (Trollope). "Dreams and *predictions* ought to serve but for winter talk by the fireside" (Bacon).

Predominate (v & adj), **Predominately** (adv). *Predominate* as a verb means to be a stronger element or force, to be numerically superior, or to prevail. "Their good or bad disposition arises, according as such and such principles *predominate* in their constitutions" (Addison). So far we are on sound ground, but many commentators contend that the adjective *predominate* and the adverb *predominately* are mistaken variants of *predominant* and *predominantly*. There can be no question that literary use favors the latter two, although the former long have been and continue to be in good use. "He gave way to his *predominate* bias" (Richardson). "Persons of a *predominately* worldly turn of mind" (Manning).

Pregnant (adj). *Pregnant* means with child, carrying offspring within the body, or teeming and is usually followed by the preposition *with*. "His town, as fame reports, was built of old / By Danae *pregnant* with almighty gold" (Dryden). The adjective also has the figurative sense of momentous or significant. "O detestable, passive obedience! did I ever imagine I should become thy votary in so *pregnant* an instance" (Arbuthnot).

Prerequisite: See **Perquisite** and **Requisite**.

Prescribe (v), **Prescription** (n); **Proscribe** (v), **Proscription** (n). *Prescribe:* To set down in writing or otherwise as a rule or guide; to enjoin. "He *prescribes* to the news-mongers in London what they are to write" (Swift). *Prescription:* An instruction; a right or rule authorized by custom; a direction, especially one written by a physician to a pharmacist for preparation of a drug. "It is silliness to live when to live is torment; and then have we a *prescription* to die when death is our physician" (Shakespeare). See also *Receipt. Proscribe:* To prohibit or denounce or condemn; to banish or exile; to announce publicly the name of someone condemned to death. "A declaration was signed by all the Powers, which *proscribed* Napoleon as a public enemy, with whom neither peace nor truce could be concluded" (Alison). *Proscription:* Interdiction or prohibition; announcement of condemnation to death or infamy. "You took his voice who should be prickt to die/In our black sentence and *proscription*" (Shakespeare).

Presentiment (n); **Presentment** (n). A *presentiment* is a foreboding or a sense of something about to happen. "Some *Presentiment* told me this agreeable Gentleman would certainly succeed" (Manley). *Presentment* is now a fairly rare word, though occasionally mistaken for *presentiment,* and means simply the act of presenting. "Such *presentments* are now usually made once a year at the archdeacon's or bishop's visitation" (*Church Law*).

Presumptuous (adj); **Presumptive** (adj). Both words spring from the same Latin root but have different meanings. *Presumptuous* means impertinently bold or arrogant. "Man only—rash, refined, *presumptuous* man/Starts from his rank and mars creation's plan" (Canning); *presumptive* means assumed or based on inference, as in *presumptive* heir to the throne.

Pretension (n), **Pretentious** (adj). *Pretension:* A claim to dignity, merit, or position; a pretense, pretext, or ambition. "To give up *pretensions* is as blessed a relief as to get them gratified" (William James). *Pretentious:* Showy, ostentatious, fatuous, affected, presumptuous. "Round your *pretentious* sentences, and discharge your concentrated malignity on the defenceless" (Newman).

Preventative (n & adj); **Preventive** (n & adj). There is nothing actually wrong with *preventative,* and both words mean serving to prevent or hinder, but the law of economy in language forbids use of long when short will do, so that now some dictionaries fail even to list *preventative*, and *preventive* holds undisputed sway. "A *preventive* war, grounded on a just fear of invasion, is lawful" (Fuller).

PRF. In electronics an acronym for Pulse Repetition Frequency—a pulse repetition rate independent of the time interval over which it is measured.

Primeval (adj); **Primitive** (adj). *Primeval* means pertaining to or characterized by the first age or ages of anything, especially the world. "He sleeps with the *primeval* giants" (Carlyle). But *primitive* means not only early or earliest but also unaffected by civilizing influences and, by extension, simple, old-fashioned, unsophisticated, crude. "But he shaved with a shell when he chose—/'Twas the manner of *Primitive* Man" (Lang).

Principal (n & adj); **Principle** (n). Perhaps not the substance but the spelling of these words is often confused. The noun *principal* means a chief person or party and also, specifically, the director or head of a school. It also means either the main body of an estate, as distinguished from income, or a capital sum, as distinguished from interest or profit. As an adjective it means chief, foremost, highest in rank or authority. "Wisdom is the *principal* thing; therefore get wisdom: and with all thy getting get understanding" (Proverbs). *Principle* means a rule of ethical conduct or a general law or truth from which others spring. "Damn your *principles*! Stick to your party" (Disraeli).

Probable: See Feasible.

Problem (n), **Problematic** (adj), **Problematical** (var). A *problem* in mathematics is a statement requiring solution and, in general, any matter involving difficulty or uncertainty. "Good Lord, what is man!/With his depths and his shallows, his good and his evil,/All in all, he's a *problem* must puzzle the devil" (Burns). The adjectives *problematic* and *problematical* share the meaning of doubtful or uncertain, but some style manuals rule out *problematical* as an unnecessary variant of *problematic*. Nonetheless, both continue in good use, but Johnson gives *problematical* the more specific meaning of arguable, disputable. "Diligent inquiries into remote and *problematical* guilt, leave a gate wide open to the whole tribe of informers" (Swift).

Proceed: See **Precede.**

Prodigal; Prodigious; Profligate (adj's). *Prodigal:* Given to reckless expenditure, extravagant, wasteful. "Here patriots live, who for their country's good,/In fighting fields were *prodigal* of blood" (Dryden). Bryson and others say that because of the parable of the *Prodigal Son,* many believe *prodigal* to mean wandering, but if this is so, it is difficult to find such misuse in literature. *Prodigious:* Extraordinary, huge, wonderful, marvelous. "The Rhone enters the lake, and brings along with it a *prodigious* quantity of water" (Addison). *Profligate:* Utterly immoral, dissipated, or recklessly wasteful. "Our fathers have been worse than theirs,/And we than ours; next age will see/A race more *profligate* than we" (Roscoe).

Program. A set of instructions composed for the solution of a specific problem by a computer.

Prolegomenon (n). A *prolegomenon* [PRO luh **GOM** uh non] is a foreword, an introductory essay, or a scholarly preface or preamble to a learned work. "It provided the best *prolegomenon* to *Comus* any modern reader could have" (T. S. Eliot). Its plural, *prolegomena,* is like that of *phenomenon* (q.v.), sometimes mistakenly used as singular, as in "a *prolegomena* to any future philosophy" (Morris). However, this mistaken use is quite rare so that Latinists may rest easy.

Promethean (adj). Prometheus disobeyed the gods by forming man and stealing fire from Olympus for man's use, making man a rival of the gods. Thus *Promethean* describes anything wonderfully creative, generative, or boldly original. "I know not where is that *Promethean* heat/That can thy light relume" (Shakespeare).

Prompt. Any message given to an operator by any operating system, whether in telecommunications or in electronics.

Proponent (n); Protagonist (n). *Proponent* means simply an advocate, a person who supports a cause or doctrine, an adherent. "These two Ends are alike valued by their respective *Proponents*" (Norris). A *protagonist* is literally the leading actor in a play, especially in ancient Greek drama, and hence also the leading figure in the play itself. Fowler therefore adamantly contends that it cannot have a plural and should not carry the figurative sense of an advocate or proponent. But the figurative use and the plural number are abundant in literature. "Marie Antoinette was the *protagonist* of the most execrable of causes" (Morley). "The chief losers in all this are the two original *protagonists*—Britain and Persia" (Shonfield).

Propose (v); Purpose (n & v), Purposive or Purposeful (adj); Purport (n & v). *Propose:* To offer a matter or idea for consideration or action. To nominate a person to some position. To propound a question or riddle. To make an offer of marriage. To intend. "Man *proposes*, but God disposes" (Thomas à Kempis). *Purpose:* To set as an aim or design for oneself. To plan with deliberate intent. "What can be avoided/Whose end is *purpos'd* by the mighty gods?" (Shakespeare). The noun *purpose* has similar meanings: design, intention, determination. "The Englishman never enjoys himself except for a noble *purpose*" (Herbert). *Purposive* or *purposeful:* Having or adapted to a *purpose*, determined, resolute. "To exemplify the *purposive* or adaptive principle in creation" (Owen). *Purport:* To profess or claim, often falsely; to imply. "Jack Downing . . . who *purported* to accompany the presidential party and chronicle its doings" (Quincy). But the noun *purport* signifies the import or meaning or sense of something. "I endeavoured to give the general *purport* of what was actually said" (Jowett).

Proscribe: See Prescribe.

Prosecute: See Persecute.

Prospective: See Perspective.

Prostrate (adj); Prone (adj); Supine (adj), Supinely (adv). These words have a common general meaning: Lying flat. But each has its individual signification. *Prostrate:* Physically weak or exhausted; submissive; overcome or overthrown. "The violent reaction which had laid the Whig party *prostrate*" (Macaulay). *Prone:* Lying face downward but also having a natural inclination or tendency to some act or state. "I hope you do not think me *prone* to any iteration of nuptials" (Congreve). *Supine:* Lying with the face upward, but *supine* has also the connotative meanings of submissive or passive: "Decent, easy men, who *supinely* enjoyed the gifts of the founder" (Gibbon).

Protagonist: See **Proponent.**

Protection.   A technique in computer operation for preventing interference between units of software or areas of data.

Protuberance (n), **Protuberant** (adj).   A *protuberance* is a projection, bulge, or protrusion; *protuberant* is protruding or bulging out from the surface of something. "If the world were eternal, by the continual fall and wearing of water, all the *protuberances* of the earth would have infinite ages since been levelled" (Hale). "Mountains vastly uneven and *protuberant*" (Hervey). The words are included here primarily because they are often misspelled *protruberance* and *protruberant*.

Prudent (adj), **Prudently** (adv); **Prudential** (adj). *Prudent:* Wisely judicious or cautious, provident, especially in financial or practical affairs. "A *prudent* man will avoid sinning against the stranger" (Jowett). *Prudential* means characterized by prudence or having discretionary authority in business or financial matters. But some critics say that *prudential* should not be used to describe acts of prudence or persons acting *prudently*. Rather, it describes motives or considerations leading to a *prudent* act or resulting from prudence. "To this I might add many other religious, as well as many *prudential* considerations" (Addison). But all dictionaries allow us *prudential* people as well as *prudential* considerations. "To take care of the town affairs under the denomination of *prudential* men" (Sullivan).

Psychedelic (adj), **Psychodelic** (var).   *Psychedelic:* Denoting a profound sense of intensified emotional or sensory perception, accompanied by feelings of euphoria, enthusiasm, or despair; also pertaining to mind-altering drugs that produce a sense of well-being and sometimes hallucination. "In Salvador Dali brilliance and genius were combined with a kind of *psychedelic*, tongue-in-cheek surrealism to produce art of striking and unforgettable effect" (Heilbrunn).

Ptarmigan (n). A collective name for several grouses of the genus *Lagopus*. "The *ptarmigan* that whitens ere his hour/Woos his own end" (Tennyson). However unlikely, it is possible to find *ptarmigan* [TAHR muh gun] used instead of *termagant* (a brawling woman). "His wife was a *ptarmigan*, and he cut her off in his will" (*Delaware County Times*). She was a grouser, not a grouse.

Pugnacious: See **Bellicose.**

Punctual (adj); **Punctilious** (adj). Both words derive from Latin *punctum* (point or dot), but *punctual* means simply on time or prompt, whereas *punctilious* means given to nicety or exactness in the observance of formalities, amenities, or rules. " 'Madam, you will be on time?' 'I will be *punctual* to the minute' " (Congreve). "Some depend on a *punctilious* observance of divine laws, which they hope will atone for the habitual transgression of the rest" (Rogers). However, in older English literature *punctual* meant consisting in a fine point, minutely attentive, exact, precise. "I should as soon think of dissecting a rainbow as of forming grave and *punctual* Notions of Beauty" (Beaumont).

Puritan, Puritanism, Pilgrim, Roundhead, Dissenter (n's). *Puritans* were the extreme Calvinistic Protestants of sixteenth- and seventeenth-century England who demanded simplification of doctrine and worship and enforcement of strict moral discipline. Calvinism knows few joys, and Santayana said of *Puritanism* that "it does not keep us from sinning—only from enjoying it." The *Pilgrims* were the *Puritans* who left England for Holland in 1608 and arrived at Plymouth Rock in 1620. The *Roundheads* (so-called because of their no-nonsense, close-cropped hair) were the *Puritan* followers of Oliver Cromwell in the struggle between the forces of Parliament and those of Charles I. Cromwell may not have been quite so rigid in doctrine as his stiff-necked *Puritan* supporters, to whom he once wrote, "I beseech you, in the bowels of Christ, think it possible you may be mistaken." *Dissenters* were later English nonconformists who dissented from the Church of England, especially after the restoration of monarchy brought about harsh legislation against the *Puritans* and reestablishment of episcopacy. Johnson offers a surprisingly temperate definition of *Dissenter:* "One who, for whatever reasons, refuses the communion of the English church."

Purpose and **Purport** See **Propose.**

Purposely (adv); **Purposefully** (adv). *Purposely:* Intentionally, deliberately. "A fine new yacht . . . built *purposely* for his majestie" (Luttrell). But *purposefully* has the connotation of intention accompanied by resolute determination. "Her feet pattering most *purposefully* along the flagged passages" (Crockett).

Purview (n). This is a word not so much misused as loosely used. Its meanings are specific and precise. *Purview:* (1) The range of operation or authority. (2) The range of vision or understanding. (3) In law that which is provided or enacted in the body of a statute or the purpose and scope of a statute. (4) The full scope of a document, statement, or pronouncement. "We will assume then that the statute intended to include in its *purview* all the circumstances of the consecration" (Gladstone).

Pusillanimity (n), **Pusillanimous** (adj). *Pusillanimity:* Cowardice, fearfulness, meanness of spirit. "The Chinese sail where they will; which sheweth, that their law of keeping out strangers is a law of *pusillanimity* and fear" (Bacon). *Pusillanimous* [PYOOH suh **LAN** uh mus]: Mean-spirited, cowardly, faint-hearted. "What greater instance can there be of a weak *pusillanimous* temper, than for a man to pass his whole life in opposition to his own sentiments?" (*The Spectator*). (See also *Timidity*.)

Qaid (n) or **Caid** (n). This entry is solely for Scrabble players, for *qaid* is one of the very few words in actual use in which "q" does not have its customer trailer "u." A *qaid* is a minor Muslim municipal officer, celebrated in a limerick:

> An aide with a Muslim master
> Is a *qaid* more incensed than myrrh.
> Said the aide with a sneer
> To his base overseer,
> "You're nought but an alabaster."

Queue: See Cue.

Quiddity (n). From its Latin, the "whatness" of anything—essence or intrinsic nature. "He could reduce all things to acts,/And knew their natures and abstracts,/Where entity and *quiddity*,/The ghosts of defunct bodies fly" (Samuel Butler). *Quiddity* is also a triffling nicety, a cavil, a captious question. "Misnomers in our laws, and other *quiddities,* I leave to the professors of law" (Camden).

Quidnunc (n). From its Latin (what now?) it has come to mean in English a gossip, busybody, scandalmonger. "He was a sort of scandalous chronicle for the *quidnuncs* of Granada" (Irving).

Quincunx (n). A word made famous for the moment by Charles Palliser's *Quincunx*, it is still in only rare use and means any arrangement of five objects, with the specific meaning in botany of an arrangement of five overlapping petals.

Quintessence (n). The pure concentrated essence of something. It is a more distinctive distillation than *essence*, because it is the fifth essence (the others air, fire, earth, and water) that is the constituent matter of heavenly bodies. "If all the heavenly *quintessence* they still/From their immortal flowers of Poesy,/Yet should there hover in their restless heads/One thought, one grace, one wonder at the least,/Which into words no virtue can digest" (Marlowe).

Quixotic (adj). An interesting word. It means impossibly chivalrous or romantic, visionary, foolishly impractical. "All public ends look vague and *quixotic* beside private ones" (Emerson). In 1596 Spenser published Book Two of his unfinished *Faerie Queene*—a paean to the ideals and romantic fantasies of chivalry. Less than twenty years later Cervantes published Part II of *Don Quixote de la Mancha*—a sardonic elegy on the death of chivalry. Its hero is so deranged by reading the romances of chivalry that he sets out to redress all the wrongs of the world. Accompanied by his rustic, ignorant squire Sancho Panza (*panza* means "paunch" in Spanish), he mistakes flocks of sheep to be armies, roadworkers to be oppressed gentlefolk, and windmills to be giants (thus giving us the phrase "tilting at windmills"). Sancho Panza is well aware of the befuddlement of his mock-heroic knight, but he loves him nonetheless, for Don Quixote is an idealist frustrated and mocked in a materialistic world he does not see. There lingers over Cervantes' hero and over the word *quixotic* a touch of the honest in a corrupt world, of the selfless in a meretricious world where only private ends are realized.

Quondam (adj); Erstwhile (adj & adv). Both adjectives are rather fancy synonyms for former, but both are in considerable use. "This is the *quondam* king, let's seize upon him" (Shakespeare). "After all, my *erstwhile* dear,/My no longer cherished,/Need we say it was not love,/Just because it perished?" (Millay). *Erstwhile* as an adverb means formerly, although such use is now uncommon. When it does appear, it almost always modifies an adjective. "The requirements of modern war have outgrown the *erstwhile* satisfactory formal organization" (Vannevar Bush).

Railroad (n & v); Railway (n). The distinction between the two words is rarely observed, but, in fact, *railroad* means a complete system of rail transportation, including rolling stock, rail beds, ticket offices, and the like. "There was a rocky valley between Buxton and Bakewell, divine as the valley of Tempe. . . . You enterprised a *railroad* and blasted its rocks away. . . . Now every fool in Buxton can be at Bakewell in half-an-hour, and every fool in Bakewell at Buxton" (Ruskin). The verb *railroad* means to supply a system of rails and also to push forward with undue haste. "The way men are *railroaded* to the gallows in that country" (*American Law Review*). But *railway* means simply a track providing runway for wheeled equipment. "On is nose there was a Cricket,/In his hat a *Railway* Ticket" (Lear).

Raise (n & v); Rear (n & v); Rise (n & v); Raze (v). *Raise* (n): An increase in the amount of something or the specific quantity of such increase. "By continued *raises* Potlatch had everything he possessed at stake" (Welcker). *Raise* (v): To move to a higher position, to lift up, to elevate; also to build or to activate. "Plots, true or false, are necessary things,/To *raise* up commonwealths and ruin kings" (Dryden). *Rear* (n): The back of anything. "My desires only are, and I shall be happy therein, to be but the last man, and bring up the *rear* in heaven" (Browne). *Rear* (v): To take care of and support up to maturity or to build or erect. There was a time when one could *rear* children but not *raise* them; one *raised* only corn or Cain. But that somewhat artificial distinction has fallen into oblivion. "Our Polly is a sad slut! nor heeds what we have taught her./I wonder any man alive will ever *rear* a daughter!" (Gay). *Rise* (v: pt, rose; pp, risen): To get up from a reclining or supine position; to become active in opposition; to spring up or grow. "Some *rise* by sin/and some by virtue fall" (Shakespeare). *Rise* (n): The act of rising, an incline or elevation; coming into existence, notice, or power, as in The *Rise* and Fall of the Roman Empire. This last is often misused as the title of Edward Gibbon's great classic, whose actual title is *The Decline and Fall of the Roman Empire*. *Raze* (v): To tear down or demolish—an antonym and homonym of *raise*. "Canst thou not minister to a mind diseas'd,/Pluck from the memory a rooted sorrow,/*Raze* out the written troubles of the brain?" (Shakespeare).

Rational (adj); **Rationale** (n). *Rational* means reasonable or sensible; exercising reason, judgment, or good sense—sometimes used in distinction to emotional. "With men he can be *rational* and unaffected; but when he has ladies to please, every feature works" (Austen). The noun *rationale* means the fundamental reason for or logical basis of an act, principle, or belief. "This gives us the true *Rationale* of the Mosaick law" (Parker).

Ravage (v); **Ravish** (v). The two verbs are from the same French root *ravir* (to carry off or enrapture), but each has a distinctive meaning. To *ravage* is to plunder or destroy, to work havoc on. "Already Caesar/Has *ravaged* more than half the globe, and sees/Mankind grown thin by his destructive sword" (Addison). *Ravish* has three separate meanings: (1) To seize and carry off by force. "The British are not so overfond of St. Patrick as to *ravish* him into their country against his will" (Fuller). (2) To imbue or overcome with great emotion, especially joy or delight; to enrapture. "Be thou *ravished* always with her love" (Proverbs). (3) To violate or rape. "They cut thy sister's tongue and *ravish'd* her" (Shakespeare). Occasionally the two words are confused, as in Farrell's "Coming whenever he wanted to *ravage* her."

Readable (adj); **Legible** (adj). *Readable* means capable of being read—but, by extension, it also means easy or interesting to read. "Of all the needs a book has the chief need is that it be *readable*" (Trollope). But *legible* means only capable of being read or discerned in both literal and figurative senses. "I trow that countenance cannot lie/Whose thoughts are *legible* in the eye" (Roydon).

Realize (v), **Realization** (n); **Know** (v), **Knowledge** (n). *Realize* means to understand clearly; also to give reality to or to bring vividly to mind. "He thought he saw an Elephant,/That practised on a fife;/He looked again, and found it was/A letter from his wife,/'At length I *realize*,' he said,/'The bitterness of life!' " (Carroll). *Know* also means to perceive or understand, but it does not suggest the completeness and thoroughness of *realize*. "When I say that I *know* women, I mean I *know* that I don't *know* them" (Thackeray).

Reassure: See Assure.

Rebound (v); **Redound** (v). *Rebound:* To spring back from force of impact or to recoil or recover. "I never think I have hit hard, unless it *rebounds*" (Johnson). *Redound:* To have an effect upon a person or thing, the effect being one either of advantage or of disadvantage, either of credit or discredit. "Which could not but mightily *redound* to the good of the Nation" (Milton).

Rebut (v); **Refute** (v); **Repudiate** (v). *Rebut* means to oppose an opinion or argument with contrary proof. "The plaintiff may answer the rejoinder, upon which the defendant may *rebut*" (Blackstone). *Refute* means to demonstrate that a statement or opinion is incorrect or false. "Would you not seek everywhere for proofs to *refute* the accusation?" (Manning). *Repudiate* means to reject, disown, cast off. "*Repudiate* the repudiators" (Pitt). (See also *Refute*.)

Recalcitrance (n), **Recalcitrant** (adj). *Recalcitrance:* Dissension from authority, resistance, reaction against, disobedience. "The Senate showed signs of indignant *recalcitrance* against the attacks" (Farrar). *Recalcitrant:* Refractory, hard to handle or deal with, unheeding. "In oaths both French and

English he called upon the *recalcitrant* Anatole" (Thackeray). Both words have the connotation of obdurate resistance. "For a time it was necessary to suspend the more *recalcitrant* ministers" (Green).

Receipt (n); **Recipe** (n); **Prescription** (n). In the sense of a formula for preparing food or medicine, either *receipt* or *recipe* is as good as the other, but in actual practice *prescription* has replaced both of them as medical formula, and *recipe* has become the usual word for a set of directions for preparing food, while *receipt* has returned to its meaning of receiving or acknowledging payment. Thus "Fit to be entrusted with the *receipt* and expenditure of large sums of money" (Mill), and "The man must have a rare *recipe* for melancholy, who can be dull in Fleet Street" (Lamb). Of course, *prescription* has a wider meaning than that of its medical use, signifying anything prescribed. "Conservatism discards *Prescription*, shrinks from Principle, disavows Progress; having rejected all respect for antiquity, it offers no redress for the present, and makes no preparation for the future" (Disraeli).

Record. In electronics a unit of data representing a particular transaction or the basic element of a file of a number of interrelated elements.

Recourse (n); **Resource** (n). These words are but infrequently confused; nevertheless, the distinction between them should be noted. *Recourse:* Access to a person or to means for support or protection. "If threats and persuasions proved ineffectual, he had often *recourse* to violence" (Gibbon). *Resource:* A source of supply or support. Its plural form usually means either the collective wealth or natural wealth of a nation or property that can be converted into money—assets. "Alexander Hamilton smote the rock of national *resources,* and abundant streams of revenue gushed forth. He touched the dead corpse of Public Credit, and it sprung upon its feet" (Webster).

Recriminate: See Incriminate.

Recur (v), **Recurring** (pres p); **Reoccur** (v), **Reoccurrence** (n); **Frequent** (adj & v), **Frequency** (n), **Frequently** (adv). These are words of similar meaning, but there are distinctions among them that should be observed. To *recur* is to occur again, but with the implication of repetition more than once of an experience or event. "In every part of the book two thoughts are continually *recurring*" (*The Saturday Review*), whereas *reoccur* suggests a single repetition: "Whenever it is applied in such measure to these several subjects, they will *reoccur*" (Atwater). Hence *recurring* describes anything that happens repeatedly as does *frequent*, but the latter implies occurring at short intervals or habitually. "The auld wife sat at her ivied door,/A thing she had *frequently* done before" (Calverley). The verb *frequent* means to visit often or to be often in some site or place. "Myself when young did eagerly *frequent*/Doctor and Saint, and heard great argument" (Fitzgerald).

Redundancy (n); **Tautology** (n); **Pleonasm** (n). *Redundancy* and *tautology* mean essentially the same thing: Unnecessary repetition of words or ideas. In "free gift," "true fact," "consensus of opinion," and "hostile malevolence," each of the nouns already contains the idea of its modifier. A *pleonasm* [PLEA oh NAZ im] (sometimes misspelled *pleonism*) has the connotation of repetition of idea for the sake of emphasis and attention. For example, "hear with one's own ears," "return back to," "visible to the eye," and "only just begun" contain within themselves a duplication of idea, but such repetitions may serve to intensify meaning or even provide a welcome pause in the flow of words. Every child plays with a "great big round ball" and often enough "falls down." Of course, "I myself, with my every own eyes, have personally seen" is a pretty circuitous way of saying "I saw."

Reduplication (n). The word may seem an unnecessary tautology but is in reasonable use with the meaning of a doubling or redoubling or counterpart. "A crowd is but the *reduplication* of ourselves" (Hunt). In philology it has the specific meaning of repetition of a word element, especially of its first syllable, as in French *bonbon* or English *murmur*.

Referee: See **Umpire.**

Refraction (n), **Refractive** (adj), **Refractory** (adj). *Refraction* is a technical term denoting deflection from a straight path by a ray of light, heat, sound, or the like in passing from one medium to another and, specifically in ophthalmology, the determination and correction of *refractive* errors of the eye. *Refractive*, then, means of or pertaining to *refraction*, whereas *refractory* means obdurate, intractable, unmanageable. "*Refractory* mortal! if thou will not trust thy friends, know assuredly, before next full moon, that thou wilt be hung up in chains" (Arbuthnot).

Refute (v); **Deny** (v); **Refutable** (adj); **Irrefutable** (adj). *Refute* is in its primary sense a stronger word than *deny*. To *refute* is to prove by fact or evidence that an opinion or charge is either erroneous or false. "Who can *refute* a sneer?" (Paley). To *deny* is to state that something believed to be true is not true. It is also to withhold, to refuse access to, to disallow agreement or approval, to gainsay. "I must go down to the seas again, for the call of the running tide/Is a wild call and a clear call that may not be *denied*" (Masefield). *Refutable* and *irrefutable* are antonyms—*refutable* describing charges or statements that can be disputed or disproved, and *irrefutable* describing statements or charges that are incontestable or incontrovertible. "It is not in the abstract, but in the concrete that it is *refutable*" (Godwin). And "Though our Argumentations for an Immaterial Soul in the Body of man be solid and *irrefutable*" (More).

Regretful (adj); **Regretfully** (adv), **Regrettable** (adj), **Regrettably** (adv). *Regretful* means filled with sorrow or regret or anguish because of something done or lost. "They soon forgot the *regretful* impressions of the day" (du Maurier). But *regrettable* means deserving of or arousing regret or sorrow. "These raids are very *regrettable*" (*The [London] Times*). *Regretful* and *regrettable* in writing almost always maintain their respective meanings of showing regret and causing regret, but their adverbs are now confused and *regretfully* often appears as a synonym for *regrettably*, as in "*regretfully*, that is no grounds for leniency" (*New Statesman*).

Reiterate (v); **Iterate** (v). Since there is a verb *iterate* (to say or do again), some purists contend that *reiterate* contains an inbuilt redundancy and ought to mean to resay or redo again, to say or do repeatedly. In actual use no such distinction is preserved, *reiterate* is used simply as a synonym for repeat, and *iterate* is scarcely used at all. However, *reiterate* often does have the sense of forcible or frequent repetition. "Repeatedly *reiterates* his view that the Supreme Court's decision was wrong" (*Boston Globe*).

Relevant (adj), **Relevance** (n), **Relevancy** (var). *Relevant* as an adjective once had a clear and useful meaning: bearing upon, relating to, pertinent. "We either admit those objections as *relevant*, or obviate them as unfounded" (Stewart). But in the midtwentieth century, *relevant* suddenly became a voguish word meaning socially important or vital. "In academic circles these days it is the fashion to be *relevant*" (cited by *WDEU*). *Relevance* and *relevancy* (once meaning appropriateness or pertinence) have taken on the broader meaning of social significance. "*Relevance* in all studies is now the cry of students" (cited by Gummere). It is, however, observable that this popular meaning of *relevance* is fading from constant view. (See also *Germane*.)

Remedial (adj), **Remediable** (adj). Follett and others contend that *remedial* (curative) and *remediable* (curable) are sometimes confused, and Follett cites "Believed that evil was mere sickness of the soul, therefore temporary and *remedial*," in which one might suppose that evil was being touted as a therapeutic agent. But the two words seem generally to be used correctly. "Every good political institution must have a preventive operation as well as a *remedial*" (Burke). "Where injustice, like disease, is *remediable*, there the remedy must be applied in word or deed" (Jowett).

Remonstrance (n), **Remonstrative** (adj). *Remonstrance* [ree MAHN struns] is objection or opposition or protest but often with the implication of strongly held or disputatious objection. "We had better not say anything having the appearance of *remonstrance*" (Dickens). *Remonstrative* means argumentative, protesting, or expostulatory. "I wrote a *remonstrative* letter to the Governour" (cited by *OED*).

Remorse (n); **Repentance** (n). *Remorse* derives from Latin *re* plus *mordere* (to bite again), reflected in the Old English "Ayenbite of Inwyt"—the Again Bite of Conscience. It means painful regret for wrongdoing, self-reproach, or compunction. Just as one man's Mede is another man's Persian, so Ogden Nash's "One man's *remorse* is another man's reminiscence." *Repentance* is a synonym for *remorse,* but its sense of contrition may also imply doing penance for past wrongdoing. "The hardest sinner in the whole lot to convert is the one who spends half his time sinning and the other half in *repentance"* (Josh Billings).

Renaissance (n); Renascence (n); Recrudescence (n). The first two nouns both mean rebirth or a renewal of life, interest, or zest. "The souls have a kind of *renascence,* or a new Life, a new World" (Burnet). Capitalized *Renaissance* [REN aye ZANS] has the specific meaning of the rich development of Western intellect, science, and art, marking the transition from medieval to modern times, that began in Italy in the fourteenth century and spread throughout Europe. "The word *Renaissance* indeed is now generally used to denote a whole complex activity of which the revival of classical antiquity was but one element or symptom" (Pater). *Recrudescence* is not rebirth but reappearance, revival, or renewal, especially the resurgence of something morbid, dangerous, or disagreeable. "The recent victories have occasioned, as might have been expected, a *recrudescence* of calumny and malignity" (*The Saturday Review*).

Repel (v); Repulse (v), Repulsion (n), Repulsive (adj). Because both words in origin mean to drive back, they are mistakenly used as synonyms. To *repel* is to drive or force back or to resist effectively. "It remains that we retard what we cannot *repel,* that we palliate what we cannot cure" (Johnson). But *repel* has also the connotation of arousing distaste or aversion, "Such extravagances *repel* minds that have a sense of truth" (Hare), whereas *repulse* means primarily to turn away, to refuse or reject, and is essentially without the implication of arousing revulsion. "Hope may vanish, but can die not;/Truth be veiled, but still it burneth;/Love *repulsed*—but it returneth" (Shelley). But *repulsion* does have the meaning of antipathy or aversion and *repulsive* that of odious or offensive. "There was something so *repulsive* about the woman" (MacDonald).

Repent (v); Regret (v). The two words are near synonyms. But to *repent* is to feel self-reproach or contrition
because of a past act, with an implication of atonement in addition to remorse. "Let this hour be but/A year, a month, a week,
a natural day,/That Faustus may *repent* and save his soul"
(Marlowe). Whereas *regret* is not so powerful a word. It too
means to feel remorse or sorrow but without the implication of
redress. It may even mean simply to feel disappointment or to
express polite refusal. "He *regretted* that he was not a bird"
(Roche). (See also *Remorse.*)

Repertoire (n). A *repertoire* [REP ur twahr] is a list
of performances that a theatrical company, a musician, or an
actor is capable of providing. "I got hold of the *repertoire* and
studied up all the parts I knew I should have to play" (Jerome).
It is also in computer operation the range of characters or codes
available in a system of coding.

Repugnance (n), Repugnant (adj); Revulsion (n),
Revulsive (adj). *Repugnance* is distaste, aversion, antipathy.
"I feel not in myself those antipathies that I can discover in
others; those national *repugnances* do not touch me" (Browne).
Repugnant means distasteful, objectionable, offensive. "It is a
thing plainly *repugnant* to the Word of God . . . to minister the
Sacraments in a tongue not understood of the people" (*Prayer
Book*). Originally *revulsion* meant the act of revolving or, in
medicine, drawing humours from a remote part of the body, but
it has also long meant a feeling of strong dislike, distaste, or
disgust. "There comes a natural *revulsion* to the puerility into
which Wordsworth too often fell" (Kingsley). The adjective
revulsive is used almost entirely in the sense of distasteful.
"Nothing could be more cold, distant and *revulsive* to me than
the conduct of ministers in this and every other point" (Burke).

Reputed (pp); Reported (pp); Reportedly (adv).
Reputed means supposed or held to be such. "He had no opinion
of *reputed* felicities below" (Browne). Whereas *reported* means
simply related or made known. "Cases *reported* with too great
prolixity" (Caxton). However, *reportedly* has the connotation
of by rumor as well as by report. "The picture of those *reportedly* gownless backs had depressed him abominably" (Malet).

Required (pp); **Prescribed** (pp). Whatever is *required* is obligatory, necessary, or demanded. "To whom nothing is given, of him can nothing be *required*" (Fielding). That which is *prescribed* is recommended, enjoined, or laid down as a course to be followed or designated for use or other purpose. "On the *prescribed* day the Sheriff's officers ventured to cross the boundary" (Macaulay).

Requisite (n & adj); **Prerequisite** (n); **Requisition** (n & v). A *requisite* is something necessary or indispensable to some purpose or goal, and the adjective *requisite* means needed or required. "There is nothing more *requisite* in business than dispatch" (Addison). A *prerequisite* is something required or needed beforehand. "The *prerequisite* of all German political parties is a daily newspaper in which to preach the party's gospels" (Shirer). A *requisition* is a demand for something to be done or supplied. "There can be no ballot except on a *requisition* signed by the proprietors" (Macaulay). The verb *requisition* means to demand or require and often has the specific meaning of demand by military or civic authorities for materials necessary to martial or public purpose. "They drove about the country *requisitioning* provisions" (cited by *OED*).

Reservation (n). A noun of many meanings, but the most common is an exception or qualification made either overtly or tacitly. "We expressly disavow all evasions and mental *reservations* whatsoever" (Addison). The term also means the allocation of memory areas in a multiprogrammed computer.

Resolution (n); **Motion** (n). In parliamentary procedure both these words mean a formal expression of opinion or a formal proposition, but a *motion* is a proposal made to a deliberative or governing body requiring a vote thereon or other action. "Then they all with one consent said to this Bramble, do thou Reign over us. So he accepted this *motion* and became the King of the Town of Mansoul" (Bunyan). A *resolution* may be no more than an expression of the opinion that something is true or desirable and hence need not result in action. Of course, *resolution* has the less formal meaning of firmness of purpose or resolve. "Great actions are not always true sons/Of great and mighty *resolutions*" (Butler).

Resource: See Recourse.

Respectful (adj), **Respectfully** (adv); **Respectable** (adj), **Respectably** (adv); **Respective** (adj), **Respectively** (adv). *Respectful* means showing respect or deference, while *respectable* means worthy of respect or esteem. "For I *respectfully* decline/To dignify the Serpentine/and make hors-d'oeuvres for fishes" (Dobson). And "In the bosom of her *respectable* family resided Camilla" (Burney). But *respective* means pertaining individually to each of a number of persons or things or to each person or thing in the order named. "The Waters under the heavens were now gathered together into their *respective* and distinct places" (Whiston).

Restaurateur (n), **Restauranteur** (var). *Restaurateur* is a French word meaning restaurant-keeper and the English *restauranteur* has the same meaning and is in substantial use, but it is difficult to justify *restauranteur*. French *restaurateur* has nothing to do with a restaurant; it derives from the verb *restaurer* (to restore or provide or refresh). Hence *restauranteur* is about as logical as *hoteleur* would be to replace French *hotelier*. Forget the "n."

Restive (adj); **Restless** (adj). No question about it, *restive* originally meant unruly, stubborn, balky, impatient. "Your colonies become suspicious, *restive* and untractable" (Burke). The sense of impatient in the word has somehow extended its meaning to synonymy with *restless*. In such a phrase as Willa Cather's "*restive* under the monotonous persistence of the missionary," there is the feeling of *restless* impatience rather than unruly reaction. This is probably the sense in which *restive* is commonly used today, and *restless* should be reserved to mean never at rest, agitated, unquiet, uneasy in heart or mind. "We find our souls disordered and *restless*, tossed and disquieted by passions, ever seeking happiness in the enjoyments of this world, and ever missing what they seek" (Atterbury).

Restore. In computer use, to set a counter or indicator to some previous value.

Resume (v), **Resumption** (n); **Continue** (v), **Continuance** or **Continuation** (n). To *resume* is to take up again after interruption, whereas to *continue* is to engage in the same activity without interruption. "The way to *resumption* is to *resume*" (Chase). But "A man ought warily to begin charges which once begun will *continue*" (Bacon). And *continuance* or *continuation* means the act or state of *continuing.* "Patient *continuance* in well doing" (Acts of the Apostles). In law *continuance* has the specific meaning of the adjournment or postponement of an action pending in court to a subsequent day of the same or later term.

Reticent (adj), **Reticence** (n); **Taciturn** (adj), **Taciturnity** (n). Both terms signify a reluctance to speak, but *reticence* implies shyness or withdrawal, whereas *taciturnity* implies sullenness or severity. "Mr. Glegg was extremely *reticent* about his will" (Eliot), but "After which brief reply John relapsed into *taciturnity*" (Mulock).

Return address. In computer operation a branch instruction that is used to exit from a routine in order to return to some desired point in a program.

Revenge: See Avenge.

Reverend (adj); **Reverent** (adj). *Reverend:* Worthy to be revered, deserving of reverence. "What is buzzing in my ears?/Now that I come to die,/Do I view the world as a vale of tears?/Ah, *reverend* sir, not I!" (Browning). Especially in England *Reverend* is regarded not as a title but as an adjective. Hence it should be preceded by *the* and followed by a title or surname, as in *The Reverend* Dr. Smith, not simply *Reverend* Smith. But clearly in America *Reverend* or *Rev.* Smith is quite acceptable. *Reverent:* Feeling or characterized by reverence or deeply pious or respectful. "Shall I, the gnat which dances in thy ray,/Dare to be *reverent*?" (Patmore).

Reversal (n); **Reversion** (n). *Reversal* means the act of reversing and hence also a mishap or misfortune. "Believing the judgment of the court to be erroneous, they might have sought its *reversal* by a writ of error" (Manning). *Reversion* means the act of returning to a former practice, custom, belief, or condition. It is sometimes used with the significance of returning to a more primitive or less acceptable condition. "Regrowth of supernumerary digits in man may be an instance of *reversion* to an enormously remote and multidigitate progenitor" (Lyell).

Revolution (n). *Revolution* has various technical meanings. In mechanics: rotation; in astronomy: the orbiting of one heavenly body around another; in geology: the earth's upheaval and formation of mountains. In everyday use Robespierre and Lenin have given the word its distinctive significance: "In politics an abrupt change in the form of misgovernment" (Bierce).

Rhubarb (n). The *rhubarb* is a purplish purgative plant that some regard as edible. "What *rhubarb*, senna, or what purgative drug/Would scour these English hence" (Shakespeare). But now it got to mean also a quarrel, fracas, or dispute is veiled in mystery. *The Dictionary of American Slang* says flatly that it came from the practice in radio and movies of saying "*rhubarb*" over and over again to simulate the menacing talk of crowds. Somehow fanciful but no more so than the idea that it is some kind of corruption of Red Barber, who for many years broadcast the disputatious baseball games of the Brooklyn Dodgers.

Rostrum: See Dais.

Rotomontade (n), **Rhotomontade** (var). A word once in considerable use, it now appears but rarely. It derives from *Rodomonte*—a braggart figure from the pen of Ariosto—and means boisterous boasting or vainglorious bragging. "A profusion of barbarous epithets and wilful *rhodomontade*" (Hazlitt).

Round. In computer operation, to enter the value of digits at the least significant end of a number to allow removal of digits.

Rout (n & v); **Route** (n & v). Both words have several meanings, but the primary meaning of the noun *rout* is a defeat attended by disorderly retreat. "The only difference after all their *rout,*/Is that the one is in, the other out" (Churchill). The verb *rout* means to search or rummage or to turn over or dig up with the snout. "If you find pigs *routing* in your enclosure, you may kill one" (Kingsley). The noun *route* means a course or road or passage. "Wide through the fuzzy field, their *route* they take,/Their bleeding bosoms force the thorny brake" (Gay). *En route* also should be mentioned, for it is a French phrase so common in English that it no longer need be italicized. However, because of its pronunciation it is quite often misspelled *on route*. "In spite of the fact that, *on route* to the show, the van brakes failed" (cited by *WDEU*). The verb *route* means to send or forward by a fixed course. "Goods *routed* this way are taken by rail to Duluth" (*Pall Mall Gazette*).

Row (n & v). A word ill used more by reporters than by correspondents. The noun *row* has two distinct pronunciations ("ro" and "rou") and meanings. The first that of a number of persons or objects arranged in a straight line. "The soldier-saints, who *row* on *row,*/Burn upward each to his point of bliss" (Browning). The second is that of a noisy dispute or quarrel: "You can do no good to yourself or anyone else by making a *row*" (Anstey). But because of its convenient three-letter length *row* is frequently misused in headlines to mean a serious international dispute or even strife. In fact, it means a noisy but casual commotion. The verb *row* means to propel a boat by the leverage of oars. "'Ha! Ha!' quoth he, 'full plain I see,/The Devil knows how to *row*'" (Coleridge). But it too can mean to dispute raucously—by words rather than deeds.

Rural (adj); **Rustic** (adj). The two adjectives are not precise synonyms. *Rural* means pertaining to the countryside or to agriculture, whereas *rustic* has the connotation of simple, artless, unsophisticated. "The two divinest things the world has got,/A lovely woman in a *rural* spot" (Hunt). "This is fulsome and offends me more than *rustic* coarseness would" (Cowper).

Sacred (adj); Sacrosanct (adj). *Sacred* means devoted to a deity or to some religious purpose and also entitled to veneration or reverence. "Poet and Saint! to thee alone are given/The two most *sacred* names of earth and Heaven" (Cowley). But *sacrosanct* means superlatively sacred and carries with it the sense of inviolability. "Truth, which alone of words is essentially divine and *sacrosanct*" (Morley).

Sacrilegious (adj). A word easily misspelled *sacreligious*. Perhaps a guide to correct spelling is that *sacrilegious* does not derive from *religious* but from the Latin word *sacrilegus* (one who steals sacred objects). However, *sacrilegious* does mean violating or profaning anything sacred. (See also *Simony.*) "Still green with bays each ancient altar stands,/Above the reach of *sacrilegious* hands" (Pope).

Sadist (n); Masochist (n). Like the sybarite (q.v.) and the ascetic, the *sadist* and *masochist* are at polar opposites in the pursuit of pleasure. The *sadist* takes pleasure in inducing pain in his sexual partner. He takes his name from the Marquis de Sade, whose life was fragmented by violent scandals over his sexual conduct and by extended imprisonments over the licentious and unnatural character of his many books. His life was an endless succession of perversions, imprisonments, escapes, and rearrests. He was committed again to prison in 1803 and died incarcerated in 1814. During his lifetime his works were considered to be the monstrous ravings of a delirious criminal mind, but recent criticism has turned its attention to their eloquence, profundity, and psychological insight. The *masochist* takes pleasure in his own physical pain and humiliation visited upon him by his sexual partner. He takes his name from the Austrian novelist Leopold von Sacher-Masoch, who relentlessly pursued in his writing the idea of pleasure in abuse as part of the sexual act. Unlike those of the Marquis de Sade, his novels have never been considered as even remotely interesting except as aberrations.

Salon (n); **Saloon** (n). These words were once indistinguishable, but a difference between them is now carefully preserved. *Salon:* A drawing room or reception hall or a gallery in which works of art are exhibited. "Ambassadors and other Great Visitors are usually received in the *Salon*" (Chambers). A *saloon* is a place where alcoholic beverages are sold and consumed. "A rather first-class *saloon*, bar and restaurant on Broadway" (Leland). But the word still also means a large room for public use, as in a ship's dining *saloon*. "Solomon of *saloons*/And philosophic diner-out" (Browning).

Sanguine and **Sanguinary: See Optimism.**

Sapphic (adj); **Lesbian** (adj). Sappho was one of the most famous of Greek lyric poets whose verse, although it exists only in fragments, is exquisitely wrought. In *Don Juan*, Byron evokes "The isles of Greece, the isles of Greece!/Where burning Sappho lived and sung." She lived out her life on the Island of Lesbos and, though married, was sensually attracted to other young women. Hence both *sapphic* and *lesbian* mean characterized by female homosexuality, but *sapphic* or *Sapphic* also describes the four-line verse form in which Sappho wrote.

Sardonic (adj). The word *sardonic* (derisive, bitter, contemptuously amusing, cynically, scornful) apparently arises from an herb native to Sardinia that induces meaningless compulsive laughter. "The *sardonic* historian, whose rule it is to exhibit human nature always as an object of mockery" (Taylor).

Sartorial (adj), **Sartorially** (adv). *Sartorial* means pertaining to tailors and their trade or pertaining to clothes and their style. The first meaning is intended in Carlyle's amusing satire "Sartor Restarus" ("The Tailor Retailored"). In its second meaning, it is in common use but scorned by those who think it too "dressy," Fowler calling it "pedantic humour." But their scorn neglects the circumstance that there is no satisfactory synonym for *sartorial* or *sartorially*. "When she puts her foot upon my *sartorially* immaculate knee" (Locke). "*Sartorial* elegance" is still a ringing useful phrase in which one is hard put to replace Fowler's pedantic "humour."

Satisfy (v). No elucidation of *satisfy* is needed, except to comment on a minor controversy as to whether *satisfy* (to fill desires, expectations, needs) can also mean "to convince." *WDEU* quotes part of an article from Dr. Alice Hamilton: "'Satisfied' is straying into the place long properly filled by 'convinced' or even the lowly 'sure.' The result is sometime startling: 'The man's family is *satisfied* that he was murdered.' Of course that may be literally so, but the family did not mean to tell the world so." Still, to *satisfy* has long meant to convince. Johnson and modern lexicographers include the meaning in their definitions. "He declares himself *satisfied* to the contrary" (Dryden).

Satyr (n), **Satyriasis** (n); **Nymphomania** (n). A *satyr* [SAYT ur] was a mythological creature half man and half horse or goat who attended upon the festivities of Bacchus and was known for riotousness, lasciviousness, and lechery. "So excellent a king; that was, to this/Hyperion to a *satyr*" (Shakespeare). *Satyriasis* [SAT ur RYE uh sis] is hence lechery, lewdness. The mythological nymphs also emulated the free-swinging sex lives of the gods so that *nymphomania* means excessive or uncontrolled sexual desire in women. The *OED* cites this somewhat curious passage from an early *Manual of Psychiatric Medicine*: "*Satyriasis* and *nymphomania*, as examples of Monomania, are, therefore, liable to the objection that they are spinal or cerebro-spinal affections."

Savant (n). A *savant* is a person of profound or extensive learning, but, like solon (q.v.), the word is now used but rarely and then often with ironic twist. "In reading, say, a book review by one of the apple-cheeked *savants* of the quarterlies or one of the pious gremlins who manufacture puns for *Time*" (Updike).

Scan (v); Scanner (n). A curious word, for *scan* once meant to scrutinize carefully or examine minutely. "The actions of men in high stations are all conspicuous, and liable to be *scanned* and sifted" (Atterbury). But it now more frequently means to glance over hastily. "I *scanned* the story rapidly and felt better" (Baker). However, this later sense is often conveyed by addition of such adverbs as *quickly* or *rapidly*, as in the example above. In electronics a *scanner* is a photoelectric device that corrects color copy and produces color separations ready for proofing or printing.

Scarify (v). An older *scarify* (from the Latin root *scarifare*) means to make scratches or to incise. "Washing the salts out of the eschar, and *scarifying* it, I dressed it" (Weisman). There is no *scare* in *scarify*, but suddenly it has taken on the meaning of to frighten or even terrify. "Vivid snapshots of the Paris barricades . . . and a few *scarifying* pictures of both sides' firing squads" (cited by *WDEU*). There can be no etymological justification for this extended meaning, but it seems here to stay.

Scenario (n). *Scenario* once had the specific meaning of a plot or outline for a play or movie or a radio or television program. In the late twentieth century *scenario* began to mean any plan or scheme or a projection of events to occur. Commentators have frowned on this usage, although it is, in this sense, one of the favorite words of journalists and columnists. "His *scenario* for a settlement envisages the eventual reunification of Vietnam" (Harrison).

Script (n); Scrip (n). *Script* is handwriting and hence, by extension, any manuscript or document. "Mrs. Campbell has had the *script* of 'Tess' on her hands for quite a while" (*Western Gazette*). *Scrip* is paper money, usually of small denomination, issued for temporary use and redeemable at some later date for actual currency. "You find a dying railway, you say to it, Live, blossom anew with *scrip*" (Carlyle).

Seasonable (adj); Seasonal (adj). *Seasonable:* Timely, opportune, or appropriate to the season, as in *seasonable* rains. "Are not these times *seasonable* for such a subject as is here handled?" (Gouge). *Seasonal:* Associated with or accompanying the various seasons of the year. "The regular *seasonal* lack of work is no dire calamity" (*The Forum*).

Sector. In mathematics, geometry, engineering, and navigation *sector* has a wide range of technical meanings. In general use it means simply a distinct part, as in the economic *sector.* In computer operation it is a section of a larger block of storage contained either on track or disk.

Semantic (adj), Semantics (n). *Semantic* means pertaining to differences in the meaning of words, and *semantics* is the linguistic science of analyzing and classifying words by their various meanings. "The heroic but witless charge of the light brigade was initiated by *semantic* misapprehension" (*Informal Introduction*). "The term *semantics,* although relatively new, refers to a variety of disciplines. . . . A single rubric for these diverse disciplines is warranted by their common concern with signs and meanings" (Edwards).

Seminar (n), Seminary (n), Seminarian (n). A *seminar* is either a small group of students devoted to the study of a special subject or the meeting of such a group. Perhaps this memorandum from the Department of Psychology of the State University of New York at Buffalo had been better used to illustrate *jargon:* "To all faculty and students interested in participating in the self-statements-rational emotive-attributional bag lunch *seminar* rap group." But a *seminary* is either a school of theology or a school of secondary level for young ladies. "Three little maids who, all unwary/Come from a ladies' *seminary*" (Gilbert). Curiously, the word *seminarian* does not include those participating in the "bag lunch *seminar* rap group" but refers only to a student of theology. "Protecting the *seminarian* from the knowledge of awkward facts" (Tyrrell).

Sense (n); Sensible (adj); Sensitivity (n); Sensibility (n). *Sense* is a noun of varied meanings. Primarily any of the faculties (sight, hearing, taste, touch, and smell) by which a person perceives the external world. By extension it takes on such meanings as a faculty of the mind, as in the moral *sense;* or a special capacity for perception, as in a *sense* of humor; or an undefined impression or feeling, as in a *sense* of security; or recognition of something incumbent, as in a *sense* of duty; or an opinion or judgment, as in the *sense* of the meeting. Finally it takes on the meaning of practical intelligence. "'The woman had a bottom of good *sense.*' The word *bottom* thus introduced was so ludicrous, that most of us could not forbear tittering. . . . 'Where's the merriment? I say the *woman* was *fundamentally sensible*'" (Boswell on Johnson). In older usage *sensible* did not mean, as it did to Johnson and as it does today, of sound, practical intelligence or reasonable but had a wide range of meanings relating to the senses, to perception, and to awareness. Such use has not disappeared but is becoming less common. *Sensible* in the meaning of aware of or perceiving or perceptible is often followed by *of* and sometimes by *to.* "The versification is as beautiful as the description complete; every ear must be *sensible of* it" (Broome on the *Odyssey*). "Air is *sensible to* the touch by its motion and by its resistance to bodies moved in it" (Arbuthnot). *Sensitivity* implies the state or quality of sensing or of being sensitive to, often in unusual degree. "An eloquent exuberance characterizes the style of our author, and a *sensitivity* of imagination which makes even the minutest phaenomenon important to his attention" (Taylor). *Sensibility* (acute consciousness, keen appreciation, or fine-honed feeling) has never had any connection with the practical side of *sensible.* In *Sense and Sensibility* Jane Austen gives it a flavor of overrefined feeling, of the highly impractical, whereas Addison will go along unreservedly with the idea of delicacy of feeling. "Modesty is a kind of quick and delicate feeling in the soul: it is such an exquisite *sensibility* as warns a woman to shun the first appearance of anything hurtful" (*The Spectator*). And Henry James will give it the sense of acute awareness: "Experience is never limited, and it is never complete; it is an immense *sensibility,* a kind of huge spider-web suspended in the chamber of consciousness, and catching every air-borne particle in its tissue."

Sensual (adj); **Sensuous** (adj). These words are frequently confused but have quite different meanings. *Sensual* means inclined to or preoccupied with gratification of the senses; carnal, voluptuous. "Of music Dr. Johnson used to say that it was the only *sensual* pleasure without vice" (Seward). *Sensuous* means perceived by or affecting the senses, especially those involved in appreciation of poetry, music, or nature: "The external or *sensuous* qualities of art" (Gullick). There is some evidence that Milton invented the word *sensuous* to avoid *sensual* because he wanted to indicate esthetic pleasure rather than physical gratification: "To this poetry would be made precedent, as being less subtile and fine; but more simple, *sensuous*, and passionate."

Sententious (adj); **Tendentious** (adj). The two words are not related, but both can often be applied to didactic speech or writing. *Sententious* means characterized by terse aphorisms or abounding in maxims and adages; hence also moralistic, pompous. "Sallust was a *sententious* pedant" (Bishop Berkeley). *Tendentious* means having a purpose or bias or markedly espousing an idea or doctrine. "Xenophon's *Cyropedia* is a mere edifying, *tendentious* romance, intended to recommend to the Athenians the Spartan type of education" (Davidson). The visibly slanted biography of Cyrus is also *sententious*.

Serendipity (n), **Serendipitous** (adj). *Serendipity* is the lucky fortune of finding something good or valuable in the pursuit of something else. The word was coined by Horace Walpole in allusion to *The Three Princes of Serendip*, because the three princes in their wanderings "were always making discoveries by accident and sagacity of things they were not in quest of." In fact, their sagacious description of a one-eyed camel they had never seen was so apt that they were arrested for stealing the animal. In Johnson's *Rasselas, Prince of Abyssinia*, a similar fable of peregrination, the prince and his sister escape the utopian "Happy Valley," where they are confined, to seek happiness in the real life of humans. They make the *serendipitous* discovery that the wisdom of age, romantic love, flights of imagination, the speculations of philosophy, and the daring ideas of science lead but to false hopes and despair. They return to the unreal Happy Valley no happier but wiser.

Serial (adj & n); Seriatim (adv). *Serial* as an adjective: consisting of or arranged in a series rather than occurring simultaneously. "They preserve a *serial* arrangement: their aggregation is little more than that of close linear succession" (Spencer). In electronics: pertaining to the performance of data-processing operations one at a time (distinguished from *parallel* performance). As a noun: "A literary work . . . creeping through several issues of a newspaper or magazine. Frequently appended to each installment is a 'synopsis of preceding chapters' for those who have not read them; but a direr need is a synopsis of succeeding chapters for those who not intend to read *them*" (Bierce). *Seriatim:* One after another, one by one in succession. "Mr. & Mrs. Kenwigs thanked every lady and gentleman, *seriatim*, for the favour of their company" (Dickens).

Set (v). Everyone knows how to use the verb *set* even though the *Random House Dictionary* offers eighty-two definitions, some with subentries. Unnoticed by present-day lexicographers is the once-common invitation of rural America: "Come in and *set* a spell." It is curious how this archaic use makes palpable the idea of leisure and welcome. It recalls a past when there was more time for unadorned sociability. Johnson disposes of such use fairly abruptly under one of his innumerable definitions of *set:* "It is commonly used in conversation for *sit*, which, though barbarous, is sometimes found in authors."

Sewage (n); Sewerage (n). *Sewage* is the waste matter that passes through sewers, whereas *sewerage* is either a system of sewers or the process of removing refuse through drains and underground watercourses. Examples of their proper use would be odious.

Shall (v); Will (v). Although one cannot deplore that this distinction has broken down, careful writers still use *shall* in the first person and *will* in the second and third persons to express futurity. "When I was a little boy, I had but little wit,/'Tis a long time ago and I have no more yet;/Nor ever *shall* until that I die,/For the longer I live the more fool am I" (*Wit and Mirth*). And "Where is the man who has the power and skill/To stem the torrent of a woman's will?/For if she *will*, she *will*, you may depend on't;/And if she won't, she won't; so there's an end on't" (Anon.). In general, *should* and *would* follow the same principle of usage, except in their special meanings of *should* in the sense of obligation and *would* in the sense of habituation. "We *would* go every day to our broken-down rural school" (O'Hara).

Shambles (n). This is another of those curious words that have developed new meanings in modern times. Originally it meant a bench, a money changer's table, a butchery or slaughterhouse. It is this last meaning that Shakespeare intended in *Henry VI*: "Far be the thought of this from Henry's heart/To make a *shambles* of the parliament-house." Nevertheless, there is in it the modern sense of a scene of destruction or chaos. "The apartment was usually in disorder, except on the day the maid came in, when it became a *shambles*" (Perelman).

Shavian (adj). Characteristic of the Irish playwright, critic, and social philosopher George Bernard Shaw; hence, witty, sardonic, dissident, caustic. Creator of some of the wittiest and most biting comedies of the English language, Shaw was himself idealistic, somewhat prudish, distrustful of intimacy, and often shy. His reformist and mocking plays are the vehicles of his ideas, not the reflection of his self—*My Fair Lady* but a pale image of his *Pygmalion*. His fame was worldwide, but during World War I his attacks on British policy so outraged reactionary sentiment in England that he became a decidedly unpopular figure. He, nevertheless, continued to speak his mind freely and write as he pleased and to create some of his most memorable works, including *Major Barbara* and *Androcles and the Lion*. Perhaps an even greater creation than his plays and criticisms was his single-handed creation of G. B. Shaw—the self-devised caricature of himself. G.B.S.—outspoken, of barbed wit, revolutionary—gives us *Shavian*, not descriptive of a literary form but suggesting the iconoclastic, comic, contrary curmudgeon Shaw would have us see in him. A hundred quotations would not do full justice to his acerbic wisdom, but perhaps a few of his terse definitions will set the *Shavian* tone. "All great truths begin as blasphemies" (*Annajanska*). "When a stupid man is doing something he is ashamed of, he always declares that it is his duty" (*Caesar and Cleopatra*). "A lifetime of happiness! No man alive could bear it—it would be hell on earth" (*Man and Superman*). "How can what an Englishman believes be heresy? It is a contradiction in terms" (*St. Joan*).

Shibboleth (n); **Superlative of Two.** These are related only in the sense that the second is an example of the first. A *shibboleth* was originally a peculiarity of language or its use that markedly distinguished one group from another—the literate from the illiterate, the sophisticated from the ignorant. It is now rarely so used except in the sense of a catchword that characterizes a party or sect, but it has also come to mean a mindlessly repeated dogma or opinion. It's in this sense that it may be applied to the tenet of grammarians who have been telling us over and over again that we cannot have a *superlative of two*. One cannot be the best of two, only the better of two. In fact writers of all degrees and ages have paid no attention to this *shibboleth* of purists. Who will fault Jane Austen's "We cannot agree as to which is the *eldest* of the two Miss Plumbtrees"? Even Fowler says of *dinghy* and *dingey* that the first is *best*.

Ship: See Boat.

Sight (n); **Spectacle** (n). A *sight* is anything seen, but a *spectacle* is something seen of unusually interesting, attractive, or puzzling character. "Prepost'rous *sight!* the legs without the man" (Cowper). But "This great *spectacle* of human happiness" (Smith). Both words may be used in a derogatory sense, as in "you are a *sight*" or "you have made a *spectacle* of yourself."

Simile (n); **Metaphor** (n). *Simile:* A figure of speech in which comparison is made between like or unlike things through use of "like" or "as." "Making it momentary as a sound,/Swift as a shadow, short as any dream;/Brief as the lightning in the coiled night" (Shakespeare). But a *metaphor* is a figure of speech in which comparison is made through identification of one thing with another. "Roses are her cheeks,/And a rose her mouth" (Tennyson). "How infinite," wrote Churchill, is the debt owed to *metaphors* by politicians who want to speak strongly but are not sure what they are going to say." Ogden Nash would later add: "One thing that literature would be greatly the better for/Would be a more restricted employment by authors of *simile* and *metaphor.*" In any event, public servants are unabashed users of *mixed metaphors.* "The Rt. Hon. Gentleman is leading the people over the precipice with his head in the sand" (cited by Fowler): a strange confusion of identity between Gadarene swine and ostriches.

      Simony (n); **Sinecure** (n). There are a thousand synonyms for thievery or fraud, but *simony* is the only word meaning either profiting by commerce in sacred objects or the sale or purchase of ecclesiastical preferments. Simon the Sorcerer gives us the word, for upon his conversion to Christianity he committed the sin of attempted purchase of spiritual powers from the Apostles. He is thought by some to be the prototype of Doctor Faustus. "No *simony* nor *sinecure* were known,/Nor would the bee work honey for the drone" (Garth). *Sinecure,* too, is essentially an ecclesiastical term. It means literally "without care," and Ayliffe so defines it: "A *sinecure* is a benefice without care of souls." It has come now to have the meaning of any office or position secured through favoritism or purchase, requiring little or no work, and affording a pleasant recompense. "The Magistracy of the city of London have adopted this ward only as a *sinecure* for the senior alderman" (Entick). The word in a figurative sense also means any effortless pursuit. "Love in this part of the world is no *sinecure*" (Byron).

      Simple (adj); **Simplified** (pp); **Simplistic** (adj). Each of these words means uncomplicated or plain; but *simple* means naturally plain or easy to understand or unadorned: "I sought the *simple* life that Nature yields" (Crabbe); whereas *simplified* means made simple or easy to comprehend: "It furnishes a *simplified* account of other countries" (Morse); and *simplistic* means overly *simple:* "The facts of nature and of life are more apt to be complex than *simple. Simplistic* theories are usually one-sided and partial" (Clarke). No doubt because of the nature of the times, *simplistic* has become a vogue word, and everyone from abecedarians to zealots is accused of *simplisticity,* to coin a word that is now needed.

Simulate (v); Stimulate (v); Simulation (n). The two verbs have no relationship except that occasionally one is written for the other. *Simulate:* To make a pretense of or to assume the appearance of. "Many caterpillars, beetles, moths, butterflies *simulate* the objects by which they are commonly surrounded" (Spencer). See also *Dissimilate. Stimulate:* To rouse to action or effort; to act as a stimulus. "You have *stimulated* my curiosity" (Lever). In electronics, *simulation* is the representation of problems allowing physical processes or factors to be expressed mathematically.

Single out; Signal out. The first is fine; the latter does not exist but is in frequent use, no doubt because of confusion with the verb signalize. To *single out* is to pick or choose one from many as an example, model, or the like. "*Singling out* from the entire body of the Clergy a man under suspicion of heresy" (Burgon).

Site: See Cite.

Sizing. Evaluation of the resources and facilities needed to perform a data-processing task.

Slack (adj, n, & v); Slake (v). These words are often confused in both spelling and use. *Slack* in all its parts of speech shares the meaning of not tight, negligent, remiss, dull, careless. "In marriage, a man becomes *slack* and selfish, and undergoes a fatty degeneration of his moral being" (Stevenson). The verb *slake* means to allay thirst, to cool or refresh. "A crystal draught/Pure from the lees, which often more enhanc'd/The thirst than *slak'd* it" (Cowper). *Slake* can also mean to diminish in intensity. "The indignation against them will shortly *slake* of it selfe" (Stafford).

SNAFU; Snafu (v). An acronym for Situation Normal All Fouled Up. Its origin is not certain, but it came into wide military use during World War II and was applied with some justice to the handling of supplies, food, and mail. It means a situation confused by lack of intelligent direction, a stupid blunder, a plan gone haywire. There is a variant meaning of *SNAFU* whose appearance here discretion does not allow. Occasionally, one sees *snafu* used as a verb in the sense of muddle, as in "The printers *snafued* the whole chapter."

Sobriquet (n). *Sobriquet* [SOH bruh kay] is a French word meaning nickname. It has largely fallen into disuse but still serves a function not in the meaning of nickname but in that of byname or secondary name. "Eternal City" for Rome and "Emerald Isle" for Ireland are not nicknames but *sobriquets.* Fowler does not object to the word itself but to use of the device. "Now," he says, "the *sobriquet* habit is not a thing to be acquired, but a thing to be avoided." Still, he must concede that to insist on "came over with William I" in preference to "with William *the Conqueror*" would be absurd.

Sodomite (n), Gomorrean (n). Sodom and Gomorrah were ancient cities destroyed for their evil ways. "The men of Sodom," the Book of Genesis says, "were wicked sinners before the Lord exceedingly." Equally wicked were the people of Gomorrah. The Lord "rained upon Sodom and upon Gomorrah brimstone and fire, and he overthrew those cities . . . and all of the inhabitants of the cities." The wickedness of their ways is not specified, but it is assumed to have been anal or oral copulation and bestiality. Hence a *Sodomite* or *Gomorrean* is one given to "unnatural" sexual practices. "Whores as they are, yea . . . vile and shameful *Sodomites* committing such heinous and abominable acts that it is horrible to think of" (Calvin).

Software. The programs used to direct the operations of a computer and, specifically, the instructions to devise and write effective programs.

Solecism (n); Solipsism (n), Solipsistic (adj). The two nouns are sometimes confused but are, in fact, of entirely different meanings. The word *solecism* is said to come from the corruption of the Attic dialect among the colonists of Soloi. It means incorrect grammar or, by extension, any error or impropriety in the use of language. "There is scarce a *solecism* in writing which the best author is not guilty of, if we be at liberty to read him in the words of some manuscript" (Addison). This is mildly mysterious. Does it mean that eighteenth-century publishers routinely repaired the *solecisms* of their authors? *Solipsism* in philosophy is the theory that only the self exists. "*Solipsism,* if not inconceivable, is in the highest degree incredible" (Barratt). But in everyday speech it means self-absorption, preoccupation with one's own feelings or desires. The adjective *solipsistic* is more likely to have this extended meaning than its philosophical significance. "They should not be made self-centered and *solipsistic* at an age when altruism should have its golden day" (*The Forum*).

Solid (adj); **Stolid** (adj). *Solid:* Having three dimensions; firm, hard, or compact; without break; and, by extension, real or genuine, sound or good. "A *solid* man of Boston,/A comfortable man, with dividends,/And the first salmon, and the first green peas" (Longfellow). *Stolid:* Not easily stirred, unemotional, impassive. Perhaps with justice *stolid* could be substituted for *solid* in the verse from Longfellow.

Solon (n). *Solon*, a Greek poet and statesman, instituted reforms in Athenian law that had the effect of our own Bill of Rights. Hence *solon* means a wise lawgiver or statesman, but in the twentieth century the word has fallen into disuse and, when it is used, is sometimes given an ironic twist. "Many of the *solons* still had rotgut whiskey fueling their affection for education" (cited by *WDEU*).

Solstice: See Equinox.

Somebody (pron), **Someone** (pron). These are among those vexatious indefinite pronouns that carry singular verbs but are often referred to by plural pronouns. Purists tell us that only singular pronouns should be used, as in "*Somebody* left *his* hat on the rack." But when the indefinite pronoun has a plural significance, the plural in its referred pronoun seems proper. Here is a somewhat complex quotation from Sir Francis Bacon that illustrates the point: "If there be a tacit league, it is against *somebody:* who should *they* be? Is it against wild beasts? No. It is against such routs and shoals of people as have utterly degenerated from the laws of nature."

Sometime (adv & adj); **Sometimes** (adv). *Sometime* as adverb means at some indefinite or indeterminate time. "His Holiness will arrive *sometime* next week" (*The New York Times*). As adjective it means former. "Therefore our *sometime* sister, now our queen" (Shakespeare). *Sometimes* means on some occasions, now and then, at times. "I do love I know not what;/ *Sometimes* this, and *sometimes* that" (Herrick). There are instances where the adjective *some* and the noun *time* are written as two words, as in "We haven't seen him for *some time.*" The distinction is here quite apparent but is not always so, as in "He arrived *some time* ago." *WDEU* provides an easy rule by which to decide whether one or two words is correct. "Insert *quite* before *some* and see if the passage still makes sense. If it does, *some* and *time* should be written separately." In "He arrived (*quite*) *some time* ago," the construction makes sense and justifies *some time* as the proper choice.

Somnolence (n), Somnolent (adj); Hypnosis (n), Hypnotic (n & adj); Fantasy (n); Morphine (n). Somnus was the Roman god of sleep, so that *somnolence* means sleepiness and *somnolent* sleepy. "The people had dined and the usual *somnolence* followed" (MacDonald). *Somnolent* also has the implication of inattentive as well as drowsy: the "*somnolent* student" is clearly one not overeager to learn. The god Somnus was also called Hypnos, so that *hypnosis* and *hypnotic* reflect the idea of sleep. Although *hypnosis* is the artificially induced trancelike state in which a subject is oblivious to all else but responds readily to suggestions from a hypnotist, the word *hypnotic* as both noun and adjective is used in medicine primarily to mean sedative or soporific: "The droning voice of a heavy reader on a dull subject is often a most effectual *hypnotic*" (Carpenter). Phantasus was an assistant to Hypnos and induced hallucinations in sleepers so that *fantasy* (an imagined event, image, or action) has the implication of dreamlike imagining. "By the power of *fantasy* we see colours in a dream, or a madman sees things before him which are not there" (Newton). *Morpheus,* the son of Somnus and the god of dreams, gives his name to *morphine,* an addictive narcotic. "Took *morphine* last night and slept some" (Jane Carlyle).

Sophist (n), Sophism (n), Sophistry (n); Sophisticated (adj). The *sophists* were learned scholars and educators of ancient Greece, but eventually they came to be regarded as overly subtle and even deceptive in their fine-spun syllogisms so that now a *sophism* is a specious theory or fallacious reasoning. "When a false argument puts on the appearance of a true one, then it is properly called a *sophism*" (Watts), and *sophistry* is likewise deceptively subtle reasoning or a spurious argument. "These men have obscured and confounded the natures of things, by their false principles and wretched *sophistry*" (Southey). *Sophisticated,* although it means knowledgeable, worldly wise, and discriminating in manners, tastes, and ideas, also has the connotation of overrefined and even deceptively clever. "Who resist the truth by argument or explain it away by *sophisticated* interpretations" (Horsley). But *sophisticated* when used in relation to machines, inventions, or research retains its meaning of subtle, complex, ingeniously devised. "The experiments Fleming and Florey used to demonstrate the nature of penicillin were not *sophisticated* but rather simple in nature" (Greenberg).

Sort. In computer operation, to arrange information or data into groups according to the identifying keys of each item. Usually the arrangement of the keys follows a predetermined order so that the information can be retrieved sequentially.

Sort of: See **Kind of.**

Special (adj), **Specially** (adv); **Especial** (adj), **Especially** (adv). The adjectives are etymologically identical, but they are not precise synonyms. *Special* means of a distinct or particular character and appears in innumerable fixed phrases such as *special* delivery, *special* session, *special* effect, *special* agent, and so on. "The salad, for which, like everybody else I ever met, he had a *special* receipt" (George du Maurier). *Especial* is a more emphatic word meaning exceptional, outstanding, extraordinary. "Dissected in minute detail but with *especial* glee" (Palmer). The adverbs too have somewhat different meanings. *Specially:* Particularly, to an extent beyond what is usual. "The plants have been *specially* selected to associate well" (Hay). *Especially:* Principally, chiefly, in an uncommon degree or manner. "Providence hath planted in all men a natural desire and curiosity of knowing things to come; and such things *especially* as concern our particular happiness" (Burnet).

Specie (n); Species (n); Specious (adj). *Specie* is a coin or minted currency. "Whether we send our Coin in *Specie* or melt it down here and send it in Bullion" (Locke). *Species:* A class of individuals having characteristics or traits in common. "I describe not men, but manners; not an individual but a *species*" (Fielding). *Specious* has nothing to do with either *specie* or *species* and means superficially pleasing or plausible, though without real merit. "What are these *specious* gifts, these paltry gains?" (Crabbe).

Spectacle: See Sight.

Spiritual (adj & n), Spiritous (adj). The adjective *spiritual* means pertaining to or characterized by the spirit or soul, as distinguished from the physical body or world. "An outward and visible sign of an inward and *spiritual* grace" (*Book of Common Prayer*). A *spiritual* is a religious hymn or song, especially one sung by slaves. "I had for many years heard of this class of songs under the name of 'Negro *Spirituals*'" (Higginson). *Spiritous* once meant ethereal or of the nature of spirit. "More refined, more *spiritous,* and pure" (Milton). In contemporary use, *spiritous* means containing alcohol produced by distillation. "Not allowing me to take anything *spiritous*" (Smith).

Split infinitive. Another topic in whose discussion countless reams of paper have been used to no avail. There is no immutable law against use of the *split infinitive,* nor should there be, for its contrived avoidance often results in awkwardness of structure and ambiguity of meaning. Here are two simple guidelines that may help: (1) Let natural structure and cadence prevail. "Students try *to really understand* the rules of grammar" is without fault, because to move *really* before *to* is to make the adverb modify *try* and to move it after *understand* is to produce gibberish. (2) Avoid the *split infinitive* if the necessary change does no harm. "The legislators hoped *to substantially* raise the living standards of unskilled laborers" reads just as smoothly and clearly in "The legislators hoped *to raise substantially* the living standards of unskilled laborers."

Spooling. A method for achieving effective use of computer hardware by which an input/output device is keyed to buffers in main and secondary storage.

Spoonerism: See **Malapropism.**

Sprain (n); **Strain** (n); **Stress** (n). *Sprain:* Wrenching or tearing of the ligaments around a joint, but without dislocation. "The treatment to be adopted for *sprains* is the immediate application of leeches" (*Penny Cyclopedia*). *Strain:* Injury to a muscle or tendon due to excessive use or tension. A severe demand on physical or emotional resources. "*Strains* are often attended with worse consequences than broken bones" (Buchan). "I should not have been surprised if he had dropped down dead, so terrible was his *strain* upon himself" (Gaskell). *Stress:* Physical, mental, or emotional tension. "Pious virgins, under *stress* of these things, swoon" (Hewlett).

Stalactite (n); **Stalagmite** (n). Both are deposits, usually conical, of calcium carbonate formed by the dripping of water. A *stalactite* is a column that hangs down; a *stalagmite* is one that builds up from the floor. "Some calcareous *stalactites* pendent from the roof" (Mills). "The rich *stalagmites* that grew up from the bottom reflected a golden light through the water" (Catlin).

Stanch (v); **Staunch** (adj); **Stench** (n). These words are not likely to be confused, although *staunch* sometimes appears when *stanch* is meant. *Stanch:* To stop the flow of. "Where was gentle Mary to *stanch* thy tears?" (Dusseau). *Staunch:* Firm, steadfast. "And you are *staunch* indeed in learning's cause" (Cowper). *Stench:* An offensive smell, but a word more likely than *odor* to be used figuratively. "The *stench* of the usual rotten politics in our mismanaged city" (*Daily News*).

Stanza: See **Verse.**

Stash: See **Cache.**

Stationary (adj); **Stationery** (n). *Stationary:* Having a fixed position; not movable. "A field hospital is a very different affair from a *stationary* base hospital" (*Daily*

News). *Stationery:* Writing paper and, less commonly, writing materials. "A rush was generally made to the desk where the *stationery* was kept" (Russell).

Statistic (n). A *statistic* is simply a figure, sometimes exemplifying, sometimes specifying as in a rate of incidence or percentage of survival. With the *statistic* (a numerical fact) we are in the accountant's realm—generally conceded to be an unemotional domain. Hence Stalin's "A single death is a tragedy, a thousand deaths a *statistic*."

Stevedore: See **Longshoreman.**

Stimulate: See **Simulate.**

Straight (adj & adv); **Strait** (n & adj); **Straitjacket** (n); **Straitlaced** (adj). *Straight* (adj): Without a bend or curve, direct. "The voice of one crying in the wilderness, Prepare ye the way of the Lord, make his paths *straight*" (St. Matthew). *Straight* (adv): In a *straight* course; directly to or from a place. "This piece of eloquence moved me so much that I went *straight* to his Excellency" (Herbert). *Strait* (n): A narrow passage of water. "They may return through the *strait* of Magellan" (Hakluyt). Hence the adjective *strait* means narrow, confined, and, by extension, strict. "*Strait* is the gate, and narrow is the way, which leadeth unto life, and few there be that find it" (St. Matthew). Further, the correct spelling is *straitjacket*, not *straightjacket*. In short, a confining rather than a straight jacket. *Straitlaced* is the correct spelling. The word derives from *strait* and means either tightly laced or excessively moralistic or prudish. "Richardson seemed to be a narrow *straitlaced* preacher" (Sir Leslie Stephen on *Pamela*). However, just as *straitjacket* has become *straightjacket*, so *straitlaced* too is misspelled, but, alas, the error has become so common that most lexicons recognize the erroneous spelling as an allowable variant. Perhaps soon "straitened circumstances" will become "straightened circumstances" and so take on a new, more pleasant meaning.

Strain, Stress: See **Sprain.**

Strange: See **Funny.**

Strategy (n), **Stratagem** (n), **Strategic** (adj); **Tactics** (n), **Tactic** (n). *Strategy:* Specifically, planning and direction of large military operations. More generally, any plan or method for obtaining a desired goal or result. "It has been too often the *strategy* of theological argument, in dealing with books or persons with whom we differ, to give no quarter" (Stanley). But a *stratagem* is a specific trick or scheme used to surprise or deceive an enemy and, by extension, any artifice or ruse used to secure a result or an advantage over an adversary. "For her own breakfast she'll project a scheme,/Nor take her tea without a *stratagem*" (Young). *Tactics:* The art of disposing and maneuvering military or naval forces in battle in accordance with a *strategic* plan. "The soldier—that is, the great soldier—of today is . . . a quiet, grave man, busied in charts, exact in sums, master of the art of *tactics*, occupied in trivial detail" (Bagehot). A *tactic*, like a *stratagem*, is a specific maneuver or expedient. "Great Coquettes have another *tactic*" (cited by *OED*).

Stream. In computer operation, the data route from a resource to a controller.

Style. A thousand manuals have been written on style, often enough by not very skilled stylists. Here we are concerned with *style* in computer language: the distinctive optical proportions of characters that remain constant whatever the size of the character.

Subjective: See Objective.

Subjunctive (n & adj). The *subjunctive* mood of verbs is a mood of iffiness, conditionality, and wishfulness, and since the eighteenth century, commentators have been lamenting its demise. In 1936 Mencken declared the *subjunctive* "virtually extinct in the vulgar tongue," but by 1948 he had somewhat revised his obituary. "On higher levels, of course, the *subjunctive* shows more life and there is ground for questioning the conclusion of Bradley, Fowler and other authorities that it is on its way out." It may be questioned whether the *subjunctive* has indeed disappeared from common parlance. It is preserved in many phrases of everyday speech—"so *be* it," "if need *be*," "Heaven *forbid*," "Come what *may*," "Far *be* it from me," and many others. Further, even in what Mencken calls the "vulgar tongue," it is not uncommon to hear "If I *were* he, I'd go to Australia" or "If he *were* in Memphis, he would have called by now," or "Would that I *were* President, then you'd see the fur fly." No literate person would use "was" in place of the italicized "were."

Subreption (n); **Surreptitious** (adj). *Subreption* is not a common word, but it is in common law and means either a concealment of pertinent facts or fallacious representation in a legal proceeding. The even more uncommon *subreptitious* probably gives us *surreptitious:* secret, clandestine, furtive, obtained or done by stealth. "Counterfeiting Copper Coyns and bringing them in by strange *surreptitious* ways, as in . . . hollow Masts" (Howell).

Subroutine. That part of a computer program that performs a self-sufficient logical section of the overall program and is available to a particular set of instructions.

Subsequent (adj); **Consequent** (adj), **Consequential** (adj). For obscure reasons these words are often misused. *Subsequent* means occurring or coming later, following in order or succession. "And he smiled a kind of sickly smile, and curled up on the floor,/And the *subsequent* proceedings interested him no more" (Harte). But *consequent* means following as a result or effect or following as a logical conclusion. "The satisfaction or dissatisfaction, *consequent* to a man's acting suitably or unsuitably to conscience" (South). However, the word *consequential* has departed from *consequent* and in modern idiom means only something of consequence or importance, sometimes used ironically to mean self-important. "Mr. C. bustled about . . . feeling himself the most *consequential* man in the town" (Martineau).

Substantial (adj); **Substantive** (adj). *Substantial:* Real, large, imposing, solid. "O blessed! blessed night! I am afraid,/Being in night, all this is but a dream;/Too flattering sweet to be *substantial*" (Shakespeare). *Substantive:* Pertaining to the real or actual nature of something; essential; having an important or practical effect; independent and self-subsistent. "We have no direct cognizance of what may be called the *substantive* existence of the body" (Newman).

Succubus, Incubus, Concubine, Concupiscence (n's). The *Succubus* is a legendary female demon who has sexual intercourse with men in their sleep, hence in lowercase a strumpet or harlot. "For forty years Benedict of Berne had kept up an amatory commerce with a *succubus*" (Sharpe). An *Incubus* is a mythological demon who possesses women in their sleep, hence in lowercase a nightmarish dream or an oppressive force or burden. "The dire superstition which sits like an *incubus* upon them" (Buckle). The word *concubine* derives from Latin *concubina* (a whore) but is related etymologically to *incubus* and means a harlot not of lofty character but of commercial acuity. The *concubine* consorts with princes of power and ministers of state while the prostitute provides paid-for pleasure to ordinary people of ordinary means. (Among polygamous peoples a *concubine* is a secondary wife of inferior social position maintained for sexual pleasure.) "I know I am too mean to be your queen/And yet too good to be your *concubine*" (Shakespeare). *Concupiscence* [kahn CUE pis ense] is ardent sexual desire, lust, lechery. "In our faces evident the signs/Of foul *concupiscence*" (Milton).

Sufficient (adj), **Sufficiency** (n); **Superfluous** (adj), **Superfluity** (n). *Sufficient* and *sufficiency* mean enough. *Superfluous* and *superfluity* more than enough. "I have had an elegant *sufficiency*. Anything more would be a *superfluous* superabundancy" (Anon.). "A quiet mediocrity is still to be preferred before a troubled *superfluity*" (Suckling).

Superlative of two: See Shibboleth.

Supine: See Prostrate.

Supportive (adj). *Supportive* (affording support or sustaining) is an old and until modern times rarely used word. "These laws are not destructive but *supportive* of one another and all *supportive* of Man" (cited by *OED*). But psychology has now made it a popular word of somewhat extended significance (providing emotional support or encouragement). "A very withdrawn young woman who might have been expected to require some more *supportive* type of therapy" (*Psychological Abstracts*).

Surprise: See **Amaze.**

Sustain (v), **Sustainment** (n); **Sustenance** (n). The verb *sustain* has a wide variety of meanings generally related to the idea of support. (1) To bear the weight of, to hold up. "Vain is the force of man,/To crush the pillars that the pile *sustain*" (Pope). To support, to buttress. "If he have no expectations of another life to *sustain* him under the evils of the world, he is of all creatures the most miserable" (Tillotson). (3) To maintain, to provide for. "What food/Will he convey up thither to *sustain*/Himself and army?" (Milton). (4) To help, to assist. "His sons who seek the tyrant to *sustain*,/And long for arbitrary lords again,/He dooms to death" (Dryden). (5) To bear, to endure. "Shall Turnus then such endless toil *sustain*,/In fighting fields, and conquer towns in vain" (Dryden). (6) To suffer, to undergo. "If you omit/The offer of this time, I cannot promise,/But that you shall *sustain* more new disgraces" (Shakespeare). Finally, *sustain* can also mean to prolong. "The Earl of Harewood said he did not realise he had backed into a parked car because he was listening to a Mozart wind serenade on his car radio and might have confused the sound of a burglar alarm, which was set off on the parked car, with a *sustained* clarinet note" (*London Daily Telegraph*). Incidental note: Lord Harewood, a cousin of the queen, was cleared of all charges. The noun *sustainment* in general shares the various meanings of support. "An unnatural and artificial *sustainment* of the language and imagery" (*Quarterly Review*). But *sustenance* means whatever provides a vital necessity of life, especially nourishment. "There are sundry means for the *sustenance* of our bodies, many sorts of raiment to clothe our nakedness" (Hooker).

Swiftian (adj). *Swiftian:* Ironic, acerbic, misanthropic, sardonic, dissident. From Jonathan Swift, who in *Gulliver's Travels* has given us an enduring masterpiece of elegant prose and satiric bitterness. In the travels of Lemuel Gulliver to Lilliput, Brobdignag, Laputa, and Houyhnhnmland it represents Swift's acrid reflections on man's corruption of his highest attribute—reason. At once sardonic, fantastic, and somber, it has always been immensely popular, although an Irish bishop said of it upon publication that it was full of improbable lies and that, for his part, he hardly believed a word of it. Swift's bitterness and irony reached their apogee in "A Modest Proposal," in which the terrible suffering and starvation of the Irish people are revealed in the mock suggestion that the poor should devote themselves to rearing children to be killed and sold for eating. Swift gives cogent reasons for his proposal and offers enticing recipes. Appointed dean of St. Patrick's Cathedral in Dublin, he there died chained to his chair, embittered, mad, and in fearful agony—but able to write his *Swiftian* epitaph: *Ubi saeva indignatio ulterius cor lacerare nequit* (Where fierce indignation can no longer tear his heart).

In O'Casey's *Red Roses for Me* a kindly rector and callow inspector watch the weary and starving night loungers along the river Liffey:

> INSPECTOR: *Swift, too, must have walked about here with the thorny crown of madness pressing ever deeper into his brain.*
> RECTOR (indicating the men and women): *Who are these?*
> INSPECTOR (indifferent): *Those? Oh, flotsam and jetsam. A few of them dangerous at night, maybe; but harmless during the day.*
> RECTOR: *I've read that tens of thousands of such as those followed Swift to his grave.*
> INSPECTOR: *Indeed, sir? A queer man, the poor demented Dean; a right queer man.*

Sybarite (n), **Sybaritic** (adj); **Ascetic** (n & adj). The *sybarite* and the *ascetic* are at opposite ends of the pole of pleasure. Sybaris, a Greek city of Italy, was known for the pleasure-seeking and luxury-loving habits of its people. Hence the *sybarite* is a hedonist and voluptuary, and the adjective *sybaritic* shares this meaning. "It was a *sybaritic* repast, in a magnificent apartment, and we were all of us young voluptuaries of fashion" (Thackeray). An *ascetic* is either a person of spartan tastes who abstains from the normal pleasures of life or one who dedicates his life to the pursuit of ideals or practices self-mortification for religious reasons—in the early Christian church a monk or hermit. "He that preaches to man, should understand what is in man; and that skill can scarce be attained by an *ascetic* in his solitudes" (Atterbury). Here the adjective *ascetic* is used in its religious sense of abstemious or austere.

"None lived such long lives as monks and hermits, sequestered from plenty to a constant *ascetic* course of the severest abstinence" (South).

Sycophant (n), **Sycophantic** (adj). A *sycophant* is a servile flatterer, a fawning parasite. "Men know themselves void of those qualities which the impudent *sycophant,* at the same time, both ascribes to them, and in his sleeve laughs at them for believing" (South). *Sycophantic* is meanly flattering, basely obsequious. "His *sycophantic* arts being detected, that game is not to be played the second time" (Johnson).

Symbiosis (n), **Symbiotic** (adj). In biology *symbiosis* is the living together of or intimate association between dissimilar organisms. Parasitism, commensalism, and mutualism are *symbiotic* states. In psychiatry *symbiosis* is the mutual cooperation or interdependence of two persons, as between mother and son or husband and wife. In general use *symbiosis* has become any interdependent or mutually beneficial association between organisms, persons, or groups. "As an instance of *symbiosis* take the rhinoceros and the yellow tickbird. The tickbird dines on parasites infesting the rhinoceros's horny skin; the rhinoceros itches less and is warned of danger when the tickbird, sharp-eyed and skittish, abandons him" (Edwards).

Sympathy: See Empathy.

Synchronous (adj). *Synchronous* has a variety of technical meanings that are also in nontechnical use. (1) Occurring at the same time. (2) Proceeding at the same rate and precisely together, recurring simultaneously. (3) In physics, having the same frequency. (4) In electronics and telecommunications, using fixed-time intervals controlled by a clock to secure simultaneity of operation. (5) In astronomy, characterizing rotation of a satellite in which the period of rotation is the same as the period of orbit. (6) In general, coincident in time or regularity. "The beats of a bird's two wings are always exactly *synchronous*" (Argyll).

Syncretize (v). A useful verb but one now rarely used, although it would seem to suit the meliorative temper of our times. It means to attempt to unify opposing or differing groups or interests. "One cannot merely *syncretize* religions" (cited by *OED*).

Syndrome (n). *Syndrome* is a medical term meaning neither a disease nor a symptom but the aggregate of signs and symptoms associated with a morbid process and constituting the clinical picture of a disease. Like many technical terms that pass into common use, it is now both overused and misused. Medically, *syndrome* cannot mean a predictable difficulty, but that is what it seems to mean in "This second book suffers from a mild case of sequel *syndrome*. It simply does not rise to the same heights as the first" (cited by *WDEU*).

Synergy (n), **Synergistic** (adj), **Synergism** (n). From its Greek roots *synergy* means working together, but it is a working together the effect of whose joint efforts is greater than the sum of its individual efforts. *Synergy* is now a faddish word, and a short step takes us from the laboratory to the boardroom where executives decide that the merger of two competing companies will have the *synergistic* effect of creating sales in excess of their individual totals. *Synergism* is a synonym for *synergy*, but it also has a specific religious significance: the doctrine that redemption may be achieved only by cooperation between divine grace and human will. "*Synergism* can best be understood as an ethical protest against attitudes which paralyze the conscience and leave the church powerless in its struggle against moral chaos" (Edwards).

Syntax (n). In the past *syntax* (grammar) could justly be called the science of language, but specialization has introduced philology as the science of language, and *syntax* has become the science of the arrangement of words and the construction of sentences. "I can produce a hundred instances to convince any reasonable man that they do not so much as understand common *syntax*" (Swift). In computer operation, *syntax* has identical significance: The rules for correctly forming statements in a source language.

Syzygy: See **Zyzzyva.**

Taciturn: See **Reticent.**

Tactics: See **Strategy.**

Tactile (adj); **Tactual** (adj); **Textile** (n & adj). *Tactile:* Endowed with or affecting the sense of touch. "The *tactile* sensation is a symbol to us of some external event" (Foster). *Tactual* is a less common word than *tactile* and is a near synonym for it, but it also has a somewhat different, more precise meaning: arising from or due to the sense of touch. "Thy existence is wholly an Illusion and optical and *tactual* Phantasm" (Carlyle). *Textile* is any woven material and, as adjective, it describes anything in general pertaining to weaving. "The *textile* mills lie near the links;/At noon of every day/The working children may look out/And see the men at play" (nineteenth-century workmen's ballad).

Tadpole (n); **Taper** (n & v); **Tapir** (n). The first two words in lowercase mean what they have always meant, but capitalized *Tadpole* and *Taper* are sly characters who made their furtive way through two satiric novels by Benjamin Disraeli (*Coningsby* and *Sybil*), and their names have become epithets for political flunkies. A *tapir* (sometimes spelled *tapyr*) is one of several stout, three-toed ungulates of Central and South America. Their species is so seriously endangered that soon *tapir* may cease to exist except as a crossword word.

Talented (adj). Today the scorn once heaped upon *talented* as an adjective seems unlikely and unreal. Coleridge called such use "vile and barbarous," and Bierce was not far behind in round condemnation. The furor has died down and *talented* is now in acceptable use in both speech and writing as a synonym for skilled, gifted, or endowed with special ability. "Of science and logic he chatters/As fine and fast as he can;/ Though I am no judge of such matters,/I'm sure he's a *talented* man" (Praed).

Tangent (n), **Tangential** (adj), **Tangible** (adj). The words come from Latin *tangere* (to touch). Hence a *tangent* in geometry is a straight line touching a curve at only one point. "Tables of *tangents* and cotangents were constructed and used by the Arab mathematicians of the 9th and 10th centuries" (cited by *OED*). But *to go off on a tangent* is to digress suddenly from one course of action or thought to another. *Tangential* means touching slightly or only partially relevant; erratic, digressive. "Emerson had only *tangential* relation with the experiment" (Holmes). "A collection of mixed and *tangential* information" (Addison). *Tangible* means capable of being touched, discernible by touch; substantial, actual, not imagined: "Without any *tangible* ground of complaint" (Grote).

Tank. A colloquialism for an acoustic delay line in which mercury is used to recirculate sonic signals.

Tantalus (n); **Tantalize** (v). *Tantalus*, a son of Zeus, is believed to have served up his son as a dish for the gods. His punishment was eternal confinement in a lake whose waters reached his chin but receded when he wished to drink and above whose surface hung choice fruits just beyond his starving reach. Hence to *tantalize* is to torment or to frustrate by raising expectations that are never realized. "Thy vain desires, at strife/Within themselves, have *tantaliz'd* thy life" (Dryden). A *tantalus* is also a stand containing usually three cut-glass decanters that, although apparently available, cannot be withdrawn until a grooved bar is released. "He crossed to a recess, and touched the spring of a *tantalus*. It flew back with a harsh click" (cited by *OED*).

Tasteful (adj); **Tasty** (adj). *Tasteful* means having or displaying good taste, whereas *tasty* means having a pleasing flavor. "The *tasteful* publisher of the Aldine Poets" (Singer), but "A famous pie or pilau, with rice and a *tasty* sauce" (Curzon).

Tatterdemalion (n). A word whose origin is obscure enough to have aroused some fanciful guesses. Johnson, who never fudged such matters, says forthrightly: "*Tatterdemalion: n.* (*tatter* and *I know not what*). A ragged fellow." He adds a somewhat strange quotation, from L'Estrange: "As a poor fellow was trudging along in a bitter cold morning with never a rag, a spark" [a showy splendid man—Johnson's definition] "that was warm clad called to this *tatterdemalion*, how he could endure the weather?" Johnson himself was not always warm clad, and one wonders if he too endured senseless questions.

Tautology: See **Redundancy.**

Teach: See **Learn.**

Tedium (n); **Trivia** (n). *Tedium* no more has a plural *tedia* than *trivia* a singular *trivium*. *Tedium:* The state of being bored; irksomeness; ennui. All agree that it comes from Latin *taedium* (weariness), but one or two irreverent commentators contend with tongue in cheek that it is nothing more than the first two words of the Latin hymn *Te Deum Laudamus.* "One or two sleek clerical tutors, with here and there a *tedium*-stricken squire" (Carlyle). *Trivia:* Trifles, things unimportant or inconsequential. "'Tis scarce worth discussing such *trivia*" (Davis). If a singular must be used, *a trivial matter* will do, but accuracy compels the reminder that there is a word *trivium*—one no longer in use—that means a place where three ways meet and in the Middle Ages the lower division of the seven lively arts—grammar, rhetoric, and logic.

Telecast (v), **Televise** (v). There is a distinction between the two verbs. To *telecast* is to broadcast by television, and to *televise* is to record for the purpose of later broadcasting.

Here the verbs are used correctly: "Models being *televised* before . . . station WBHQ *telecasted* on Monday a complete showing" (cited by *WDEU*). But now the words are often used interchangeably, perhaps with no great loss. "He shuddered at the enormous cost of *televising* the show in color" (Smith).

Telephone (n); **Telescope** (n). *"Telephone:* An invention of the devil which abrogates some of the advantages of making a disagreeable person keep his distance. *Telescope:* A device having a relation to the eye similar to that of the telephone to the ear, enabling distant objects to plague us with a multitude of needless details" (Bierce). Were Bierce still with us, he would have a word to say about fax machines, Xerox copies, and modems.

Temporal (adj); **Temporary** (adj). Both words refer, of course, to time, but *temporal* has the extended meaning of concern with present life, and hence worldly or secular, as distinguished from ecclesiastical. "His Scepter shows the force of *temporal* power" (Shakespeare). *Temporary* means existing or effective for only a short time. "The use of force alone is but *temporary*. It may subdue for a moment; but it does not remove the necessity of subduing again" (Burke).

Temporize (v); **Extemporize** (v). *Temporize* means to gain time by delay, hence to compromise temporarily. "I have behaved like a fool: I ought to have *temporized* with this singular being, learned the motives of its interference, and availed myself of its succour" (Scott). To *extemporize* is to speak with no or slight preparation. "Preachers are prone either to *extemporize* always or to write always" (Phelps).

Tendentious: See Sententious.

Terminal. Any device for entering data into a computer or receiving information from it, usually consisting of a keyboard with video display unit.

Terpsichore (n), **Terpsichorean** (adj); **Euterpe** (n), **Euterpean** (adj). *Terpsichore* [turp SIK ur ee] was the Greek goddess of dance and choral song; hence *tepsichorean* means pertaining to the dance. "The loving couples hold themselves aloof from the busy hum, or mix in it for *terpsichorean* purposes only" (*Daily News*). *Euterpe* was the patron goddess of music; hence *euterpean* means musical. "A performance that would have been barely creditable to the '*Euterpean*' or 'Philharmonic' society of a country town" (cited by *OED*).

Text. The information element of a computer message, excluding characters or bits used to facilitate transmission.

Textile: See Tactile.

Thankfully (adv). *Thankfully* as a sentence modifier has been subject to the same but less extensive criticism that greets *hopefully* (q.v.) in such use. "*Hopefully*," Follett writes, "appeals to speakers and writers who do not think about what they are saying. . . . How readily the rotten apple will corrupt the barrel is seen in similar use of other adverbs: 'the suicide needle which—*thankfully*—he didn't see fit to use.'" No question about it, *thankfully* should be replaced with "we are thankful to say." But perhaps in speech we may allow "*Thankfully*, it didn't rain on our picnic" (wedding reception, Easter parade, fireworks display, or whatever).

Thanking you in advance (phrase). Of all trite epistolary phrases, this is one of the worst, with its uncivil implications that the requested favor will be granted and that no later acknowledgment of it should be expected. Say instead something like "With many thanks for your consideration."

That (pron); **Which** (pron). Perhaps millions of editorial blue pencils have been used to the nub to enforce the distinction between *that* and *which*, but usage continues to pay scant attention to editorial preference. Nevertheless, the distinction is both real and simple. *That* is restrictive and defining; *which* is simply descriptive. "This is the house *that* Longfellow built." Here *that* defines the house. "This is Longfellow's house, *which* was built in 1837." Here the house is already defined and *which* simply describes it. One should also note that nonrestrictive clauses beginning with *which* are set off by commas.

Theater (n), **Theatre** (Brit. var), **Theatrical** (adj). A *theater* is a building or hall or outdoor arena, usually fitted with tiers of seats, for the presentation of dramas, operas, musicals, recitals, motion-picture shows, or demonstrations. "So long as there is one pretty girl left on the stage, the professional undertakers may hold up on their burial of the *theater*" (Nathan). It is also by extension any place of action or area of activity. "The *theater* of operations of an army embraces all the territory it may desire to invade and all that it may be necessary to defend" (Mendell). *Theatrical* means pertaining to the *theater*, but it also has the connotation of stagy, histrionic, extravagant, ostentatious, as in "his *theatrical* display of grief."

Their (pron); **There** (adv & pron); **They're** (contraction). *Their* is a possessive, attributive pronoun. "Mine and all *their* free and sovereign king" (Swinburne). *There* is an adverb meaning in or at that place and a pronoun used to introduce a sentence or clause in which the verb precedes its subject. "As I was going up the stair/I met a man who wasn't *there*. He wasn't *there* again today./I wish, I wish he'd stay away" (Mearns). And "From all these things *there* resulted consequences of vast importance" (Buckle). *They're* is a contraction for they are. "*They're* Rogues as sure as Light's in Heaven" (Ward).

Thence (adv); **Whence** (adv). *Thence* is an infrequently used adverb meaning from that place, therefrom, from that time, and *whence* similarly means from what place, cause or source, wherefrom. A fairly bitter dispute has arisen among critics as to whether one may say *from thence* or *from whence* when the *from* is implicit in both adverbs, Johnson even calling the unnecessary *from* "a vicious mode of speech." Certainly "*Whence* comest thou?" is both clear and correct, but who will fault Swift's "I suppose he will write to us *from thence*" or Franklin's "He went soon after to Carolina *from whence* he sent me two long letters"? Perhaps an old rhetorical rule applies here as elsewhere: "Leave it in if it sounds right; take it out if it sounds strange."

Therefore (adv); **Therefor** (adv). These were once variant spellings of the same word, but now each has a distinctive meaning of its own. *Therefore* means in consequence of, as a result of. "I think, *therefore* I am" (Descartes). *Therefor* means in exchange for or in place of something. "Argument being at an end, recourse was then had to the common substitute *therefor*, ridicule" (Hall).

Thesaurus (n). From the Greek *thēsaurós* (treasure house, vault), it has come to mean a storehouse of knowledge and in the Renaissance became the title of erudite dictionaries of Greek and Latin. "In a complete *thesaurus* of any language, the etymology of every word should exhibit both its philology and its linguistics" (Marsh). Today the word is almost confined in meaning to a dictionary of synonyms or of synonyms and antonyms. "You should keep a *thesaurus* right next to your dictionary" (*Family Word Finder*). Its plural may be either *thesauri* or *thesauruses*, but the later is much more common.

Thinking man (phrase). The phrase often takes the form of *no thinking man* and is clearly intended to discourage disagreement by suggesting that it would be offered only by a thoughtless person. Fowler therefore says it puts the reader's back up and inclines him to reject the view that is being forced on him. However, the phrase *thinking man* of itself and not as a weapon of argument is in good and inoffensive use. "Mr. Ustinov is a *thinking man* with a satiric mind" (*The Saturday Review*).

Think to (phrase). A phrase called both colloquial and objectionable by many critics, it still is in daily use to mean expect (I did not *think to* see him there") or remember ("Did you *think to* ask the postman for his address?") or intend ("The writer *thinks to* succeed by piling up an accumulation of detail" [Leacock]). Certainly such use is idiomatic but can scarcely be called objectionable.

Thread. A group of beads that forms a complete computer program. Beads are small nodules that perform specific functions and can be written and tested individually before being combined in *threads*.

Thrive (v), **Thrifty** (adj). To *thrive* is to grow vigorously, to flourish. "Bold knaves *thrive* without one grain of sense" (Dryden). *Thrifty* (deriving from *thrift*) means economizing, frugal, saving, pennywise. "I am glad he has so much youth and vigour left, of which he hath not been *thrifty*, but wonder he has no more discretion" (Swift). But *thrifty* (deriving from *thrive*) means flourishing, vigorous, prospering. "The bush looked wonderfully *thrifty*, considering its many drawbacks to growth" (Mary Wilkins).

Thrust (v & n). Both verb and noun have long been in steadfast use and of clear meaning. *Thrust* as verb: To push or drive into or among with force; to shove. "Except I shall see in his hands the print of the nails . . . and *thrust* my hand into his side, I will not believe" (St. John). As noun: A forcible stroke, push, shove, or lunge. "Science is nothing but trained and organized common sense, . . . and its methods differ from those of common sense only as far as the guardman's cut and *thrust* differ from the manner in which a savage wields his club" (T. Huxley). However, in the last few decades, *thrust* has taken on the figurative meaning of essential point, design, or purpose. Several critics regard such use as "pretentious jargon," but in this figurative use the ideas of force and vigor implicit in *thrust* give it an edge over its synonyms. "Touting mayhem has been the principal promotional *thrust* of wrestling" (*Sports Illustrated*).

Thusly (adv). Few words in actual use have attracted more vigorous denunciation. Its kindest epithet is "superfluous," and it is usually said to be "illiterate and incorrect" as a substitute for *thus*, but *thusly* now appears with some frequency, especially in meanings somewhat different from those of *thus*. "Stories never lose anything in the recital, and consequently this one grew *thusly*" (Lady Barton).

Timber (n); **Timbre** (n). *Timber:* The wood of growing trees suitable for structural use or a stand of such trees. "It is the love of the people; it is their attachment to their government, . . . which gives you your army and your navy, and infuses into both that liberal obedience, without which your army would be a base rabble, and your navy nothing but rotten *timber*" (Burke). *Timbre:* The quality or character of a sound distinguishing it from other sounds of similar pitch and intensity.

"There are scarcely any two individuals who have exactly the same *timbre* of voice" (Blaserna).

Timidity (n); **Temerity** (n), **Temerarious** (adj). *Timidity* is fearfulness, shyness, lack of self-assurance. "The hare figured pusillanimity and *timidity* from its temper" (Brown's *Vulgar Errours*) (*figured* is used here in the sense of represented). *Temerity* is the antonym of *timidity:* audacity, boldness, courage, rashness. "Marlborough might have been made to repent his *temerity* at Blenheim" (Johnson). *Temerarious* (the rarely used adjective form of *temerity*): Rash, bold, audacious, reckless, venturesome. "The King was one of the first that entered the breach, choosing rather to be thought *temerarious* than timorous" (Speed).

Tirade: See **Harangue.**

Titan (n), **Titanic** (adj). The first children of Uramus and Gaea were the twelve *Titans*—six male and six female giants. Hence *titanic* means huge, immense, colossal, gargantuan. "He has assailed heaven itself with *titanic* audacity" (Kelly).

Titillate (v); **Titivate** (v). These words are rarely confused, for the good reason that the second is rarely used. *Titillate:* To excite agreeably, to tickle the fancy. "Not to *titillate* his palate, but to keep up his character for hospitality" (Macaulay). *Titivate:* To make smart or spruce up. "It was drawn through the Fair by eight oxen *titivated* with ribbons and flowers" (*Daily News*). Somehow an unlikely picture.

To all intents and purposes (phrase). The phrase has been the object of severe criticism, mostly because it says in five words what *in effect* says in two and because it has a certain hackneyed flavor. Still, it appears often enough in the work of good writers to suggest that it need not be avoided. "His courteous response was, *to all intents and purposes,* no response at all" (Roth).

Toothsome (adj); **Toothy** (adj). *Toothsome* can mean both delicious and enticing or attractive. "Hard to please if they cannot select something *toothsome* from the menu"

(Callow) or "To coax his *toothsome* secretary into a close relationship" (cited by *WDEU*). But recently *toothsome* has begun to mean *toothy:* Having numerous large or prominent teeth. Such use cannot possibly be justified, and so far it appears only in sports columns, where good usage plays second fiddle to catchy expression.

Tortuous (adj), **Tortuosity** (n); **Torturous** (adj). *Tortuous:* Full of twists and turns, bending, winding, and hence, by extension, deceitfully indirect. "The unscrupulous cunning with which he assisted in the execution of the schemes of his master's *tortuous* policy" (Scott). *Tortuosity:* A twisted form or course, convolution, deviousness. "These the midwife contriveth unto a knot close unto the body of the infant, from whence ensueth that *tortuosity,* or complicated nodosity, called the navel" (Brown's *Vulgar Errours*). "The charge of deliberate *tortuosity* of action and double-dealing" (cited by *OED*). *Torturous:* Characterized by excruciating pain or by torture. "Outworn with sorrow, with hours of *torturous* anguish" (Ellis).

Transcendent (adj); **Transcendental** (adj). The words are related, both meaning surpassing usual standards, going beyond ordinary limits. "Such *transcendent* goodness of heart" (Richardson). But *transcendental* has the further meaning of abstract, mystic, metaphysical; beyond the accidental knowledge of human experience; describing what, in fact, Carlyle called *"transcendental* moonshine."

Transient (n & adj); **Transitory** (adj). The noun *transient* means a temporary person or thing, someone or something passing through a place or situation. It has also the slight connotation of a tramp or hobo. "My grandmother held these *transients* in low esteem" (Mrs. Rollins). The adjective is without such connotation and means momentary, short-lived, fleeting. "Love hitherto a *transient* guest/Ne'er held possession in his breast" (Swift). *Transitory* too means of short duration, temporary, but it also has the implication of brief lived and destined to change, as in "Fame is *transitory.*" "Religion prefers those pleasures which flow from the presence of God evermore, infinitely before the *transitory* pleasures of this world" (Tillotson).

Translator. In telecasting (q.v.) a relay station that receives a program on one frequency and rebroadcasts it on another. In computer operation a program that converts statements written in one programming language to another, for example, from a source language to machine code.

Translucent and Transparent See Opaque.

Transmute (v), Transmutation (n); Transmogrify (v), Transmogrification (n); Transubstantiate (v), Transubstantiation (n). *Transmute:* To change from one nature, substance, or form to another (usually followed by the preposition *to* or *into*). "Melville *transmutes* the lowly fact into a meditation on mankind" (Updike). *Transmutation* shares the meaning of the verb but has the special significance of changing less valuable ores into gold or silver. "The great aim of alchemy is the *transmutation* of base metals into gold" (Johnson). To *transmogrify* is also to change in appearance or form but especially to alter grotesquely. "Thou art so *transmogrified,* and bedaubed, and bedizened" (Smollett). *Transmogrification* almost always implies strange or grotesque alteration. "The *transmogrification* of the Macrobian children into Swans" (Motteux). To *transubstantiate* is likewise to alter or *transmute* but especially in theology to change bread and water into the body and blood of Christ in the Eucharist. "After consecration there is no longer the substance of Bread, but the Bread is *transubstantiated* and turned into the substance of Christ's body" (Cartwright). *Transubstantiation* almost always denotes the miraculous transformation of the Eucharist. "How is a Romanist prepared easily to swallow, not only against all probability, but even the clear evidence of his senses, the doctrine of *transubstantiation?*" (Locke).

Transpire (v), Transpiration (n). *Transpire* was originally a technical term meaning to pass through a membrane, as vapor through the surface of a leaf or gas through the pores of a vessel. "Not only are gases occluded, but they are also *transpired* under favourable conditions of temperature and pressure" (Anderson). *Transpire* has also come to mean to be revealed, to escape from secrecy to notice, and this use has been often denigrated, Johnson calling it "a sense lately innovated from France without necessity." With or without necessity, such meaning is justified in the extended sense of *transpire* to leak through or out. "This letter goes to you in confidence. . . . And you will therefore not let one word of it *transpire*" (Lord Chesterfield). But the use of *transpire* to mean happen or take place cannot be justified, although it occurs occasionally. "It *transpired* that he fell out with his friends" (Downey). However, *transpiration* is used almost entirely in its technical sense of passage, exhalation, or evaporation. "Plants give off a watery vapour by *transpiration* through the stomata" (Macnab).

Trap. A branch operation initiated automatically by hardware on detection of an unusual condition in the running of a computer program.

Travail (n & v). The noun *travail* arises from the medieval Latin *trepalium* (a three-pronged instrument of torture) and so means burdensome work, drudgery, suffering, or anguish, especially the pain of childbirth. "As everything of price, so this doth require *travail*" (Hook). "In the time of her *travail* twins were in her" (Genesis). The verb *travail* (to harass, vex, or fatigue) is no longer in great use but was commonplace in the eighteenth century. "As if all these troubles had not been sufficient to *travail* the realm, a great division fell among the nobility" (Hayward).

Treachery (n); Treason (n). Both words mean the deliberate, conscious betrayal of trust or confidence, but *treason* means only betrayal of one's country, faithlessness of allegiance to one's land. "I am justly kill'd with my own *treachery*" (Shakespeare). But "If this be *treason*, make the most of it" (Patrick Henry).

Tremble (v); Tremor (n); Tremulous (adj); Tremendous (adj). The four words derive from Latin *tremere* (to shake), and *tremble, tremor,* and *tremulous* share this meaning. "Indeed I *tremble* for my country when I reflect that God is just" (Jefferson). "He fell into a universal *tremor* of all his joints" (Harvey). "His voice unstrung grew *tremulous*" (Cowper). *Tremendous* means huge, gigantic, colossal, for it once meant causing *trembling* or quaking with awe at the great size or majestic image of something. "And is it true? And is it true,/This most *tremendous* tale of all,/Seen in a stained-glass window's hue,/A Baby in an ox's stall?" (Betzeman, *Christmas*). *Tremendous* and *fantastic* have become the two most faddish words in newspaper and broadside advertising, whose appeal lies in the two unshakable convictions that whatever is cheap is a bargain and whatever is expensive is good.

Tribute (n). Fowler says flatly that *tribute* means only a periodical payment made by one country or domain to another in token of submission or as the price of protection. Hence the use of *tribute* as "a testament to" is "a slipshod extension of the less excusable kind." Slipshod or not, countless testimonial dinners, festivities, ceremonies, and commentaries pay *tribute* to someone or something and are not likely to stop doing so. "The building was a considerable *tribute* to human ingenuity" (Cheever). Perhaps in La Rouchefoucauld's "Hypocrisy is a *tribute* which vice pays to virtue" there is the meaning of both testament and impost.

Triumphal (n & adj); **Triumphant** (adj). *Triumphal* and *triumphant* as adjectives both mean exulting in victory or success, but the noun *triumphal* usually denotes official celebration of victory or achievement. "O come, all ye faithful,/Joyful and *triumphant*" (translation of *Adeste Fideles*). "So strook with dread and anguish fell the Fiend;/And to his crew, that sat consulting, brought/Joyless *triumphals* of his hop't success,/Ruin, and desperation, and dismay" (Milton).

Trivia: See **Tedium.**

Truculent: See **Bellicose.**

Truncate (v). To *truncate* is to shorten by cutting, to lop off. "The examples are too often injudiciously *truncated*" (Johnson). In computer operation to *truncate* is to suppress insignificant digits of a number.

Trustee (n); **Trusty** (n). Confusion between the words is rare, but it does occur. A *trustee* is someone to whom property is committed in trust, and a *trusty* is a prisoner considered trustworthy and so allowed special privileges. Here the former is used to mean the latter: "Judson Kaines had been a *trustee,* a favorite of the warden's" (cited by *WDEU* from *Psychiatry*).

Tumult (n), Tumultuous (adj); Turmoil (n). Both nouns mean confusion and agitation, but to the purist *tumult* applies only to people and *turmoil* to both people and things. However, *tumultuous* applies to both. "The promised Prince of Peace should not be sought amongst the *tumultuous* hosts of warre" (Jackson).

Turgid (adj); Turbid (adj). *Turgid* [T U R jid]: Swollen, distended, and, hence, overblown, bombastic. "The advocates, who filled the Forum with the sound of their *turgid* and loquacious rhetoric" (Gibbon). *Turbid:* Not clear, opaque, obscured, confused, muddied. "Clear writers, like fountains, do not seem so deep as they are; the *turbid* look the most profound" (Landor).

Turkey (n). A generally agreeable, fearless, and delicious bird. "It was a *turkey*! He never could have stood upon his legs, that bird! He would have snapped 'em off short in a minute, like sticks of sealing wax" (Dickens, *Christmas Carol*). But the word itself is surrounded by mystery. Where did it come from? Apparently guinea hens imported from Africa, through Turkey and into England, were called turkey hens, Johnson defining *turkey* as a "large domestic fowl brought from Turkey." Somehow the indigenous American bird was confused with the similar African bird and also called "*turkey*," although *Columbia Encyclopedia* says without fear of contradiction that its name derives from its "turk-turk" call. How does it come about that a person getting down to the real point of an issue is said to "talk *turkey*"? There is an old and unlikely story that an Indian, being paid by a white trader in crows instead of promised turkeys, made the point that they shouldn't talk birds but should "talk *turkey*." Perhaps. Why is a stage performance that is exceptionally dull, poorly written and produced, and a financial failure called a "*turkey*"? Why too is a person inept, objectionable, incompetent, and disliked also called a "*turkey*"? No one really knows why a flop or a numbskull is called a *turkey*. And here we have Jane Austen using *turkey* in a figurative sense not of dud or flop but of fine embellishment. "A large income is the best recipe for happiness I ever heard of. It certainly may secure all the myrtle and *turkey* part of it."

Turncoat (n). A *turncoat* is one who forsakes his principles or his party, a renegade, a traitor. "Wine is a *turncoat* (first a friend, then an enemy)" (Herbert). When feudal lords maintained their own armies, each had a special livery for his swordsmen. A vassal leaving one master for the service of another turned his livery coat inside out so that he would not be mistaken for an enemy as he approached the land of his new feudal master. "*Turncoat* Windham to no party true" (Wolcott).

Turpitude (n). "As to Jimmy Carter the man, his integrity, his moral *turpitude*, his commitment to government and to family, he is unimpeachable" (cited by Safire). Clearly meant as unalloyed approbation, but unfortunately *turpitude* means baseness or depravity. Perhaps the writer had in mind "rectitude."

Typography (n), **Typographical** (adj); **Typology** (n), **Typological** (adj). *Typography* is the art of printing from type and the practice of its related processes and is also the appearance or character of printed matter. "The *typography* of both editions does honour to the press" (Boswell). But *typology* is the study of symbolic representations, especially those of religious literature; the classification of types and symbols. "The *Typology* of Scripture has been one of the most neglected departments of theological science" (Fairbairn). However, the adjective *typological* can also mean pertaining to the art of printing. "Future writers on the Invention of Printing should treat the question from a purely historical and *typological* point of view" (Trubner).

Ubiquity (n), **Ubiquitous** (adj). *Ubiquity:* Omnipresence, the state of or capacity for being everywhere, and by extension anything widely diffused. "Glittering generalities! They are blazing *ubiquities*" (Emerson). *Ubiquity* also has in theology the sense of the omnipresence of God. *Ubiquitous:* Omnipresent, everywhere, pervasive. "The *ubiquitous* and unabashed British tourist" (*Pall Mall Gazette*).

Ultima Thule (phrase). *Thule* is the ancient name of an island or point of land far north of Britain. Pliny says, "It is an island in the Northern Ocean discovered by Pytheas after sailing six days from the Orcades" (Orkney Islands). It was considered to be the northernmost limit of the earth and hence *Ultima* (farthest) *Thule* means the last extremity or end of the world. Virgil referred to *Ultima Thule* in the *Georgics* and meant by it the outermost boundary of the world, but it is sometimes used in lowercase to mean any mysterious distant region or remote objective.

Umbilicus (n), **Umbilical** (adj). *Umbilicus:* The navel, the omphalos, "the pit in the center of the abdominal wall marking the point where the *umbilical* cord entered in the fetus" (Stedman). *Umbilical:* Pertaining to the omphalos or the navel cord. "Birds are nourished by *umbilical* vessels, and the navel is manifest a day or two after exclusion" (Brown's

Vulgar Errours). *Umbilical* also has the extended meaning of conveying or central, as in an *umbilical cable* in rocketry or "The Chapter-house is large, supported as to its arched Roof, by one *umbilical* pillar" (Defoe).

Umbrage (n), **Umbrageous** (adj). *Umbrage* [UM brij] is actually the shade or shadow cast by foliage, but it has come to mean offense, distaste, and displeasure, and in this meaning is almost always used with *take*. " 'It appears the Americans have *taken umbrage.*' 'The deuce they have! Whereabouts is that?' " (*Punch*). But *umbrageous* is still primarily used to mean shady. "No cooling Grottoes, no *Umbrageous* Groves,/To win the Graces and allure the Loves" (Cumberland).

Umpire (n); **Referee** (n). Both words mean a person to whom something is referred for decision—one who adjudicates, as a *referee* in bankruptcy. However, in some sports a *referee* decides, but in others an *umpire* does. There is no rational basis for the difference. "Britton claimed the fight on a foul, but the *referee* disallowed the claim" (*Sportsman*). Or "And in case they can't Decide such Differences, then they shall be referr'd solely to the Decision of the said Sir Thomas Parkyns as *Umpire*" (*Wrestling*).

Un- (prefix). *Un* is a useful and engaging simple prefix. It means "not." What is not likely is unlikely. Whoever is not disturbed is undisturbed. Robert Lynd tells in a long-ago essay of some Dutch sailors in Portsmouth who became rollicking drunk and then belligerent, eventually punching and even biting some respectable British subjects. At the conclusion of their trial the magistrate addressed the Dutch sea captain gravely, "It is very Unenglish to bite people, and I should like you to impress this on your men." To which the captain replied with equal gravity, "It is very Undutch too, your worship." Here we see that *Un-* before national designations has a limited and chauvinistic use. The *Oxford English Dictionary* gives un-American a fairly ancient lineage. Under the date of 1818 it supplies this example: "Ninety marble capitals have been imported at vast cost from Italy and shew how *un*-American is the whole plan." The sentence illustrates that delicate use of *un-* in its connotation that anything not customary to or practiced by one's own people is either wrong or wrongheaded. Lynd asked a Scotchman if he had ever heard anyone use the adjective Unscotch, and he said he could not imagine it except in reference to Irish whiskey.

Unction (n), **Unctuous** (adj), **Unctuousness** (n); **Unguent** (n). *Unction:* The act of anointing or the anointing oil itself; in theology the bestowal of divine grace. "Thy blessed *Unction* from above,/Is comfort, life, and fire of love" (*Prayer Book*). An *unction* is also anything soothing but sometimes with the implication of self-serving or false comfort. "Mother, for love of grace,/Lay not that flattering *unction* to your soul" (Shakespeare, *Hamlet*). *Unctuous:* Oily, slick, suave, and, by extension, cloyingly pious or excessively smug. "The corrupt and *unctuous* forms of a mechanical religious profession" (Morley). *Unctuousness:* Oiliness and especially self-righteous smugness or pietistic display. "The coarse, self-exhibiting *unctuousness* with which his book overflows" (cited by *OED*). An *unguent* is an ointment, salve, or oil with none of the connotation of *unction*. "With *unguents* smooth, the lucid marble shone" (Pope).

Unequivocal (adj); **Equivocate** (v). To *equivocate* is to say one thing and mean another, to hedge one's statements, to prevaricate. "The witness shuffled, *equivocated,* pretended to misunderstand the questions" (Macaulay). Hence *unequivocal* means clear, unambiguous, having only one possible meaning and also unqualified, absolute, as in "acts of *unequivocal* hostility against his country" (Thirlwall).

Uninterested: See Disinterested.

Unique (adj). *Unique* means single or solitary in type or character; it is applicable only to what is in some respect the only existing specimen, the precise like of which cannot be found. Hence *unique* is an adjective without comparative or superlative degrees. No *unique* thing is more or less *unique* than another. Of course one does not often encounter uniquer or uniquest, but one does see the misuse of *more unique* and *most unique*. Here we see the word in its sense of singularity: "A thing so totally *unique*/the great collectors would go far to seek" (Taylor). But *unique*, when used with *to*, also means distinctively characteristic of, as in President Reagan's "This is not a condition *unique to* California."

Unless and until (phrase). Several critics make the same objection to this pointless combination of words as they do to "if and when." It is quite true that each of the conjunctions means something, but together they mean nothing that one or the other of them does not convey. *"Unless and until* the quota is met" means the same thing if either of the conjunctions is used alone, nor is the meaning made explicit if for *and* one substitutes *or.* A phrase, like "thanking you in advance" (q.v.), to be avoided.

Unmoral: See **Amoral.**

Unorganized (pp); **Disorganized** (pp). Both words mean lacking order or unity, but *disorganized* also implies upsetting or overturning an existing orderliness. "A succession of revolutions; a *disorganized* administration" (Macaulay). "The sustained fire threw their dense and *unorganized* masses into rapid confusion" (Froude). And, of course, *unorganized* also means not unionized. *"Unorganized* workers are powerless" (Browder).

Unqualified (pp); **Disqualify** (v), **Disqualified** (pp). *Unqualified:* Lacking the required qualifications. "It is no use sueing a quack. Why did you employ him? You know he is *unqualified"* (Kingslake). *Disqualified:* Deprived of qualifications. From *disqualify:* To divest of credentials or privileges; to render *unqualified.* "Strong passions and keen sensibilities may easily *disqualify* a man for domestic tranquility" (Stephen).

Unsatisfied (pp); **Dissatisfied** (pp). *Unsatisfied:* Feeling that expectations have not been met; discontent. "He seemed a good deal *unsatisfied* that the Spanish Ambassador had received the Advice from England" (Temple). *Unsatisfied* also means unpaid: "He was deeply in debt and had a number of *unsatisfied* judgments out against him" (Hitchman). *Dissatisfied:* Displeased, offended, disappointed. "I think I could turn and live with animals, they are so placid and self-contain'd;/ . . . Not one is *dissatisfied,* not one is demented with the mania of owning things" (Whitman).

Untimely death (phrase). "A common but really quite inane expression. When ever was a death timely?" (Bryson). The objection is valid, but it is also true that in this overused phrase *untimely* really means premature, and the WCTUer may justly lament the *untimely death* of the Volstead Act.

Urban (adj); Urbane (adj), Urbanity (n). *Urban* means pertaining to or characteristic of a city or city life. "For Cambridge people rarely smile,/Being *urban*, squat, and packed with guile" (Brooke). But *urbane* means having the polish and sophistication that are presumed to be characteristic of the social life of great cities. "A man remarkable for his talents and *urbane* manners" (Tooke). And *urbanity* means the character of being *urbane*, courtesy, refinement, or elegance of manner. "In the *urbanities* of social life, Athens was without an equal" (Felton).

Utopia (n), Utopian (adj). In the early sixteenth century Sir Thomas More published a book about an island called *Utopia* (*Nowhere*, from its Greek root), whose inhabitants enjoyed a life of tranquillity, sensible customs and laws, and unobtrusive government. Hence *utopian* means visionary, ideal, but sometimes with the implication of quixotic impracticality. More was a man of brilliant gifts, an idealist, and a devout Catholic. In 1529 he succeeded Cardinal Wolsey as lord chancellor of England but in 1532 refused to take the oath acknowledging the supremacy of Henry VIII over the pope. He was imprisoned and a year later executed for the principles and beliefs set out in his *Utopia*. Wordsworth too was in his youth a *utopian*, but in "The Prelude" he gives *Utopia* the sense of an unreal place. "Not in *Utopia* . . ./But in the very world, which is the world/Of all of us,—the place where in the end/We find our happiness, or not at all." Later, Samuel Butler would publish his bitter satiric novel *Erewhon* (an anagram of Nowhere) in which he brilliantly ticked off the English attitudes toward religion, science, custom, and law that make *Utopia* an unrealizable dream. And in his doomsday book, *1984*, George Orwell recognized that some of the very ideals of *Utopia* may be subverted—that efficiency, ease, and security may be purchased at terrifying cost, that law and order may become cruel oppression, that individual rights surrendered are freedom lost. Perhaps it was foreseen by Burton in *The Anatomy of Melancholy:* "*Utopian* parity is a thing to be wished for rather than effected."

Vacillate: See Fluctuate.

Vacuum (n); Vacuity (n), Vacuous (adj); Vacuousness (n). *Vacuum* (from Latin *vacuus*—empty) means a space devoid of matter; emptiness, void. "It is contrary to reason to say that there is a *vacuum* in which there is absolutely nothing" (Descartes). Hence the noun *vacuity* (emptiness, inanity) and the adjective *vacuous* (without content or ideas; witless, fatuous). "Thus the understanding takes repose in indolent *vacuity* of thought" (Cowper). "With that *vacuous* leer that distinguishes his lordship" (Thackeray). There is a noun *vacuousness*, a synonym for *vacuity*, that is no longer in great use but was once used to mean vacancy of countenance or fatuity of thought rather than mere emptiness. "The mistiness and *vacuousness* of abstract expression" (Gilchrist).

Vagary (n); Vagrant (n & adj). *Vagary* [vuh GAR ee *or* VAY gur ee] derives from the Latin *vagari* (to wander) and so means an unpredictable action, a caprice, a whimsical idea. "They chang'd their minds,/Flew off, and into strange *vagaries* fell" (Milton). *Vagrant* derives from the same root and, as an adjective, means wandering, nomadic, unsettled; as a noun, a wanderer, vagabond, beggar, or tramp. "That beauteous Emma *vagrant* courses took,/Her father's house and civil life forsook"

(Prior). *"Vagrants* who on falsehood live,/Skill'd in smooth tales and artful to deceive" (Pope).

Valuable (adj); **Valued** (pp). Anything *valuable* is of great worth or merit. "We present you with this Book, the most *valuable* thing that this world affords. Here is Wisdom; this is the royal Law; these are the lively Oracles of God" (English Coronation Service). But what is *valued* is esteemed, highly regarded, cherished—but it may or may not be *valuable*. "Secrets with girls, like loaded guns with boys,/Are never *valued* till they make a noise" (Crabbe).

Varied (adj); **Various** (adj); **Various and Sundry** (phrase). *Varied:* Characterized by variety; diverse, changed, altered; made different. "No man hath walked along our roads with step/So active, so inquiring eye, or tongue/So *varied* in discourse" (Landor on Browning). *Various:* Of different kinds, distinct, differing. "Unlike the hard, the selfish, and the proud,/They fly not sullen from the suppliant crowd,/Nor tell to *various* people *various* things,/But show to subjects what they show to kings" (Crabbe on books). *Various and sundry:* One of those descriptive but senseless phrases. Both words mean what each means.

Varlet (n); **Varmint** (n). A *varlet* was originally a servant or footman but has become a scoundrel, rascal, or rogue. "Thou, *varlet*, dost thy master's gains devour;/Thou milkst his ewes and often twice an hour" (Dryden). But a *varmint* has always been either vermin or an animal or person disliked, annoying, troublesome, or contemptible. "'These beaver,' said he, 'are the knowingest *varmint* I know'" (Irving).

Vehicle (n), **Vehicular** (adj). A *vehicle* is any means by which someone or something is transported or conveyed. "A private passenger *vehicle* is one registered to an individual with a gross weight of less than 8000 pounds" [*Meredith (New Hampshire) News*]. Almost all of us will qualify. In its figurative sense a *vehicle* is a medium of communication or expression. "Quarles was a kind of journalist to whom the *vehicle* of verse came more easily than the *vehicle* of prose" (Saintsbury). But *vehicular* almost always has the meaning of pertaining to a *vehicle* in its literal sense. "Places inaccessible to *vehicular* conveyances" (Byron).

Venal (adj); **Venial** (adj). These look-alikes have entirely different meanings. *Venal:* Willing to betray a trust; open to bribery; corruptible. "As the Senate is smaller . . . the vote of each member is of more consequence, and fetches, when *venal*, a higher price" (Bryce). *Venial:* Pardonable, excusable, not seriously wrong, trifling. "Our own laws not long ago punished forgery and even more *venial* crimes with death" (Yeats). Hence a *venial sin* is for Catholics a transgression against God's law committed without full awareness of its seriousness and so not depriving the soul of divine grace.

Verbiage (n). In its usual sense *verbiage* means wordiness. "The Matter, when cleared from the Perplexity of his abounding *Verbiage,* lies open to this easy answer" (cited by *OED*). But *verbiage* also means diction, wording, verbal expression without any connotation of excess. "Independently of this distinctiveness of *verbiage* there is a wide difference between the two Epistles" (Farrar).

Verdure (n), **Verdant** (adj). *Verdure:* Foliage, vegetation, especially grass or herbage. "Let twisted olive bind those laurels fast,/Whose *verdure* must forever last" (Prior). *Verdant* hence means green with vegetation, covered with plants or grasses. But from the idea of "green," it also means inexperienced, unsophisticated, immature. "I spoke of simple facts in my own experience with the idea of warning *verdant* purchasers" (cited by *OED*).

Veritable (adj). Many commentators dislike the word, especially Fowler, who regrets its nineteenth-century revival and says it "has always the effect of taking down the reader's interest a peg or two." Why? Because its function is often to prepare the reader or listener for an exaggeration that the writer or speaker avows to be the absolute truth. In its origin *veritable* meant simply truthful or factual, and Shakespeare uses it in this established sense. But here too there is some implication of truth not quite so truthful as it is claimed to be: "Most *veritable,* therefore look to't well."

Verse (n); **Stanza** (n). The word *verse* has many meanings, but technically it signifies one line of a poem and is often confused with *stanza,* which means an arrangement of consecutive lines of poetry unified by a pattern of rhyme or meter and making up one of several like divisions that, together, constitute a complete poem. "For rhyme the rudder is of *verses,/* With which like ships they steer their courses" (Butler). "I have adopted the *stanza* of Spenser—a measure inexpressibly beautiful" (Shelley).

Viable (adj). *Viable:* Literally, capable of living, appearing in this sense in *"viable* fetus." It has, however, become a faddish word meaning workable or practicable, capable of growth or stimulation. In this use it has attracted unfavorable notice, *The Saturday Review* saying it threatens "to become as fashionable among intellectuals and their camp-followers as *ambivalent* and *dichotomous."* Fowler joins the attack: "Nothing is durable, workable, lasting, effective, practicable any longer; *viable* must always be the word." No doubt the criticism is just, but *viable* in its new-fashioned sense is a highly popular, even expressive word. Can one really fault Max Lerner's *"viable* international order" or Joyce Carol Oates's *"viable* subjects for serious fiction"? (cited by *WDEU*).

Vicar (n), **Vicarious** (adj). A *vicar* is the incumbent of a benefice or a person acting in the place of the rector of a parish. The *vicar's* life is not always an easy one if we may judge by a limerick newspaper ad quoted by Baring-Gould: "Evangelical *vicar,* in want of a portable second-hand font, would dispose, for the same, of a portrait in frame, of the Bishop, elect, of Vermont." The sixteenth-century *vicar* was often buffeted by the winds of doctrine, but somehow the *Vicar* of Bray managed to retain both life and living during the religiously turbulent reigns of Henry VIII, Edward II, Mary Tudor, and Elizabeth I. He is memorialized in song. "And this is the law I will maintain/Until my dying day, Sir,/That whosoever king shall reign,/I'll still be the *Vicar* of Bray, Sir" (cited by Espy). A *vicar* is also a substitute, as in "God's *vicar* on earth." "An archbishop may not only excommunicate and interdict his suffragans, but his *vicar* general may do the same" (Ayliffe). And so *vicarious* means substitutive or participating in the experience of another through imagination. "I shall be considered as exercising a kind of *vicarious* jurisdiction" (Johnson).

Victim: See Martyr.

Vivid: See Livid.

Volatile memory. Memory that does not retain information when power is lost. Does this refer only to computers?

Volume. A unit of magnetic storage connected to a computer system.

Vulgar: See Popular.

Vulnerable (adj). *Vulnerable* (deriving from Latin *vulnerare*—to wound) means capable of being wounded. But in modern usage it almost always means open to attack, criticism, or temptation. "How delighted I am that I have found out where you are *vulnerable*" (Scott).

Warp (n); **Woof** (n). These words are no longer in common use, but together they mean the underlying basis upon which something is built, as in "English common law is the *warp and woof* of our judicial system" (Black). But separately, the words have distinctive meanings. The *warp* is a set of parallel threads running vertically on a loom; the threads running horizontally between these are the *woof* or *weft*. The fabric that results is the *web*. "Weave the *warp* and weave the *woof*,/The winding-sheet of Edward's race./Give ample room, and verge enough/The characters of hell to trace" (Gray).

Wax (v); **Wane** (v). Because these words are now rarely used, they are sometimes misused. *Wax* means to grow larger, to increase in strength or power, whereas *wane* means to decline in strength or power, to decrease or diminish. "Yon rising moon that looks for us again./How oft hereafter will she *wax* and *wane;*/How oft hereafter rising look for us/Through this same garden—and for *one* in vain!" (Fitzgerald).

Way (n), **Ways** (n); **Weigh** (v). The word *way* has many meanings: manner or mode; characteristic or habitual practice; a method for attaining a goal; a respect or particular; a path or course. However, *way* is in colloquial usage misused to mean away and to mean situation, as in "he is in a bad *way*." *Ways* is simply the plural of *way*, but, despite congressional precedent, the phrase *ways and means* is redundant, for both words mean the same thing. "Seated upon the convex mound/Of one vast kidney, Jonah prays/And sings his canticles and hymns,/making the hollow vault resound/God's goodness and mysterious *ways*,/Till the great fish spouts music as he swims" (Huxley). *Weigh* has nothing to do with the foregoing words, except that in nautical use, it is sometimes confused with *way*. A ship, in short, gets under *way* only when its anchor is *aweigh*—that is, free from the bottom or *weighed*. "I found about sixty of the convoy had lost their anchors in attempting to *weigh*" (Wellington).

Whence (adv); **Whither** (adv). *Whence* means from what place or what position, whereas *whither* means to what place or position. "Drink! for you know not *whence* you came, nor why:/Drink! for you know not why you go nor where" (Fitzgerald). "*Whither*, O splendid ship, thy white sails crowding,/Leaning across the bosom of the urgent West,/That fearest nor sea rising, nor sky clouding,/*Whither* away, fair rover, and what thy quest?" (Bridges).

Whereby (adv & conj); **Whereat** (adv & conj). Both words have been criticized by commentators as archaic or excessively formal, but both continue in good use. *Whereby:* By which or by what. "You take my life,/When you do take the means *whereby* I live" (Shakespeare). *Whereat:* At what or at which. "*Whereat*, I wak'd, and found/Before mine eyes all real, as the dream/Had lively shadow'd" (Milton).

Wherefore (adv). *Wherefore* means why, not where. "O *wherefore* was my birth from heav'n foretold/Twice by an angel?" (Milton). Confusion in its use may arise from the odd circumstance that *wherefore* is now primarily a noun meaning the reason for. "Good to know the whys, hows and *wherefores* of what you are seeing" (cited by *WDEU*).

Whether: See **If.**

Whether or not (phrase). Economy in use of words suggests that the *or not* is scarcely necessary, but the phrase is in constant good use. "Never knew *whether or not* to insert the names of his parents" (Updike). And when the clause so introduced has an adverbial function the *or not* should be retained, as in "Adhere to some kind of methodology, *whether or not* it works" (Daniels).

Which: See That.

Whippersnapper (n). An impudent, saucy fellow— someone younger, pushier, and more callow than the observer. *Young* is somehow implicit in the word, as if there could be no such thing as an old *whippersnapper*. "A *whippersnapper* of an attorney's apprentice . . . I'll teach him to speak with more reverence of the learned professions" (Scott). A good although, in Johnson's words, "injudiciously truncated example," for there may be lurking in it the slightest of implications that the saucy young fellow's disrespect for an ancient but devious profession had in it more truth than impudence.

Whither: See Hither.

Who (pron), **Whom** (pron). The rule for correct use can be stated simply. "*Whom* is used when it is the object of a preposition ('To *whom* it may concern') or of a verb ('The man *whom* we saw last night') or the subject of a complementary infinitive ('The man *whom* we took *to be* your father'). *Who* is used on all other occasions" (Bryson). But, alas, there is a proper but dismaying exception. When the pronoun follows a preposition but is the subject of a relative clause, it is the latter function that governs correct form. "They rent it to *whomever* needs it" (*Fortune*) is incorrect because the pronoun is the subject of the verb "needs." The sense of the construction is seen if the sentence is considered to say, "They rent it to any person *who* needs it." All clear as a bell, as in "For *Whom* the Bell Tolls," except for the awkward circumstance that wonderfully skilled writers often disdain the awkward *whom*. "Polonious: 'What is the matter, my lord?' Hamlet: 'Between *who*?' Polonious: 'I mean the matter that you read, my lord.'" Shakespeare wrote a century before strict grammarians would have had him say *whom*, but modern writers too sometimes favor an incorrect *who* over an ungraceful *whom*. "They become leaders. It doesn't matter *who* they lead" (Hemingway). What we don't know is whether Hemingway was careless, indifferent, unknowing, or consciously choosing a grammatically wrong but right-sounding word. If the last, one may imagine his oathful indignation at some blunderbuss editor's attempt to add the *m*.

Who's (contraction); **Whose** (poss pron). *Who's* is a contraction of who is, and *whose* is the possessive form of the pronoun who. Confusion between them arises because *who's* seems to have a possessive form. "*Who's* the Potter, pray, and who the Pot?" (Fitzgerald). "Yes, lad, I lie easy,/I lie as lads would choose;/I cheer a dead man's sweetheart,/Never ask me *whose*" (Housman).

Will: See Shall.

-wise (suffix). It all began with *clockwise*, but suddenly there was an unlikely rage for use of the suffix *-wise* to denote reference to, or manner, direction, or position of, in every conceivable and inconceivable way. Fortunately, a counterclockwise movement set in and the fever abated, but one can still admire the owl anxiously inquiring of his wife how their little owlet is doing wise*wise*.

Witness (v). To *witness* is to see or observe (especially in a legal context), but Bernstein and others say that one can *witness* an event, action, or occurrence but never a thing. In general this rule is followed—one may see the Brooklyn Bridge or *witness* its building. But there are instances in which the distinction between a thing and an occurrence may not be clearcut, as in Katherine Anne Porter's "The most bitter scene I had ever *witnessed*."

Won't (contraction); **Wont** (n & adj). *Won't* is a contraction of will not. "Will you, *won't* you, will you, *won't* you, will you join the dance?" (Carroll). *Wont* as noun means custom and as adjective accustomed. "Her lodger gave her, contrary to his *wont*, a signal to leave the room" (Scott). And "He might have more good qualities than she was *wont* to suppose" (Austen).

Woof: See Warp.

Would: See Shall.

Wrath (n), **Wrathful** (adj); **Wroth** (adj). *Wrath* is fierce anger, stern indignation. "Come not between the dragon and his *wrath*" (Shakespeare). *Wrathful* and *wroth* are both adjectives signifying angry, incensed, enraged. "Sad be the sights and bitter fruits of war,/And thousand furies wait on *wrathful* swords" (Spenser). "The Lord said unto Cain, why art thou *wroth*" (Genesis).

Wreak (v), **Wreck** (v). To *wreak* is to inflict or execute punishment or vengeance, to vent rage, malice, or ill humor, and is in modern times almost always used with *havoc*. "Nor is the feisty crew beyond *wreaking havoc* among themselves" (cited by *WDEU*). Occasionally *wreck* (to ruin or destroy) is wrongly used in place of *wreak*: "The isolationists *wrecked* their *havoc* by asserting that military and economic assistance were two different things" (*New Republic*).

Write. To transcribe data onto one form of storage from another form, for example, to transfer data onto a magnetic tape from the main memory of a computer. To *write* otherwise is neither so mechanical nor so easy. "He who would not be frustrate of his hope to *write* well hereafter in laudable things ought himself to be a true poem" (Milton).

Wrought (v). *Wrought* is a peculiar word. It is not the past tense of *wreak*, as is sometimes thought, but an archaic preterit and past participle of *work* that is still in substantial use. "What God hath *wrought*?" is a sentence from Numbers quoted by Samuel Morse in the world's first telegraph message. *Wrought* appears as the past participle of *work* in *wrought-up:* aroused, stimulated, perturbed. "Excited as I had been by my painful and *wrought-up* interest in his recital" (Bulwer-Lytton). But *overwrought* does not mean *overworked;* it means extremely agitated or distressed. "Spirits *overwrought*/Were making night do penance for a day/Spent in a round of strenuous idleness" (Wordsworth).

"X is a letter, which, though found in Saxon words, begins no word in the English language" (Johnson, *A Dictionary of the English Language,* 1755).

Xanthate, Xanthein, Xanthene, Xanthin, Xanthone (n's). These words do not appear in everyday speech, but both their meanings and spellings are frequently confused. *Xanthate:* An ester of xanthic acid. *Xanthein:* The water-soluble part of the coloring matter in yellow flowers. *Xanthene:* A chemical compound. *Xanthin:* The part of the coloring matter of yellow flowers that is not water soluble. *Xanthone:* A nitrogenous compound. Examples of usage would make tedious an otherwise instructive lesson.

Xanthippe or **Xantippe.** Socrates appears to have spent a fair amount of time away from home, and perhaps with reason, for he made his wife's name *Xantippe* [zan TIP ee] a byword for shrew; a quarrelsome, peevish wife. "An errant Vixen of a wife. . . . By this *Xantippe* he had two sons" (Fielding).

Xenophobia (n), **Xenophobic** (adj); **Xenolith** (n). *Xenophobia* is an unreasoning fear or dread of strangers or foreigners, and *xenophobic* means fearful of whatever is unfamiliar or alien. "The French peoples's notorious and inescapable *xenophobia"* (cited by *OED*). The word derives from the prefix *xeno-* (strange or alien, as in *xenolith*, a stone occurring in a stratum of rock to which it does not belong). One occasionally sees *xenophobia* ascribed to Xenophon, who, as a self-appointed Spartan patriot, no doubt hated foreigners but is better known for a kind of indulgent disregard for facts such as distinguished his biography of Cyrus.

Yarborough (n). A term beloved of complaining bridge players, and most bridge players are chronic complainers. Named after the Second Earl of Yarborough, born to nobility and losing at cards, it means a hand at whist or bridge in which no card is higher than the nine spot. "I have held *Yarboroughs* and been doubled and roughed all the evening" (*Blackwell's Magazine*).

Year (n). Proper use of the word *year* presents no problem except that it is sometimes not realized that after a man has had his fiftieth birthday he is in his fifty-first year, although he has not yet attained the age of fifty-one. In short, we are always one year ahead of our age in the sense of what year we are in. A newborn infant is in his first year; after his first birthday he will be in his second year.

Yester- (prefix). A combining form denoting an immediately prior period of time to the present time. For some reason other combinations than *yesterday* seem incongruous except in poetry. It is obvious that *yestereve* is shorter than yesterday evening, but what the word gains in economy it loses in a kind of false elegance. But perhaps *yesteryear* is acceptable. "Where are the snows of *yesteryear*?" (Villon).

Zany (n & adj). "A popular character in old Italian plays, who imitated with ludicrous incompetence the *buffoon,* or clown, and was therefore the ape of an ape; for the clown himself imitated the serious characters of the play" (Bierce). *Zany* as an adjective: Ludicrously comical, clownish, foolish. "He will make some of your *zany* squires shake in their shoes" (Blackmore).

Zeal, Zealous, Zealot: See Jealous.

Zenith (n); **Nadir** (n). Both *zenith* and *nadir* are terms taken from astronomy but, for no discernible reason, sometimes confused. *Zenith:* The point on the celestial sphere vertically above a given position—hence highest point or culmination. *Nadir:* The point on the celestial sphere directly beneath a given position—hence the lowest point or depth. "God's suffering for man was the *Nadir,* the lowest point of God's humiliation; man's suffering for God is the *Zenith,* the highest point of man's exaltation" (Donne). (See also *Nadir.*)

Zero (n); **Absolute zero; Zero in on.** The most interesting and useful of all numerals, *zero* means nothing, the absence of quantity, a goose egg. It is the foundation of the decimal system of numbers and the metric system of measurement. (Can one imagine multiplying roman numerals?) Discovered independently by Hindu, Babylonian, Arabian, and Mayan mathematicians, its absence was a severe handicap to the otherwise subtle mathematics of ancient Greece, for it alone makes feasible calculation in numbers of vast dimension, without which modern chemistry, physics, and astronomy would be impossible. Added to or subtracted from another number, it alters the order of its magnitude but leaves the number itself unchanged. Any number multiplied by *zero* is *zero*, but division by *zero* is undefined—there is no number that represents the value of a number so divided. "Unless my algebra deceives me, Unity itself divided by *Zero* will give Infinity" (Carlyle). *Absolute zero* is not an absolute cipher but the temperature (–273.15° Celsius or –459.67° Fahrenheit) at which all motion of atoms and molecules theoretically ceases. The phrase *zero in on* (to concentrate or focus on) arises from the simple circumstance that the center of a target is a round naught.

Zoology (n). Not a troublesome word except for its pronunciation. As Espy says, "There's no zoo in zoology." It's pronounced "zoh AHL uh jee," and it means the biologic science dealing with animals. "The term *Zoology* is practically restricted to the science of the outward characters, habits, properties and classification of animals" (cited by *OED*).

Zyzzyva (n); **Syzygy** (n). These words are scarcely on every tongue and are mostly for crossworders, double crosticians, and Scrabblers. But they are real, sometimes, confused, and often misspelled. *Zyzzyva:* A tropical weevil. *Syzygy:* The configuration of the earth, moon, and sun lying in a straight line. "Said a termite with sardonic leer,/'May I ask is the bar tender here?/I'll have a sweet *syzygy*/Or a *zyzzyva* maybe,'/ Said the bar, 'Have instead a small bier.'"

Z.Z.'Z." Progressive degrees of contraction. Also the sound a reader makes when he or she has gotten this far in the book.

Part two

Useful Foreign Words and Phrases

This is essentially a book on troublesome English words, so the reader may well ask why a section on foreign words and phrases. In the preface it is said that they too are frequently misspelled and misused and that is indeed so. A posh Los Angeles restaurant offers "Choice thin-sliced beef dipped in au jus." No doubt hustled in à la carte. But there is another reason for their inclusion—one, perhaps, more convincing to the author than the reader. In the course of finding suitable examples of the proper use of words from classical English literature, the author also began to turn up engaging foreign phrases. Some of them so compelling that this second section seemed a pleasant thing to put together. Who could resist the Spanish proverb, *Ante la puerta del rezador, nunca eches tu trigo al sol*? "Never put out your corn to dry before the door of a man of prayer." "A proverb," said Bertrand Russell, "is one man's wit and all men's wisdom." In the phrases to follow, the wisdom of philosophers will be but little represented. Poets will speak instead, for poem and proverb have the power to transfix ideas.

It is said that Boswell, hardly an expert linguist, kept a card file of classical Latin quotations and memorized selections from them for his endless talkfests with Johnson in which he managed to insinuate slyly subjects to which his quotations would be appropriate. Perhaps the reader too will occasionally spice up his or her own speech or writing with the sage observations of foreign authors. Like Boswell's lists, the foreign words and phrases appear under categories so that quotations suitable to a specific purpose or discussion may be readily discovered. This writer, too, must acknowledge some limitation in his choices arising from a scarcely expert knowledge of only Latin, Greek, French, and German, but acquaintanceship with Latin has allowed quotations rich in homely wisdom from Italian and Spanish sources. No one can manage all necessary feats. As the Spanish say, "No se puede repicar y andar en la procesión" ("You can't ring the bells and, at the same time, walk in the procession").

Absence

l'absence diminue les médiocres passions, et augmente les grandes, comme le vent éteint les bougies, et allume le feu (Fr, *La Rochefoucauld*): Absence diminishes commonplace passions and increases great ones, as the wind extinguishes candles and kindles fire.

Advices

a chi consiglia non duole il capo (It): The man with advice has no headache. Advice costs nothing. Advice is easier to give than to take.

à fripon fripon et demi (Fr): Set a thief to catch a thief.

aide-toi, le ciel t'aidera (Fr, *La Fontaine*): If you help yourself, heaven will help you. God helps those who help themselves.

aude sapere (Lat): Dare to be wise. Pay no heed to opposition of just ideas.

cantabit vacuus coram latrone viator (Lat, *Juvenal*): Travel light and you can sing in the robber's face. The beggar fears no thief.

Advices (cont.)

carpe diem, quam credula postero (Lat): Seize the day; believe
not in tomorrow. Eat, drink, and be merry, for tomorrow you may
die.

cave quid dicis, quando et cui (Lat): Take care what you say,
when and to whom you say it.

c'est une folie à nulle autre seconde, de vouloir se mêler à
corriger le monde (Fr, *Molière*): Of all human follies there's
none greater than trying to render our fellowmen better.

crede quod habes, et habes (Lat): Believe that you have
something, and you have it.

dans le doute, abstiens-toi (Fr): When in doubt about something,
don't do it.

défiez-vous des premiers mouvements parce qu'ils sont bons (Fr,
Comte de Montrond): Have no truck with first impulses as they
are always generous ones.

esto quod esse videris (Lat): Be what you seem to be.

fuyez les dangers de loisir (Fr): Avoid the dangers of leisure.

hänge nicht alles auf einen Nagel (Ger): Literally, don't hang
everything on one nail. Don't put all your eggs in one basket.

ignoscito saepe alteri, numquam tibi (Lat): Forgive others often,
never yourself.

il est bon de parler, et meilleur de se taire (Fr): It is good to
speak but better to keep silent. Speech is silver; silence is
golden.

il faut attendre le boiteux (Fr): It is necessary to wait for the
lame man. By implication—do not be too hasty both for the
sake of others and of yourself.

il faut cultiver notre jardin (Fr, *Voltaire*, the concluding words
of *Candide*): We must cultivate our garden. We must attend to

our daily duties and let the outside world do what it will. Work is the antidote to inevitable misfortune.

il faut manger pour vivre, et non pas vivre pour manger (Fr, *Molière*): One should eat to live, not live to eat.

illegitimi non carborundum (Pig Lat): Don't let the bastards grind you down!

il ne faut jamais défier un fou (Fr): Never argue with a fool.

il ne faut pas éveiller le chat qui dort (Fr): Do not waken the sleeping cat. Let sleeping dogs lie.

iniquum petas ut aequum feras (Lat): Ask for what is unfair that you may obtain what is fair.

in vino veritas (Lat): In wine there is truth. Discuss with drink; decide when sober.

jugez un homme par ses questions, plutôt que par ses réponses (Fr): Judge a man more by his questions than by his answers.

lauda la moglie e tienti donzello (It): Praise a wife but remain a bachelor.

maggiore fretta, minore atto (It): More haste, less speed. Haste makes waste.

minima ex malis (Lat): Choose the least of evils.

ne cede malis (Lat): Do not yield to misfortune.

ne fronti crede (Lat): Literally, do not trust the face. Don't be deceived by appearances. Don't judge a book by its cover.

ne puero gladium (Lat): Don't give a sword to a boy. Don't send a boy on a man's errand.

ne sutor supra crepidam (Lat): Shoemaker, stick to thy last.

ne tentes aut perfice (Lat): Either don't make the attempt or determine to succeed at it. If you try, try hard.

nimium ne crede colori (Lat): Put little trust in appearances.

Advices (cont.)

nitor in adversum (Lat): Struggle against adversity.

noli irritare leones (Lat): Don't vex lions.

noli turbare circulos meos (Lat): "Do not disturb my circles." The words of Archimedes to a Roman soldier who obstructed his view of a problem in physics that engaged his attention. The angered soldier is said to have killed the scientist.

non ex quovis ligno Mercurius fit (Lat): You can't make a statue of Mercury from any old log. You can't make a silk purse out of a sow's ear.

on ne choisit pas pour gouverner un vaisseau celuy des voyageurs qui est de la meilleure maison (Fr, *Pascal*): We do not choose as the skipper of the ship the best born among the passengers.

operibus credite, et non verbis (Lat): Put your trust in deeds, not words.

ora et labora (Lat): Pray and work. The motto of St. Benedict and of the Benedictine Order.

palmam qui meruit ferat (Lat): Let him wear the palm who has won it. The motto of Lord Nelson.

pars sanitatis velle sanari fuit (Lat, *Seneca*): To be cured, you must wish to be cured.

paulo majora canamus (Lat): Let us sing of more important matters.

percontatorem fugito, nam garrulus idem est (Lat, *Horace*): Avoid the inquisitive person, for he is certain to be a scandalmonger.

prends mois tel que je suis (Fr): Take me just as I am.

recoge tu heno mientras que el sol luciere (Sp): Make hay while the sun shines.

rem tene et verba sequentur (Lat): Master the matter and the words will follow.

respice, adspice, prospice (Lat): Look to the past, the present, and the future. A motto of many institutions.

respice finem (Lat): Look to the end of life. See things in the perspective of mortality.

respondeat superior (Lat): Let the superior answer. Let the principal reply for his agents.

revenons à nos moutons (Fr): Let us return to our sheep. Let's get back to the matter at hand. Sometimes quoted as "retournons à nos moutons."

sauve qui peut (Fr): Let everyone look out for himself.

spes sibi quisque (Lat): Let every man put his hope in himself.

surtout, point de zèle (Fr, *Talleyrand*): Above all, don't be too zealous (advice to politicians).

sutor ne supra crepidam (Lat): Shoemaker, stick to thy last.

tempori parendum (Lat): We should move with the times.

tiens à la vérité (Fr): Hold to the truth.

ut tamquam scopulum sic fugias insolens verbum (Lat): Avoid the exotic word as if it were a dangerous cliff. Caesar's advice to orators.

vérité sans peur (Fr): Literally, truth without fear. Speak truthfully and fear not.

vestigia nulla retrorsum (Lat): There are no returning footsteps. This is based on the fable of the fox who failed to visit the sick lion because there were no returning footsteps. But it's often used to mean: One can't go backward.

Anger

aeternum servans sub pectore vulnus (Lat, *Virgil*): Forever remembering an offense. Nursing one's wrath to keep it warm.

ut fragilis glacies, interit ira mora (Lat, *Ovid*): Like ice, anger melts if held for a while.

Aphorisms

à beau jeu, beau retour (Fr): One good turn deserves another; tit for tat.

à bon commencement bonne fin (Fr): A good beginning makes a good end.

absent le chat, les souris dansent (Fr): When the cat's away, the mice will play.

à chaque saint sa chandelle (Fr): Literally, to each saint his candle—honor to whom honor is due.

a chi fa male, mai mancano scuse (It): The wrongdoer will never lack excuses.

a chi vuole, non mancano modi (It): Where there's a will, there's a way.

ad astra per aspera (Lat): To the stars through hardship. Nothing good is gained without difficulty.

ad impossibile nemo tenetur (Lat): No one is held responsible for what is impossible.

ah, la belle chose que de savoir quelque chose (Fr, *Molière*): Ah, it's a lovely thing, to know a thing or two.

al primo colpo, non cade l'albero (It): At the first blow the tree does not fall. Rome was not built in a day.

amore è cieco (It): Love is blind.

animum fortuna sequitur (Lat): Fortune follows courage.

ante victoriam ne canas triumphum (Lat): Do not rejoice in triumph before victory. Don't count your chickens before they're hatched.

après la mort, le médicin (Fr): After death, calling the doctor. Locking the barn after the horse is stolen.

audentes fortuna juvat (Lat, *Virgil*): Fortune favors the brave.

aunque la mona se vista de seda, mona se queda (Sp): The monkey in silks is a monkey still.

au royaume des aveugles les borgnes sont rois (Fr): In the land of the blind, the one-eyed man is king.

aus den Augen, aus dem Sinn (Ger): Out of sight, out of mind.

batti il ferro mentre è caldo (It): Strike the iron while it is hot. Seize the moment.

beaucoup de bruit, peu de fruit (Fr): Lots of talk, little result.

boni pastoris est tondere pecus, non deglubere (Lat): It is the part of a good shepherd to shear his flock, not to skin it!

bonis nocet quisquis pepercerit malis (Lat): Whoso spares the evil harms the good.

Borgen macht Sorgen (Ger): Borrowing makes worrying. Who goes a-borrowing goes a-sorrowing.

buey viejo surco derecho (Sp): The old ox plows a straight furrow. A new broom sweeps clean, but the old broom gets in the corners.

cada uno es hijo de sus obras (Sp, *Cervantes*): Everyone is the result of his own actions.

(la) caridad bien entendida empieza por sí mismo (Sp): Sensible charity begins at home.

cassis tutissima virtus (Lat): Courage is the best protection.

Aphorisms (cont.)

celsae graviore casu decidunt turres (Lat): Literally, high towers fall with a greater crash. The bigger they come, the harder they fall.

c'est double plaisir de tromper le trompeur (Fr, *La Fontaine*): It is doubly pleasing to trick the trickster.

c'est un vin pur et généreux; mais nous avons bu trop du notre (Fr, *Taine*): [Equality] is a pure and noble wine, but we have drunk too much of ours.

(un) chien regarde bien un évêque (Fr): A cat can look at a king (literally, a dog can stare at a bishop).

chi fonda in sul populo fonda in sul fango (It, *Machiavelli*): He who builds on the people, builds on mud.

chi niente sa, di niente dubita (It): He who knows nothing has no doubts.

chi no fa, non falla (It): He who does nothing commits no errors.

(le) coeur a ses raisons que la raison ne connâit pas (Fr, *Pascal*): The heart has reasons that reason knows not of.

cogito, ergo sum (Lat, *Descartes*): I think, therefore I am.

consuetudo fit altera natura (Lat): Habit becomes second nature.

cucullus non facit monachum (Lat): The cowl does not make the monk. Appearances are deceiving.

culpam majorum posterio luunt (Lat): Descendants pay for the faults of their ancestors. The sins of the fathers are visited upon the children.

da Dios nueces al que no tiene muelas (Sp): God gives nuts to the toothless.

dalla rapa non si cava sangue (It): You can't get blood out of a turnip.

damnunt quod non intelligunt (Lat): They condemn what they do not understand.

decepit frons prima multos (Lat): First appearances are deceiving. The beard does not make the philosopher.

de gustibus non est disputandum (Lat): There's no arguing about tastes.

del dicho al hecho hay gran trecho (Sp): There's a long way from saying to doing.

delle ingiurie il remedio e lo scordarsi (It): The remedy for wrongs sustained is to forget them.

desunt inopiae multa, avaritiae omnia (Lat): Poverty has many wants, but greed wants everything.

di buona volontà sta pieno l'inferno (It): Hell is paved with good intentions.

Dieu défend le droit (Fr): God defends the right.

digo, paciencia y barajar (Sp, *Cervantes*): What I say is, patience, and shuffle the cards.

dolce far niente (It): It is nice to do nothing.

dolendi modus, timendi non item (Lat): There is an end to grief but not to fear.

(la) donna è mobile (It): Woman is fickle—an aria in Verdi's *Rigoletto*.

dove l'oro parla, ogni lingua tace (It): When gold talks, everyone else is silent.

due teste valgono più che una sola (It): Two heads are better than one.

dum vivimus, vivamus (Lat): While we live, let us live.

durum et durum non faciunt murum (Lat): Strong measures do not make a strong wall. Repressive acts do not provide security.

Aphorisms (cont.)

eadem, sed aliter (Lat): The same things but in a different way. Nothing changes but change.

Eile mit Weile (Ger): The more hurry, the less speed. Haste makes waste.

eine Schwalbe macht keinen Sommer (Ger): One swallow does not a summer make.

ejus nulla culpa est, cui parere necesse sit (Lat): The man who is forced to do something is not guilty of his act.

e meglio esser mendicante che ignorante (It): Better to be a beggar than an ignoramus.

e meglio tardi che mai (It): Better late than never.

empta dolore docet experientia (Lat): Painful experience is a good teacher. The burnt child shuns the fire.

ende gut, alles gut (Ger): All's well that ends well.

e sempre l'ora (It): Always the right time is now.

es ist nicht alles Gold was glänzt (Ger): All that shines is not gold. It is curious that Gray's "Nor all that glisters, gold" is almost always misquoted as "Nor all that *glitters*, gold."

exceptio probat regulum (Lat): The exception proves the rule.

exempla sunt odiosa (Lat): Examples are odious.

ex Oriente lux; ex Occidente frux (Lat): Out of the East light, from the West fruit. The Orient has given us religion and philosophy, the Occident productive industry and practical ideas.

experientia docet stultos (Lat): Experience teaches even the dull.

expertus metuit (Lat): Having had experience, he fears it. This refers to experience such as friendship of the powerful—so pleasant to the uninitiated, so bitter to the experienced.

faber quisque fortunae suae (Lat): Every man is the builder of his own fortune.

facile est inventis addere (Lat): It is easy to add to what has already been discovered.

facilis descensus Averno (Lat): The descent to hell is easy.

faire d'une mouche un élephant (Fr): To make an elephant out of a fly. To make mountains out of molehills.

fama nihil est celerius (Lat): Nothing travels more swiftly than scandal.

(la) fame vuol leggi (It): Hunger recognizes no law.

fata viam invenient (Lat, *Virgil*): The Fates will find a way.

felicitas multos habet amicos (Lat): Prosperity makes many friends.

felix quem faciunt aliena pericula cautum (Lat): He is fortunate whose caution arises from the errors (or perils) of others.

ferme acerrima proximorum odia (Lat): Hatred among close relatives is the bitterest hatred.

ferrum ferro acuitur (Lat): Iron is sharpened by iron. The brave are made braver by bravery.

fiat justitia ruat caelum (Lat): Let justice be done though the heavens fall.

fide, sed cui vide (Lat): Trust, but be careful whom you trust.

finis origine pendet (Lat): The end depends on the beginning.

flamma fumo est proxima (Lat): Where there's smoke there's fire.

Aphorisms (cont.)

forma bonum fragile (Lat): Beauty is fragile, a transitory blessing.

forma flos; fama flatus (Lat): Beauty a flower, fame a breath.

fortes fortuna juvant (Lat, *Terence*): Fortune favors the brave.

forti et fideli nihil difficile (Lat): Nothing is difficult to the courageous and the loyal.

fortis cadere, cadere non potest (Lat): The brave may fall but cannot yield.

fortuna fortibus favet (Lat, *Pliny*): Fortune favors the bold.

fortuna meliores sequitur (Lat): Fortune follows the better man. Successful men have all the luck.

fortuna multis dat nimis, satis nulli (Lat): Fortune gives to many too much—to nobody enough.

fou que se tait passe pour sage (Fr): The fool who is silent passes for a wise man.

fraus est celare fraudem (Lat): To conceal fraud is fraud.

froides mains, chaud amour (Fr): Cold hands, warm heart.

frugalitas miseria est rumoris boni (Lat): Frugality is wretchedness with a good name.

frustra laborat qui omnibus placere studet (Lat): He labors in vain who tries to please everyone.

fugit irreparabile tempus (Lat, *Virgil*): Irretrievable time flies by.

furor arma ministrat (Lat, *Virgil*): Rage provides arms.

gaudeamus, igitur, juvenes dum sumus (Lat): Therefore let us rejoice while we are young. "Gather ye rosebuds while ye may" (Herrick).

gaudet tentamine virtus (Lat): Virtue rejoices in temptation.

(la) génie c'est la patience (Fr): Genius is patience.

(les) gens qui hésitent ne réussissent guère (Fr, *Napoleon*): Those who hesitate rarely consummate.

gleich und gleich gesellt sich gern (Ger): Birds of a feather flock together.

(la) gloire et le repos sont choses qui ne peuvent loger en même gîte (Fr, *Montaigne*): Fame and tranquillity can never be bedfellows.

(i) grande dolari sono muti (It): Great sorrows are silent.

grande fortune, grande servitude (Fr): A great fortune is slavery.

gratia gratiam parit (Lat): Kindness begets kindness. Grace engenders grace.

grosse tête, peu de sens (Fr): Big head, little sense.

gutta cavat lapidem, non vi sed saepe cadendo (Lat, *Ovid*): Constant dripping wears away the stone.

(l') habitude est une seconde nature (Fr): Habit is (or becomes) second nature.

hasta la muerte todo es vita (Sp, *Cervantes*): While there's life there's hope.

heureux les peoples dont l'histoire est ennuyeux (Fr): Happy the people whose history is dull.

heute rot, morgen tot (Ger): Here today, gone tomorrow.

hodie mihi, cras tibi (Lat): Mine today, yours tomorrow—an inscription often found on old tombstones.

(l') homme absurde est celui qui ne change jamais (Fr): The foolish man is one who never changes his opinions.

Aphorisms (cont.)

homo homini lupus (Lat, *Plautus*): Man is a wolf to his fellowman.

homo mensura (Lat): Man is the measure of all things—a Latin condensation of a Platonic aphorism.

homo proponit, sed Deus disponit (Lat, *Thomas à Kempis*): Man proposes, but God disposes.

homo solus aut deus aut daemon (Lat): A man alone is either a god or a devil.

honi soit qui mal y pense (Fr): Shame to him who evil thinks.

honores mutat mores (Lat): Honors change manners or the characters of men. The elevated forget their humble origins.

honos habet onus (Lat): Honors bring responsibility.

horas non numero nisi serenas (Lat): I count only the sunny hours—an inscription often found on sundials.

(el) huesped y el pez hieden al tercero día (Sp): Guests and fish stink on the third day.

Hunde, die bellen, beissen nicht (Ger): Dogs who bark do not bite.

(l')hypocrisie est un hommage que le vice rend à la vertu (Fr, *La Rochefoucauld*): Hypocrisy is a tribute that vice pays to virtue.

iacta alea est (Lat, *Julius Caesar*): The die is cast (said by Caesar upon his crossing the Rubicon).

ich kenne mich auch nicht und Gott soll mich auch davor behuten (Ger, *Goethe*): I do not know myself, and God forbid that I should.

ignorantia facti excusat (Lat): Ignorance of the fact excuses. An honest error is not reprehensible.

ignoti nulla cupido (Lat, *Ovid*): One cannot want what he does not know.

il a les défauts de ses qualités (Fr): He has the defects of his virtues. The thrifty man becomes stingy; the brave man foolhardy.

il connaît l'univers, et ne se connaît pas (Fr, *La Fontaine*): He knows the universe but not himself.

il faut noter, que les jeux d'enfants ne sont pas jeux: et les faut juger en eux, comme leurs plus sérieuses actions (Fr, *Montaigne*): It should be noted that children at play are not playing about; their games should be seen as their most serious-minded activity.

il faut que la jeunesse se pas (Fr): Youth must have its way. Boys will be boys.

il n'y a guère d'homme assez habile pour connaître tout le mal qu'il fait (Fr, *La Rochefoucauld*): There is scarcely a single man sufficiently aware to know all the evil he does.

il n'y a pas de grand homme pour son valet-de-chambre (Fr): No man is a hero to his valet.

il n'y a que ceux qui ne font rien, qui ne se trompent (Fr): Only those who do nothing make no errors.

il n'y a qu'un seul vice dont on ne voie personne se vanter, c'est l'ingratitude (Fr, *Gérard de Nerval*): There is only one vice of which no one boasts—ingratitude!

il rit bien qui rit le dernier (Fr): He laughs best who laughs last. Await the outcome before rejoicing.

ils commencent ici par faire pendre un homme et puis ils lui font son procès (Fr, *Molière*): Here [in Paris] they hang a man first, and try him afterward.

il sent le fagot (Fr): He smells of the fagot. He is suspected of heresy. He is in trouble.

Aphorisms (cont.)

il y a peu de métiers honnêtement exercés, ou peu d'honnêtes gens dan leurs métiers (Fr, *Diderot*): Either there are too few professions conducted honestly, or there are too few honest people in the professions.

ingenium res adversae nudare solent, celare secundae (Lat, *Horace*): Adversity reveals, prosperity conceals genius.

in nocte consilium (Lat): Night brings wisdom.

in un giorno non si fe' Roma (It): Rome was not built in a day.

invidia festos dies non agit (Lat): Envy takes no holidays.

in vili veste nemo tractatur honeste (Lat): In shabby clothes no one is treated justly.

(le) jeu ne vaut pas la chandelle (Fr): The game's not worth the candle.

jus summum saepe summa est malitia (Lat, *Terence*): Law rigorous in the extreme is often wrong in the extreme.

labor ipse voluptas (Lat): Work itself is a pleasure.

labor omnia vincit improbus (Lat): Work overcomes every difficulty.

liberté, égalité, fraternité (Fr): Liberty, equality, fraternity—ideals of the French Revolution.

(dos) linages sólus hay en el mundo, como decía una abuela mia, que son el tenir y el no tenir (Sp, *Cervantes*): There are only two families in the world, as a grandmother of mine used to say: the haves and the have-nots.

lis litem generat (Lat): Strife begets strife.

locos y niños dicen la verdad (Sp): Madmen and children speak the truth.

lontan dagli occhi, lontan dal cuore (It): Literally, far from the eyes, far from the heart. Out of sight, out of mind.

(il) lupo cangia il pelo, ma non il vizio (It): The wolf may change his coat but not his character.

magna civitas, magna solitudo (Lat): A great city is a great seat of loneliness.

magna est veritas et praevalet (Lat): Truth is great and will prevail.

magna est vis consuetudinis (Lat): Great is the force of habit.

magnas inter opes inops (Lat, *Horace*): Poor in the midst of plenty.

magnum vectigal est parsimonia (Lat, *Cicero*): Frugality is a great source of income.

(la) mala erba cresce presto (It): Weeds grow fast.

male parta, male dilabuntur (Lat): Ill-gotten goods are ill disposed.

malheurs ne vient jamais seul (Fr): Misfortunes never come singly. Sorrows come not single spies but whole battalions.

mali principii malus finis (Lat): A bad end to a bad beginning.

mañana es otro día (Sp): Tomorrow is another day.

Man kann, was man will, wenn man nur will, was man kann (Ger): One can do what he wills if he wills to do what he can.

manus manum lavat (Lat): One hand washes the other. No one is altogether independent.

más han muerto porque hicieron testamento que porque enfermaron (Sp): More people have died because they made their will than because they were sick.

más vale saber que haber (Sp): Better wise than rich.

más vale tarde que nunca (Sp): Better late than never.

Aphorisms (cont.)

mater artium necessitas (Lat): Necessity is the mother of arts.

maxima bella ex levissimis causis (Lat): The greatest wars arise from the slightest causes.

maximum remedium est irae, mora (Lat, *Seneca*): Delay cures anger.

(le) méchant n'est jamais comique (Fr): The wicked man is never funny.

mendacem memorem esse oportet (Lat, *Quintilian*): A liar should have a good memory.

mens sana in corpore sano (Lat, *Juvenal*): A sound mind in a sound body (much-quoted phrase).

metter il carro innanzi ai buoi (It): To put the cart before the horse.

mi casa es su casa (Sp): My house is your house.

(les) morts sont toujours tort (Fr): The dead are always wrong.

mos pro lege (Lat): Custom has the force of law.

multis utile bellum (Lat): War benefits many.

mundus vult decipi (Lat): Most people want to be deceived.

muta est pictura poema (Lat): A picture is a silent poem.

mutato nomine de te fabula narratur (Lat, *Horace*): Change the name and the story could be told of you. The drama of life is universal.

natura lo fece, e poi ruppe la stampa (It, *Ariosto*): Nature made him and then broke the mould. Said of someone whose achievement is unique.

natura non facit saltum (Lat): Nature does not proceed by leaps but gradually and slowly.

natura vacuum abhorret (Lat): Nature abhors a vacuum (*Rabelais* citing a principle of ancient science).

necessitas non habet legem (Lat): Necessity respects no law.

nec lusisse pudet, sed non incidere ludum (Lat, *Horace*): The shame lies not in having a fling, but in not cutting it short.

nec scire fas est omnia (Lat, *Horace*): It is not permitted to know all things.

nemo dat quod non habet (Lat): No one can give what he does not have.

nemo judex in causa sua (Lat): No one should be a judge in his own case.

nemo mortalium omnibus horis sapit (Lat, *Pliny*): No mortal is wise at all times.

nemo propheta acceptus est in partia sua (Lat, *St. Luke*): No one is a prophet in his own country.

nemo repente fuit turpissimus (Lat, *Juvenal*): No one ever suddenly became depraved.

nemo solus sapit (Lat): No one is wise all by himself. All need the counsel of others.

neque quicquam hic nunc est vile nisi mores mali (Lat, *Plautus*): The only cheap thing around here nowadays is immortality.

nicht die Kinder bloss speist man mit Marchen ab (Ger, *Lessing*): Children aren't the only ones to whom fairy tales are told.

niente più tosto si secca che lacrime (It): Nothing dries so quickly as tears.

nil dictum quod non dictum prius (Lat): Nothing is ever said that has not been said before. There's nothing new under the sun.

Aphorisms (cont.)

nitimur in vetitum semper, cupimusque negata (Lat, *Ovid*): We always seek what is forbidden and desire what is denied. "Everything I like to do is either illegal, immoral, or fattening" (Alexander Wollcott).

nobilitas sola est atque unica virtus (Lat, *Juvenal*): The one and only nobility is virtue.

no hay cerradura si es de oro la garzua (Sp): There is no lock that a golden key will not open. Only a well-filled palm opens every door.

non datur tertium (Lat): No one gets a third chance.

non ogni fiore fa buon odore (It): Not every flower has a lovely fragrance.

non omne licitum honestum (Lat): Not every lawful act is honorable.

non omnia possumus omnes (Lat, *Virgil*): Not all of us can do everything.

non semper erit aestas (Lat): Summer does not go on forever.

noscitur a sociis (Lat): A man is known by his companions.

nous avons tous assez de force pour supporter les maux d'autrui (Fr, *La Rochefoucauld*): We always have enough strength to endure other people's misfortunes.

nul bien sans peine (Fr): No pains, no gains.

nulla nuova, buona nuova (It): No news is good news.

nullum est jam dictum quod non sit dictum prius (Lat, *Terence*): Nothing is ever said that hasn't been said before.

nunc patimur longae pacis mala (Lat, *Juvenal*): We are now suffering the evils of a prolonged peace.

obra de común, obra de ningun (Sp): Everyone's business is no one's business.

obscurum per obscurius (Lat): Explaining an obscurity by something still more obscure. The difficult made more difficult.

obsequium amicos, veritas odium parit (Lat): Acquiescence makes friends, the truth enemies.

(l') occasion fait le larron (Fr): Opportunity makes the thief.

o fortunatos nimium, sua si bona norint! (Lat, *Virgil*): How happy they would be if only they recognized their own blessings.

ogni bottega ha la sua malizia (Sp): Every shop has its tricks. There are tricks in all trades.

ogni medaglia ha il suo rovescio (It): Every medal has its reverse side. We only see one side of the story.

ogni pazzo vuol dar consiglio (It): Every fool's ready to give advice.

olet lucernam (Lat): It smells of midnight oil. It is a labored production.

omne ignotum pro magnifico est (Lat): Anything unknown is presumed to be magnificent.

omne solum forti patria est (Lat, *Ovid*): Every soil is a brave man's homeland.

omne tulit punctum, qui miscuit utile dulci (Lat, *Horace*): He pleases all who mixes the useful with the agreeable.

omne vitium in proclivi est (Lat): The road to vice is downhill.

omnia bona bonis (Lat): To the good all things are good—good men are often credulous.

omnia mutantur, nos et mutatamur in illis (Lat): All things change, and we change with them.

Aphorisms (cont.)

Omnia vanitas (Lat): All is vanity—in the old sense of in vain.

omnis comparatio claudicat (Lat): Every comparison limps. All comparisons are odious.

omnis definitio periculosa est (Lat): Every definition is hazardous. The watchword of lexicographers.

on connaît l'ami au besoin (Fr): You discover a true friend when you are in need. A friend in need is a friend indeed.

on doit se regarder soi-même un fort long temps, avant que de songer a condamner les gens (Fr, *Molière*): We should look long and carefully at ourselves before we pass judgment on others.

on ne se blâme que pour être loué (Fr): One belittles himself only to be praised.

on n'est jamais si malheureux qu'on croit, ni si heureux qu'on espère (Fr, *La Rochefoucauld*): One is never as unhappy as one thinks, nor as happy as one hopes.

opse theon aleousi myloi, aleousi de lepta (Gr): Though the mills of God grind slowly, yet they grind exceedingly small.

orator fit, poeta nascitur (Lat): The orator is made, the poet born.

otia dant vitia (Lat): Leisure makes vice.

où la chèvre est attaché, il faut qu'elle broute (Fr): Where the goat is tethered, there it must browse. Make the most of what's available.

(la) paix est forte bonne de soi; mais le quoit sert-elle avec des ennemies sans foi? (Fr, *La Fontaine*): Peace is good in itself; but what good is it if your enemies cannot be trusted?

(el) pan comido y la compañia deshecha (Sp, *Cervantes*): With the bread eaten up, up breaks the company.

panton metron anthropos estin (Gk): Man is the measure of all things.

para el que viene del cielo es la paciencia; para el que del suelo, la prudencia (Sp, *Gracian*): Patience is the virtue of the angels; for us, here on earth, prudence will do.

par le droit du plus fort (Fr): By the right of the strongest.

parturient montes, nascetur ridiculus mus (Lat, *Horace*): The mountains will labor and bring forth a laughable little mouse.

parva leves capiunt mentes (Lat): Little minds are captivated by little things.

pas à pas on va bien loin (Fr): Step by step one goes a long way.

pas de nouvelles, bonnes nouvelles (Fr): No news is good news.

(la) patience est amère, mais son fruit est doux (Fr, *Rousseau*): Patience is tart, but its fruit is sweet.

pedibus timor addidit alas (Lat, *Virgil*): Fear adds wings to the feet.

(i) pensieri non pagano dazio (It): Thoughts pay no duty. Ideas cross borders free of charge.

per angusta ad augusta (Lat): Through trials to triumphs. Same as *per aspera ad astra:* Through straits to stars.

pereunt et imputantur (Lat): The hours pass away and are charged to our account. An inscription frequently appearing on sundials.

periculum in mora (Lat): There's peril in procrastination.

peritis in sua arte credendum (Lat): The skilled artisan should be trusted to do his own thing.

per più strade si va a Roma (It): One may go to Rome by many ways. There are many ways of doing something.

Aphorisms (cont.)

petit à petit, fait l'oiseau son nid (Fr): Little by little the bird builds her nest.

petit chaudron, grandes oreilles (Fr): Little pitcher, big ears.

pietra mossa non fa muschio (It): A rolling stone gathers no moss.

plus aleos quam mellis habet (Lat): He has more gall than honey.

plus ça change, plus c'est la même chose (Fr): The more things change, the more they stay the same.

poca roba, poco pensiero (It): Little wealth, little care.

pondere non numero (Lat): By weight not number—by substance, not quantity.

possunt quia posse videntur (Lat): They can do it because they think they can.

prendre la lune avec les dents (Fr): To take the moon by your teeth. To reach for impossibilities.

presto maturo, presto marcio (It): The sooner ripe, the sooner rotten.

pretio parata vincitur pretio fides (Lat, *Seneca*): Faithfulness won by bribes is lost by bribes.

prior tempore, prior jure (Lat): First in time, first by right. First come, first served.

probitas laudatur et alget (Lat, *Juvenal*): Honesty is praised, but left to shiver.

prudens quaestio dimidium scientiae (Lat): A shrewd question is half of discovery.

quae fuerunt vitia mores sunt (Lat, *Seneca*): What were once vices are now customs.

quae nocent docent (Lat): Things that injure instruct. The child learns to walk by falling.

qualis vita, finis ita (Lat): As a life has been, so will its end be.

quand je me joue à ma chatte, qui sait si elle passe son temps de moi plus que je ne fais d'elle? (Fr, *Montaigne*): When I play with my cat, who knows whether she isn't amusing herself with me more than I am with her?

quand les vices nous quittent, nous nous flattons de la créance que c'est nous qui les quittons (Fr, *La Rochefoucauld*): When our vices abandon us we flatter ourselves with the belief that we abandoned them.

quand on ne trouve pas son repos en soi-même, il est inutile de le chercher eilleurs (Fr): When you find no repose in yourself, it is useless to look for it elsewhere.

quand on parle du loup, on en voit la queue (Fr): Talk of the wolf and you'll soon see his tail. Speak of the Devil, and there he'll be.

quantula sapientia regitur mundus (Lat): How little wisdom rules the world.

que aprovecha el candil sin mecha! (Sp): What use is a candle without a match?

que la nuit parait longue à la douleur qui veille (Fr): How long is the night to sleepless grief.

quel che pare burla, ben sovent è vero (It): Many a true word is spoken in jest.

quem deus vult perdere prius dementat (Lat): Whom the gods would destroy they first drive mad.

quem di diligunt adolescens moritur (Lat): Whom the gods love die young.

qui a bu boira (Fr): He who has drunk will drink again. Once a drunk, always a drunk.

Aphorisms (cont.)

quicquid praecipies esto brevis (Lat, *Horace*): Whatever your advice, let it be brief.

quid enim differt, barathrone dones quidquid habes an numquam utare paratis? (Lat, *Horace*): What is the difference whether you squander all you have, or never use your savings?

quid faciant leges, ubi sola pecunia regnat (Lat, *Petronius*): What use are laws where money alone holds sway?

qui docet discit (Lat): He who teaches learns.

qui donne tôt, donne deux fois (Fr): He who gives quickly gives twice.

quien calla otorga (Sp): Silence lends consent.

quien madruga, Dios le ayuda (Sp): God helps the man who rises early. The early bird catches the worm.

quien tiene dineros, tiene compañeros (Sp): Whoever has money has friends.

quieta non movere (Lat): Don't disturb things at rest. Let sleeping dogs lie. Don't fix what is working.

qui facit per alium facit per se (Lat): He who acts through another acts for himself. By acting through an agent a man cannot avoid responsibility for his acts.

qui me amat, amet et canem meum (Lat): Love me, love my dog.

qui nimium probat, nihil probat (Lat): He who tries to prove too much proves nothing.

qui non proficit deficit (Lat): He who does not go forward goes backward.

qui s'excuse, s'accuse (Fr): He who excuses himself accuses himself.

qui timide rogat, docet negare (Lat, *Seneca*): To ask timidly is to ask for refusal.

quod non opus est, asse carum est (Lat): What is of no use is dear at a penny.

quod volumus, facile credimus (Lat): We readily believe whatever we want to believe.

quoque magis tegitur, tectus magis aestuat ignis (Lat, *Ovid*): Hidden fires are fiercest.

quot homines, tot sententiae (Lat, *Terence*): As many opinions as there are men. Consensus is hard to come by.

radix omnium malorum est cupiditas (Lat): Cupidity is the root of all evils.

(la) reconnaissance de la plupart des hommes n'est qu'une secrète envie de recevoir de plus grands bienfaits (Fr, *La Rochefoucauld*): In most of mankind gratitude is merely a secret hope for greater favors.

(die) Religion ist das Opium des Volkes (Ger): Religion is the opium of the people. A famous phrase from *Karl Marx.*

rem acu tetigisti (Lat, *Plautus*): You have hit the nail on the head.

rex regnat, sed non gubernat (Lat): The king reigns but he does not rule.

rien n'est nouveau sous le soleil (Fr): There is nothing new under the sun.

rien de plus éloquent que l'argent comptant (Fr): Nothing speaks louder than money.

rien n'arrive pour rien (Fr): Nothing comes for nothing.

rien ne pèse tant qu'un secret (Fr): Nothing weighs so heavily as a secret.

Aphorisms (cont.)

rira bien qui rira le dernier (Fr): He laughs best who laughs last.

(el) sabio muda consejo; el necio, no (Sp): The wise man changes his ideas; the foolish man, never.

. . . s'altri puote offender di nascosto, e gran sciocchezza il nemico assalir palesemente (It, *Giraldi*): It is very foolish to attack one's enemy openly, if one can injure him in secret.

sanan cuchilladas, mas no malas palabras (Sp): The knife wound heals—not the cut from the tongue.

sans pain, sans vin, amour n'est rien (Fr): Without bread, without wine, love's not so fine.

scelere velandum est scelus (Lat, *Horace*): The criminal act requires concealment by another criminal act.

sdegno d'amante poco dura (It): The lover's wrath soon cools.

semper avarus eget (Lat, *Horace*): The avaricious man is always in need.

semper timidum scelus (Lat): The guilty live always in fear.

se non è vero, è ben trovata (It): If it's not the truth, at least it's a clever imitation.

sero venientibus ossa (Lat): Those who come late get the leavings.

sic transit gloria mundi (Lat): Thus passes away the glory of the world (spoken at the ordination of the pope).

sic vos non vobis (Lat, *Virgil*): Thus you labor but not for yourselves. The analogy here is to the beasts of the field who labor not for themselves but for others.

si jeunesse savait, si vieillesse pouvait! (Fr): If youth could only know; if age could only do.

similis simili gaudet (Lat): Like is pleased with like. Birds of a feather flock together.

si possis recti, si non, quocunque modo rem (Lat, *Horace*): Make money. Honestly if you can; if not, make it anyhow.

sit ut est aut non sit (Lat): Let it be as it is or not at all.

si vis pacem, para bellum (Lat): If you want peace, be prepared for war.

si vous lui donnez un pied, il vous en prendra quatre (Fr): Give him an inch and he'll take a mile.

sola nobilitas virtus (Lat): The only nobility is virtue.

(un) sot savant est sot plus qu'un sot ignorant (Fr, *Molière*): A knowledgeable fool is a greater fool than an ignorant fool.

sotto umbilico ne religione ne verità (It): Below the navel there is neither religion nor truth.

stemmata quid faciunt? (Lat, *Juvenal*): Of what use are pedigrees?

(le) style c'est l'homme (Fr): Writing style is the man himself. One of the aphorisms from Buffon's *Discours sur la Style*.

suaviter in modo, fortiter in re (Lat): Gentle in manner; resolute in deed. "Speak softly and carry a big stick."

sublata causa, tollitur effectus (Lat): Remove the cause, and the effect disappears.

summun jus, summa injuria (Lat, *Cicero*): The most rigorous law creates the most oppression. Justice in the extreme is injustice in the extreme.

sum quod eris, fui quod sis (Lat): I am what you will be; I was what you are. A gentle reminder on tombstones.

suppressio veri, suggestio falsi (Lat): To suppress truth is to suggest deception.

Aphorisms (cont.)

surgit amari aliquid quod in ipsis floribus angat (Lat, *Lucretius*): Something bitter always occurs to poison our sweetest joys.

tacent, satis laudant (Lat, *Terence*): Their silence is praise enough.

tel brille au second rang qui s'éclipse au premier (Fr, *Voltaire*): He who fails in the first rank may well shine in the second.

tempus edax rerum (Lat): Time devours all things.

tempus omnia revelat (Lat): Time discloses all things.

timeo Danaos et dona ferentes (Lat, *Virgil*): I fear the Greeks even when they bring gifts.

timeo hominem unius libri (Lat): I fear the man of one book. This can be interpreted in several ways. One of its principal meanings is: I fear the zealot, that is, the man whose learning comes from only one source.

tôt gagné, tôt gaspillé (Fr): Soon gained, soon spent. Easy come, easy go.

toujours l'épine est sous la rose (Fr): No rose without a thorn.

tout chemin mène à Rome (Fr): All roads lead to Rome. This can be interpreted as there's more than one way to get where you're going—or the end, not the means, is the important thing.

tout comprendre c'est tout pardonner (Fr): To understand all is to forgive all.

tout est bien qui finit bien (Fr): All's well that ends well.

tout le monde est sage aprés le coup (Fr): Everyone is wise after the event.

tout le monde se plaint de sa mémoire, et personne ne se plaint de son jugement (Fr): Everyone complains of his memory, but no one complains of his judgment. One of *La Rochefoucauld's* happier maxims.

(la) troppa familiarità genera disprezzo (It): Familiarity breeds contempt.

tutius erratur ex parte mitiore (Lat): It is better to err on the gentle side.

ubi jus, ibi officium (Lat): Where there is a right, there is also a responsibility.

ubi mel, ibi apes (Lat): Where there is honey, there are bees.

Übung macht den Meister (Ger): Apprenticeship makes the master. Practice makes perfect.

(l') ultima che se perde è la speranza (Sp): The last thing we lose is hope.

una golondrina no hace verano (Sp, *Cervantes*): One swallow does not make a summer.

una volta furfante e sempre furfante (It): Once a knave always a knave.

un bienfait n'est jamais perdu (Fr): An act of kindness is never lost.

un sot trouve toujours un plus sot qui l'admire (Fr): A fool will always find a greater fool to admire him.

usus est optimus magister (Lat): Experience is the best teacher.

vanitas vanitatum, et omnia vanitas (Lat, Ecclesiastes): Vanity of vanities, all is vanity.

varium et mutabile semper femina (Lat, *Virgil*): Woman is ever changeable and capricious.

vaso vuoto suona meglio (It): An empty pot makes the loudest noise.

Aphorisms (cont.)

venenum in auro bibitur (Lat): Poison is drunk in golden vessels. The poor need not fear the poisoner.

venter non habet aures (Lat): The belly has no ears. A hungry man is not interested in words, especially words of good advice.

vera prosperita e non necessita (It): True prosperity is to have no wants.

verba docent, exempla trahunt (Lat): Words instruct the mind, examples attract the mind.

veritas odium parit (Lat): Truth begets hatred.

veritas vos liberabit (Lat, St. John): The truth shall make you free.

veritatis simplex oratio est (Lat): The language of truth is simple.

vestis virum facit (Lat, *Erasmus*): Clothes make the man.

via il gatto ballano i sorci (It): When the cat's away, the mice will play.

via trita, via tuta (Lat): The beaten path is the safe path.

(la) vida es sueño (Sp): Life is a dream.

vincam aut moriar (Lat): I shall conquer or die.

vincit omnia veritas (Lat): Truth conquers all.

vincit qui patitur (Lat): He who is patient wins.

vincit qui se vincit (Lat): He conquers who conquers himself.

violenta non durant (Lat): Violence does not endure.

vir sapit qui pauca loquitur (Lat): He is wise who speaks but little.

virtutis fortuna comes (Lat): Good fortune is the companion of valor.

(la) visija quebrantada es la que nunca se acaba de romper, que enfada con su durar (Sp, *Gracian*): It is the cracked vessel that never gets completely broken that annoys you by its durability.

vitiis nemo sine nascitur (Lat, *Horace*): No one is born without faults.

volto sciolto e pensieri stretti (It): An open face but hidden thoughts.

vox et praeterea nihil (Lat): A voice and no more. Sound without sense or substance.

(le) vrai n'est pas toujours vraisemblable (Fr): Verity has not always verisimilitude. Truth is sometimes hard to believe or stranger than fiction.

vultus animi janua et tabula (Lat): The countenance is the portal and picture of the mind.

vultus est index animi (Lat): The face is the mirror of the soul.

was ich nicht weiss, macht mich nicht heiss (Ger): Whatever I know not doesn't make me hot. I don't get excited about things I know nothing of.

Weisheit is nur in der Wahrheit (Ger): Wisdom exists only in truth.

wie gewonnen, so zerronen (Ger): Easy come, easy go.

zartem Ohre, halbes Wort (Ger): To a sharp ear half a word is enough.

Appetite

à bon appétit il ne faut point de sauce (Fr): When there is good appetite, no sauce is needed.

Arms and Warfare

à main armée (Fr): By military force.

cedant arma togae (Lat): Let arms yield to the gown; military power should be governed by civil authority. Beware the military-industrial complex.

Eisen und Blut (Ger): Iron and Blood—Bismarck's motto for unrestrained use of force. Often translated in English as "Blood and Iron."

enfants perdus (Fr): Literally, lost children. Usually used in the military sense of a suicide squad or of troops in an indefensible position.

en grande tenue (Fr): In full military or formal dress.

flagrante bello (Lat): While war is still raging.

ils ne passeront pas (Fr): They shall not pass. Battle cry of the French at Verdun.

inter arma leges silent (Lat, *Cicero*): In time of war the laws are silent.

(der) Krieg ist lustig den unerfahrnen (Ger): War is an adventure to those who have not experienced it.

Macht geht vor Recht (Ger): Literally, might goes before right. The Bismarckian policy of reliance on the power of armed might.

nervi belli, pecunia infinita (Lat, *Cicero*): The sinews of war are limitless money.

paritur pax bello (Lat): Peace is born of war.

quarante hommes, huit chevaux (Fr): Forty men, eight horses. The indicated capacity of French boxcars during World War I. A famous phrase that inspired many societies of this name.

ubi solitudinem faciunt, pacem appellant (Lat, *Tacitus*): When men create a desert they call it peace.

ultima ratio regum (Lat): The ultimate argument of kings is war.

(une) victoire racontée en détail, on ne sait plus ce qui la distingue d'une défaite (Fr, *Sartre*): Once you hear the details of a victory, it is hard to distinguish it from a defeat.

vi et armis (Lat): By force of arms.

wollt ihr immer leben? (Ger): Do you want to live forever? Frederick the Great's question to his troops.

Art

alto relievo (It): High relief. Figures that project from a wall.

ars est celare artem (Lat): True art lies in concealing art. Art is without artifice.

ars gratia artis (Lat): Art for art's sake.

bas relief (Fr): Relief sculpture in which the figures project only slightly from their background.

chiaroscuro (It): The art of contrasting light and shade in painting.

école des beaux arts (Fr): School of fine arts.

pinxit (Lat): He or she painted it. Followed on paintings by the artist's name. Sometimes written *pnxt.*

sculpsit (Lat): He or she sculptured the work.

trompe l'oeil (Fr): A visual deception. A phrase used to describe paintings in which objects are rendered in such extreme detail as to give the illusion of tactile or spatial qualities. The phrase means literally "(it) fools the eye."

vita brevis, ars longa (Lat, *Seneca*): Life is short, art long. Often quoted as "ars longa, vita brevis."

Art (cont.)

xoanon (Gk): A simple carved image in which the original block of stone or wood is apparent.

Capability

aliquis in omnibus, nullus in singulis (Lat): Jack of all trades, master of none.

Cleverness

c'est une grande habileté que de savoir cacher son habileté (Fr, *La Rochefoucauld*): The height of cleverness is to be able to conceal it.

Criticism

equidem pol vel falso temen laudari multo malo, quam vero culpari (Lat, *Plautus*): I much prefer false compliments to sincere criticisms.

Courage

un équipage cavalier fait les trois quarts de leur vaillance (Fr, *La Fontaine*): A uniform provides three fourths of a man's valour.

Death

cineri gloria sera venit (Lat, *Martial*): Fame is too late bestowed on a man's ashes.

ho thanatos toioutos, hoion genesis, phuseos mustērion (Gk, *Marcus Aurelius*): Death, like birth, is one of nature's secrets.

in articulo mortis (Lat): At the point of death.

je veus . . . que la mort me trouve plantant mes choux, mais nonchalant d'elle, et encore plus de mon jardin imparfait (Fr,

Montaigne): I want death to find me planting my cabbages, but caring little for it, and much more for my imperfect garden.

lasciate ogni speranza, voi ch'entrate (It, *Dante*): All hope abandon, ye who enter here. Inscription on the gates of hell in Dante's *Inferno*.

l'on a le temps d'avoir les dents longues, lorsqu'on attend, pour vivre, le trépas de quelqu'un (Fr, *Molière*): You can get very hungry while waiting, if your livelihood depends on someone's death.

memento mori (Lat): Remember you must die.

mors communis omnibus (Lat): Death is common to all.

nos morituri te salutamus (Lat): We who are about to die salute thee. The greeting of Roman gladiators to their emperor.

Determination

la volonté aussi est une solitude (Fr, *Camus*): Determination is also a solitude.

ce n'est que le premier pas qui coûte (Fr): It is only the first step that is difficult.

Education

cum laude (Lat): With praise. *Magna cum laude* means with great praise, and *summa cum laude* with highest praise. These are phrases often used in the conferring of degrees.

education, c'est délivrance (Fr, *Gide*): Education is deliverance from bondage.

jurare in verba magistri (Lat, *Horace*): To swear by the words of a teacher. To believe implicitly in authority.

occidit miseros crambe repetita magistros (Lat, *Juvenal*): That cabbage hashed up again and again proves the death of the wretched teachers.

Evil

malum in se (Lat): Evil in itself. A crime against nature.

malum prohibitum (Lat): That which is wrong because it is prohibited, not because it is essentially or morally wrong.

muchas veces empeoran los malos con los remedios (Sp): Evils are often made worse by their remedies.

Exclamations

Deus avertat! (Lat): God forbid!

ecce homo! (Lat): Behold the man! The words with which Pilate presented Christ, crowned with thorns, to his accusers.

écrasez l'infâme! (Fr): Crush the vile system! The slogan of Voltaire and other forerunners of the French Revolution.

eheu! fugaces labuntur anni (Lat): Alas, how the fleeting years slip by.

e pur si muove! (It): "It still moves so." Recent evidence indicates that Galileo actually said this after he recanted his conclusion that the earth moves around the sun.

et tu, Brute (Lat): "And thou too, Brutus." In Shakespeare's *Julius Caesar* the last words spoken by Caesar in sorrow and surprise at the perfidy of his friend.

Eureka! (Gk): I have found it! An exclamation of triumph attributed to Archimedes upon his discovery of a method for detecting gold alloy.

flagellum dei (Lat): The scourge of God—a name given to Attila the Hun.

Hannibal ad portas (Lat): Hannibal is at the gates—a cry of alarm.

horribile dictu (Lat): Horrible to relate.

Italia irredenta (It): Unredeemed Italy. A phrase referring to Italian lands still not belonging to Italy after its unification.

mirabile dictu (Lat): Wonderful to relate.

mirabile visu (Lat): Wonderful to see.

miserabile dictu (Lat): Miserable to relate.

(une) nation boutiquière (Fr): A nation of shopkeepers. Napoleon's belittling phrase for the British.

O! si sic omnia (Lat): Literally, O! if all things were thus. Usually interpreted as: would that we had always acted so.

O Liberté, O Liberté, que de crimes on commet en ton nom! (Fr): O Liberty, O Liberty, what crimes are committed in thy name! Said by Mme. Roland just before her execution. Her husband had tried to save the life of Louis XVI.

O tempora! O mores! (Lat): O the times! O the customs! Cicero denouncing the degenerate ways of his day.

perfide Albion (Fr): Perfidious Albion. An epithet applied to England by the Emperor Napoleon.

place aux dames! (Fr): Make place for the ladies. Ladies first!

retro me, Satana (Lat): Get thee behind me, Satan.

vae victis! (Lat): Woe to the vanquished!

Fashion

beau monde (Fr): The world of fashion.

déshabillé (Fr): Informally or revealingly dressed.

en déshabille (Fr): Scantily clad. Wearing a dressing gown or peignoir.

haute couture (Fr): High fashion.

Food

à la carte (Fr): According to the menu. Apart from a dinner at fixed price.

au jus (Fr): Served in its own juice.

haute cuisine (Fr): Fine cooking. The preparation of food as an art.

haut goût (Fr): High seasoning.

vol-au-vent (Fr): A light flaky pastry filled with delicacies, often meat, in a sauce.

Friendship

ami de cour (Fr): A court friend; a false or unreliable friend.

si tous les hommes scavoient ce qu'ils disent les uns des autres, il n'y auroit pas quatre amis dans le monde (Fr, *Pascal*): If everyone knew what each said about the other, there would not be four friends left in the world.

ut pignus amicitiae (Lat): As a token of friendship.

Government

comitas inter gentes (Lat): Civility or courtesy between nations.

imperium in imperio (Lat): A state within a state.

Küche, Kirche, und Kinder (Ger): Kitchen, church, and children. An antifeminist slogan and policy of Nazi Germany.

laissez-faire (Fr): Literally, allow to pass. The name given the doctrine of noninterference in people's affairs, especially the theory of nonintervention by governments in the natural economic order of things.

oderint dum metuant (Lat): Let them hate so long as they fear— the philosophy of tyrants.

(la) parole a été donnée à l'homme pour déguiser sa pensée (Fr): "Speech was given to man in order to disguise his thoughts." Talleyrand said this in relation to the language of diplomacy.

plenum (Lat): Literally, full. A space filled with matter, as opposed to *vacuum*. Also a full or joint legislative assembly.

Realpolitik (Ger): Power politics. Policy based solely on material considerations.

salus populi suprema lex esta (Lat): The good of the people shall be the supreme law.

seditio civium hostium est occasio (Lat): Civil discord affords the enemy his opportunity.

siècle d'or (Fr): The golden age of Louis XIV.

(l')union fait la force (Fr): In union there is strength.

vivat republica (Lat): Long live the republic.

Greetings and Farewells

alla vostra salute (It): Your good health.

a rivederci (It): Till we meet again.

ave atque vale (Lat): Hail and farewell.

à votre santé (Fr): To your health.

a vuestra salud (Sp): To your health.

bene ambula et redambula (Lat, *Plautus*): Fare well and fare well when you return.

buena suerte (Sp): Good luck!

Dominus vobiscum (Lat): May the Lord be with you.

felice ritorno (It): Welcome back!

hasta la vista (Sp): Till we meet again.

Greetings and Farewells (cont.)

macte virtute esto (Lat): Go forth and prosper.

pax vobiscum (Lat): Peace be with you.

prosit (Lat): May it profit you. To your health.

vade in pace (Lat): Go in peace.

vale *or* valete (Lat): Farewell.

vaya con Dios (Sp): Go with God; farewell.

High Office

ad vitam aut culpam (Lat): For life or until fault is found. A phrase used to describe and limit tenure of appointed office.

chargé d'affaires (Fr): A substitute or stand-in for a high-ranking diplomat. An envoy to a state to which an ambassador is not sent.

functus officio (Lat): Having performed his duties—hence no longer in office.

sic temper tyrannis (Lat): "Thus always to tyrants." Words shouted by John Wilkes Booth after shooting President Lincoln.

sine cura (Lat): Literally, without care. An office without duties. A sinecure.

toga candida (Lat): The white toga worn in Rome by candidates for office. The badge of office seeking.

virtute officii (Lat): By virtue of the office one holds.

Honor

(la) honra el trono de al entereza (Sp): Honor is the throne of integrity.

mourant sans déshonneur, je mourrai sans regret (Fr, *Corneille*):
If I die without dishonor, I shall die without regret.

Knavery

buena fama hurto encubre (Sp): A good reputation may mask
thievery.

cosa nostra (It): Literally, our affair. The name of a secret
underworld society devoted to crime and manipulation of public
officials.

Knowledge

ab uno disce omnes (Lat, *Virgil*): From one example, you may
judge all the rest.

(les) gens de qualité savent tout sans avoir jamais rien appris
(Fr, *Molière*): People of quality know everything without ever
having been taught anything.

gnosis (Gk): Knowledge.

nous avons changé tout cela (Fr, *Molière*): "We've changed all
that." This is Sganarelle's answer in *The Physician in Spite of
Himself* when objection is taken to his statement that the heart
is on the right side of the body. The expression is used to
ridicule those who defend indefensible errors or those who
pretend to knowledge they do not have.

pons asinorum (Lat): Bridge of asses, a name given to the fifth
proposition of the first book of Euclid. Hence also a stumbling
block for the not so very bright.

Language and Literature

ab incunabulis (Lat): From the cradle. Also used to designate
books published from the invention of printing to the beginning
of the sixteenth century. Such works are called *incunabula*.

(la) belle dame sans merci (Fr): A beautiful lady without
pity—a phrase made famous as the title of a poem by Keats.

Language and Literature (cont.)

c'est une belle langue que l'anglais; il en faut peu pour aller loin (Fr, *Beaumarchais*): English is a fine language; a little of it goes a long way.

c'est une étrange entreprise que celle de faire rire les honnetes gens (Fr, *Molière*): It's an odd job, making decent people laugh.

c'est un métier que de faire un livre, comme de faire une pendule: il faut plus que de l'esprit pour être auteur (Fr, *La Brugère*): Making a book is a craft, as is making a clock; it takes more than wit to become an author.

chanson de geste (Fr): An epic poem telling of the exploits of medieval knights.

(La) Comédie Humaine (Fr): *The Human Comedy*—the title of Balzac's works portraying French society.

curiosa felicitas (Lat, *Petronius*): Nicety of expression, with the connotation of felicity achieved by studied effort.

de profundis (Lat): Out of the depths (of despair, sorrow, grief, etc.). The title of Oscar Wilde's essay of confession and despair written to Lord Alfred Douglas when Wilde was imprisoned.

Dichtung und Wahrheit (Ger): Fiction and fact; poetry and truth. The title of Goethe's autobiography.

double entendre (Fr): Double meaning or ambiguity. Used as a synonym for *double intente:* an expression that has two meanings, one of which is indelicate or risqué.

editio princeps (Lat): First edition.

(l')empire des lettres (Fr): The republic of letters.

errata (Lat): A list of errors in a published book.

(la) farce est jouée (Fr, *Rabelais*): The farce is over. His last words.

hiatus valde deflendus (Lat): A gap much to be regretted. Used at a break in ancient texts or when a person's performance falls short of expectation.

incipit (Lat): Here begins. Placed at the beginning of Latin manuscripts with the author's name and title of the work.

Index Librorum Prohibitorum (Lat): Index of forbidden books, a list issued by the Holy Office of the Roman Catholic Church of books to be read only in expurgated editions or by special canonical permission.

in medias res (Lat, *Horace*): In the middle of things. A technique of story telling in which one begins at a dramatic point and then backtracks.

je prends mon bien où je le trouve (Fr): "I take my stuff where I find it." Molière's response to the accusation of plagiarism.

licentia vatum (Lat): Poetic license.

lingua franca (Lat): The mixed language used between Europeans and natives of the Levant. Any language used as a means of communication among speakers of different language.

literae humaniores (Lat): Humane letters—studies of ancient languages, logic, ethics, metaphysics, and so on.

littera scripta manet (Lat): The written word remains. A phrase used to mean both the permanency of letters and a caution against rash writing.

livre de circonstance (Fr): A book worked up for the occasion. Sometimes in Hollywood a novel is commissioned in order that a film already underway may be described as based on a published book.

locus classicus (Lat): A frequently cited passage in a classical text.

lucidus ordo (Lat, *Horace*): An orderly arrangement, especially in a literary work.

Language and Literature (cont.)

Lysistrata (Gk): The title and heroine of a comedy by Aristophanes in which the wives of Athens and Sparta agree to withhold themselves from their husbands until the Pelopennesian War, then in its twenty-first year, be concluded. Lysistrata eventually dictates the terms of peace. Hence her name has become the symbol of feminist pacifism and feminine determination.

notitia linguarum est prima porta sapientiae (Lat, *Roger Bacon*): Knowledge of languages is the gateway to wisdom.

nugae literariae (Lat): Literary bagatelles.

omnis Gallia in partes tres divisa est (Lat, *Caesar*): All Gaul is divided into three parts—the famous beginning of Caesar's *De Bello Gallico*.

ore rotundo (Lat, *Horace*): Literally, with full round voice. Polished speech.

pereant qui nostra ante nos dixerunt (Lat, *Donatus*): May they perish who have said these things before we could!

raconteur (Fr): A teller of interesting stories.

rechauffé (Fr): Warmed over. Hence used to describe derivative literary works.

rogo, ut artificem, quem elegeris, ne in melius quidem sinas aberrare (Lat, *Pliny*): I ask that the copier you choose should not depart from the original, even to improve it!

roman à clef (Fr): A novel in which real persons are portrayed under fictitious names.

scribendi recte sapere est et principium et fons (Lat, *Horace*): The source of good writing is good sense.

scripta manent, verba volent (Lat): Written words stay, spoken fly away.

sic passim (Lat): It is so here and there or everywhere. Used to indicate that a word, phrase, or idea occurs repeatedly elsewhere in the same book.

stet (Lat): Let it stand. Often used in proofreading to indicate that material canceled or altered should be let stand as written.

variorum notae (Lat): The notes of commentators or the notes of differences in various texts of the same original.

virginibus puerisque (Lat): For girls and boys. Also the title of a collection of delightful essays by Robert Louis Stevenson.

Wahrheit und Dichtung (Ger): Truth and poetry. A phrase much in use among the German writers of the *Sturm und Drang* period. Also *Dichtung und Wahrheit:* Fiction and fact.

Laughter

je me presse de rire de tout, de peur d'être obligé d'en pleurer (Fr, *Beaumarchais*): I hasten to laugh at everything, for fear of being obliged to weep.

Law

accusare nemo se debet (Lat): No one is obliged to give testimony incriminating himself.

actus curiae (Lat): Act of the court.

agent provocateur (Fr): An undercover agent who encourages criminals or dissidents to commit crimes in which they will be apprehended.

amicus curiae (Lat): Literally, a friend of the court. An appointee to a court for the purpose of advice in a difficult legal issue.

argumentum ad hominem (Lat): An argument to the individual man—that is, to his interests or prejudices. Also an argument addressed to the character of an opponent rather than to the justice of his cause.

Law (cont.)

argumentum ad ignorantiam (Lat): An argument based on an opponent's ignorance of the facts at issue.

bon avocat, mauvais voisin (Fr): A good lawyer makes a bad neighbor.

cause célèbre (Fr): A celebrated case at law or a trial attracting wide attention.

corpus delecti (Lat): The basic element in a crime. The facts necessary to prove the perpetration of a criminal act. Literally, the body of the offense—not the body of a victim.

Corpus Juris Civilis (Lat): The body of civil law—Roman law as collected and codified by the Emperor Justinian.

Dei judicium (Lat): The judgment of God. Trial by ordeal. The survivor was considered innocent.

de internis non judicat praetor (Lat): The court does not consider a defendant's intentions.

de minimis non curat lex (Lat): The law does not concern itself with small matters.

droit du mari (Fr): The rights of a husband.

droit du seigneur (Fr): A nobleman's right to enjoy the bride of his vassal upon her wedding night.

Esprit des Lois (Fr): The spirit of laws—title of a greatly admired book by Montesquieu.

habeas corpus (Lat): Literally, you may have the body. In law a writ requiring a person to be brought before a court for investigation of restraint of liberty. Writs beginning with these words are a protection against illegal imprisonment.

habendum et tenendum (Lat): To have and to hold—a legal phrase often found in deeds.

ignorantia legis neminem excusat (Lat): Ignorance of the law excuses no one.

in camera (Lat): In the chamber of the judge; secretly, confidentially.

in custodia legis (Lat): In custody of the law.

in facie curiae (Lat): In the presence of the court.

in flagrante delicto (Lat): In the very act of committing a crime or offense against morals.

ipso jure (Lat): Legally; by the operation of laws.

ita lax scripta est (Lat): Thus the law is written.

judex damnatur ubi nocens absolvitur (Lat): The judge is condemned when the criminal is acquitted.

judicium parium aut leges terrae (Lat): Judgment by one's peers or by the laws of the land. One of the fundamental concessions to civil liberty granted by King John in the Magna Carta.

jure divino (Lat): By divine law.

jure humano (Lat): By human law.

jure uxoris (Lat): By a wife's right.

jus canonicum (Lat): Canon law. The laws of the Roman Catholic Church.

jus civile (Lat): Civil law. Specifically, rules and laws derived from Roman custom and legislation as opposed to those derived from other nations.

jus civitatis (Lat): The right of or to citizenship.

jus gentium (Lat): The law of nations—international law.

jus gladii (Lat): The right of the sword or the right to bear a sword.

jus hereditatis (Lat): The right of inheritance.

Law (cont.)

jus mariti (Lat): The right of a husband to his wife's property.

jus naturae (Lat): The natural law.

jus non scriptum (Lat): Unwritten law.

jus possessionis (Lat): The right of possession. Possession is nine tenths of the law.

jus proprietatis (Lat): Property rights.

jus relictae (Lat): The right of a widow to her husband's property.

jus sanguinis (Lat): Literally, the right of blood. The principle that the right of citizenship of a child is determined by the citizenship of his parents.

jus soli (Lat): Literally, the right of soil. The principle that the citizenship of a child is determined by the land where he is born.

jus suffragii (Lat): The right to vote.

justo titulo (Lat): By legal title; lawfully by reason of deed or privilege.

jus ubique docendi (Lat): The right to teach everywhere. An important license conferred by ecclesiastical authorities to university students in the Middle Ages.

laesa majestas (Lat): Lese majesty. Any crime or offense, especially high treason, against the sovereign power of a state, or an affront against the dignity or authority of a monarch.

laissez-passer (Fr): Literally, allow to pass. A permit, especially permission to leave one's country without a passport.

lex scripta (Lat): Written as opposed to unwritten law.

lite pendente (Lat): While litigation is pending or during a trial.

locus criminis *or* locus delicti (Lat): The scene of a crime.

locus standi (Lat): Literally, ground to stand on. The right to have a case heard in court.

(les) lois sont toujours utiles à ceux qui possedent et nuisibles à ceux qui n'ont rien (Fr, *Rousseau*): The law is always useful to the haves and vexatious to the have-nots.

Magna Carta (Lat): The Great Charter—the constitutional guarantees forced upon King John of England in 1215; now any bill of rights.

mandamus (Lat): We command—a legal writ commanding performance of a particular act.

mens legis (Lat): The spirit rather than letter of the law.

nemo bis punitur pro eodem delicto (Lat): No one should be twice punished for the same offense.

nihil dicit (Lat): Literally, he says nothing. A judgment that may be handed down against a defendant who makes no reply to the plaintiff's declaration.

nolle prosequi (Lat): A legal term meaning entry on the record that a plaintiff or prosecutor will proceed no further in a suit or action.

nolo contendere (Lat): Literally, I do not wish to contest. A defendant's plea that does not admit guilt but subjects him to punishment.

non est inventus (Lat): He has not been found. A statement of failure to deliver a subpoena.

nunc pro tunc (Lat): Literally, now for then. In law a phrase describing acts allowed to be done after they should have been done.

onus probandi (Lat): The burden of proof.

Law (cont.)

ope consilio; *sometimes written* ope et consilio (Lat): By aid and counsel. A term in civil law applied to accessories—same as the "aiding and abetting" of common law.

oyer and terminer (Fr): A half-French phrase applied to the assizes from the direction to the judges empowering them to "inquire, *hear, and determine* all treasons, felonies, and misdemeanors."

Oyez! (Fr): Hear ye! A word used in courts by the public crier to command attention when a proclamation is about to be made. Usually pronounced three times.

pacta conventa (Lat): The conditions agreed upon—used in either a legal or diplomatic context.

pactum illicitum (Lat): An illegal agreement.

pari delicto (Lat): Equally guilty or at fault.

pars rationabilis (Lat): That part of a man's estate required by law to belong to his wife and children.

particeps criminis (Lat): An accessory in crime.

partus sequitur ventrem (Lat): The offspring follows the mother. The brood of an animal belongs to the owner of the dam—a maxim of British common law usually applied only to animals.

patria potestas (Lat): Power of the father. In ancient Rome this extended to power over life and limb.

peine forte et dure (Fr): Cruel and unusual punishment. The phrase refers to pressing heavy weights on criminals until they confessed or died—a practice presumably abolished in the eighteenth century.

le pendente lite (Lat): Pending the outcome of litigation.

per curiam (Lat): By the court. Used in law to describe an opinion of the whole court as distinguished from one written by a single judge.

permissu superiorum (Lat): With the permission of superiors. A phrase found in approved Catholic books that has the force of *nihil obstat* or *imprimatur.*

per stirpes (Lat): By roots or stocks. In law the principle of dividing an estate by which descendants of a deceased legatee share as a group in the portion of the estate to which the deceased would have been entitled.

post litem motam (Lat): After the start of litigation. Depositions made after court proceedings have begun are so called.

potior est conditio possidentis (Lat): Literally, he who possesses is in a stronger position. Possession makes right.

prima facie (Lat): At first glance; presumably. In law used to describe a fact or evidence presumed to be true unless disproved by evidence to the contrary.

pro confesso (Lat): For or as confessed. To take for granted. A term applied to a bill in equity where the defendant has made no answer to it.

propter delictum (Lat): For or on account of crime. To take exception to a juror on grounds of past crime.

res adjudicata—*more correctly spelled* res judicata (Lat): A point or question that was in dispute and has been authoritatively settled by a court decision.

rustici (Lat): In feudal law the natives of a conquered country.

rusticum forum (Lat): An unlearned or unlettered tribunal. A term often applied to arbitrators in a case who are not expert in the law.

salvo jure (Lat): Without prejudice to one's rights.

Law (cont.)

scire facias (Lat): Literally, to cause to know. A judicial writ requiring a defendant in a lawsuit to show cause why the plaintiff should not have full knowledge of facts and records.

secundum legem (Lat): According to law.

sine praejudicio (Lat): Without prejudice. A phrase sometimes used at law to mean without already formed judgment.

strictum jus (Lat): The law strictly interpreted.

sub poena (Lat): Under penalty. A writ ordering a person to appear in court under pain of punishment. The usual method of procuring witnesses. Usually written as one word in English.

ubi jus, ibi remedium (Lat): Where there is a law, there is also a remedy.

ubi jus incertum, ibi jus nullum (Lat): Where the law is uncertain, there is no law.

ultra vires (Lat): Beyond authority. The exercise of power beyond legal limits.

u.s. (ubi supra, Lat): Where cited above. A notation in judicial acts directing that what precedes should be reviewed.

venia necessitati datur (Lat): Indulgence is granted to necessity. Necessity is above the law.

vis major (Lat): A superior force. A legal term covering circumstances beyond one's control.

volenti non fit injuria (Lat): No injustice is done to a consenting party.

Life

apologia pro sua vita (Lat): A defense of his life—not an apology—and so meant as the title of John Newman's autobiography.

Love

amor gignit amorem (Lat): Love engenders love.

il n'y a que d'une sorte d'amour, mais il y en a mille differéntes copies (Fr, *La Rochefoucauld*): There is only one kind of love, but there are a thousand different versions.

omnia vincit amor (Lat, *Virgil*): Love conquers all.

omnis amans amens (Lat): Every lover is a little bit crazy.

tomava la por rosa mas devenia cardo (Sp): I took her for a rose, but she proved to be a thistle.

Magic

elixir vitae (Lat): Essence of life; a magical potion that prolongs life.

lapis philosophorum (Lat): The philosopher's stone. An imaginary substance that turns base metal into gold—the object of unceasing search by medieval alchemists and sorcerers.

Palladium (Gk): The statue of Pallas Athene said to safeguard Troy. Hence anything that safeguards or provides protection.

Marriage

(le) divorce est si naturel que, dans plusieurs maisons, il couche toutes les nuits entre deux époux (Fr, *Chamfort*): Divorce is so natural that, in many houses, it sleeps nightly between husband and wife.

hombre cassado, burro domado (Sp): The married man is a tamed burro.

il y à de bons mariages, mais il n'y en a point de délicieux (Fr, *La Rochefoucauld*): There are good marriages, but no delightful ones.

Marriage (cont.)

mariage de conscience (Fr): A private marriage but also a marriage performed to satisfy some illegality or doubt in an existing marriage.

mariage de convenance (Fr): A marriage of convenience—one based on motives of material interest rather than on love.

mésalliance (Fr): Marriage in which one of the parties is of significantly lower social rank.

nuptias non concubitus sed concensus facit (Lat): Marriage is made not by cohabitation but by agreement.

Medicine

aegrescit medendo (Lat): He becomes ill from the treatment. The cure is worse than the disease.

belle indifférence (Fr): A neurosis characterized by indifference to one's condition.

caduceus (Lat): Insignia of Mercury; symbol of peace and of medicine.

c'est un homme expéditif, qui aime à depecher ses malades; et quand on a à mourir, cela se fait avec lui le plus vite du monde (Fr, *Molière*): He's an expeditious man, who likes to hurry his patients along; and when you have to die, he sees to it that it goes quickly.

crux medicorum (Lat): A puzzle for doctors—a difficult case.

Gott macht gesund, und der Doktor bekommt das Geld (Ger): God cures us, and the doctor takes the money.

graviora quaedam sunt remedia periculis (Lat, *Publilius Syrus*): Some cures are more dangerous than the disease.

hôtel Dieu (Fr): A hospital.

in perturbato animo sicut in corpore sanitas esse non potest (Lat): In the disturbed mind, as in the disturbed body, health is not possible.

materia medica (Lat): The remedial substances of medicine. Also the science of sources, characteristics, and use of drugs— pharmacognosy.

medice, cura te ipsum (Lat): Physician, heal thyself.

morbus Gallicus (Lat): The French disease—syphilis.

odium medicum (Lat): Hatred of physicians.

pia mater (Lat): Tender mother. Also the membrane enveloping the brain and spinal cord.

placebo (Lat): Literally, "I shall please" from the Office of the Dead. In medicine a substance of no pharmacologic effect but given to a patient either to please him or to study the effects of another, presumably effective drug agent.

post partum (Lat): After birth. In medicine, *postpartum*—the period following childbirth.

primum non nocere (Lat): First of all, do no harm. An aphorism of both Greek and Roman medicine.

sequela (pl. sequelae) (Lat): Consequence; result; in medicine an abnormal condition resulting from a previous disease or from therapy.

vis medicatrix naturae (Lat): The healing power of nature.

Moderation

aurea mediocritas (Lat): The golden mean.

est modus in rebus (Lat): Moderation in all things.

in medio stat virtus (Lat): Virtue exists in the middle. Moderation is the wisest course.

Moderation (cont.)

mediocria firma (Lat): Moderate ways are the most dependable.

tertium quid (Lat): Literally, a third something. A point in between two diametrically opposed positions. Something intermediate.

via media (Lat): The middle way or moderate course.

Old Age

bis pueri senses (Lat): Old men again are boys. In advanced years the aged become children.

senectus insanabilis morbus est (Lat): Old age is a disease that cannot be cured.

zhizn' nasha v starosti—iznoshennýi khalat: I sovestno nosit' ego, i zhal' ostavit' (Rus, *Vyazemsky*): Our old age is like a worn-out dressing gown; it shames us to wear it, yet we cannot bring ourselves to throw it away.

The Past

ab actu ad posse valet illatio (Lat): The past reveals the future. Literally: From what has happened can be estimated what will happen.

ancien régime (Fr): The former order of things. Often used to describe the social situation of France before the Revolution.

mais où sont les neiges d'antan? (Fr, *Villon*): "But where are the snows of yesteryear?"

Patriotism

amor patriae (Lat): Love of one's country.

ducit amor patriae (Lat): Love of country guides me.

dulce et decorum est pro patria mori (Lat, *Horace*): It is both sweet and honorable to die for one's country.

patria cara, carior libertas (Lat): My country is dear but freedom dearer.

ubi bene, ibi patria (Lat): Where all goes well, there is my fatherland.

ubi libertas, ibi patria (Lat): Where there is liberty, there is my homeland.

People

ad hominem (Lat): Literally, to the man. Directed to an individual's interest or character; personally. See also *argumentum ad hominem.*

(les) grands seigneurs ont des plaisirs, le peuple a de la joie. (Fr, *Montesquieu*): Great lords have their pleasures, but the people have fun.

interdum vulgus rectum videt (Lat, *Horace*): Sometimes the rabble sees what is right.

(le) monde ordinaire a la pouvoir de ne pas songer à ce qu'il ne veut pas songer (Fr, *Pascal*): Ordinary people are able to free from their minds those things they do not want to think about.

non Angli, sed angeli (Lat): "Not Anglos but angels." Pope Gregory I was supposed to have said this upon seeing fair-haired, fair-skinned Englishmen.

(la) petite bourgeoisie (Fr): The lower middle class—in France consisting largely of tradesmen.

posse comitatus (Lat): The force or power of the country. The whole population of a country above the age of fifteen that a sheriff may summon to his assistance in emergency situations.

vox populi, vox Dei (Lat): The voice of the people is the voice of God.

Philosophy

De Consolatione Philosophiae (Lat, *Boethius*): *The Consolation of Philosophy*—a once highly influential work.

ex nihilo nihil fit (Lat): Out of nothing nothing comes. A philosophic axiom justifying the eternity of matter.

hypotheses non fingo (Lat): "I do not make hypotheses." Sir Isaac Newton said this to indicate the factual rather than theoretical basis of his scientific ideas.

logos (Gk): Literally, a word or thought. In philosophy, the rational principle that governs the universe. In theology, the divine word incarnate in Jesus Christ.

nihil tam absurde dici potest, quod non dicatur ab aliquo philosophorum (Lat, *Cicero*): There is nothing so absurd but some philosopher has said it.

oderint dum probent (Lat): Let them hate as long as they approve—the philosophy of the complacent.

panta rei (Gk): Everything is in a state of flux. The philosophic doctrine of Heraclitus.

post hoc; ergo propter hoc (Lat): After this; therefore because of it. The fallacy of assuming that what goes before is the cause of what happens after.

primum mobile (Lat): The source of motion, the mainspring, the primeval force. In Ptolemaic astronomy the outermost of the ten concentric spheres of the universe.

(le) silence eternel de ces espaces infinis m'effraye (Fr, *Pascal*): "The eternal silence of infinite space frightens me." From Pascal's *Pensées*—fragments of a projected defense of Christianity.

Weltanschauung (Ger): A philosophical overview of the world.

Piety

ah, pour être dévot, je n'en suis pas moins homme (Fr, *Molière*): I am not the less human for being devout.

ante la puerta del rezador, nunca eches tu trigo al sol (Sp): Never put out your corn to dry before the door of a man of prayer.

nunca bien venerará la estatua en el ara el que la conocio tronco en el huerto (Sp, *Gracian*): The image on the altar will never be properly revered by the man who knew it when it was but a tree trunk in the garden.

Religion

ad majorem Dei gloriam (Lat): To the greater glory of God.

advocatus diaboli (Lat): The devil's advocate. Often used to describe one who argues for an unpopular cause or for the argument's sake. Also in the Roman Catholic Church an official appointed to present arguments against beatification or canonization.

anathema sit! (Lat): Let him be accursed. A phrase used in the condemnation of heretics.

apocrypha (Gk): Of unknown or doubtful authorship. Also the 14 books of the Old Testament not considered canonical and usually omitted from Protestant editions of the Bible.

beneficium clericale (Lat): Benefit of clergy—a medieval phrase meaning exemption from trial by civil authorities.

censor deputatus (Lat): A censor empowered to examine manuscripts before publication lest they contain things contrary to faith, morals, and law.

Corpus Christi (Lat): Literally, the body of Christ—a festival celebrating the Eucharist.

De Civitate Dei (Lat): *The City of God*—a famous tract by St. Augustine.

Religion (cont.)

Deum cole, regem serva (Lat): Worship God; serve the king.

Deus vult (Lat): God wills it—a battle cry of the Crusades.

en Dieu est tout (Fr): In God are all things.

ex cathedra (Lat): Literally, from the chair. A phrase describing utterances of the pope affecting the dogma of the Church or matters of faith and morals.

(eine) feste Burg ist unser Gott (Ger): A mighty fortress is our God. First line of a famous hymn by Luther.

gloria in excelsis Deo (Lat): Glory to God in the highest.

habeas papam (Lat): "We have a pope." Words spoken upon the election of a pope.

in hoc signo vinces (Lat): In this sign shalt thou conquer. The words seen in the heavens by the Emperor Constantine before his decisive victory over Maxentius.

in manus tuas commendo spiritum meum (Lat): "Into Thy hands I commend my spirit." Words of Christ spoken on the cross.

in nomine Domini (Lat): In the name of the Lord.

Kyrie eleison (Gk): The petition, "Lord, have mercy," used in various offices of the Greek Catholic Church and the Roman Catholic Church.

lavabo (Lat): The ritual washing of the hands of those celebrating Mass.

mater dolorosa (Lat): Mother of Sorrows—the Mother of Christ sorrowing for her Son.

no todos podemos ser frailes y muchos son los caminos por donde lleva Dios a los suyos al cielo (Sp, *Cervantes*): We cannot all be friars, and many are the ways by which God leads his own to eternal life.

odium thelogicum (Lat): Hatred among theologians.

ora pro nobis (Lat): Pray for us.

O sancta simplicitas! (Lat): "O holy simplicity!" Words spoken by John Huss when an old woman added a fagot to the fire in which he was being burned for heresy.

pontifex maximus (Lat): The Chief Priest or head of the Pontifical College of Rome. Literally, the word *pontifex* means bridgemaker.

pro Deo et ecclesia (Lat): For God and church.

quod Deus vult (Lat): What God ordains.

quo vadis? (Lat): "Whither goest thou?" The words spoken by Christ to Saint Peter when the deeply discouraged apostle was leaving Rome.

Religio Medici (Lat): *A Doctor's Religion.* The title of the best-known work of Sir Thomas Browne, in which he arrived at a warm and vital faith acceptable to the scientist.

Roma locuta, causa finita (Lat): Rome has spoken; the case is ended. When the pope renders a decision, debate ceases.

sanctum sanctorum (Lat): Holy of holies.

si Deus nobiscum, quis contra nos? (Lat): If God be with us, who shall stand against us?

si Dieu n'existait pas, il faudrait l'inventer (Fr, *Voltaire*): "If God did not exist, it would be necessary to invent him."

si Dieu veult (Fr): If God so wills.

Stabat Mater (Lat): Literally, the Mother was standing. The title of a thirteenth-century hymn commemorating the sorrows of the Virgin Mary at the Cross.

tantum religio potuit suadere malorum! (Lat, *Lucretius*): For how many evils has religion been responsible.

Religion (cont.)

uberrima fides (Lat): Absolute faith.

via dolorosa (Lat): The way of Christ to Golgotha. A sorrowful course or series of events.

viva il papa (It): Long live the pope.

vox clamantis in deserto (Lat, St. Matthew): The voice of one crying in the wilderness.

Remembrance

ad perpetuam rei memoriam (Lat): In perpetual memory of an event or occasion.

(les) bons souvenirs sont des bijoux perdus (Fr, *Valéry*): Good memories are lost jewels.

de mortuis nil nisi bonum (Lat): Speak nothing but good of the dead.

feig, wirklich feig ist nur, wer sich vor seinen Erinnergunen fürchtet (Ger, *Canetti*): He who is afraid of his own memories is truly cowardly.

j'ai plus de souvenirs que si j'avais mille ans (Fr, *Baudelaire*): I have more memories than if I were a thousand years old.

jucundi acti labores (Lat, *Cicero*): The recollection of past labors is pleasant.

memorabilia (Lat): Things worthy of remembrance. Things kept in memory of someone.

si monumentum requiris, circumspice (Lat): If you seek his monument, look about you. Engraved on Sir Christopher Wren's tomb in St. Paul's Cathedral.

Royalty

après moi le déluge (Fr): After me the deluge, said by Louis XV. Hence a phrase symbolizing despotism and wastefulness.

Dieu et mon droit (Fr): God and my right. Motto of the royal arms of England. There is some question here whether *droit* means right cause or right arm. If the latter, the sense is somewhat that of *Dieu est toujours pour les plus gros bataillons:* God is always on the side of the larger battalions.

(l') état c'est moi (Fr): "I am the state." The reply of Louis XIV to the president of parliament when the latter made suggestions concerning affairs of the state. Hence a symbol of autocracy.

Fidei defensor (Lat): Defender of the Faith, one of the titles of English sovereigns.

fleur de lys (Fr): Blossom of the lily. Heraldic emblem of French royalty.

(le) petit caporal (Fr): The little corporal. A sobriquet for Napoleon I.

(le) roi est mort. Vive le roi! (Fr): The king is dead. Long live the king! The salute by French courtiers to the new king when they had learned that the old had died. Hence also a greeting to any new departure or change.

(le) roi soleil (Fr): The Sun King—a name given Louis XIV.

tel est notre plaisir (Fr): Such is our pleasure. Words of approval by French kings.

vivat regina (Lat): Long live the queen.

vivat rex (Lat): Long live the king.

Self-interest

argumentum ad crumenam (Lat): An appeal to profit, that is, to one's self-interest.

The Stage

basso buffo (It): A bass singer in comic opera.

cape et epée (Fr): Cloak and dagger melodrama.

chant du cygne (Fr): Swan song—a final public appearance.

commedia dell' arte (It): Comedy of the guild of sixteenth-century Italian actors famous for improvisation.

così fan tutte (It): What all women do—the title of a comic opera by Mozart.

dramatis personae (Lat): A list of characters in a play. Sometimes used to mean the people involved in a real-life situation.

entr'acte (Fr): The interval between acts of a play.

exeunt omnes (Lat): All leave—a stage direction.

jeu de théâtre (Fr): A stage trick. An illusion.

mise en scène (Fr): A stage setting.

petite pièce (Fr): A minor theatrical production. Sometimes used to mean a curtain-raiser.

Travel

yā rayt kānū al-mutarjimin kulla-hum yikhrasū (Arabic): If only all guides were dumb!

Useful Words and Phrases

ab imo pectore (Lat): From the bottom of the heart.

ab initio (Lat): From the beginning.

à bon droit (Fr): With good reason.

à bon marché (Fr): At a bargain price.

ab ovo usque ad mala (Lat): From egg to apples—from soup to nuts.

absit invidia (Lat): Let there be no ill will. No offense intended.

absit omen (Lat): May this not prove to be an evil omen. The equivalent of "knock on wood."

a capite ad calcem (Lat): From head to toe; entirely.

accouchement (Fr): Act of giving birth; delivery. The period of confinement before and after childbirth.

à coeur overt (Fr): With open heart; frankly.

à contre coeur (Fr): Against inclination, unwillingly.

à coup sûr (Fr): With sure aim; accurately.

actus Dei (Lat): Act of God.

ad arbitrium (Lat): At will; by choice.

ad cautelam (Lat): For the sake of caution; prudently.

ad unguem (Lat): Literally to the nail. To a nicety; exactly.

ad unum omnes (Lat): To the last man.

ad valorem (Lat): According to its value; often used to describe a tax or import duty based on the value of goods.

aequabiliter et diligenter (Lat): Equably and diligently.

aequo animo (Lat): With a calm mind.

affaire d'amour (Fr): A love affair.

affaire d'honneur (Fr): An affair of honor; a duel.

affaire du coeur (Fr): An affair of the heart.

à fond (Fr): Literally at bottom; thoroughly or fundamentally.

a fortiori (Lat): With stronger reason; all the more so.

Useful Words and Phrases (cont.)

à haute voix (Fr): In a strong voice; loudly.

à huis clos (Fr): Behind closed doors; secretly.

aide de camp (Fr): Field aide, liaison agent for a general or other high-ranking officer.

à la belle étoile (Fr): Under the stars; in the open air.

à la bonne heure (Fr): In good time. Well done.

à la campagne (Fr): In the country.

à la dérobée (Fr): Stealthily; furtively.

à la lettre (Fr): Literally.

à la mode (Fr): According to the custom or fashion. Also, with ice cream.

al fresco (It): In the open air. Also painting on fresh plaster.

à l'improviste (Fr): Unexpectedly.

allons (Fr): Let's go.

alma mater (Lat): Fostering (dear) mother. Also a school from which one has graduated.

alter ego (Lat): Another self; a close friend.

alter idem (Lat): Another exactly similar.

alumna (pl. alumnae) (Lat): Foster daughter; female graduate of a teaching institution.

alumnus (pl. alumni) (Lat): Foster son; male graduate of a teaching institution.

amanuensis (Lat): Clerk; stenographer; secretary. Literally: Hand servant.

a maximis ad minima (Lat): From the largest to the smallest.

ambigendi locus (Lat): Room for doubt.

ame perdue (Fr): A lost soul.

à merveille (Fr): To a wonder; very well done.

amicus humani generis (Lat): Friend to humankind.

à moitié (Fr): By halves.

à mon avis (Fr): In my opinion.

amor fati (Lat): Acceptance of fate—even cherishing whatever ills life brings.

amour propre (Fr): Self-respect, self-esteem, vanity.

animo et fide (Lat): With courage and faithfulness.

animus (Lat): Mind; intention; disposition. Also hostile feeling.

annus mirabilis (Lat): Amazing Year—often used in reference to the year 1666, when plague and conflagration visited London.

ante bellum (Lat): Before the war. Specifically, before the Civil War in the United States.

à perte de vue (Fr): As far as the eye can reach; beyond one's view.

a point (Fr): Precisely, correctly, just in time.

a posteriori (Lat): A conclusion reached from data rather than from pure reason. See *a priori*.

a primo ad ultimum (Lat): From first to last; from beginning to end.

a priori (Lat): Reasoning derived from hypothetical propositions rather than from data. See *a posteriori*.

à propos de rien (Fr): Apropos of nothing; with reference to nothing in particular.

arcana caelestia (Lat): Celestial mysteries.

Useful Words and Phrases (cont.)

arcana imperii (Lat): State secrets.

argot (Fr): Thieves' slang; jargon.

argumenti gratia (Lat): For argument's sake.

argumentum ad invidiam (Lat): An appeal to envy or jealousy.

argumentum ad judicium (Lat): An argument appealing to judgment or fairness.

argumentum ad misericordiam (Lat): Appeal to pity or sympathy.

argumentum a fortiori (Lat): Argument by analogy or by previous concession.

arrière pensée (Fr): Mental reservation.

athenaeum (Gk): Temple of Athena—goddess of wisdom. Hence a meeting place of philosophers, writers, or men of learning; a lecture hall.

à tort et à travers (Fr): At random; without reflection.

à tort ou à raison (Fr): Rightly or wrongly.

à toute force (Fr): With all one's might.

à tout prix (Fr): At any cost.

au bon droit (Fr): Justly or rightly.

au courant (Fr): Fully acquainted with matters or with the matter at hand.

au désespoir (Fr): In despair; desperately.

au fait (Fr): Skilled; informed.

au fond (Fr): Basically.

au naturel (Fr): In natural style or in the nude.

au pis aller (Fr): At the worst.

aussitôt dit, aussitôt fait (Fr): No sooner said than done.

autres temps, autres moeurs (Fr): Other times, other customs.

avant-garde (Fr): Literally, a forward guard. By extension, leading the way in new art forms.

a verbis ad verbera (Lat): From words to blows.

bagatelle (Fr): A trifle; a brief musical composition.

ballon d'essai (Fr): A trial balloon.

bas bleu (Fr): Literally, blue stocking—a phrase used to describe women interested in matters intellectual or artistic.

beatae pacifici (Lat): Blessed are the peacemakers—one of the beatitudes.

beau geste (Fr): A generous gesture.

beau idéal (Fr): The model of perfection.

beaux esprits (Fr): Men of wit.

belles-lettres (Fr): Literature; poetry; literary criticism.

bête noire (Fr): Black beast—one's pet aversion; a bugbear.

betise (Fr): A piece of stupidity.

bien entendu (Fr): Well understood; of course; naturally.

bona fide (Lat, bonae fidei): In good faith.

bonanza (Sp): Fair weather; a run of good luck, unexpected good fortune.

bon gré, mal gré (Fr): With good or ill grace; willingly or unwillingly.

bonis avibus (Lat): Under favorable auspices.

bon mot (Fr): A witticism.

Useful Words and Phrases (cont.)

bonne bouche (Fr): A delicate morsel; a tidbit.

bonne foi (Fr): Good faith; honest intent.

(le) bon temps viendra (Fr): Good times are coming.

bon ton (Fr): Excellent fashion or appearance.

bonum commune (Lat): The common good.

bon vivant (Fr): One fond of luxury and good living; a gourmet; an epicure.

boulevardier (Fr): Pleasure-seeker; frequenter of cafés and theaters.

bourse (Fr): Purse; stock exchange.

bravura (It): A display of great dexterity or spirit.

brutum fulmen (Lat): A harmless thunderbolt; an idle threat; a paper tiger.

caballero (Sp): Knight; cavalier; gentleman.

cacoethes scribendi (Lat, *Juvenal*): The writer's itch; the urge to write.

cadit quaestio (Lat): The argument falls; there is no need for further discussion.

caeca est invidus (Lat): Envy is blind.

ça ira (Fr): It will go on. A phrase applied to the hanging of aristocrats during the French Revolution.

cambio (Sp): Change; exchange.

camera lucida (Lat): Bright chamber. A device to project an image on drawing paper.

camera obscura (Lat): Dark chamber. A device to project an inverted image on a surface. Precursor of the box camera.

canis in praesepi (Lat): Dog in the manger. A phrase used to describe those who prevent others from enjoying a benefit of which they themselves cannot partake.

cap à pie (Fr): From head to foot.

carpe diem (Lat): Literally, seize the day. Enjoy the present.

carte blanche (Fr): Literally, a blank page. The opportunity or right to do what one wishes.

cartouche (Fr): An ornament with space for an inscription; any oval design.

castella in Hispania (Lat): Castles in Spain. Daydreams.

casus belli (Lat): The cause, justification, or pretext for war.

casus fortuitus (Lat): A matter of luck.

catalogue raisonné (Fr): A catalog of books or other articles developed according to a plan and in which each item is described or appraised.

causa sine qua non (Lat): An indispensable cause or condition.

caveat emptor (Lat): Let the buyer beware.

caveat venditor (Lat): Let the seller beware.

cavendo tutus (Lat): Safe through prudence.

cela m'est égal (Fr): It's all the same to me.

cela ne fit rien (Fr): That makes no difference.

cela va sans dire (Fr): It goes without saying.

c'est à dire (Fr): That is to say.

c'est la guerre (Fr): That's war for you. Blame it on the war.

c'est la vie (Fr): That's the way life is.

Useful Words and Phrases (cont.)

c'est le commencement de la fin (Fr): It is the beginning of the end.

cetera desunt (Lat): The rest is missing or here there is a break.

ceteris paribus (Lat): Other things being equal.

chacun à son goût (Fr): Everyone to his own taste.

chacun à son marotte (Fr): Everyone follows his own notions.

chacun tire de son côté (Fr): Everyone favors his own side.

chef d'oeuvre (Fr): A masterpiece.

cherchez la femme (Fr, *Dumas*): Literally, seek for the woman. There's a woman at the bottom of most difficulties, problems, and crimes. A favorite motto of fictional detectives.

che sarà sarà (It): What will be will be. Accept things as they come.

chevalier d'industrie (Fr): One who lives by his wits—a rogue or swindler.

chi ama, crede (It): He who loves also trusts.

chi los sa? (It): Who knows?

chi tace acconsente (It): Silence means consent.

chi tace confessa (It): He who keeps silent confesses guilt.

circulus vitiosus (Lat): A vicious circle.

civis Romanus sum (Lat): I am a Roman citizen—once a badge of distinction and almost a universal passport.

clarior e tenebris (Lat): Made brighter by darkness.

clarum et venerabile nomen (Lat): An illustrious and venerable name.

codex (Lat): A collection of laws. A manuscript written on parchment.

coloratura (It): Embellishments in vocal music. A soprano who sings such parts.

comme ci comma ça (Fr): So-so. Neither good nor bad.

comme il faut (Fr): As it should be; as is proper.

commune bonum (Lat): The common good.

compos mentis (Lat): Of sound mind.

compte rendu (Fr): An account rendered; a report of affairs or proceedings.

concièrge (Fr): Janitor or hotel service clerk.

(la) condition humaine (Fr): The human condition.

con dolore (It): Sorrowfully.

con molta passione (It): A musical term meaning with fire or passion.

consilio et prudentia (Lat): With wisdom and prudence.

contra bonos mores (Lat): Against good manners or morals.

contra mundum (Lat): Against the whole world. A phrase used to describe those who hold to their own ideas despite overwhelming contrary opinion.

copia verborum (Lat): A rich supply of words; fluency or articulateness.

cordon bleu (Fr): Literally, blue ribbon. It describes anyone of great distinction in his or her field, especially an excellent chef. Sometimes also applied to a particularly fine dish or recipe.

cordon sanitaire (Fr): A line of guards to prevent the spread of contagion or pestilence. Also a buffer zone between hostile countries.

Useful Words and Phrases (cont.)

cornucopia (Lat, cornu copiae): Horn of plenty; symbol of peace and prosperity.

corrigenda (Lat): A list of errors to be corrected in a book already printed. Same as *errata*.

così così (It): So-so. Tolerable or tolerably.

coup de bourse (Fr): A successful stock transaction.

coup d'éclat (Fr): A brilliant stroke.

coup de grâce (Fr): A finishing stroke; death blow. Also a merciful killing.

coup de main (Fr): A bold stroke.

coup de maître (Fr): A master stroke.

coup d'état (Fr): The sudden overthrow of a government—usually by force or the threat of force.

coup de théâtre (Fr): An unexpected turn of events.

coute que coute (Fr): No matter at what cost.

crassa negligentia (Lat): Gross negligence.

crème de la crème (Fr): The cream of the crop.

cui bono? (Lat): To whose benefit or advantage?

cui malo? (Lat): To whose harm or disadvantage?

cum grano salis (Lat): With a grain of salt; skeptically.

cum privilegio (Lat): With authorized license or privilege.

cum tacent, clamant (Lat): While they are silent, they speak. Silence is itself an admission of guilt.

cura animarum (Lat): The care of souls.

curriculum vitae (Lat): The details of one's life—especially those appropriate to a job application or a petition.

custos morum (Lat): The guardian of manners or morals.

damnum absque injuria (Lat): Damage done without intent.

danse macabre (Fr): A fiendish dance; the dance of death.

dare pondus fumo (Lat): To give weight to smoke; to attach importance to trivial matters.

de bon augure (Fr): Of good omen. Under good auspices.

de bonis propriis (Lat): Paying out of one's own pocket.

de bonne grâce (Fr): With good grace; willingly.

deceptio visus (Lat): An optical illusion. See also *trompe l'oeil* (**Art**).

de facto (Lat): In fact, actually.

défense de . . . (Fr): One is forbidden to—followed by a verb infinitive, such as *défense de fumer* (no smoking), *défense d'afficher* (post no notices).

dégagé (Fr): Free and easy; unrestrained.

de gaieté de coeur (Fr): From sheer joy.

de haut en bas (Fr): Literally, downward. In a contemptuous or supercilious manner. Also *du haut en bas.*

déjà vu (Fr): Literally, seen before. The sense of having seen or experienced something previously.

de jure (Lat): Rightfully or legally.

de mal en pis (Fr): From bad to worse.

(le) demi-monde (Fr): The world of women who are not quite respectable.

Useful Words and Phrases (cont.)

dénouement (Fr): Unknotting; the unraveling of a story plot; the resolution of complications.

de nouveau (Fr): Afresh; anew.

Deo adjuvante (Lat): With God's help.

de pilo pendent (Lat): It hangs by a hair. By the skin of our teeth.

de proprio motu (Lat): Willingly.

de rien (Fr): Not at all.

de rigueur (Fr): Compulsory, required by etiquette or fashion.

(le) dernier cri *or* **(le) dernier mot** (Fr): The last word; the latest fashion.

(le) dernier resort (Fr): The last resort.

desideratum (pl. **desiderata**) (Lat): That which is needed or desired.

de temps en temps (Fr): From time to time.

de trop (Fr): Too many, too much.

deus ex machina (Lat): Literally, a god from the machine. Hence in drama and fiction any contrived or unnatural ending.

dictum factum (Lat): No sooner said than done.

Dies Irae (Lat): The Day of Wrath or of Judgment (said in the Requiem Mass).

dionysia (Gk): Dances or festivals in honor of Dionysius or Bacchus.

divertissement (Fr): Diversion; a brief sketch or other lively entertainment given between the acts of a play.

divide et impera (Lat): Divide and conquer.

docendo discimus (Lat): We learn by teaching.

(la) dolce vita (It): The sweet and luxurious life—the title of a famous Italian movie directed by Fellini.

dos à dos (Fr): Back to back. Originally a term applied to back-to-back seats but now, in the United States, a call in square dancing.

dossier (Fr): File; systematic notes; personal records.

douane (Fr): Customs office.

d'outre mer (Fr): From overseas.

doux yeux (Fr): Soft glances.

droit au travail (Fr): The right to work.

durante absentia (Lat): While absent.

durante vita (Lat): During life.

ecce signum (Lat): Behold the sign or behold the proof.

éclat (Fr): Brilliant success; prestige.

e consensu gentium (Lat): An argument based on universal agreement.

(l') élan vital (Fr): The vital force. The idea of a life force is central to the philosophy of Henri Bergson, and he popularized the phrase.

elapso tempore (Lat): The time having elapsed.

embarras de richesses (Fr): An embarrassment of riches. Having more good things than one can use or enjoy.

embarras du choix (Fr): A difficulty of choice arising from too many possibilities.

embonpoint (Fr): Plumpness.

en arrière (Fr): Behind—in arrears.

Useful Words and Phrases (cont.)

en avant (Fr): Forward!

en badinant (Fr): In jest.

en bloc (Fr): As a unit.

enceinte (Fr): Pregnant with child.

en deux mots (Fr): In two words; in brief.

en famille (Fr): With one's family; at home.

enfant de famille (Fr): A child of good breeding, of proper background.

enfant de son siècle (Fr): A child of his times.

enfant terrible (Fr): A child difficult to manage or one that makes disconcerting remarks. A holy terror.

(l')ennemi du genre humain (Fr): An enemy of mankind.

en plein jour (Fr): In the full light of day.

en revanche (Fr): In repayment; in compensation.

en suite (Fr): In succession.

entablature (Fr): An architectural unit surmounting columns.

entente cordiale (Fr): A cordial understanding, especially one between nations.

entourage (Fr): A body of courtiers and retainers; a group of admirers or disciples.

en tout cas (Fr): In any case. By extension describing an all-weather tennis court.

entre deux feux (Fr): Between two fires.

entre nous (Fr): Between ourselves.

e pluribus unum (Lat): From many one. The motto on the great seal of the United States.

e re nata (Lat): According to necessity.

errare humanum est (Lat): To err is human.

esprit de corps (Fr): A sense of shared purpose animating an organization or any group acting together in a common cause.

esprit de finesse (Fr): Shrewdness or sharpness of mind.

et al. (et alii, et aliae, Lat): And others. It also means *et alibi:* and elsewhere.

et passim (Lat): And everywhere; scattered throughout a written work.

ex aequo et bono (Lat): According to what is fair and good. Equitably.

ex animo (Lat): With spirit; sincerely.

ex capite (Lat): Literally, from the head. From memory.

excerpta (Lat): Short selections or summary statements.

ex curia (Lat): Out of court; without litigation.

ex debito justitiae (Lat): By reason of a valid debt.

exempli gratia (Lat): By way of example.

ex gratia (Lat): By special favor or dispensation.

ex libris (Lat): From the library of.

ex more (Lat): According to custom.

ex necessitate rei (Lat): Arising from the urgency of the case or matter.

ex officio (Lat): By virtue of holding an office or official position.

Useful Words and Phrases (cont.)

ex opere operato (Lat): By outward acts.

ex ore infantium (Lat): Out of the mouths of infants.

ex parte (Lat): From one side only. Hence describing an argument prejudiced or based on self-interest.

experimentum crucis (Lat): A decisive experiment; a critical test.

experto crede (Lat): Believe the experienced.

explication de texte (Fr): Detailed and elaborate exegesis of difficult classical texts.

ex post facto (Lat): After the deed is done. In retrospect or retroactively.

expressis verbis (Lat): In so many words.

ex professo (Lat): Openly—without secret reservation.

ex tacito (Lat): Implicitly.

ex tempore (Lat): Extemporaneously, impromptu.

extra muros (Lat): Outside the walls.

extra ordinem (Lat): Out of the natural order.

ex vi termini (Lat): From the meaning of the term. By definition.

ex voto (Lat): In fulfillment of a vow or according to a promise.

facile princeps (Lat): Easily the leader. The undisputed chief.

façon de parler (Fr): Manner of speaking.

facta, non verba (Lat): Deeds, not words.

factotum (Lat): Jack-of-all-trades, a handyman.

faire bonne mine (Fr): To put a good face on the matter.

faire l'homme d'importance (Fr): To assume an air of importance.

faire mon devoir (Fr): To do my duty. To do, not to say.

fait accompli (Fr): A thing done or accomplished, usually with the sense of irreversibility.

fata obstant (Lat): The Fates are opposed.

faute de mieux (Fr): For want of anything better.

faux ami (Fr): A false friend.

femme couverte (Fr): A married woman.

femme fatale (Fr): A seductive woman.

femme galante (Fr): An adventuress. A courtesan.

femme savante (Fr): A learned woman.

femme seule (Fr): An unmarried woman.

fendre un cheveu en quatre (Fr): To split a hair in fours. To make an oversubtle distinction.

festina lente (Lat): Make haste slowly.

Festschrift (Ger): Commemorative volume; a collection of learned papers in honor of a scholar.

feu de joie (Fr): A fusillade as a sign of rejoicing. A bonfire.

fiat lux et lux erat (Lat, Genesis, Vulgate): Let there be light, and there was light.

fide, non armis (Lat): By faith, not by arms.

fide et amore (Lat): By faith and love.

fide et fortitudine (Lat): By faith and fortitude.

fidus et audax (Lat): Faithful and courageous.

filius nullius (Lat): A son of no one—an illegitimate son.

Useful Words and Phrases (cont.)

filius terrae (Lat): A son of the earth. A peasant.

fille de joie (Fr): A daughter of pleasure. A prostitute.

fils à papa (Fr): A favored son of a favored father.

fin de siècle (Fr): End of the century. Also characterized by the customs, ideas, and art forms of the end of the nineteenth century.

finem respice (Lat): Look to the end or goal.

finesse d'esprit (Fr): Shrewdness of mind or character.

floruit (Lat): He flourished. Used when the exact dates of a person's life are unknown.

flux de bouche *and* flux de paroles (Fr): Flow of words; garrulity.

foi en tout (Fr): Faith in everything.

folie de grandeur (Fr): Delusions of grandeur.

force de frappe (Fr): A sudden striking force—sometimes used to describe an atomic onslaught.

force majeure (Fr): Literally, a greater force. Circumstances beyond one's control.

fortiter, fideliter feliciter (Lat): Boldly, faithfully, effectively.

fortiter et recte (Lat): With courage and with right.

fortiter in re (Lat): With firmness or resolution of action.

fortunae filius (Lat): A child of fortune. A spoiled child.

(la) forza del destino (It): The power of destiny. The title of a Verdi opera.

furor scribendi (Lat): The urge to write. Writer's itch.

gage d'amour (Fr): A pledge of love.

gaieté de coeur (Fr): Joy of heart.

garde du corps (Fr): Bodyguard.

gardez bien (Fr): Take care.

gardez le foi (Fr): Keep faith.

gaudium certaminis (Lat): The joy of conflict or battle.

Geist (Ger): Spirit; intellect.

genius loci (Lat): A presiding spirit or deity of a place.

genre (Fr): Type; style; kind—especially applied to artwork or writing.

gens de condition (Fr): People of rank or high standing.

gens d'église (Fr): Churchmen.

gens de la même famille (Fr): Birds of a feather.

gens de robe (Fr): Officials of the law—judges, magistrates, and so on.

gens du monde (Fr): People of the world; the upper crust.

genus homo (Lat): The human race.

Gestalt (Ger): Form; configuration; pattern; a unified whole.

grande chère et beau feu (Fr): Good cheer and a good fire. Comfortable quarters or pleasant living.

grande dame (Fr): A lady of queenly aspect. Sometimes applied to one who gives herself airs.

grande parure or grande toilette (Fr): Full dress.

grand merci (Fr): Many thanks.

grand seigneur (Fr): An aristocrat of the highest rank.

Useful Words and Phrases (cont.)

gratia placendi (Lat): For the sake of pleasing.

gratis dictum (Lat): A mere allegation; an unsupported statement.

graviora manent (Lat): Greater afflictions await. More serious matters remain.

habitué (Fr): One who is in the habit of frequenting a place.

haud longis intervallis (Lat): At intervals of no great length.

haute bourgeoisie (Fr): The upper middle class.

helluo librorum (Lat): A bookworm.

Hibernis Hiberniores (Lat): More Irish than the Irish. Said of settlers who become ardent partisans of their new country and its ways.

hic et ubique (Lat): Here and everywhere.

hoc age (Lat): Do this or pay attention to this.

homo factus ad unguem (Lat): A polished or cultivated man.

homo multarum litterarum (Lat): A man of great learning.

homo sapiens (Lat): The human species.

homo sui juris (Lat): A man who is his own master, a man of independent character.

hors de combat (Fr): Out of the fight—no longer able to fight.

hors de concours (Fr): Out of the race.

hors de la loi (Fr): Beyond the law.

hors de propos (Fr): Out of place; irrelevant.

hors de saison (Fr): Out of season.

hostis humani generis (Lat): An enemy of mankind.

Ibid. (abbreviation of ibidem, Lat): In the same place. Often used in citations to literature.

idée fixe (Fr): A fixed idea—an obsession. A stubborn opinion.

ignis fatuus (Lat): Literally, foolish fire. An evanescent vapor—will-o'-the-wisp. Anything deluding or misleading.

ignotum per ignotius (Lat): Elucidation of the difficult by explanation that is still more difficult.

il avait le diable au corps (Fr): He's full of the devil.

il conduit bien son barque (Fr): He knows how to row his own boat.

il n'entend pas raillerie (Fr): He can't take a joke.

il n'y a pas de quoi (Fr): It's nothing—don't mention it. You're welcome.

imbroglio (It): Confusion; complication; a perplexing state of affairs.

imo pectore (Lat): From the bottom of the heart.

impedimenta (Lat): Literally baggage or army supplies. Hence obstacles to progress.

imprimatur (Lat): It may be printed. The official term for ecclesiastical authorization to publish.

in absentia (Lat): In absence, often used in conferring a degree or honor to a person not present.

in aeturnum (Lat): Forever.

in corpore (Lat): In body or substance.

in delicto (Lat): In or at fault.

in dubio (Lat): In doubt or doubtfully.

in equilibrio (Lat): In balance.

Useful Words and Phrases (cont.)

in esse (Lat): In being; in actuality.

in extenso (Lat): At length; fully.

in extremis (Lat): At the point of death.

in forma pauperis (Lat): As a pauper.

in foro conscientiae (Lat): Before the tribunal of conscience.

infra dignitatem (Lat): Beneath one's dignity. This appears in slang as *infra dig.*

in infinitum (Lat): To infinity.

in initio (Lat): In the beginning.

in limine (Lat): On the threshold.

in loco parentis (Lat): In the place or role of a parent.

in nubibus (Lat): In the clouds; in a fog; muddled.

in nuce (Lat): In a nutshell.

in omnia paratus (Lat): Prepared for all things.

in ovo (Lat): In the egg; as yet unborn.

in perpetuum (Lat): Forever.

in pios usus (Lat): For pious uses. A term used to describe a religious bequest.

in principio (Lat): In the beginning; at the outset.

in propria persona (Lat): In one's own person. Personally present.

in puris naturalibus (Lat): Naked.

in re (Lat): In the matter of.

in rerum natura (Lat): In the nature of things.

in situ (Lat): In its original place or situation.

insouciance (Fr): Freedom from care or anxiety; indifference.

in statu quo (Lat): In the state in which anything was or is.

in statu quo ante bellum (Lat): As things were before the war.

intaglio (It): A decoration cut into the surface of a precious stone; any design so incised.

in tenebris (Lat): In darkness or shadows.

in terrorem (Lat): As a warning or threat.

inter vivos (Lat): Among the living.

in totidem verbis (Lat): In so many words.

intra vires (Lat): Within one's powers or abilities.

introit (Fr): Any introduction, especially that of a musical composition or the High Mass.

in utero *or* in ventre (Lat): In the womb; unborn.

inverso ordine (Lat): In inverse order.

in vitro (Lat): Within glass. In a test tube.

ipse dixit (Lat): He himself said it—an assertion without proof.

ipso facto (Lat): By the very fact; by the fact itself.

jacta alea est (Lat): "The die is cast." A much-repeated phrase first pronounced by Julius Caesar as he crossed the Rubicon. Also spelled *iacta alea est.*

j'ai bonne cause (Fr): I have good cause.

januis clausis (Lat): Behind closed doors; secretly.

je ne sais quoi (Fr): Literally, I know not what—an indefinable, elusive quality, especially a pleasing one. Also used when one is unable to summon precisely the right word. A something or other.

Useful Words and Phrases (cont.)

jeter de la poudre aux yeux (Fr): To throw powder in the eyes. To deceive someone.

jeu de main (Fr): A practical joke; horseplay.

jeu de mots (Fr): Play on words; a pun.

jeu d'esprit (Fr): A display of wit; a witticism.

joie de vivre (Fr): Delight in being alive. Carefree enjoyment of life.

judicium Dei (Lat): The judgment of God.

junta (It, Sp): Legislative council. (Lat): secret political unit.

Jupiter pluvius (Lat): Jupiter of the rain. Wet weather.

jure belli (Lat): By rules of warfare.

(le) juste milieu (Fr): The golden mean.

lacuna (pl. lacunae) (Lat): Literally, a ditch or furrow. Hence a gap or any missing part.

laissez-faire (Fr): Let things go as they will. Unrestrained freedom. Noninterference by government in human affairs.

lana caprina (Lat): Goat's wool. Hence anything of slight value.

language des halles (Fr): Language of the marketplace. Rough, abusive talk.

lapsus calami (Lat): Slip of the pen.

lapsus linguae (Lat): Slip of the tongue.

lapsus memoriae (Lat): Lapse of memory.

lares et penates (Lat): Roman household gods who protected home, field, and family.

Lebensraum (Ger): Additional territory desired by a nation, often for the expansion of trade. A favorite rallying word in Nazi Germany.

Leitmotiv (Ger): Guiding principle; a recurring theme in music or writing.

lèse-majesté (Fr): Treason or treachery, especially against a sovereign. Hence an attack on any custom or institution held sacred.

lettre d'avis (Fr): Letter of advice; a notice.

lettre de cachet (Fr): A sealed letter, especially one containing a royal warrant for imprisonment without trial.

lettre de change (Fr): Bill of exchange.

lettre de créance (Fr): Letter of credit.

lettre de marque (Fr): A letter of reprisal.

lex loci (Lat): The law or customs of a place.

liaison (Fr): Originally contact between military units. Now any similar contact between units of an institution or group. Also an illicit relationship between a man and woman.

literatim (Lat): Literally.

littérateur (Fr): Man of letters.

locum tenens (Lat): Literally, holding the place. A temporary substitute, especially for a physician or a clergyman.

lucri causa (Lat): For the sake of profit.

lux mundi (Lat): Light of the world.

ma foi! (Fr): Upon my faith! My word!

magister ceremoniarum (Lat): Master of ceremonies.

magnum opus (Lat): Masterpiece.

Useful Words and Phrases (cont.)

maintiens le droit (Fr): Cling to what is right.

maître des basses oeuvres (Fr): Literally, master of the low works—a sewer cleaner.

maître des hautes oeuvres (Fr): Literally, master of the high works—an executioner.

maître d'hôtel (Fr): Steward, butler, or head waiter.

major domo (Lat): A chief steward; one in charge of the management of a household.

maladroit (Fr): Awkward; fumbling.

mala fide (Lat): In bad faith; treacherously.

mal à propos (Fr): At a bad time.

malgré nous (Fr): In spite of ourselves.

malgré soi *or* malgré lui (Fr): In spite of himself.

mali exempli (Lat): By way of a bad example.

malis avibus (Lat): Literally, with unlucky birds. Under unlucky portents.

malo modo (Lat): In a bad or evil manner.

malus pudor (Lat): False shame; false modesty.

manibus pedibusque (Lat): With hands and feet; with all one's strength.

manu forti (Lat): With a strong hand.

manu propria (Lat): With one's own hand. By one's own volition.

mare clausum (Lat): A closed sea—one in which commerce or navigation is restricted.

mare nostrum (Lat): Our sea—the Roman name for the Mediterranean.

mater familias (Lat): Mother of a family. Also matriarch.

mauvais coucheur (Fr): Literally, a bad bedfellow. Anyone touchy, quarrelsome, or difficult to get on with.

mauvaise honte (Fr): Bashfulness or false modesty.

mauvaise plaisanterie (Fr): A bad joke.

mauvais goût (Fr): Bad taste.

mauvais sujet (Fr): A worthless scamp. A bad egg.

maximus in minimis (Lat): Very great in very small matters.

mea culpa (Lat): My fault or through my fault.

ménage à trois (Fr): A domestic arrangement under which a man and wife share the same household with one of their lovers.

meo periculo (Lat): At my own risk.

merum sal (Lat): Literally, pure salt. Pure wit.

miserabile vulgus (Lat): The wretched mob.

mobile perpetuum (Lat): Perpetual motion.

mobile vulgus (Lat): The fickle crowd.

modus operandi (Lat): Manner of working or method of operation.

modus vivendi (Lat): Manner of living. By extension, a temporary arrangement between parties at dispute to continue as things were until the disagreement is settled.

mon Dieu! (Fr): My God! But in France this is a mild exclamation, and its English equivalent is something more like "For goodness' sake."

Useful Words and Phrases (cont.)

monologue intérieur (Fr): Interior monologue; stream of consciousness.

more majorum (Lat): In the manner of our ancestors.

mot juste (Fr): The precise word.

mots d'usage (Fr): Commonplace words.

moulin à paroles (Fr): A wordmill; a windbag.

moyen âge (Fr): The Middle Ages.

multa gemens (Lat): With many a groan.

multum in parvo (Lat): Literally, much in little. A phrase spoken in praise of brief aphorisms or brief condensations.

mutatis mutandis (Lat): With the necessary changes.

mutuus concensus (Lat): Mutual consent.

Naturwissenschaft (Ger): Natural science.

nemine contradicente (Lat): With no one opposing.

nemine dissentiente (Lat): With no one dissenting.

ne nimium (Lat): Literally, not too much. Avoid excess.

ne plus ultra (Lat): Literally, nothing further. The ultimate.

nexus (Lat): Tie, link, bond. Also a connected series or group.

nihil ad rem (Lat): Nothing to the point. Inappropriate.

nihil obstat (Lat): Literally, nothing stands in the way. Official approval of publication.

nil admirari (Lat): To be astonished at nothing. (A jaded or blasé attitude.)

nil desperandum (Lat): There is no reason for despair.

ni l'un ni l'autre (Fr): Neither one nor the other.

nimbus (Lat): A cloud or aura surrounding a thing or person; a shining halo surrounding a deity when on earth.

noblesse oblige (Fr): Rank imposes obligations. Those born to nobility must act nobly.

nolens volens (Lat): Willing or unwilling.

noli me tangere (Lat): Touch me not. The words of Jesus appearing to Mary Magdalene after his resurrection. Hence anyone or anything that may not be touched or interfered with.

nom de plume (Fr): A pen name.

nom de théâtre (Fr): A stage name.

non compos mentis (Lat): Not of sound mind. Incapable of managing one's affairs.

non constat (Lat): It is not clear. It is not evident.

non culpabilis (Lat): Not guilty.

non deficiente crumena (Lat): Literally, the purse not failing. As long as the money lasts.

non multa sed multum (Lat): Not many but much. Quality, not quantity.

non placet (Lat): It is not pleasing. A phrase indicating disapproval—something like Queen Victoria's "We are not amused."

non sequitur (Lat): It does not follow. A false conclusion.

notatu dignum (Lat): Worth note.

nous verrons ce que nous verrons (Fr): We shall see what we shall see, implying a skeptical attitude.

nouveau riche (Fr): The newly rich, with the implication of ostentatious display of wealth.

Useful Words and Phrases (cont.)

novus homo (Lat): Literally, a new man. One who has raised himself from obscurity—an upstart.

novus ordo seclorum (Lat): The new order of the ages. Motto on the reverse side of the Great Seal of the United States.

nuda veritas (Lat): The naked truth.

nudis oculis (Lat): With the naked eye.

nudis verbis (Lat): In plain words.

nudum pactum (Lat): An agreement unconfirmed in writing or by earnest money.

nulli secundus (Lat): Second to none.

nunc aut nunquam (Lat): Now or never.

nunc dimittis (Lat): From the canticle beginning with the words of Simeon, "Lord, now lettest thou thy servant go in peace" Permission to depart.

nuncio (It): Diplomatic representative of the papacy.

obiit sine prole (Lat): He died childless.

obiter dictum (Lat): Something said in passing, often in the plural *obiter dicta.*

objet d'art (Fr): A work of art of some value.

oeil-de-boeuf (Fr): Literally, a bull's-eye but actually a small, round window.

oeil-lade (Fr): An amorous glance, ogle.

oleum addere camino (Lat): To throw oil on the fire. To incite further.

omnem movere lapidem (Lat): To leave no stone unturned.

omnibus has litteras visuris (Lat): To whom it may concern. To all who read this writing.

omnium gatherum (Lat): A miscellaneous collection. "Gatherum" is, in fact, a made-up word intended to give a twist of unlikelihood to the collection.

ora e sempre (It): Now and forevermore.

orbis terrarum (Lat): Circle of the earth; the globe; the whole world.

otium sine dignitate (Lat): Leisure without dignity. Or its opposite—otium cum dignitate: Leisure with dignity.

oui-dire (Fr): Hearsay.

outré (Fr): Extreme; eccentric; exaggerated.

pace tua (Lat): By your leave.

panache (Fr): An ornamental plume of feathers. Hence a grand or flamboyant style, verve, flair.

panem et circenses (Lat): Bread and circuses. The rallying cry of Roman mobs.

Pantheon (Gk): The temple erected by Hadrian in Rome to celebrate all gods. Also a public building containing the bodies of the illustrious dead of a nation, or a place for the celebration of the heroes or idols of any group.

parbleu! (Fr): Certainly! A mild expletive derived from *par Dieu:* by God!

par ci, par là (Fr): Here and there.

par complaisance (Fr): Out of a desire to please.

parfaitment bien (Fr): Perfectly well or perfectly done.

pari causa (Lat): With equal right.

par negotiis neque supra (Lat): Equal to his business but not above it.

Useful Words and Phrases (cont.)

parole d'honneur (Fr): Word of honor.

par rapport (Fr): By reason of.

pars adversa (Lat): The opposing party.

part du lion (Fr): The lion's share.

parti pris (Fr): A preconceived opinion.

parvenu (Fr): Upstart.

pas à pas (Fr): Step by step.

pas si bête (Fr): Not so stupid.

passim (Lat): Throughout; here and there.

pastiche (Fr): A literary, musical, or artistic work consisting of themes or motifs borrowed from various sources.

pater familias (Lat): The head of the household.

patina (Lat): Literally, a shallow dish, but also a film or encrustation, especially that produced by oxidation on the surface of old bronze. Hence any sheen indicative of antiquity or value.

patte de velours (Fr): The velvet glove, sometimes concealing the iron hand.

paucis verbis (Lat): In a few words.

pauvre diable (Fr): Poor devil.

pax orbis terrarum (Lat): The peace of the world. Motto found on many Latin coins.

pax Romana (Lat): The Roman peace. A peace maintained by force of Roman arms.

penetralia mentis (Lat): Secret depths or innermost recesses of the mind.

penumbra (Lat): The partial shadow outside the complete shadow of an opaque body. Hence any shadowy or indefinite area.

per contra (Lat): On the contrary or on the other hand.

père de famille (Fr): Father of the family.

per mare, per terras (Lat): By sea and land.

perpetuum mobile (Lat): Perpetual motion.

per procurationem *or* per procuratorem (Lat): By proxy.

persona grata *and* persona non grata (Lat): An acceptable *and* an unacceptable person. Phrases used in diplomacy but now carried over to everyday life.

per totam curiam (Lat): By the whole world. Sometimes used to mean unanimously.

petetio principii (Lat): Begging the question.

pièce de résistance (Fr): The principal dish of a meal or the principal event, incident, article, or work of a series.

pied à terre (Fr): A temporary or occasional lodging.

pis aller (Fr): The last resort or resource.

placet (Lat): It pleases—a yes vote.

plein de soi-même (Fr): Full of himself; egotistical.

pleno jure (Lat): With full right.

plus royaliste que le roi (Fr): More of a royalist than the king. A mark of extreme attitudes.

plus sages que les sages (Fr): Wiser than the wise.

point d'appui (Fr): Point of support. A fulcrum or base.

pomum Adami (Lat): Adam's apple. A reference to the tradition that Eve's apple stuck in Adam's throat.

Useful Words and Phrases (cont.)

poste restante (Fr): The department of a post office in which mail is held until called for.

post mortem (Lat): After death.

post tenebras lux (Lat): After darkness, light; the dawn.

prenez garde! (Fr): Take care. Look out!

pro bono publico (Lat): For the common good.

pro et contra (Lat): For and against.

profanum vulgus (Lat): The profane rabble.

pro forma (Lat): As a matter of form. In importation the phrase is used to describe an invoice presented in advance to arrange for payment or permits with the understanding that it may not correspond to the later, actual invoice.

pro hac vice (Lat): For this occasion.

pro rata (Lat): In proportion. According to a certain rate.

pro ratione aetatis (Lat): In proportion to age.

pro re nata (Lat): According to what occurs. In respect to the matter at hand.

pro salute animae (Lat): For the good of one's soul.

pro se quisque (Lat): Everyone for himself.

pro tempore (Lat): For the time being. Sometimes written *pro tem*.

pro virili parte (Lat): According to one's strength.

Punica fides (Lat): Carthaginian faith, that is, treachery.

pur sang (Fr): Pure-blooded; thoroughbred.

quamdiu se bene gesserit (Lat): So long as he conducts himself well. During good behavior.

quand même (Fr): In spite of everything. Nevertheless; notwithstanding.

quanti est sapire (Lat): How desirable is wisdom.

quantum (Lat): Literally, how much or how great. The indivisible unit of any substance. Also a theory of physical mechanics.

quid faciendum? (Lat): What is to be done?

quid nunc (Lat): What now? In English a *quidnunc* is a scandalmonger.

quid pro quo (Lat): One thing for another. Tit for tat.

qui vive (Fr): Literally, who goes there? The phrase *on the qui vive* means watchful, alert.

quod vide (Lat): Which see. Often used in citations as q.v.—a cross-reference.

raison de plus (Fr): All the more reason.

raison d'état (Fr): Literally, reason of state. For the good of the country.

raison d'être (Fr): Reason or justification for being or existence.

rara avis (Lat): Literally, a rare bird. By extension anything unique or wonderful.

recherché (Fr): Esoteric; of affected refinement or elegance.

reculer pour mieux sauter (Fr): To go back in order to go forward.

reddite quae sunt Caesaris, Caesari; et quae sunt Dei, Deo (Lat, St. Matthew): Render therefore unto Caesar the things that are Caesar's and unto God the things that are God's.

Useful Words and Phrases (cont.)

reductio ad absurdum (Lat): A reduction to absurdity. The refutation of a proposition by demonstrating the absurdity of the conclusion to which it logically leads.

regnat populus (Lat): Let the people rule.

re infecta (Lat): The business being unfinished.

relata refero (Lat): I tell the story as it was told to me.

renaissance (Fr): Literally, rebirth. When capitalized, the rebirth of humane studies, especially of Greek and Latin literature, in the fifteenth and sixteenth centuries first in Italy and later in Europe generally.

rencontre (Fr): An encounter. Sometimes used to mean a hostile meeting or a collision.

res ipsa loquitur (Lat): The thing speaks for itself. Said of whatever is self-evident.

res publica (pl. res publicae) (Lat): In singular form, the state or commonwealth. In plural, things belonging to the public; public property.

ride si sapis (Lat): Smile if you are wise.

rire dans sa barbe (Fr): To laugh in one's beard. To laugh up one's sleeve.

ruat caelum (Lat): Let the heavens fall.

sang froid (Fr): Literally, cold blood. Coolness of mind; composure.

sans pareil (Fr): Without equal.

sans peur et sans reproche (Fr): Without fear and without reproach—a motto of French chivalry.

sans rime et sans raison (Fr): Without rhyme or reason.

sans souci (Fr): Without care. Also, capitalized, the palace of Frederic II in Potsdam.

sans tache (Fr): Without spot—stainless or blameless.

satis superque (Lat): More than enough.

Saturnalia (Lat): Capitalized, the festival of Saturn celebrated in December in ancient Rome. In lowercase, any fete of unrestrained revelry.

savoir faire (Fr): Tact; knowing how to act.

savoir vivre (Fr): Good manners.

secundum naturam (Lat): According to nature.

secundum ordinem (Lat): In due process.

secundum usum (Lat): According to custom.

semel pro semper (Lat): Once and for all.

semper idem (Lat): Always the same; unchanging.

sero sed serio (Lat): Serious but late.

sic (Lat): Literally, so. A word inserted in a quotation to point out an error in the original.

sic eunt fata hominum (Lat): Such is man's fate.

siècle des ténèbres (Fr): The Dark Ages.

simplex munditiis (Lat): Elegant in simplicity.

simulacrum (Lat): Likeness; image; sometimes meaning slight likeness.

sine die (Lat): Without a day being appointed. Adjournment without a date set for reassembly.

sine qua non (Lat): Literally, without which not. An indispensable condition.

sophia (Gk): Wisdom.

sotto voce (It): In a stage whisper. In a soft voice.

Useful Words and Phrases (cont.)

souffler le chaud et le froid (Fr): To blow both hot and cold.

sous tous les rapports (Fr): In all respects.

speculum vitae (Lat): Mirror of life.

sponte sua (Lat): Voluntarily.

stare super vias antiquas (Lat): To hold fast to old ways.

status quo ante bellum (Lat): The state of things as they were before the war.

Sturm und Drang (Ger): Storm and stress. A literary movement in late eighteenth-century Germany leading to romanticism.

sua cuique voluptas (Lat): Every man to his own pleasures.

sub rosa (Lat): Literally, under the rose. Secretly, confidentially.

sub silentio (Lat): In silence or without notice.

sub verbo (Lat): Under such and such a word. A form of cross-reference in dictionaries.

succès d'estime (Fr): Critical rather than popular success.

succès fou (Fr): Thundering success.

sui generis (Lat): In a class by itself; unique.

summum bonum (Lat): The supreme good.

suo loco (Lat): In its proper place.

suo periculo (Lat): At one's own risk.

sur le pavé (Fr): Literally, on the street. Destitute.

suum cuique (Lat): To each his own.

tabula rasa (Lat): A clear slate. A mind not yet affected by impressions and experiences. Locke's description of the mind at birth.

taedium vitae (Lat): Weariness of living; boredom, satiety.

tangere ulcus *or* tangere vulnus (Lat): To touch a sore spot.

tant mieux (Fr): So much the better.

tant pis (Fr): So much the worse.

tant s'en fait (Fr): Far from it.

te judice (Lat): In your judgment.

tempus fugit (Lat): Time flies.

tempus ludendi (Lat): Time for play.

terminus ad quem (Lat): Literally, the end to which. Goal, objective.

terminus a quo (Lat): Literally, the end from which. The starting point; the point of departure.

terra firma (Lat): Solid earth. A secure foothold.

terra incognita (Lat): Unexplored or unknown land. By extension an unexplored subject.

tête-à-tête (Fr): Literally, head to head. A private conversation or interview.

thesaurus (Lat): Treasure; collection. Also a dictionary arranged according to ideas or themes.

to kalon (Gk): The good, the beautiful.

totis viribus (Lat): With all one's might.

tôt ou tard (Fr): Sooner or later.

touché (Fr): An expression used in fencing to indicate a hit—hence also used to describe a telling remark or rejoinder.

Useful Words and Phrases (cont.)

toujours l'amour (Fr): Love, ever love.

toujours perdrix (Fr): Always partridge. Always the same thing over and over again.

tour de force (Fr): A feat of exceptional strength, brilliance, or cleverness. A stroke of genius. But also a feat done more for the sake of its own cleverness or difficulty than for other purpose.

tourner casaque (Fr): To change one's coat. To change sides.

tout bien ou rien (Fr): All or nothing.

tu quoque (Lat): You too. A retort charging an opponent with the same offense he charges against you.

tutum est (Lat): It is your own. The assumption is that however humble it's still yours.

ult. (ultimo, Lat): In or of the month preceding the current one.

Ultima Thule (Lat): The place believed by the ancients to be the northernmost point of the world. Hence the farthest point of any journey or the highest degree attainable in any deed or project.

ultimum vale (Lat): The last farewell.

ultra licitum (Lat): Beyond what is allowable.

una voce (Lat): With one voice; unanimously.

unguibus et rostro (Lat): With tooth and nail.

uno animo (Lat): With one mind; in complete accord.

Untergang (Ger): Decline; fall. A word made famous in the title of Oswald Spengler's *Untergang des Abendlandes*—The Decline of the West.

unum post aliud (Lat): One thing after the other. One thing at a time.

usque ad nauseam (Lat): To the point of disgust.

ut infra (Lat): As stated or shown or cited below.

ut quocumque paratus (Lat): Prepared for any emergency.

ut sup. (ut supra, Lat): As above or before.

vade mecum (Lat): Literally, go with me. A handy reference volume.

vedi Napoli e poi mori (It): See Naples and then die. When you've seen Naples, you've seen everything.

veni, vidi, vici (Lat): I came, I saw, I conquered. Julius Caesar's inscription displayed at his Pontic triumph.

ventis secundis (Lat): With favoring winds.

verbatim (Lat): In exactly the same words; word for word.

verbatim et litteratim (Lat): Word for word and letter for letter.

verbum sapienti sat est (Lat): A word to the wise is sufficient.

veritas numquam perit (Lat): Truth never dies.

veritas vincit (Lat): Truth conquers.

via lactea (Lat): The Milky Way.

vice versa (Lat): Conversely; in reverse order.

vigilate et orate (Lat): Watch and pray.

virtute et fide (Lat): By courage and faith.

vis-à-vis (Fr): Opposite; face to face.

vis vitae (Lat): Life force.

voilà une autre chose (Fr): That's an entirely different thing.

voir le dessous des cartes (Fr): To see the underside of the cards. To be in the know.

Useful Words and Phrases (cont.)

volens et potens (Lat): Willing and able.

Vorspiel (Ger): Prelude, especially a musical overture.

vulgo concepti (Lat): Illegitimate children.

vulgus ignobile (Lat): The vulgar mob.

vulnus immedicabile (Lat): An irreparable injury.

Wanderlust (Ger): Desire for travel; an instinctive impulse to see the world.

Wein, Weib, und Gesang (Ger): Wine, woman, and song.

Weisheit auf der Gasse (Ger): Wisdom of the street. Proverbial truth.

xenia (Gk): An epithet of Athena meaning hospitable.

xenophobia (Gk): An unreasoning dread of or aversion to foreigners—from the Greek historian Xenophon or the prefix xeno- (alien).

Zeitgeist (Ger): The spirit of the age.

Zeitschrift (Ger): Periodical or journal.

zonam perdidit (Lat): He has lost his purse. He is in straitened circumstances.

Communication: An Epilogue

Dance, fire, drum, bell, symbol, and word are all ancient means of communication. Today language, written or spoken, in prose, verse, or song, has become our primary means of expression so that there is an almost mythic attachment to the word, especially the right and graceful word. Felicity of expression makes ideas memorable and compelling.

How powerful words are. They open miraculously onto other realms. In the slums of Cairo people greet each other with garlands of words. "Morning of blessing! Morning of light!" they say, and a moment of grace has been conjured up in the mean and squalid streets of poverty. In our own lives so simple a phrase as "Once upon a time . . ." is the key to the magical kingdom of childhood in which there is a world above reality and a beauty beyond experience.

Once upon a time the incomparable Sarah Bernhardt was playing Cleopatra on the London stage to sellout audiences. In her final scene she stabbed to death the slave who brought her news of Mark Antony's defeat at Actium. She stormed, raved, wrecked the scenery in her frenzy, and, finally, as the curtain fell, dropped to the stage in a shuddering, wailing, convulsive heap. Tumultuous applause always greeted this performance, and once, as it died down, a British matron was heard to say to her neighbor, "How different, how *very* different, from the home life of our dear Queen Victoria."

How very different the brave new world of writing and publishing threatens to be. Behind the attraction of elec-

415

tronic storage, retrieval, and communication of knowledge is the curious notion that knowledge has somehow outstripped our capacity to assimilate it. That we can create what we cannot understand seems at best a dubious proposition. But, more important, there is at the heart of this naive belief in the might of the machine not only the powerful force of laziness but subconscious belief in magic. Men will always seek some button to press to obtain wisdom, some mumbo-jumbo to achieve salvation. The magic we must work is neither in mystic numbers nor in machines, only in the capacity to think hard and well.

The information-storing machine can be the instrument of only established doctrine, but fashions of the mind and spirit and even the shapes of truth do change. In the seventeenth century the chancellor of Cambridge, Dr. John Lightfoot, culminated years of meticulous study in his announcement that "heaven and earth, center and circumference, were created all together, in the same instant, and this work took place and man was created by the Trinity on October 23, 4004 B.C., at nine o'clock in the morning." Lightfoot could not have known that on the very morning before the hour he so precisely specified, a highly cultivated people, and one well equipped to savor the achievements of science, crowded the great cities of Egypt, all unaware that their world had not yet been created.

In one vision of a changed future, books of course will not disappear, but they will take on a character quaint and ornamental. The library will be a cunning contrivance of tangled tape and circumambient circuitry. In this technological rat's nest will be an antiquarian alcove containing a few ancient examples of the bookmaking art and perhaps even a stuffed editor reminiscent of Jeremy Bentham, who can still be seen seated behind his desk in a closet of the University of London. And the learned journal? It too will depart. The scientist will subscribe not to a journal but to a push-button answering service, and the answering service will give back the abstracted views of the contemporary chancellor of Cambridge, Dr. John Lightfoot. But this is a vision that may not be realized, and the book may survive as depository of information and source of knowledge.

*   *   *

Now that the weary pen is laid down, the jigsaw pieces of leftover manuscript cleared from the kitchen table, and the light dimmed, perhaps the author of this book may speak for himself.

I have enjoyed its writing, for it has renewed acquaintanceship with splendid writers and their enchanted words. It is a work that could readily be either half or twice its present size, so that decisions have become a constant part of its doing. I shall be content if these were reasonably well taken, for I have never really known how I decided what words are difficult and what are not, what words are common enough to be included and what uncommon enough to be excluded.

I shall conclude by adapting to myself St. Augustine's famous words: "O Lord, give me chastity and continency, but do not give it yet." I shall say, "O Lord, take from me the burden of my writer's cramp and my writer's itch—but not just yet."

J.L.D.

$\mathcal{R}_{\text{eferences}}$

In the list of books and essays to follow, fewer than a score have been used liberally in this compilation, but of these the one that has been the richest source of apt quotation and astute definition is the *Oxford English Dictionary*. So thorough is its scholarship and so splendid its detail that it can justly be described as the single most valuable reference source in linguistics ever published. Perhaps then a brief account of its doing may be of interest. Its history is beautifully told by Elisabeth Murray in her *Caught in the Web of Words*.

In 1866 a position is to be filled in the British Museum Library. A twenty-nine-year-old bank clerk applies for it:

> I have to state that Philology, both Comparative and special, has been my favourite pursuit during the whole of my life, and that I possess a general acquaintanceship with the languages & literature of the Aryan and Syro-Arabic classes—not indeed to say that I am familiar with all or nearly all of these, but I possess that general lexical & structural knowledge which makes the intimate knowledge only a matter of a little application. With several I have a more intimate acquaintance as with the Romance tongues, Italian, French, Catalan, Spanish, Latin & in a less degree Portuguese, Vaudois, Provençal & various dialects. In the Teutonic branch, I am tolerably familiar with Dutch (having at my place of business correspondence to read in Dutch, German, French & occasionally other languages)

Flemish, German, Danish. In Anglo-Saxon and Moeso-Gothic
my studies have been much closer, I having prepared some
works for publication upon these languages. I know a little of the
Celtic, and am at present engaged with the Sclavonic, having
obtained a useful knowledge of Russian. In the Persian,
Achaemenian Cuneiform, & Sanscrit branches, I know for the
purposes of Comparative Philology. I have sufficient knowledge
of Hebrew & Syriac to read at site the *O.T.* and *Peshito;* to a less
degree I know Aramaic Arabic, Coptic and Phenician to the
point where it was left by Gesenius.

The applicant, James A. H. Murray, son of a tailor in
the small town of Denholm, did not get the job, but this did not
diminish for an instant his conviction that to acquire an intimate knowledge of anything is "only a matter of a little application."

But Murray was fortunate in that his passion for
philology, for elucidation of the organic development of linguistic forms, and for the fine splendor of the English language
were recognized by F. J. Furnivall, founder of the Early English
Text Society, and by Walter Skeat, the great Anglo-Saxon
scholar. Although English society was still caste-ridden, somehow Murray's humble origins and status as a schoolmaster and
correspondence clerk in the Chartered Bank of India, Australia
& China were overlooked; Furnivall and Skeat had their way,
and Murray was appointed editor of the *Oxford English Dictionary* to be.

Its preparation was beset by every conceivable difficulty. Lack of space, lack of money, lack of qualified help, lack
of support from the fretful delegates of the University Press
were symbolized by the damp, inadequate, desperately over-
crowded garden shed in which Murray and his staff worked.
These handicaps did not deter him in the emerging plan for a
dictionary of unprecedented scope, erudition, and excellence.
The delegates of the press were not slow to express their mis-
givings: "The more we endow the Dictionary, the slower it
goes"; "Surely the number of quotations can be reduced"; "What
excuse can there be for including so outlandish a technical term
as 'appendicitis'?"

Murray persisted in his determined but hazardous
course, giving between eighty and ninety hours a week to the
monumental task. He serenely worked himself to death, dying

on July 26, 1915, just as he was completing the letter T. Many of the entries to which he had given his life are miniature treatises on crucial social and philosophic aspects of Western imagination and science. They will captivate men's minds so long as language endures.

Just as the high-flown dons of the university had taken Murray's renown and knighthood in lofty stride, so it is today curious that the second edition of *The Reader's Encyclopedia* cannot seem to squeeze in the name of James Murray. "His monument and its derivatives stand matchless. They are the living history of the English tongue and the dynamic embodiment of its spread over the earth. The master wordsmiths in modern letters—Joyce, Nabokov, Anthony Burgess, John Updike—are Murray's debtors. Where speech is vital and exact, it springs from the *OED* and enriches it in turn. It carries within its dark-blue boards the libraries of fact and of feeling. Dip into it anywhere and life itself crowds at you" (Steiner).

American Heritage Dictionary of the English Language. 1969. Ed. William Morris. Boston: Houghton Mifflin.

Asher, Richard. 1972. *Talking Sense.* London: Pitman & Sons.

Ayer Glossary of Advertising and Related Terms. 1977. Ed. Julie M. Moss. Philadelphia: Ayer Press.

Baker, Sheridan. 1984. *The Complete Stylist and Handbook*, 3rd ed. New York: Harper & Row.

_____. 1981. *The Practical Stylist*, 5th ed. New York: Harper & Row.

Banki, Ivan S. 1981. *Dictionary of Administration and Management.* Los Angeles: Systems Research.

Barzun, Jacques. 1985. *Simple & Direct*, rev. ed. New York: Harper & Row.

_____. 1985. Behind the blue pencil. *Publisher's Weekly*, October 4.

Benet, William R. 1965. *The Reader's Encyclopedia*, 2nd ed. New York: Thomas Crowell.

Bernstein, Theodore. 1971. *Miss Thistlebottom's Hobgoblins.* New York: Farrar, Straus & Giroux.

_____. 1965. *The Careful Writer.* New York: Atheneum.

Bierce, Ambrose. 1909. *Write It Right,* reprinted 1937. New York: Union Library Assoc.

_____. 1906. *The Devil's Dictionary,* a selection reprinted 1958. Mount Vernon, N.Y.: Peter Pauper Press.

Black's Law Dictionary. 1979, rev. 5th ed. St. Paul, Minn.: West Pub. Co.

Bowler, Peter. 1979. *The Superior Person's Book of Words.* Boston: David Godine.

Brandreth, Gyles. 1948. *Famous Last Words.* New York: Sterling.

Bryant, Margaret M. 1962. *Current American Usage.* New York: Funk & Wagnalls.

Bryson, Bill. 1987. *The Penguin Dictionary of Troublesome Words,* 2nd ed. Harmondsworth: Penguin Books.

Canfield, Cass. 1971. *Up and Down and Around.* New York: Harper & Row.

Chandor, Anthony. 1980, rev. 2nd ed. *The Penguin Dictionary of Computers.* Harmondsworth: Penguin Books.

Charlton, James. 1980. *The Writer's Quotation Book.* Yonkers, N.Y.: Pushcart Press.

Collins, F. Howard. 1938. *Authors' & Printers' Dictionary,* 8th ed. London: Oxford Univ. Press.

Collison, Robert, and Mary Collison. 1980. *Dictionary of Foreign Quotations.* New York: Everest House.

Cook, Claire K. 1985. *Line by Line.* Boston: Houghton Mifflin.

Copperud, Roy H. 1960. *Words on Paper.* New York: Hawthorn.

Curme, George O. 1931. *Syntax.* Boston: D. C. Heath. Vol. 3 of *A Grammar of the English Language.*

Dampier, William C. 1957. *A Shorter History of Science.* New York: Meridian Books.

Dorland's Illustrated Medical Dictionary. 1991, 27th ed. Philadelphia: W. B. Saunders.

duGran, Claurene. 1981. *Wordsmanship: A Dictionary.* New York: Pocket Books.

Dusseau, John L. [In press.] Just words. *Perspect. Biol. Med.*

_____. 1989. Responsibility of the learned journal. *Perspect. Biol. Med.* 32:3, 344–348.

_____. 1979. The editorial me. *Perspect. Biol. Med.* 22:2, 243–249.

Edmunds, Robert A. 1985. *Prentice Hall Standard Glossary of Computer Technology.* Englewood Cliffs, N.J.: Prentice Hall.

The Encyclopedia of Philosophy. 1967. Ed. Paul Edwards, reprint ed., 8 vols. New York: Macmillan.

Espy, Willard R. 1978. *O Thou Improper, O Thou Uncommon Noun.* New York: Clarkson Potter.

Fadiman, Clifton. (Ed.) 1985. *The Little, Brown Book of Anecdotes.* Boston: Little, Brown.

Family Word Finder. 1975. Pleasantville, N.Y.: Reader's Digest Assoc.

Follett, Wilson. 1966. *Modern American Usage,* rev. ed. by Jacques Barzun. New York: Hill & Wang.

Fowler, H. W. 1965. *A Dictionary of Modern English Usage,* 2nd ed. Revised by Ernest Gowers. Oxford: Oxford University Press.

Franklin, Benjamin. 1731. Reprinted 1956. *An Apology for Printers.* Philadelphia: Bingham Co.

Frazer, James G. 1950. *The Golden Bough,* abridged ed. New York: Macmillan.

Gill, Brendan. 1975. *Here at The New Yorker.* New York: Random House.

Gingrich, Arnold. 1971. *Nothing But People.* New York: Crown Publishers.

Gowers, Ernest. 1948. *Plain Words.* London: His Majesty's Stationery Office.

Graves, Robert, and Alan Hodge. 1971. *The Reader over Your Shoulder.* New York: Random House.

Gross, Jerome S. 1978. *Illustrated Encyclopedic Dictionary of Real Estate,* 2nd ed. Englewood Cliffs, N.J.: Prentice Hall.

Guinagh, Kevin. 1966. *Dictionary of Foreign Phrases and Abbreviations.* New York: Pocket Books.

Gummere, John F. 1989. *Words, Etc.* Haverford, Pa.: Haverford Publications.

Hebb, Donald O. 1958. *A Textbook of Psychology.* Philadelphia: W. B. Saunders.

The Holy Bible. 1865. Philadelphia: J. B. Lippincott.

How to Divide the Word. 1956, rev. 7th ed. Kingsport, Tenn.: Southern Publishers.

Hutchinson, Lois T. 1976. *Standard Handbook for Secretaries,* 8th ed. New York: McGraw-Hill.

Johnson, Samuel. 1755. *A Dictionary of the English Language.* London: W. Strahan. Reprinted 1979. New York: Arno Press.

Jones, Judy, and William Wilson. 1987. *An Incomplete Education.* New York: Ballantine Books.

Jordan, Edwin P., and Willard C. Shepard. 1952. *Rx for Medical Writing.* Philadelphia: W. B. Saunders.

Lamberts, J. J. 1972. *A Short Introduction to English Usage.* New York: McGraw-Hill.

Leacock, Stephen. 1943. *How to Write.* New York: Dodd, Mead.

Lederer, Richard. 1991. *The Miracle of Language.* New York: Pocket Books.

_____. 1989. *Crazy English.* New York: Pocket Books.

The Little, Brown Handbook. 1986. Ed. H. Ramsey Fowler et al., 3rd ed. Boston: Little, Brown.

Lowth, Robert. 1762. *A Short Introduction to English Grammar.* London.

The Macmillan Handbook of English. 1982. Ed. Robert F. Willson, Jr., 7th ed. New York: Macmillan.

Mencken, H. L. 1989. *The American Language.* Rev. by Raven I. McDavid. New York: Alfred A. Knopf.

Merriam-Webster Concise Handbook for Writers. 1991. Springfield, Mass.: Merriam-Webster.

Merriam-Webster New Book of Word Histories. 1991. Springfield, Mass.: Merriam-Webster.

Merritt Glossary of Insurance Terms. 1980. Eds. Thomas E. Green, Robert W. Osler, and John S. Bickley. Santa Monica, Calif.: Merritt Co.

Moore, W. C. 1971. *The Penguin Encyclopedia of Places.* Harmondsworth: Penguin Books.

Morrison, Stanley. 1936. *First Principles of Typography.* New York: Macmillan.

Murray, Elisabeth. 1976. *Caught in the Web of Words.* New Haven, Conn.: Yale Univ. Press.

The New Columbia Encyclopedia. 1975. Eds. William H. Harris and Judith S. Levy, 4th ed. New York: Columbia University Press.

Newman, Edwin. 1975. *Strictly Speaking.* New York: Warner Books.

Newmark, Maxim. 1950. *Dictionary of Foreign Words and Phrases.* New York: Philosophical Library.

O'Donnell, Paul T., and Eugene L. Maleady. *Dictionary of Real Estate Terminology.* Philadelphia: W. B. Saunders.

Opdyke, John B. 1939. *Don't Say It.* New York: Funk & Wagnalls.

_____. 1935. *Get It Right.* New York: Funk & Wagnalls.

O'Rahilly, Ronan. 1988. Guide to writing articles in English. *Acta Anatomica,* 131, 1–2.

The Oxford Book of Literary Anecdotes. 1975. Ed. James Sutherland. Oxford: Clarendon Press.

The Oxford Dictionary of Quotations. 1980, 3rd ed. Oxford: Oxford Univ. Press.

The Oxford English Dictionary (Compact Edition). 1971, originally published 1933. Ed. James A. Murray. Oxford: Oxford Univ. Press.

Paxson, William C. 1990. *The New American Dictionary of Confusing Words.* New York: The Penguin Group.

Prentice Hall Handbook for Writers. 1988. Ed. Glenn Leggett, 10th ed. Englewood Cliffs, N.J.: Prentice Hall.

Priestley, Joseph. 1798. *The Rudiments of English Grammar.* London.

The Random House Dictionary of the English Language. 1987. Ed. Stuart B. Flexner, 2nd ed. New York: Random House.

Reber, Arthur S. 1985. *Penguin Dictionary of Psychology*. New York: The Penguin Group.

Roberts, Philip D. 1987. *Plain English: A User's Guide*. London: The Penguin Group.

Rodale, J. I. 1961. *The Synonym Finder*. Emmaus, Pa.: Rodale Books.

Safire, William. 1988. *You Could Look It Up*. New York: Times Books.

_____. 1986. *Take My Word for It*. New York: Times Books.

_____. 1984. *I Stand Corrected*. New York: Times Books.

_____. 1982. *What's the Good Word?* New York: Times Books.

_____. 1980. *On Language*. New York: Times Books.

Sandell, Richard V. 1989. *A Microcomputer Glossary*. Delray Beach, Calif.: Direct Access Maintenance.

Scott, John S. 1981. *Dictionary of Civil Engineering*, 3rd ed. New York: Halsted Press (Div. of John Wiley).

Shaw, Harry. 1975. *Dictionary of Problem Words & Expressions*. New York: McGraw-Hill.

Simon, John. 1980. *Paradigms Lost: Reflections on Literacy and Its Decline*. New York: Clarkson Potter.

Sloan, Gary. 1990. Frequency of errors in essays by college freshmen and by professional writers. *College Composition and Communication* 41:3, 299–308.

Sloan, Harold S., and Arnold T. Zurcher. 1970. *Dictionary of Economics*. New York: Barnes & Noble.

Sloane, Richard. 1987. *The Sloane-Dorland Annotated Medical-Legal Dictionary*. St. Paul: West Pub. Co.

Sloane, Sheila B. 1982. *The Legal Speller*, 2nd ed. St. Paul: West Pub. Co.

Sloane, Sheila B., and John L. Dusseau. 1984. *The Business Word Book*. Glenview, Ill.: Scott Foresman.

Statsky, William. 1985. *Legal Thesaurus/Dictionary*. St. Paul: West Pub. Co.

Stedman's Illustrated Medical Dictionary. 1982, 24th ed. Baltimore: Williams & Wilkins.

Steiner, George. 1977. Give the word. *The New Yorker,* November 21, 221–230.

Stern, J., and M. Stern. 1990. *The Encyclopedia of Bad Taste.* New York: Harper-Collins.

Stroman, J. H. 1968. *The Secretary's Manual.* Bergenfield, N.J.: New American Library.

Strunk, William, Jr. 1969. Rev. by E. B. White. *The Elements of Style.* New York: Macmillan.

Success with Words. 1983. Ed. Peter Davies. Pleasantville, N.Y.: Reader's Digest Association.

Taber's Cyclopedic Medical Dictionary. 1981, 14th ed. Philadelphia: F. A. Davis.

Taylor, John R. 1970, rev. ed. *The Penguin Dictionary of the Theatre.* Harmondsworth: Penguin Books.

Unwin, Stanley. 1960. *The Truth About a Publisher.* New York: Macmillan.

Urdang, Laurence. 1988. *The Dictionary of Confusable Words.* New York: Ballantine Books.

Van Winkle. 1818. *The Printer's Guide.* New York: Univ. of New York Press.

Webster's Biographical Dictionary. 1976. Springfield, Mass.: G. & C. Merriam.

Webster's Dictionary of English Usage. 1989. Springfield, Mass.: Merriam-Webster.

Webster's New Dictionary of Synonyms. 1968. Springfield, Mass.: G. & C. Merriam.

Webster's New World Guide to Pronunciation. 1984. (William S. Chisholm, Jr.) New York: Simon & Schuster.

Webster's Ninth New Collegiate Dictionary. 1983. Ed. Frederick C. Mish. Springfield, Mass.: Merriam-Webster.

Webster's Third New International Dictionary. 1961. Ed. Philip B. Gove. Springfield, Mass.: G. & C. Merriam.

Wentworth, Harold, and Stuart B. Flexner. 1968. *The Pocket Dictionary of American Slang.* New York: Pocket Books.

Wheelock, John H. (Ed.). 1971. *Editor to Author: The Letters of Maxwell E. Perkins*. New York: Scribners.

Whitford, Robert C., and James R. Foster. 1937. *American Standards of Writing*. New York: Farrar & Rinehart.

Why Do We Say It? 1985. Secaucus, N.J.: Castle (Div. of Book Sales).

Wyld, H. C. 1920. *A History of Modern Colloquial English*. London: T. Allen Unwin.

Zinsser, William. 1976. *On Writing Well*. New York: Harper & Row.